Policy and Politics in State Budgeting

Bureaucracies, Public Administration, and Public Policy

Kenneth J. Meier
Series Editor

Policy and Politics in State Budgeting

Kurt M. Thurmaier and
Katherine G. Willoughby

M.E.Sharpe
Armonk, New York
London, England

Library of Congress Cataloging-in-Publication Data

Thurmaier, Kurt M., 1957–
    Policy and politics in state budgeting / by Kurt M. Thurmaier and Katherine G.
Willoughby.
        p. cm. — (Bureaucracies, public administration, and public policy)
    Includes index.
    ISBN 0-7656-0293-8 (alk. paper)
    1. Budget—United States. I. Willoughby, Katherine G., 1958– II. Title.
    III. Series.

HJ2053.A1 T48 2001   00-053160
352.4´8213´0973—dc21   CIP

Printed in the United States of America

The paper used in this publication meets the minimum requirements of
American National Standard for Information Sciences
Permanence of Paper for Printed Library Materials,
ANSI Z 39.48-1984.

BM (c)   10   9   8   7   6   5   4   3   2   1

We dedicate this book
to Dan H. Willoughby, Jr., and
to the memory of Roland J. Thurmaier

Contents

List of Tables, Figures, and Boxes

Tables

Figures

Box

Preface

This book accomplishes two goals. First, it provides an in-depth description of budgetary politics and policy-making in state budget offices. The data rendered in these chapters fills a significant gap in our understanding of state budget processes, and how budgeting and policy-making are linked in state budget offices. Except for a few important attempts in the early 1960s, very little is written about state budget office activities, which is surprising given their crucial position at the nexus of budgeting and policy-making in many states. The stories we tell here help public administration and political science scholars understand how we get collective budgetary choices, how state budget examiners influence those choices, and how these examiners make decisions to influence budgetary choices.

The second goal of this book is to present a descriptive model of the decision-making processes of state budget examiners, a model that we believe has significant implications for the larger effort to create a corpus of budget theory that has positive and normative validity. The lack of a widely accepted budgetary theory of decision-making is no small matter for scholars and students alike. With a few notable exceptions, budgeting scholars seem to be gun-shy about proposing models of budgetary decision-making. This has been especially problematic at the microbudgeting level, where such a void has been increasingly filled by residual applications of microeconomic decision-making models that portray bureaucrats as self-interested and utility maximizing. The model proposed in this book rejects simplistic assumptions of bureaucratic behavior and presents a decision-making model that accounts for multiple rationalities as the basis for budget and policy decisions by state budget examiners. Budget examiners themselves, in this case those in the eleven state budget offices included in our field study, provide substantial evidence of this model.

We wrote this book with three audiences in mind. Scholars of state budgeting, state policy-making, and state politics should find this book a useful addition to their libraries. The model we construct weaves budgeting, policy, and politics together, highlighting the actors, the decision points, and the nexus of budgeting and policy-making in state budget offices. The state politics literature has lacked any significant study of how budgetary politics fits into the larger policy process with respect to the governors, and this book will fill that void as well. Research colleagues in the fields of public administration and political science will find this research highly valuable in contributing to a continuing academic discussion about how we get the collective budgetary choices we do, and the role that budget examiners play in influencing those choices.

Students of public administration, public policy, and political science will find this book useful as well. It is particularly well suited to two types of courses. First, graduate courses in public budgeting and policy analysis will benefit greatly from the book's focus on microbudgetary decision processes. It is an excellent complement to macrolevel books on budgeting (e.g., Rubin's *Politics of Public Budgeting*) and general textbooks (e.g., Lee and Johnson's *Public Budgeting Systems*). These kinds of books help students see the overall process of budgeting but gloss over how *individuals* make budgeting decisions and contribute to final budget outcomes. Students can identify with the ideal type of examiners and their work in state budget offices as presented in the second half of this book, and can follow examiners' "thinking" as they develop budget recommendations for their respective governors.

Students in state politics courses will also benefit from this book. It highlights how governors use budgets as policy instruments, identifying both the nexus and the distinctiveness of state politics and state policy-making. The book enriches our understanding of the policy-making process in states and particularly highlights the policy influence of a key set of actors (budget examiners) who often have been either ignored or lumped carelessly with the "governor's office." For example, we identify some important differences between the decision-making of state budget examiners and that of members of the governor's policy staff. The politics of budgeting is influenced by both sets of actors.

The third audience for this book is the retinue of public servants engaged in state budgeting in various agencies, state budget offices, and state legislatures. The results of our field study of state budget offices in two different regions of the United States provide practitioners of state budgeting with an important window into the "black box" of budgetary decision-making in state budget offices. We demonstrate how budget examiners develop their budget recommendations for the governor. We identify the important difference it makes for examiners (and governors) when the budget office has a stronger policy rather than control orientation. The results reported here also encourage agency budgeters and state budget examiners to have open and cooperative relationships that support a mutual goal of advancing the effectiveness of agency programs. The personal relationships between these budget actors are critical factors in the way budget office recommendations are fashioned for the governor.

Of the third audience, this book is especially useful for governors who wish to make the budget and the budget office into more effective policy instruments. To the extent that a governor desires to change the role of the budget office and the budget examiners employed therein, this book provides some footprints to follow with respect to the relationships between the governor, the budget director, and the budget examiners. It highlights the impact of a personal relationship between the governor and examiners, and how that relationship does not require examiners to compromise their "neutral competency" in an effort to provide more effective budget and policy recommendations to the governor.

Conducting some 200 interviews in eleven states is not the easiest way to perform research. It is certainly a much slower process than mailing surveys to key actors. And it is more expensive and time-consuming than either telephone or mail surveys. But the results we found are well worth the effort. Transcribing interview tapes, then reading and rereading the interviews, has imparted to us a much deeper understanding of the nuances involved in the crafting of budget recommendations for a governor. We have tried hard to impart these understandings to you, the reader. As with all successful research, perhaps we have ended with more questions than we answered. However, we hope that our work will inspire others to rise to the challenge of truly comparative state research and answer some of the questions we raise in the last chapter. Let there be little doubt, then, that we anticipate great reading in the future.

Acknowledgments

From Both Authors

There is a real dilemma in deciding whom we should thank first for help in this field project. Ultimately, however, we begin with the state budget directors and their staffs who let us into their offices and who let us probe who they are, what they do, and how they do it. Without them, we would not have a story to tell. We thank each and every one of you who let us take some of your valuable time. We hope the rewards are found is this book.

We must also thank many of our colleagues who pushed, nudged, and guided us through this process. Thank you is not enough to convey our appreciation to Tom Lauth, Julia Melkers, Irene Rubin, Barbara Romzek, George Frederickson, and Steven Maynard-Moody. Their suggestions have been fruitful. And, we want to recognize Elizabeth Granda and Patricia Kolb, who have been so patient and never lost sight of our goal and never let us lose sight of it either.

Finally, we wish to honor the late Gloria Timmer, former Kansas budget director and executive director of NASBO. Her insights into budgeting have sharpened our thinking about state budgeting. She embodied the very essence of a policy-oriented professional budgeter, and we miss her deeply.

From Thurmaier

I cannot begin to thank my wonderfully patient partner, Jeanine, who will no longer have to compete for attention with this book project. And thanks also to Anna and Emily who have given up many hours with their dad so I could spend many hours on this book. My gratitude extends to my parents, who have encouraged me to accomplish my goals from my earliest memory. A special thanks is due also to Lon Sprecher, former Wisconsin budget director, who gave me a chance to learn "the ropes" of budgeting, and to Robyn Gates, my WISBO team leader, who taught me much more than I realized at the time.

From Willoughby

I wish to express my gratitude to Lisa Keating, my graduate research assistant during a most difficult period of this project that involved the transcription of tapes. I appreciate her hard work on behalf of this research effort. I thank my father for his academic mind and his understanding of the various components of this project and, most especially, my mother, who first directed me to the study of public administration given her career in public service to the state of North Carolina. I thank them both for their loving care of my children periodically during this project. Many thanks and love to my husband, Dan, whose support and encouragement remained strong throughout the entire project, and to my children, Forrest, Hart, and Anna, in whose eyes I could always look for the reason to finish.

Acronyms

ANOVA	Analysis of Variance
BCB	Budget and Control Board
BOB	Bureau of the Budget
CC	Client counselors
EBO	Executive budget office
ECM	Economic choice model
GCM	Garbage can model
MOE	Maintenance of effort
NASBO	National Association of State Budget Officers
OECD	Organization for Economic Cooperation and Development
OMB	Office of Management and Budget
OPEC	Organization of Petroleum Exporting Countries
PAS	Policy agenda setting
PBB	Performance-based budgeting
PIC	Political-Incremental choice
RTB	Real-time budgeting
SBO	State budget office
SPL	Social-political-legal
ZBB	Zero-based budgeting

Policy and Politics in State Budgeting

1

Introduction

The Purpose of This Research

The problems facing state government officials include old ones greatly magnified and new ones just surfacing. Dramatic demographic shifts, the volatile international market, modern fiscal federalism, and heightened public awareness regarding taxing and spending issues increasingly burden these decisionmakers in state government. Recent federal devolution of programmatic responsibilities to the states has furthered interest in the fiscal capacity of states to implement a wide range of policies. For example, states have succeeded in changing the way welfare programs are provided, and they are moving forward on a number of innovations in areas like managed care for Medicaid recipients, immunization and other health-related registries and databases, sentencing of offenders, and voting by mail, to name a few. Thus, public officials and administrators are increasingly concerned with budgetary issues, as appropriations ultimately determine and support these public policies and programs.

Yet, we find that there is little information about state budgetary politics and processes that investigate decisionmakers below the level of elected official. Also, the emphasis in academic texts on budgeting is decidedly weighted toward the politics and economics of national budgeting, highlighting the tug of war between the president and Congress. While several texts discuss state and local budgeting, notably Axelrod (1995) and Gosling (1997), most scholastic literature on the topic is composed of ad hoc research on specific aspects of budgeting, often focusing on a single state or select states for analysis (Clynch and Lauth 1991). While there is much to learn from these studies, the field of public budgeting is lacking a full exposition of budgeting at the state level. We have written this book to fill in the details of budgetary politics and processes in state government.

This book is also designed to serve another purpose. There is a long list of academic laments about the lack of a budgetary theory of decision-making that explains on what basis budgeters decide to give one program X amount of dollars, while giving another program Y amount of dollars (Key 1940; Lewis 1952; Straussman 1979; Rubin 1990 and 1997). One obstacle has been the relatively easier task of creating normative or prescriptive models of budgetary behavior. There has not been a concomitant bounty of descriptive models of budgetary behavior. Another hurdle has been the traditional academic focus on budgeting at the macro level (a process-oriented approach with strong political and institutional explanations) versus budgeting at the micro level (an individual decision-making approach). Part of the problem of this focus on macro-level budgeting has involved the controversy over Wildavsky's theory of budgetary incrementalism and whether it is valid as either a descriptive or prescriptive model of budgetary behavior (LeLoup 1978; Rubin 1990). Even then, there are arguments that the point is moot, because the era of incremental budgeting is past, and another model is needed to replace it (Schick 1983; Straussman 1985; Kiel and Elliott 1992).

In this study we are concerned about budgetary decisions on the micro level as understood by James Skok (1980). In a two-year study of the budget process in Pennsylvania, Skok analyzed the distributive and redistributive nature of budgetary decision-making. He found that below the macro-level stage, budgetary decision-making is distributive. "Each program subcategory is analyzed independently on its own merits according to a battery of routine criteria (past performance, indicators of need, evaluation studies, formula mandates, prior-year appropriations, salary projections, and the like)" (Skok 1980, 457–458). However, as budgeting progresses to the macro level, decisions begin to involve redistributive versus distributive issues. Skok (1980, 458) suggests that apolitical analysis is most influential at the micro-level stages of budgetary decision-making "where questions of funding source and/or tradeoffs among program subcategories is not of primary importance."

Further, we believe it is not only possible but also desirable to develop a descriptive model of budgetary behavior. To do this, we intentionally focus our attention on budgeting in the states. Specifically, we develop a descriptive model of budgetary decision-making by a group of key budgetary actors, the examiners in the state budget offices. We focus on these budgeters deliberately. From an internal perspective, the "segmented" quality of the state government budget process involves a distinct cycle of decisions and defines the behavior of budget actors. Long considered an "executive-driven" process greatly influenced by the legal constraint of a balanced-budget requirement and limits on deficit financing, state government budgeting is actually composed of both macro- and micro-level activities. For example, micro-level budget development is comprised of three segments: the agency request, the chief executive's recommendations (recommended total budget), and the legislative appropriation (Abney and Lauth 1986; Crecine 1967; Gray 1983). These are conditioned by the macro environment of political and fiscal factors.

Each component of the state budgetary process involves a distinct set of players characterized by specific role behaviors and particular routines and responses. In this case, role behavior is understood as the "recurring actions of an individual appropriately interrelated with repetitive activities of others so as to yield a predictable outcome" (Katz and Kahn 1978, 189). This book identifies multiple roles of budget examiners because they serve at the nexus of the macro and micro levels of the state budget process and also at the nexus between the policy process and the budget process.

We argue that focusing on this group of relatively unscrutinized budgeters will reveal that (1) they are central decisionmakers in state budgetary and policy processes, (2) they exercise considerable influence on budgetary outcomes through the exercise of delegated powers from governors, and (3) their critical gatekeeping roles produce decisions that substantially affect state budget outcomes and, consequently, the governments of which they are a part. This characterization is conditioned by the decision context for examiners —namely, whether the state budget office (SBO) has a control or policy orientation.

This is not to discount the involvement and influence of the other important actors, including governors and agency heads, legislative leadership, and even media and interest groups. Nor do we argue that these other actors follow the same calculus of decisions as examiners in the budget office, although they may. Also, we understand that elected officials have the final word in budgeting—they have the votes and the veto pens that formally ascribe to them absolute authority and accountability for state budgeting decisions. Instead, we argue that the structure of state budgeting and policy processes places the SBO at the vortex where these two processes meet, and that the governor very often delegates tremendous discretion to the budget office staff through the budget director. We assess the degree of influence that individual budget examiners have in this process and hope to persuade you that it is considerable. We explain the conditions under which we expect to find different degrees of budget office influence on budgetary outcomes. In addition, we discuss the historic, cultural, and political factors that seem to give budget offices in some states more discretionary powers than their counterparts in other states.

The central question of this book is, *On what basis do budget examiners make recommendations to the governor?* In this discussion we develop a model of budget rationality or decision-making "at the center" (Axelrod 1995). We note that the demands on a positivist, micro-level theory of budgeting are formidable. Does it truly describe activity in measurable ways? Can the model account for micro-level decisions, yet be predictive of macro-level ones? Is this model predictive of behavior only under prescribed conditions? Finally, does this theory tie policy and budgetary decisions together in a sensible and meaningful way?

We briefly explore the various notions of rationality to illustrate that there are multiple conceptions of rationality, even though the current climate of discussion in the fields of political science and public administration would lead one to believe that rationality is, de facto, defined as economic rationality. The development of our model of budget rationality begins by identifying its underlying conditions and assumptions. Here we return to the issues of gubernatorial delegation of discretion to budget offices, and to the link between the budget and policy processes. It is the intimate relationship between the policy decisions and the budgetary decisions that requires a budgeting rationality more complex than the incrementalism model or decision models based purely on economic rationality. Budgets are more than simply political or economic decisions. Especially at the state level, budget decisions are rarely divorced from an "air of management" concern for how policies will actually be implemented by agencies, and whether the budgetary and other resources are available and worth the benefits of the policy. As Kenneth Howard (1973) noted more than twenty-five years ago, examiners in state budget offices have stood apart from national budgeting staff in their concern for policy implementation, long before it was fashionable in national or scholastic circles. The "air of management" is subtly infused in the decision-making by state budget examiners, and manifests itself in terms of policy implementation issues rather than simply "agency management" and efficiency.

Understanding this context of budgetary decision-making at the center, in state budget offices, permits us to outline a model of decision-making rationality that can address the multiple facets of the policy and budget problems facing state budget examiners who must recommend some type of action to the governor. We then illustrate this model by dissecting the anatomy of a budget recommendation through a year in the life of two state budget examiners. Joining them on their first day of the new job, we follow the development and evolution of their thinking as they gather information, process it, gather more, identify and frame budgetary problems, analyze them based on available information, and develop recommendations for presentation to their section managers, deputies, budget directors, or governors. Crucial aspects of the recommendation process include: the kinds of information gathered by the examiner, the sequencing of information gathering, the framing of the problem—for themselves and for their superiors—and threshold decisions about how much they will invest in arguing in support of, or opposition to, various budgeting options or solutions that they may develop or that are presented by other budgetary actors, including agency officials and interest groups.

In the end, we hope to persuade you that budgetary politics is only one of five types of budgetary decisions, and that budgetary politics is distinct from budgetary policy in the minds of professional examiners. We explain that budgetary rationality is not synonymous with economic rationality, and that budgeting decisions by examiners based solely on economic rationality are in fact irrational.

We acknowledge that we have only mined the surface of the complexity involved in state budgeting practices. There are many avenues that need exploration. In addition, we invite validation of our model through replications in regions of the country not included in this study as well as other levels of government. For example, we suspect the model is relevant to budget decisions in local government budget offices, where they exist.

The State Government Setting: Factors Influencing Budgeters' Decisions

Decision-making implies action within a specific task environment as well as evidence of a certain "willingness" on the part of the individual to make a choice (Bromiley 1981; Straussman 1979). As this study concerns the state government setting, the process of resource allocation, and the behavior of state government budgeters, it therefore considers individual action in a particular context. Thus, we consider current understanding of the special aspects of this context and the influence of such factors on budgeters' decisions.

Financial Condition

Aaron Wildavsky (1986) explains that modern state government budgeting is plagued by one of two syndromes—either a surplus or a shortfall. He illustrates that changes in budgetary process at the state level vary markedly depending upon the existence of either syndrome. Presence of a surplus necessitates questions about where to spend the overage; presence of a shortfall necessitates questions about where to cut and which potential revenue sources to tap (Wildavsky 1986, 229). Sydney Duncombe and Richard Kinney's 1986 study of state level budgeters substantiates the model of changing behavior in periods of financial shortfall. They found the most frequently mentioned factor affecting appropriations on the part of the state budget officials in their survey to be "revenue availability" or "fiscal condition of the state" or a similar phrase. They state that "for an agency budget office, the overall revenue situation is a reality of life. In good fiscal times you can strive for new or expanded programs; when times are hard you fight to maintain existing programs" (Duncombe and Kinney 1986, 115–116). Their results indicate that competition for funds becomes more heated as fiscal resources become scarce.

Certainly the state of the economy is greatly influential to gubernatorial success. We witnessed how the recession of the early 1990s dogged governors into raising taxes and cutting state programs. Because of this, many faced eroded popularity early in their tenure as chief executive (Beyle 1993, 11). On the other hand, by the end of the decade, most state governments were operating in flush environments.

Political Factors

A number of factors contribute to the political strength and influence of the governor and thereby affect the role of the central budget office and the examiners employed in them. At the onset, party composition of the two branches of government influences the ability of a governor to successfully channel policy and, in particular, the budget, through the legislative branch (Beyle 1993). Certainly the strength of a governor in terms of initiating and promoting policy is directly related to his or her relationship with legislators, a relationship founded primarily on party affiliation that would support such an agenda (Rosenthal 1990). Whether or not the legislative branch is of similar persuasion to the governor contributes mightily to support his or her budget recommendation and, ultimately, the governor's policies (Sabato 1983).

State government party split between the branches has undergone dramatic change over the last several decades—that is, strong one-party states are rare. Following the 1994 elections there were thirty Republican governors, nineteen Democrats, and one independent (Angus King of Maine). Legislative party breakdown that year indicates there were sixteen one-party states, ten in which Democratic governors shared power with predominantly Democratic legislatures, and six in which Republican governors worked with predominantly Republican legislatures (*Book of the States 1993–1994*, 1993, 113). Yet, while the executive branch in the states had swayed markedly Republican in the 1990s, state houses remained predominantly Democratic. Again, following the 1994 elections, there were twenty-four states with Democratic legislatures, just seven with Republican legislatures, and nineteen with split houses (Nebraska having a unicameral legislature). Of the eighteen split states, ten had Democratic houses and seven were predominantly Republican; one state, Michigan, had an evenly split house. Upper chambers of split states were just slightly more likely to be Republican; eight states had Republican senates, seven were Democratic, and three states (Alaska, Florida, and Illinois) had senate chambers evenly split between Democrats and Republicans.

While a party affiliation's greatest potential strength to a chief executive once elected is to promote policy success, we see that the modern governor is most likely to face a legislature in which one or both houses are of another party. Therefore, chief executives seeking to make a policy impact in their state must rely heavily on formal and other informal powers that, in conjunction with party affiliation, can contribute to successful agenda-setting and policy change. We next examine a number of powers afforded to governors that influence the impact that they can have on state government and state policy.

The formal powers of the governor obviously contribute to the state government environment and influence budgeters' decisions. Robert Crew (1992) explains a model of gubernatorial policy success as a function of personality and strategy. Strategy involves the ability of the chief executive to use his or her skills and resources within a given political and economic situation to initiate policy. Personal skill is certainly a function of educational and work background, as well as personality and leadership style. Here too we might classify the informal power of the governor to serve as the primary spokesperson of all citizens of the state, predominantly through the bully pulpit, by giving speeches and public addresses, through television, radio, and increasingly the Internet to communicate with citizens and to generate support for policy initiatives.

Then there are the formal powers of the governor that can help or hinder the chief executive vis-à-vis the legislature regarding policy success. Such powers begin with tenure and succession of the office. Typically, states provide governors a four-year term with succession for an additional term. Some governors also have the opportunity to sit out a term (having served one or two terms) and then run for re-election as chief executive again with the possibility of serving up to two more consecutive terms (for example, in Alabama and North Carolina). Vermont and New Hampshire are the only states that set a two-year tenure of office for the chief executive, although the governors of these states can serve an unlimited number of terms. Ten other states allow for unlimited successive terms. In Utah, the governor can now serve three consecutive four-year terms. In Washington, the governor is limited to eight years of service out of every 14. Finally, Virginia does not allow the governor to serve immediate successive terms (National Governors Association Online 1999).

Alan Rosenthal (1990) portrays a governor's power as a function of the budget process. That is, front-end influence is derived from a governor's ability to set the stage for budget (and thus policy) deliberation, initially with his or her inaugural address, thereafter with submission of a budget recommendation to the legislature, and then through state-of-the-state addresses, other briefings, and memos and executive orders. Early in his or her tenure, the chief executive may also call upon reorganization powers, perhaps to establish new configurations of departments and agencies or to create free-standing boards or commissions. For example, governors in twenty-four states have the ability to reorganize executive departments without legislative approval (NASBO 1999, 25). Further, savvy chief executives use their power of appointment most effectively early in their first administration to set the stage for policy focus throughout their administrations. The appointment power can be weighty. A governor may well make over 1,000 appointments during a given term of office. While the number of elected state executives has declined over the years to strengthen the governor's hand, states still vary on the berth they provide their chief executives for appointing cabinet members and agency heads in addition to judges and other agency, board, and commission members.

The budget cycle itself can be empowering to the chief executive—a biennial process allows greater latitude to a governor for both planning and implementing state policy and programs. Twenty-three states operate a biennial budget process; in some the legislature appropriates for a twenty-four-month period yet allows for reconsideration of appropriations in nonbudget years. The more typical budget cycle in state government is an annual one that requires legislative consideration of the executive budget recommendation every year and appropriation for a twelve-month period (NASBO 1999, 1).

Other aspects of the budget process and the budget format can contribute to gubernatorial success as well. For example, balanced-budget requirements of the governor, but not the legislature, give the upper hand to the legislative branch when deliberating about spending. Most states (forty-five) require that the governor submit a balanced budget to the legislature, while forty-one states require the legislature to pass a balanced budget. And thirty-five states have constitutional or statutory requirements that the governor sign a balanced budget (NASBO 1999, 32). Budget formats range from traditional, line-item approaches most empowering to legislatures to program and performance-based budgets that can offer greater flexibility and discretion to the governor and executive branch agencies and departments. It is rare these days that state governments would utilize an incremental budget approach only, however. In a survey of state budget processes, the National Association of State Budget Offices (NASBO 1999, 45) finds that only four states

(Alaska, Indiana, New Hampshire, and New York) stipulate their budget approach as exclusively incremental. Every other state indicates at least a program approach, if not a hybrid system involving program budgeting, zero- or modified zero-based budgeting, or performance budgeting along with a traditional approach.

One caveat regarding performance budgeting should be mentioned, however. In the past, this reform has been instituted by governors by using executive orders or budget guidelines as a means of gathering better information to distinguish agency performance (for management purposes). Julia Melkers and Katherine Willoughby (1998) find in recent years that legislatures are the more likely source of performance-based initiatives. Their findings substantiate that such reform continues to have the greatest impact on administration and not the cost of government. That is, performance-based budgeting's greatest value relates to organizational factors regarding agency management, program results, and coordination among branches. As such, this budget reform has indicated less impact on political factors such as addressing public concerns about spending, or fiscal factors such as appropriation levels.

One of the greatest tools of agenda-setting and potential policy success for a chief executive is sole responsibility for establishing the revenue estimate. Because state spending is confined by constitutions or statutes to the amount of revenue that can be generated under current law, responsibility for setting that estimate is very empowering. States have a number of different ways in which they ascribe responsibility for the revenue estimate. Preparation of the estimate may be the sole responsibility of the budget office, a revenue agency, a separate or special board or commission, or the legislature. Or, any of these entities may be required to work together to prepare the estimate. Over half the states assign primary authority for the revenue estimate with the executive branch (*Book of the States 1993–1994*, 1993, 322). Approximately twenty-three states require a consensus approach to the development of the forecast. Fifteen states allow the legislature to revise the forecast (NASBO 1999, 17). Slightly over half of the states (twenty-seven) allow for more than annual or biennial updates to the forecast; semi-annual, quarterly, or monthly revisions of the forecast are allowed.

Farther along in the budget process, gubernatorial ability to veto or amend legislation is a formal power that can be an effective tool for the chief executive in terms of policy direction (Abney and Lauth 1997). Governors given some form of veto can gain power and momentum for their agenda at the end of the legislative session. Not surprisingly, gubernatorial veto powers are of numerous kinds. A governor may have veto authority with respect to budget bills concerning:

- Funding for a particular line item;
- Funding for an entire program or agency;
- Language accompanying the appropriation bill explaining how money should be spent;
- Provisos or contingencies related to expenditure of appropriation; or
- The entire appropriation bill only.

Some governors have the power to reduce an appropriation or substitute a new measure for consideration by the legislature. Governors can be afforded the power to add and delete words to bills as well as to change the meaning of words. Today forty-three of fifty governors have line-item veto authority; far fewer have item veto power of selected words, and only three states afford the governor the item veto to change the meaning of words (NASBO 1999, 29).

Once the budget is passed, governors maintain influence and power by implementing the budget. Budget execution responsibilities of the governor and his or her budget staff include monitoring agency spending plans, making allotments and preparing expenditure reports, the conduct of transfers and reprogramming, and discretion regarding the use of contingency, emergency, or rainy day funds, as well as the more mundane functions of central clearance for legislation initiatives of agencies or for hiring, buying equipment, and the like. Again, state governments vary in the degrees of freedom afforded to governors regarding the flexibility they have to conduct these types of activities. NASBO's (1999) investigation of budget processes in the states indicates a number of other functions typical of budget offices in addition to agency budget review and preparation, as exhibited in Table 1.1.

Organizational Setting of the State Budget Office

The organizational placement of the state budget office within state government may influence the role it plays in budgetary decision-making (Howard 1979; Polivka and Osterholt 1985; Stone 1985). This office can be located in the governor's office, within a department of administration, finance, or administration and finance, or established as an independent office. Most states (thirty-one) place their executive budget office within another department of administration or finance, or as a division within a department of management and budget. The budget office is located within the office of the governor in eleven states. In only eight states is the budget office designated as a freestanding agency, typically within the executive branch and thus headed by the governor (NASBO 1999, 14–15).

Donald Stone (1985) suggests that regardless of physical location of the

Table 1.1

State Budget Office Functions in the United States

Budget Office Functions	Proportion of States Indicating Function Is Carried Out by Budget Office (%)
Review legislation	98
Management analysis	90
Program evaluation	88
Planning	80
Fiscal notes	80
Economic analysis	72
Revenue estimating	74
Demographic analysis	44
Debt management	42
Cash management	42
Contract approval	38
Data processing	38
Accounting	34
Pre-audit	28
Tax expenditure report preparation	26

Source: NASBO (1999). *Budget Processes in the States.* Table B, Budget Agency Functions, p. 6.

organization, being listed on the governor's office roster, or otherwise stipulated as a member of the "executive management team," provides strength to the office or officer so designated. For example, of the fifty state budget directors, twenty-eight serve as cabinet members. Stone emphasizes that the crucial nature of the budget to the functioning of the governor usually warrants strategic placement of state budget office staff within the executive office to afford easy access throughout the budget process. Similarly, Larry Polivka and Jack Osterholt (1985, 92) point out that moving Florida's Office of Budget and Planning out of the Department of Administration and into the Executive Office of the Governor in 1979 was a direct effort to enhance gubernatorial leadership and power. Essentially, where the budget office is located within the organization influences the *perceived* power of the budget examiners—the farther the office is organizationally from that of the governor, the less influential the staff is *expected* to be.[1]

Internal aspects of the budget office influence the orientations of budgeters who work within them as well. In a study of state budget examiners in Iowa, Minnesota, and Wisconsin, Gosling (1987) found that the orientation of the budget office, and particularly of the budget director (whether focused on financial management and control or a policy analysis function), influenced examiners' decision-making. Organizational focus served as a factor in defining the job of the examiners, influenced examiners' views of the job and its responsibilities, and provided patterns for future staff recruitment and selection. Specifically, examiners coming into an office with a policy analysis focus exhibited a more developed political acumen because they were exposed to more political players involved with resource allocation decisions (Gosling 1987).

In a national survey of state budget directors, James Ramsey and Merl Hackbart (1979) found that budget reform often results from the persuasive capabilities of the budget director alone. "In states with influential budget directors, the push for budget innovation may come directly from the budget office. . . . [In many states] innovation has been a function of the budget director" (Ramsey and Hackbart 1979, 69). From a general standpoint, James Conant's 1989 empirical study of the relationship between leadership and organizational change indicates that leadership often serves as an explanation for organizational change at the state level. Specifically related to budgetary decisions in the State of New Jersey, he found that the leadership of department heads "played major intervening or independent roles" in securing state dollars. Conant (1989, 7) finds that:

> The level of state resources appropriated to the [Department of Human Services] grew rapidly during the tenure of [Commissioner] George Albanese (1982–1985). Resource expansion was a key objective for Albanese, and he was adept at developing gubernatorial and legislative support for his budget requests. Economic factors . . . undoubtedly played a significant role here, too. But improving economic conditions certainly did not guarantee the kind of resource growth that Albanese was able to secure.

Conant's study illustrates the powerful role of leadership in effecting change in public organizations, and ultimately their output.

Sole responsibility for appointment of the budget director certainly strengthens the budget and policy hand of the chief executive. In 1994, just over half of the states allowed the governor alone to appoint the budget director. Nine states provide for gubernatorial approval of an appointment by the department head within which the budget office resides; nine require the senate's consent of a gubernatorial appointment. Only five states allow the department head to appoint the budget director with no approval requirement from above. Finally, most budget directors serve at the pleasure of the appointing officer.

Staff size may influence the decision orientations of examiners by contributing to the overall strength of the central budget office. From data compiled from two surveys of state budget offices conducted in 1974–75 and 1979–80, Robert Lee (1981) found staff size to be the best single predictor of centralization of spending decisions. He adds that "characteristics about the budget office professional staff provide a better indication [than general state characteristics] of what level of central control [of agency budgets] is likely to be maintained" (Lee 1981, 79). According to NASBO (1999, 12), there is great variability among executive budget offices in total positions allocated to the budget function and the number of budget examiners employed. Total positions in the budget function range from a high in New York of 354 to a low of just 5 in North Dakota. Average number of positions in an executive budget office is 35. Only eight states, including Alabama, have less than 10 positions allocated to the budget function; thirteen states have less than 10 budget examiners in the budget office. New York has the largest number of budget *examiners* (230), while West Virginia has the least (3). Finally, in most states (thirty), budget examiner positions (among others in the budget office) are appointed through the civil service system (NASBO 1999, 12).

Personal Characteristics of Budget Examiners

Level of education and training of employees also influence budgetary decisions at the state level. Primarily, these factors are attributed to the recruitment and selection of examiners by particular budget offices. State budget offices seek to employ candidates who will work well within their organization and who hold the skills necessary to understand and use the information generated by the budget office as well as the other agencies and departments (Poister and McGowan 1984, 222). For instance, Ramsey and Hackbart (1979, 67) found that budget directors listed staff capabilities as the primary impediment to budget innovation in states where change occurred.

Likewise, job experience influences the decisions of the budget examiner. Arnold Meltsner and Aaron Wildavsky (1970), in their case study of budget behavior in the City of Oakland, witnessed distinctions in the review strategies of examiners according to length of time on the job. Experienced examiners (those who have been on the job for more than two years) had a greater sense of their role in the budget process, often exhibiting "nurturing" behavior. As they become more familiar with the programs and services provided by the departments whose budgets they analyze year after year, they become advocates of department objectives. Such examiners are concerned with developing an understanding relationship with their departments and discovering "what will fly" with their governor regarding specific budget requests (Meltsner and Wildavsky 1970, 336). Katherine Willoughby (1993a) found distinctions between novice and experienced budgeters in her study of 131 state budget analysts. That is, more tenured examiners tend to weigh political factors more heavily than do inexperienced examiners. Further, novice examiners tend to adhere to (incremental) "rules of thumb" when reviewing the budgets of departments with which they have developed little rapport. Kurt Thurmaier (1992 and 1995a) also found distinctions from experience factors in his experiment regarding the decision-making of central budget bureau analysts.

State Sample Characteristics

Fiscal and Economic

Our model is based on data collected from 182 interviews with executive budget office staff in a sample of state governments of the United States. This exploratory research project takes advantage of in-depth, face-to-face interviews with these budgeters who work in eleven states, six in the Midwest and five in the South. These eleven states are collectively representative of the states nationwide, exhibiting a range of characteristics regarding population, financial well-being, political makeup, and organizational setting. Illinois is the most populous of the states included in this study, ranked sixth nationally by the *State Yellow Book* (1998). The least populous state is Kansas, ranked thirty-second with approximately 2.6 million citizens in 1994. For the five-year period from 1990 to 1995, Georgia exhibited the greatest population growth rate, 11.2 percent, compared to Iowa, which experienced the lowest population growth rate of 2.3 percent. It is interesting that the five states in the South experienced growth rates of more than 5 percent for this period. Minnesota is the lone Midwest state that experienced such growth (5.4 percent). The rest of the Midwest states experienced population growth of less than 5 percent.

The sample states also represent a mix of economies. Concerning major agricultural commodities produced by these states, most include broiler chickens, corn, and cattle, with Minnesota and Wisconsin noting dairy products and North Carolina and Virginia noting tobacco. The leading industry for most states is manufacturing, listed first in Alabama, Iowa, North and South Carolina, and Wisconsin; service industries are listed first in the rest of the states (*State Yellow Book* 1998). According to the bond rating house of Standard and Poor, the financial rating of the states regarding total employment growth in 1994 indicates that Alabama, Illinois, and South Carolina fell under the U.S. annual rate of just below 3 percent. The rest of the states met or exceeded this rate, with Georgia exhibiting the greatest gain in employment at 5 percent (Standard and Poor's DRI Regional Economic Service: http://www.dri.mcgraw-hill.com/regional/).

Other indicators show diversity of economic health. For example, many of the southern states fare poorly relative to other states regarding per capita income in 1994, with Alabama, Georgia, and North and South Carolina ranking thirtieth or lower for this indicator. (South Carolina ranked lowest at forty-fourth.) The rest of the states range in rank from ninth (Illinois) to twenty-ninth (Iowa). Consideration of percent of the population on federal public assistance indicates the highest proportions in Illinois (8.3 percent), followed closely by Georgia (8.2 percent), North Carolina (7.2 percent), and Missouri (7.0 percent) (*State Yellow Book* 1998). Alabama exhibits the highest unemployment rate in 1994 (6.3 percent) of the sample states, followed by Illinois (5.2 percent) and South Carolina (5.1 percent). The rest of the states have rates that fall between 3 and 5 percent, with the lowest unemployment rates exhibited in Iowa (3.5 percent), then Minnesota and Wisconsin (both 3.7 percent). Per capita federal aid amounts by state in 1996 coincide with indications related to the unemployment rate figures. Among the states examined here, per capita funds of this sort range from a low of $510 in Virginia to the highest aid amount of $820 in South Carolina. Illinois ($779) and Alabama ($778) are second and third from the top, respectively, on this indicator (U.S. Bureau of the Census 1999).

A look at general fund revenues, expenditures, and debt per capita helps to assess the fiscal health of these states. Table 1.2 illustrates these figures for each state, as well as comparison with United States averages for 1994. Distinctions by region are a bit unclear. More Midwest states fall above the national average for general fund revenues, expenditures, and debt per capita. States that may be deemed fairly healthy, considering relative levels of spending compared to relative levels of debt, show that fiscally healthy states include Minnesota, Iowa, North Carolina, and Kansas. States falling at the other end of the spectrum, that is, falling below the U.S. average for per capita revenues and expenditures and higher than the U.S. average for per capita debt, include Illinois, Missouri, and Virginia. Thus, the sample includes states in both regions that fall along a continuum regarding economic and fiscal health, with neither region exhibiting a distinctively poor or distinctively rich economic or fiscal environment.

Politics, Budget Powers, and Organizational Factors

At the time of this study, six of the eleven states had Republican governors. Of these states, three had predominantly Democratic legislatures (Minnesota, South Carolina, and Virginia). Citizens in Minnesota reelected incum-

Table 1.2

1994 General Fund Revenues, Expenditures, and Debt per Capita by State

State	1994 GF Rev/ Capita	State	1994 GF Exp/ Capita	State	1994 GF Debt/ Capita
Minnesota	$3,108	Minnesota	$3,051	Kansas	$ 433
Wisconsin	$2,845	Wisconsin	$2,719	North Carolina	$ 641
Iowa	$2,690	Iowa	$2,662	Iowa	$ 697
North Carolina	$2,537	South Carolina	$2,625	Georgia	$ 733
Kansas	$2,534	North Carolina	$2,492	Alabama	$ 913
South Carolina	$2,476	**U.S. Average**	$2,394	Minnesota	$ 952
U.S. Average	$2,443	Kansas	$2,389	**U.S. Average**	$1,128
Alabama	$2,376	Alabama	$2,354	Virginia	$1,208
Illinois	$2,266	Illinois	$2,221	Missouri	$1,233
Virginia	$2,262	Georgia	$2,215	South Carolina	$1,335
Georgia	$2,199	Virginia	$2,178	Wisconsin	$1,524
Missouri	$2,151	Missouri	$2,007	Illinois	$1,734

Source: Government Finances: State Finances Series, U.S. Department of Commerce, Economics and Statistics Administration, Bureau of the Census, 1990–94.

bent Republican governor Arne Carlson to a second term in November 1994. Likewise, in November 1994 South Carolinians replaced two-term Republican governor Carroll Campbell with another Republican, David Beasley. These states and Virginia were politically split across the branches. The other three states with Republican governors had split legislatures. A Republican senate and Democratic house existed in Illinois and Wisconsin; a Democratic senate and Republican house existed in Iowa (although the party split in the house was very close at fifty-one Republicans to forty-nine Democrats).

Five states had Democratic governors. Strictly Democratic states include Alabama,[2] Georgia, Missouri, and North Carolina. In November 1994, incumbent Zell Miller was voted into a second term as governor of Georgia. Governor Jim Hunt returned to office in 1992 as chief executive in North Carolina as well, having served previously for two terms as governor beginning in 1976. At the time of the study, Kansas was the only state split with a Democratic governor (Joan Finney) and a Republican legislature. This state then became one-party Republican, given the election of Bill Graves to the governor's office in November 1994.

Tenure and succession of governors in these states varies. Illinois, Iowa, Minnesota, and Wisconsin all allow governors to serve unlimited four-year terms. The rest of the states, excluding Virginia, provide constraints on succession such as limiting the governor to two consecutive terms. Virginia is the only sample state that confines the chief executive to one four-year term of office.

Of the states included in this study, several had governors with fairly long tenures as chief executive. Iowa's Terry Branstad (R) had served in the state's highest office since 1982. Tommy Thompson (R) had been Wisconsin's governor since 1986, and North Carolina's Jim Hunt (D) was first elected as governor in 1976 and served two terms before beginning another two-term tenure in 1992.

These governors are afforded various levels of flexibility and discretion related to administrative practices that influence their power vis-à-vis the legislature. For example, governors in Minnesota and Wisconsin have the ability to reorganize departments during legislative recess. Illinois, Missouri, and Virginia governors have partial ability to reorganize departments during legislative recess while governors in Kansas, North Carolina, and South Carolina must have legislative approval (NASBO 1987).

These states also differ in the budgetary power and organizational arrangements afforded to each governor and reflect the different and changing executive-legislative arrangements discussed by Edward Clynch and Thomas Lauth (1991). Every state except Alabama operates on a July-to-June budget calendar. Alabama's fiscal year runs from October through September. Six states operate on an annual budget cycle; biennial budget cycles exist in Minnesota, North Carolina, Virginia, and Wisconsin. In Kansas, nineteen agencies are on a biennial budget cycle, while the rest operate on an annual one (NASBO 1999, 5).

Seven of these state governments have budget offices located in a department of administration, finance, or management. Budget offices in Georgia, North Carolina, and Illinois are in the governor's office. The Office of State Budget in South Carolina is in the Budget and Control Board, a quasi executive-legislative body unique to the sample observed here.

Among the sample states, the governor appoints the budget director in six states (Georgia, Illinois, Iowa, Kansas, North Carolina, and Virginia). In four states the director of finance (Alabama and Minnesota) or administration (Missouri and Wisconsin) appoints the budget director, upon approval of the governor. And in South Carolina, the Budget and Control Board (BCB) is responsible for appointing the budget director. Of the eleven states included in this study, only three (Illinois, Iowa, and North Carolina) designate the budget director as an official cabinet member.

In five states the executive has the primary authority for determining the revenue estimate. Of these, Illinois and Georgia provide analytical and budget support within the office of the governor. Minnesota, Missouri, and Virginia also require that the executive prepare the revenue estimate, although the governor's budget support is located within a separate department or office. In South Carolina, the budget office is responsible for the revenue estimate, and by virtue of its location in the BCB cannot be considered a responsibility of the chief executive alone.[3]

Of the remaining states, Alabama, Iowa, and Kansas require that the revenue estimate be prepared by consensus. Wisconsin also requires a joint effort across branches. The executive branch is legally required to prepare the estimate, while the legislature's Joint Committee on Finance is able to revise it. In these four states, the executive budget office is in a department separate from the office of the governor. In North Carolina, the Fiscal Research Division within the Legislative Services Commission, an arm of the General Assembly, is responsible for preparing the revenue estimate. This state is unique in the strength afforded the legislature vis-à-vis the governor, given that the chief executive has no veto power. Nevertheless, analytical and budget support for the governor is located in the Office of Management and Budget housed in the chief executive's office.

Virginia's governor is the only one in the sample not required by law to present a balanced budget to the General Assembly. Virginia, Iowa, and Missouri do not require their legislatures to pass a balanced budget; a majority of the states do not legally require the governor to sign a balanced budget (Illinois, Iowa, Kansas, Minnesota, North Carolina, Virginia, and Wisconsin). Only Illinois is allowed to carry over a deficit (ACIR 1994, 6).

North Carolina is the only state in the sample (and in the United States) in which the governor does not have any veto powers. However, such inherent weakness is somewhat diminished in this state by the personal popularity of Governor Jim Hunt, who was returned to office in 1992 having previously served as governor of North Carolina for two terms beginning in 1976. All of the other states in the sample afford their governor some veto power, typically allowing the governor to veto line items, including an amount or a paragraph. Georgia, Illinois, and Wisconsin also allow the governor to veto syntax. In Alabama, "the governor may return a bill without limit for recommended amendments for amount and language as long as the legislature is in session" (NASBO 1999, 30). In Virginia, the governor may return the budget bill without limit for recommended amendments for amount and language. For purposes of a veto, a line item is defined as "an indivisible sum of money that may or may not coincide with the way in which items are displayed in an appropriation act. If a language paragraph designates a sum of money for a distinct purpose, it is subject to the item veto" (ACIR 1994).

Comparison of the Sample States

Assessment of the above data concerning the factors important to state government decision-making, and specific to gubernatorial power and budget office orientation, yields interesting propositions. That is, we witness that each state has characteristics that both contribute to and detract from the governor's ability to initiate and promote his or her agenda and thereby foster policy change or initiation. Looking at indicators of fiscal condition, several states sink to the bottom, relatively speaking, regarding capacity. For example, Alabama, Illinois, and South Carolina rank low or near the bottom for a few of the indicators noted. Yet, special circumstances exacerbate these states' condition in 1994. For example, the constitutional powers of the governor in Illinois are very strong, and Governor Jim Edgar's extensive state government background, use of a transition team to jump-start his administration at the start of his first term, and solid appointments to state agencies to distance himself from the previous administration contribute greatly to the view of Edgar as a potentially successful chief executive. On the other hand, he stepped into the governor's chair during a particularly bleak budget period bought on by what he termed as a "spending spree" by the previous administration. Further, the reduction of the state's bond rating by Standard and Poor drove a nail in the budget coffin, and certainly tied hands, at least during the first half of the decade of the 1990s (Gove 1992).

In Alabama, the one-party status existing in 1994 would suggest an empowering environment for the governor. However, Governor Jim Folsom Jr. was not elected to office; as lieutenant governor under Governor Hunt, he was placed in the governor's seat when Hunt was removed as the chief executive following his conviction for state ethics laws violations. Further, while this state touts an executive-empowering program budget format, the state's fund structure is actually quite hamstrung by the education fund, which automatically soaks up most state revenues (Pilegge 1978).

Other examples of state dichotomies include North Carolina and Virginia. North Carolina gets lots of credit for an advanced budget format and process, as well as for the state's very popular and experienced governor, whose party alliance is reflected in the legislature. Yet, these factors cannot completely sweep aside the fact that the chief executive in this state operates at a disadvantage compared to others in the sample in that he has no veto authority. In Virginia, the strong budget powers of the governor cannot overcome a poor budget outlook in 1994 nor the weakness of the governor given his constricted tenure.

Recognizing the distinctive characteristics of each state government, including the political environment, the budget power and authority afforded each governor, and the organizational setting within which each chief executive works, is an important first step in this research effort. While the states are different in the powers and resources that they afford their governors to manage the political circumstances and fiscal environments, the state budget office (SBO) stands out as a key instrument the governor can use to craft and implement policy priorities. This book reports on our field study of SBOs and their examiners to determine the extent to which this is true, and how this shapes budgetary decision-making inside the SBOs. We next seek understanding about how such resources and circumstances can be used by a governor as he or she wades through policy development and change while managing state government.

Interview Methodology

Interviews were conducted with 182 budgeters in the state budget offices of eleven states chosen to be included in the sample. Speaking with almost everyone responsible for budget review and spending recommendations in each office, from the newly hired examiner to state budget directors, we have explored the richness and complexity of state budget office decision-making on hours of tapes and pages of transcripts. Table 1.3 lists the states included in the study, the name of the executive budget office in each, and the number of budgeters interviewed by office. As noted, we were interested only in interviewing those budgeters chiefly responsible for budget review and development, including examiners, section managers, the deputy director(s), as well as the budget director. Additionally, at the suggestion of some SBOs, we included section managers from divisions other than budget review and development, if such managers had served as a budget examiner or section manager in budget review and development prior to their present position. Therefore, response rates by state and in total are indicative of all budgeters to which we were afforded interviews and who were responsible for budget review and development activities in 1994. Table 1.4 arrays the interviews of SBO staff by supervisory level.

As Table 1.3 suggests, this study uses a nonprobability convenience sample of states in two regions of the United States. The examiners were interviewed during the spring, summer, and fall of 1994, with the exception of Kansas's budget office examiners, who were interviewed during the summer of 1993. The examiner category includes examiners, and when available the division or section managers (team leaders) and deputy directors of the budget offices. We also interviewed the SBO budget directors, and in some states it was also appropriate to interview the secretary of administration (or the head of whatever department housed the budget office), as in Iowa. Typically, a researcher visited a budget office over a period of days, conducting interviews lasting from thirty to ninety minutes for each budgeter. On average, interviews lasted about forty-five minutes. SBO budgeters were asked a number of questions regarding how they approached their responsibilities of

Table 1.3

Number of Budgeters Interviewed by State Budget Office

State	State Budget Office	Number of Budgeters Interviewed	Number of Budgeters in SBO	Percent of Budgeters Interviewed
Southeast				
Alabama	State Budget Office in the Department of Finance	8	9	89
Georgia	Office of Planning and Budget in the Office of the Governor	18	21	86
North Carolina	Office of State Budget and Management in the Office of the Governor	12	15	80
South Carolina	Office of State Budget in the Budget and Analysis Division of the Budget and Control Board	14	14	100
Virginia	Planning and Budget Department in the Finance Secretariat	21	22	95
Midwest				
Illinois	Bureau of the Budget in the Governor's Office	28	30	93
Iowa	State Budget Division in the Department of Management	11	11	100
Kansas	Budget Division in the Department of Administration	17	18	94
Minnesota	Division of Budget Services in the Department of Finance	19	21	90
Missouri	Division of Budget and Planning in the Office of Administration	15	16	94
Wisconsin	Division of Executive Budget and Finance in the Department of Administration	19	26	73
Total		182	203	90

Table 1.4

Interviews of Budgeters by State and Supervisor Level

| | Supervisor Level | | | | |
State	Examiner	Manager	Budget Director	DOA Secretary	Total
Alabama	4	3	1		8
Georgia	15	2	1		18
Illinois	23	4	1		28
Iowa	9	NA	1	1	11
Kansas	11	5	1		17
Minnesota	15	3	1		19
Missouri	10	4	1		15
North Carolina	6	5	1		12
South Carolina	6	7	1		14
Virginia	19	2			21
Wisconsin	14	4	1		19
Total	132	39	10	1	182

agency budget review and recommendation of spending to their governor. A protocol for the loosely structured interviews is presented in Figure 1.1.

Researchers attempted to address all questions in Figure 1.1 in each interview. However, given the open-ended nature of loosely structured, face-to-face interviews, some questions may not have been addressed in any given interview. Isadore Newman and Keith McNeil (1998) might categorize this interview protocol as "partially structured," although we do provide a basic core of open-ended questions. Accordingly, we as researchers are interested in the reasons behind the responses, and we seek to explore these reasons in-depth through a relaxed or flexible interview protocol. Such a data-gathering technique allows researchers "to look into the motives behind stated actions to determine explanation for behaviors" (in this case, decisions) (Newman and McNeil 1998, 27). The best aspect of this interview method is that it allows the researcher "to make more valid interpretations of the data, which can yield more meaningful solutions to the problem under study" (Newman and McNeil 1998, 28).

The weakest aspects of validity and reliability of this type of data gathering, compared to other types of survey methods (such as by mail or telephone), are researcher bias (how questions are presented; relationship to subject in the face-to-face setting) and the objectivity of responses from subjects (Newman and McNeil 1998). For such reasons we sought to immediately establish our credentials as academics to examiners in each budget office, declaring our approach to the study for research purposes only. Both re-

Figure 1.1 **Budget Examiner Interview Protocol**

Date: _____

Name of Examiner: _____

Job Title/Position: _____

State Government: _____

1. How long have you been employed by this budget office?
2. When did you first arrive in the budget office (what time of year)?
3. What did you do before coming here? Previous work experience and educational background?
4. What division or section did you first begin working in?
5. Think back to when you first entered this budget office, what were your first assignments?
6. What did you do to prepare for these assignments? What information did you begin to collect? Where did you go for information?
7. Have you since changed assignments?
8. What were the reasons for changing assignments or sections?
9. How do you go about learning about a new assignment?
10. How do you know who to contact in an agency?
11. How do you get a sense of the priorities of the agencies that you review?
12. When you put together a recommendation for an agency/program, to what extent do you rely on site visits?
13. Do you ever have need to consult the state attorney on matters related to your agencies?
14. Do you need to assess clients of your agencies, directly or indirectly?
15. If cuts are necessary, how do you implement them? Do you give the agency a number and have them come up with the cuts, or do you make suggestions for cuts?
16. Has an agency head/program director ever been surprised by the recommendation put forward by the governor? Is this common? When might this happen? Have you been surprised by a department's request?
17. How do you get a sense of the priorities of the governor?
18. To the extent that you make recommendations, do you anticipate reaction to your recommendations from the budget director? From the governor? From the agency?
19. Would you make a recommendation that you knew might be criticized by the budget director or the governor?
20. Who is your boss? Who do you work for?
21. Do analysts in this office influence state spending? Do they influence state policy? Would you characterize the general orientation of this office toward agencies as Control? Management? Planning? Policy?
22. What do you think are the most important qualities that an analyst working in this office can have to be effective?
23. How would you describe your role with respect to your agencies? Antagonist? Adversary? Advocate? Other?
24. Do personal values come into play in your recommendation decisions? If so, how do they influence your decisions?
25. How have technological advancements changed your duties and/or workload?
26. Do you like your job?
27. What do you anticipate in your future, say five years from now, professionally speaking?

searchers had conducted extensive interviews of budget office staff at the state and local levels prior to this study and thus were comfortable with making initial contacts, describing the nature of the study and research protocol, as well as referencing past research about budget office staff and activities. Each author's previous experience as a budget examiner in the 1980s (Thurmaier was an examiner in the Wisconsin State Budget Office and Willoughby was an interning examiner in the budget office of Wake County, North Carolina) also helped establish interviewer credibility. The fact that these budgeters were being asked questions about their routine duties, activities, and decision-making on the job, and not questions of a personal nature, minimizes response bias. Also, the interviews were conducted in the examiners' own offices, or in a budget office conference room, affording a high comfort level to examiners.

Ultimately, the purpose of our exploratory interviews was to try to understand how these particular state government budgeters think and feel about the decisions that they make as part of their job and on a routine basis (Oppenheim 1992, 65–80). We considered it important to provide a structure to the interview through the questions, yet maintain flexibility during each interview to account for spontaneity of response and to pick up gaps and hesitations in the conversation as well as movement of response from one topic to another, even if such movement might break protocol flow. Further, we understand that consideration of interview data from a number of examiners from each budget office serves as a validity check regarding the responsibilities, activities, and orientations of the budget offices included in the sample. Although this study involves a judgment sample of elites, each researcher interviewed most of the examiners from each budget office in order to get a sense of its "budget orientation."

As Figure 1.1 indicates, the sessions began with an account by the examiners of the length of time they had been employed in the budget office, and their previous work experiences and educational background. Interview questions related to perceptions of the budgeter's role in the budget process, the general orientation of the budget office, what information was collected for agency budget review and how such information was collected, the factors considered most important when reviewing agency programs and services to determine spending plans for the upcoming fiscal year, who the budgeter worked for, and what characteristics were considered most important to be effective in the job. The core of the interview concentrated on the examiner's strategies for crafting budget recommendations to the budget director and governor. Several questions explored examiners' perceptions of agency and gubernatorial agendas, and their role in relaying information to both agencies and the governor. Except for the few instances when a budgeter declined permission to be taped, all interviews were recorded and then transcribed for analysis.

While the task of sorting through all of this data has been enormous, the pleasure of telling these budgeters' stories is very rewarding. We guaranteed the anonymity of respondents, so citations of quotes attributable to subjects throughout this text are omitted. We occasionally omit the state label when it might compromise anonymity. Whenever we have quoted the budget director specifically, we have tried to verify accuracy with that director since that anonymity is often impossible.

Summary: Using This Text Effectively

In this book we address three questions:

1. How do public budgeters (in this case, state government budget examiners) make decisions?
2. Can we describe a model of budget rationality that reflects this budgeter's decision-making activity?
3. Under what conditions does this model apply?

The role that states play in our federal system today, both financially and from a policy standpoint, warrants analysis of budgeting practices at this level of government. Similarly, the role of the budget examiner as a nexus between the budget and policy processes entreats us to learn about how they make spending decisions. Academics' relative lack of attention to state-level budgeting and to budget examiner activities and decisions is a primary reason that we have focused our research on this level of government and these particular budgeters.

In the preface we acknowledged the usefulness of this text to three groups of readers—scholars of political science, public administration, and public policy and their students, as well as practitioners, in particular governors and their budget office staff. We have provided a flow to the presentation of our model and research that progresses from theoretical justification to practical "application" to facilitate a learning progression that begins with traditional concepts of state government policy and budget processes, decision models, and general descriptions of state government and SBO characteristics. This first chapter presents our research questions and explains the state government budget process, expressly describing the sample state government budget office environments considered. We present a way of distinguishing states and SBOs according to political, economic, and organizational factors. The second chapter then details the budget problem and reviews budget and policy models that contribute significantly to our concept of budgetary rationality. The second chapter ends with the definition of the budget decision agenda and illustration of the SBO as the gatekeeper of information that links micro and macro decisions.

Chapter 3 begins a thorough consideration of our budget rationalities model of decision-making, explaining the need to accommodate multifaceted budget problems. The chapter defines effectiveness decisions, addressing the social, political, and legal angles of budget problems. Chapter 4 continues fleshing out our decision-making model by defining efficiency decisions through descriptions of economic and technical rationalities. This chapter concludes with a discourse on problem representation and issue framing and describes how an examiner can approach budget problems from a number of angles, thereby engaging a variety of rationalities.

Chapter 5 provides clear descriptions of the SBO budget orientation exhibited in each sample state and as told by the examiners themselves. We compare and contrast SBOs along a continuum from a strict control to strong policy orientation. We present data that confirms that communication flow and budget actor relationships contribute markedly to office orientations. This chapter affords the reader excellent comparisons among a variety of SBOs exhibiting distinctive decision contexts that fall along the control-policy continuum.

The fifth chapter sets the stage for the stories that we tell in chapters 6 and 7. In chapter 6 we shadow the prototypical examiner employed in a policy-oriented SBO. Our story is peppered with the experiences as told to us by examiners from the budget offices we visited that exhibited a strong policy orientation. We describe how the examiner approaches her work, from her first day on the job, throughout the period of budget development to recommendation of agency spending to the governor. We use the story to explain to the reader what information is important to the examiner and when, and how the examiner determines what to communicate to those working in the agencies whose budgets she oversees and, more importantly, to her superiors in the chain of command.

Chapter 7 then presents a different, although equally engaging story—we shadow the prototypical examiner employed in a control-oriented SBO. Carefully moving through the same stages in budget development and recommendation enhances a comparison with the activities and decisions of our examiner in chapter 6. The reader will find that the differences between the decision-making approaches of the two examiners are considerable.

In chapter 8 we delve into the roles that examiners play throughout the different stages of the budget process, within different decision contexts, and the influences of a control- versus policy-oriented SBO. It is here that we are able to contrast the decision styles of the control- versus policy-oriented examiners and particularly the usefulness of the various rationalities to these examiners when making budget decisions. In this chapter we explore role definition of examiners within SBOs as advocate, conduit/facilitator, policy analyst, or antagonist. Further, we illustrate how examiner roles change depending upon the SBO orientation.

The concluding chapter evaluates the extent to which we have accomplished the goals established with this research effort. Have we answered our principal questions? How do budget examiners in SBOs make decisions? Have we presented a reasonable model of such a decision process? And, knowing the components of the model, can we predict a manner of decision-making to be expected of examiners, depending upon certain characteristics of the state, the office, and the individual that we have considered? We also suggest future avenues for research that can contribute to better understanding and application of our model.

We hope that the audiences to which we have steered this work will find the layout of the text helpful. We incorporate appropriate research protocol to support telling the story of state government budgeting and specifically that of examiners and how they link state policy with budgets and state budgets with policy. We find this story to be compelling and, yes, even fantastic at times. We hope that you do too.

Notes

1. We know of no empirical test of this conventional wisdom.
2. Republican Governor Guy Hunt was removed from office in 1993 and succeeded by Democrat Jim Folsom, son of former governor "Big Jim" Folsom. Folsom lost the November 1994 election to Republican Fob James, who served previously as a Democratic governor from 1979 to 1982, making Alabama then a split state, given the overwhelmingly Democratic legislature.
3. In 1993, legislation was passed in South Carolina creating a cabinet form of government and establishing an executive budget system. This requires that the governor and not the Budget and Control Board (BCB) develop budget recommendations. In 1994, however, budgetary personnel within the Office of the Governor were extremely limited. Analysts within the Office of State Budget of the BCB reviewed agency requests and prepared budget recommendations for the governor to consider. The governor, and not the BCB, then presented budget recommendations to the General Assembly. Yet, the budget office within the BCB still is responsible for development of the revenue estimate and is therefore classified as a consensus method of forecasting.

2

The State Budget Office and the Budget Problem

The Budget Problem: Funding Policies and Programs

At its core, budgeting is a decision-making process for finding the appropriate balance between acceptable levels of expenditures, revenues, and debt. Under the broad umbrella of "balancing the budget" are subsets of budget problems that are expenditure-, revenue-, or debt-related. Each of these problems requires a decision, and the aggregation of these decisions comprises "the final decision" about the main budget problem: how to allocate public resources to finance government policies and programs. The final decision on the budget problem is usually a vote (or series of votes) on the budget package by the legislative body (including any veto override decisions). These broad aspects of budgeting, and the general process (or processes) that lead to budget votes, are generally encompassed and described as macro-budgeting.

Macro-budgeting fundamentally is reducible to an allocation problem because budgets finance government policies and programs. The proliferation of government programs at all levels of American government has meant increasing complexity in budgetary decisions. Budgeting has also become more difficult because the willingness of Americans to increase taxes has not matched their willingness to increase government spending. While public opinion polls superficially reflect a desire to cut government spending, they also reveal that fingers are usually pointing at someone else's program to be cut. The problem of balancing the budget today, as it has been in the past, is deciding how to allocate dollars across numerous and various and often competing programs, given a revenue constraint. For example, D.W. Breneman (1995, B2) affirms that states need to think the unthinkable concerning higher education in that "sweeping changes must be considered, because the combination of growing demand and limited state resources will not permit painless solutions."

Budgetary problems are integral parts of broader public policy problems. Dennis Palumbo (1995, 11) defines public policy as "the guiding principle behind regulations, laws, and programs; its visible manifestation is the strategy taken by government to solve public problems." As such, public policy is characterized as "complex, invisible, and elusive." Budget decisions finance a program plan for government action on a specific issue. Harold Smith (1945) recognized this as director of the federal Bureau of the Budget (BOB), noting that budgets reflect the program of the chief executive and must encompass the *political, economic,* and *social* aspects of that program. Similarly, Norton Long (1949, 257) argued that "administrative rationality requires a critical evaluation of the whole range of complex and shifting forces on whose support, acquiescence, or temporary impotence the power to act depends."

The Governor's Budget and Policy Problems

Most governors, with a few exceptions, are policy-minded. Coleman Ransone (1982) notes that policy formation is one function in which the governor is active personally. He argues that the process of state policy formation involves a series of large and small decisions by the governor over a period of several years. The cumulative impact of the governor's decisions during the course of his or her administration probably determines his or her effectiveness in all aspects of the policy determination role. Some decisions are much more dramatic than others. The budget and its preparation involve governors in their greatest policy-making role. "No other elected official plays as important a role as the governor in setting the policy agenda" (Bernick and Wiggins 1991, 75).

Governors promote their policy agenda through budget development and recommendation—dramatically so through their State of the State and budget presentations. Former New York budget director Dall Forsythe (1997) intones that these documents are likely to be the two most detailed statements of the governor's plans for the next year or two. Top staff needs to coordinate the two so the budget can pay for the State of the State initiatives. The governor and budget director need to plan for the chief executive's program and political initiatives. The budget director has chief responsibility for developing a preliminary financial plan—the totals of spending and revenues resulting from the baseline and revenue estimates.

James Gosling's (1991) study of gubernatorial policy agendas finds that governors have increased their use of budgets as policy vehicles, especially since the latter half of the 1980s. Burdett Loomis (1994, 43) describes the governor at work on the policy–budget link in a Kansas budget year, noting that simultaneous to constructing the budget, the governor was crafting his State of the State address, which affords the chief executive his most important opportunity to focus the state's attention on the few issues he deemed most important. Although the budget and the speechwriting processes are complementary, Loomis notes they are not identical. The governor's policy agenda is focused on a few initiatives, while the budget must encompass the expansive range of state policies and programs. Budget development and recommendation serve as the foundation for the governor's bully pulpit.

Budget requests emerge from the policy process. When a program is proposed for funding, it becomes part of the larger budget problem because it competes with other proposed and existing programs for funds. The individual funding decision for a program is itself a smaller budget problem, because the program exists as various activities using a variety of resources, most of which are reducible to money. Since there are usually alternative ways of operating a program to achieve policy goals, the micro-level budget problem for the individual budgeter is *how* to fund *which* activities to achieve a goal (or goals). Knowing how and why a public policy program exists is essential to understanding how to evaluate a budget request to fund it. Using the budget to fund policies forms a nexus of the budget process and the policy process. These two processes are distinct but interdependent. Policies demand budgetary support, while budgets exist to fund policies. Analysis of budget requests to fund policies cannot help but be tied to analysis of the policies.

V.O. Key (1940) framed the budget problem as one of allocating expenditures among different purposes to achieve the greatest return, suggesting a predilection for a budget rationality model based on economic rationality and its doctrine of marginal utility. Yet, in the end, he concludes that the economic rationality model "has a ring of unreality when applied to public expenditures. The most advantageous utilization of public funds resolves itself into a matter of value preferences between ends lacking a common denominator. As such, the question is a problem in political philosophy" (Key 1940, 1143–1144). Thus, because decisions about funding rest on value preferences, careful analysis of the factors governing the decisions of budgeters is warranted.

Verne Lewis (1952) took Key's challenge and argued that budgetary decision-making ought to be based on marginal utility analysis, rather than on a theory of political philosophy. He sought to overcome the common denominator problem of comparing "unlike things" by using the marginal costs and benefits of competing budgetary requests as the basis for decisions. Essential elements of his model are manifested to some degree in the performance budgeting and zero-based budgeting reforms in later decades. Still, his perspective was based on an economic rationality model, and by ignoring the problem of fundamental philosophical value preferences noted by Key, his model is unable to guide decisions when noneconomic values cannot be ignored.

Wildavsky (1978) was especially interested in what he termed the "social interaction" style of decision-making. He drew a stark contrast between that style and the traditionally favored information-driven style, which he termed the "intellectual-cognition" style. Dominant groups using the "social interaction" style will not collect, analyze, or present information if doing so might raise tensions that could slow the resolution of an issue, threaten the group's longer-term power base in the policy-making system, or be costly in other ways.

Wildavsky argued that this approach is more political and less rigorously analytic in nature than the cognitively driven styles of decision-making that scholars and engineers tend to prefer. However, such an approach is not necessarily less "rational." From the perspective of those in power, it can make good sense. Although a sizable body of research suggests that political behavior can undermine effectiveness because it often involves the suppression, disregard, and distortion of potentially useful information (Cyert and March 1963), a focus on "objective" analysis at the expense of attention to the power structure surrounding an issue can also lead to ineffective policy-making (Pfeffer 1981). Wildavsky therefore concludes with admonitions on the virtues of policy-making based on balancing social interaction and intellectual cognition.

Susan Frost et al. (1997) studied state policy decision-making regarding the cutoff for admissions of out-of-state students to state institutions and found politics to be the overriding determinant of how decisions were made— top–down policy with little formal input from university administrators, faculty, or students, and a position assumed by decisionmakers based on perception rather than research or fact. Instead of a focused and united front to combat top-level decision-making, arguments by faculty and university administrators for increased percentages of out-of-state students were made individually. Essentially, information played virtually no role; this policy issue was resolved almost entirely without resort to comprehensive analysis.

If it is the value preferences of budgeters that ultimately guide budget allocation decisions, then a model of budgetary decision-making needs to incorporate the ways in which those values are brought to bear on the economic aspects of budget problems facing government decisionmakers. Understanding budget problems first as policy problems leads us to think of budgeting as more than an economic efficiency exercise. Thinking about the multifaceted complexity of policy problems, then, necessitates consideration of whether each facet of the problem requires a distinctive type of decision-making process. We argue later that a comprehensive budget rationality involves the coordination of multiple decision-making processes. Let us first look at the way the policy process generates budget requests.

Policy Change and the Agenda-Setting Model

There are two general types of policy changes that generate budget requests. Most are only incremental changes to existing policies and programs; some represent substantial changes in policy and can inaugurate new programs or radically change others. Not surprisingly, there are two basic decision-making models that try to explain these types of policy changes: incrementalism and the Garbage Can Model (GCM). Charles Lindblom's (1968) policy process model describes the process for making incremental changes to policies. Wildavsky (1964, et seq.) then used the incremental decision-making model to explain budgetary changes as well.

Whereas Lindblom's and Wildavsky's recognition of incrementalism focused attention on the predictable aspects of small, successive changes to programs, others (Miller 1991; Kingdon 1995) have explored the utility of the GCM of decision-making originally developed by Michael Cohen et al. (1972) (see Box 2.1). John Kingdon (1995) successfully applies the GCM to agenda-setting in the public policy process for the United States government to explain more radical changes in public policies. Likewise, Irene Rubin's (1997) model of real-time budgeting (RTB) has a strong flavor of a GCM framework. We first explore Kingdon's decision-making model based on the GCM to extract some relevant features for understanding budgeting. Then we explore incrementalism and compare the features relevant to budgeting in state budget offices. A synthesis of these models with Rubin's RTB model begins to build a framework for understanding budget rationality in a state budget office.

Although Kingdon's policy agenda setting (PAS) model does not focus on the budgetary aspects of the policy process, his analysis enlightens us with respect to how the public policy agenda produces budget requests that are considered by the central budget office. The Kingdon model has three important features: multiple decision streams, two clusters of decision actors, and two types of decision opportunities. Kingdon treats decisions about problems, decisions about policy alternatives, and political decisions as separate streams in the policy process. The likelihood of significant shifts in policy choices (in contrast to incremental policy changes) increases greatly when

Box 2.1

The Garbage Can Model

How can one explain decision-making involving actors who operate in a system that could be characterized as an organized anarchy? Cohen et al. (1972) accomplished this task by noting that organized anarchies have three main characteristics. First, actors have problematic preferences, which is to say that they are sometimes unclear, sometimes inconsistent, and often changing. Perhaps more importantly, preferences are often unknown, and they are discovered through actions more than serving as the basis for actions. Second, the decision-making technology is poorly understood by organizational actors, which is to say that often they are unclear about the process for working on a task and largely ignorant of what other actors in the organization are doing. They resort to trial and error and various heuristic techniques to accomplish objectives. Third, participation in organization activities is fluid, which is to say that members devote uneven time and effort to different activities and readily interrupt work on one subject, perhaps to return to it again later, or perhaps not.

Solving problems in organized anarchies does not resemble the traditional, linear process prescribed by the standard synoptic model (identify problem, identify alternatives, evaluate alternatives, choose best alternative). However, the anarchy generally is not characterized by chaos; there is some structure to decision-making. These organizations are laced with four separate activity streams, which are relatively independent of each other. Problems are identified, recognized, or generated in one stream; they are measured, characterized, or redefined even though they are not matched to a solution, or they may lack identifiable solutions. Meanwhile, solutions are developed for problems; they too are analyzed, reformed, and recast, and remain available as mates for any problem that might be adaptable. Participants flow in a third stream, drifting in and out of decision activities, identifying problems and identifying and evaluating solutions. Finally, choice opportunities float apart from these other three activity streams, providing an opportunity for participants to gather and fit a problem with a solution, or a solution with a problem, or several solutions with a problem, and so on.

The choice opportunities are the basis for the garbage can metaphor, for they consist of the problems and solutions as they are generated and acknowledged by participants. What is available in a choice opportunity depends upon "the mix of [garbage] cans available, on the labels attached to the alternative cans, on what garbage is currently being produced, and on

(cont'd)

(Box 2.1 cont'd)
the speed with which garbage is collected and removed from the scene" (Cohen et al. 1972, 2). Thus, organized anarchies resemble "a collection of choices looking for problems, issues and feelings looking for decision situations in which they might be aired, solutions looking for issues to which they might be the answer, and decision makers looking for work" (Cohen et al. 1972, 2). Who shows up at a particular meeting, and the issues on the minds of participants that day, will influence the choices made at the meeting, if any.

Organized anarchies make three types of decisions: by resolution (choices resolve problems after working on them for some time), by oversight (problems are attached to other choices and a new choice is made), and by flight (problems are unresolved because problems leave the choices, allowing a decision to be made). Decisions can also combine flight and oversight, by which some problems leave choices and the remaining problems are solved. Therefore, not all problems are addressed and not all choice opportunities are taken.

Cohen et al. argue that the most important implications of the garbage can model are that decision-making by flight and oversight are much more common than by resolution. The process is also sensitive to variations in the resources required to make decisions; as energy requirements increase, problems are less likely to be resolved, flight increases, and decisions take longer. Decisionmakers and problems tend to move together from one decision opportunity to another, giving decisionmakers "a feeling that they are always working on the same problems in somewhat different contexts, mostly without results" (10). The components in the decision process can also be sharply interactive; for example, quick decisions are encouraged by restricting the ratio of choices to problems while allowing any decisionmaker to participate in the decisions.

Particularly noteworthy for us, important problems are more likely to be solved than unimportant ones, and problems that appear early are more likely to be resolved than those that arrive late. Hierarchical ranking of problems produces a queue for decisions, with the late-arriving and relatively unimportant problems waiting at the end of the queue. This is more likely when the most important problems require a lot of energy for decision-making.

Cohen et al. note that decisions (choices) are different for different types of problems. Important decisions are made by oversight and flight, and they are less likely than unimportant decisions to resolve problems. Unimportant decisions are made by resolution. A large proportion of decisions are actually made, and most decisions of intermediate importance are made. However, choice failure is concentrated among the most important and the least important choices. These outcomes result from a major feature of the garbage can process, the partial uncoupling of problems and choices. That is, "problems are worked upon in the context of some choice, but choices are made only when the shifting combinations of problems, solutions, and decision makers happen to make action possible. Quite commonly this is after problems have left a given choice arena or before they have discovered it [decisions by flight or oversight]" (16).

An important consequence of the GCM is that "the garbage can process does not resolve problems well. But it does enable decisions to be made and problems to be resolved, even when the organization is plagued with goal ambiguity and conflict with poorly understood problems that wander in and out of the system, with a variable environment, and with decision makers who may have other things on their minds" (16). In sum, the logical structure of decision-making in the garbage can model is built around the flow of relatively independent factor streams through the system, and decision outcomes are dependent upon (a) the coupling of these streams when a choice opportunity presents itself and (b) the choices available in the garbage can.

all three streams converge and actors have a "window of opportunity" to change the current policy. Problems are not necessarily matched with available solutions, and available solutions do not necessarily fit problems receiving attention by other policy actors.

The PAS model distinguishes between the governmental agenda, which lists the subjects or problems to which policy actors are paying serious attention, and a decision agenda, which is the subset of issues on the governmental agenda that are slated for an active decision. The governmental agenda is structured by the politics and problems of policy issues. Issues are unlikely to move to the decision agenda unless the politics and problems streams conjoin with the solutions stream.

A program or policy alternative floating in the policy stream must become coupled either to a prominent problem or to changes in the political stream if it is to be considered seriously in a broader context than the policy specialists' community. When an alternative can be coupled to a problem as its solution, the combination must also find support in the political stream. In this conjoined event, an alternative is seized upon by politicians and justified as a solution to the problem. "None of the streams are sufficient by themselves to place an item firmly on the decision agenda. If one of the three elements is missing—if a solution is not available, a problem cannot be found or is not sufficiently compelling, or support is not forthcoming from the political stream—then the subject's place on the decision agenda is fleeting. The window may be open for a short time, but if the coupling is not made quickly, the window closes" (Kingdon 1995, 187). Action taken during one open window can set principles that guide future decisions within a policy arena, or principles that spill over into other arenas. While some policy actors are active in all three areas of the policy process, Kingdon argues that two relatively discrete groups of policy actors tend to dominate a decision area. The specialization of activity is accentuated by the relative independence of decision-making in one decision area relative to the others.

One of the important features of the PAS model is that Kingdon divides the policy community into two general groupings of participants: a visible cluster of actors and a hidden cluster. The visible cluster receives a lot of press and public attention and includes the president, high-level political appointees, and prominent members of Congress. It also includes the media, and such elections-related actors as political parties and campaign organizations. The visible cluster, not surprisingly, dominates the political stream. Visible decisionmakers take soundings from organized interests, and try to respond to the public mood regarding a policy area. More often than not, the national mood acts as a constraint on political decisions, limiting which problems and solutions can be addressed by the political process. Swings in the national mood create opportunities for a new set of problems or solutions to be given attention. This may be the consequence of elections that change the composition of Congress (as in 1994), put a new president and administration in charge (as in 1992), or both (as in 1980). The visible cluster of actors is responsible for determining which problems move from the governmental agenda to the decision agenda. Yet they turn to the hidden cluster of actors for the set of alternatives that address the problem.

The hidden cluster is responsible for generating policy alternatives and includes policy specialists such as academics and researchers, career bureaucrats, congressional staffers, and lower-level administration appointees. Career bureaucrats (and other hidden cluster actors) take their cues from the elected officials as to what items will be on the agenda for consideration and which will not. Problems and solutions discussed in the policy community are dumped into a policy "garbage can" in which cooks "the policy primeval soup." Within this environment, policy specialists try out their policy ideas on each other, measuring problems, refining and recombining solutions as necessary to make sure their alternatives to problems are ready for the decision agenda when the time is right. The proposals that surface to the status of serious consideration in this "soup" must meet several criteria, including technical, political, and *budgetary* feasibility. This selection system narrows the set of conceivable proposals to a short list of proposals that is actually available for serious consideration. If elected officials are receptive to policy alternatives, then the specialists push their ideas. If not, they shelve the proposals and wait for a new administration or a new focus by the legislative branch. Much of the work of this cluster is done in the planning and budget shops, especially analyzing the feasibility of an idea relative to a budget constraint.

Kingdon defines two types of decision opportunities in the policy process: predictable and unpredictable "windows of opportunity." Major policy changes may happen during these windows of opportunity because this is when the three streams come together: a problem is recognized, a solution is available, the political climate is receptive to change, and other constraints do not prohibit action. Swings in national mood brought about by crisis or turmoil are unpredictable windows of opportunity. Energy policy changes that came after the 1974 Organization of Petroleum Exporting Countries (OPEC) oil embargo are an example of this situation.

The annual budget development process is an example of a predictable window. For Kingdon, the budget constitutes a particular kind of problem because the budget is a central part of governmental activity. While budget considerations can promote issues higher on the governmental agenda, more often the budget acts as a constraint because the item exceeds the costs that decisionmakers are willing to contemplate. In either case, budgetary considerations and the policy process are intertwined. The budget constraint is perceptual because it is "subject to interpretation. . . . . The budget constraint can be cited as an argument against a proposal that one does not favor on other grounds, and can be side-stepped for proposals that one does favor, by underestimating their cost or ignoring their long-range cost altogether" (Kingdon 1995, 108).

While he says little about the specific role of the budget office in the policy process, Kingdon places the Office of Management and Budget (OMB) in the position of being hidden presidential staff, largely devoted to alternative specification, but retaining its central gatekeeper function. "The Office of Management and Budget . . . has some enduring orientations that persist, regardless of the turnover of personnel within OMB or the comings and goings of administrations. . . . Everybody in government . . . can count on OMB to be interested in cutting budgets, and, in the case of new initiatives, opting for the least expensive program possible" (Kingdon 1995, 162). He notes that Larry Berman's (1979) analysis of OMB over a fifty-year span confirms a need to maintain the gatekeeper function. The credibility of OMB has been seriously questioned when its policy role has overwhelmed the control function, as occurred during the Kennedy, Nixon, and Reagan tenures. Agency budget bureaus are also annual participants in these predictable windows of opportunity in which policy actors have the opportunity to make significant changes to public policies and programs.

PAS and State Policy-Making

Kingdon's model of national agenda setting has also been applied to state policy-making. As in the PAS model, Virginia Gray and David Lowery (1999) found that Minnesota legislators relied on their own experiences and those of their constituents for problem identification, but relied heavily on the "hidden cluster" of legislative staff for policy formation. In turn, the legislative staff relied on a variety of sources of policy expertise in the hidden cluster, including executive agency officials and other legislative staff.

In one of the most explicit extensions of the PAS model to state policy-making, Burdett Loomis (1994) takes us through a "political year" of the Kansas legislature to illustrate the importance of time, timing, and deadlines to policy-making in the Sunflower State. Loomis surveys the growing literature that views many aspects of policy-making as cyclical. Nonlinear aspects of policy-making highlight the repetitive nature of many policy problems, which reappear in slightly altered forms in cyclical patterns of variable length. "Although the multifaceted concept of political time contains many implications for the electoral calculations of strategic politicians, it may contribute most to furthering an understanding of policy formulation" (Loomis 1994, 165).

The budget cycle and its deadlines to force policy decision-making are prominent features of Loomis's description of state policy-making. He argues that much of the thinking of strategic politicians can be understood as entrepreneurial and similar in their pursuit of long-term investment strategies as they forge their political careers. He observes that how officeholders view the selection of agenda items, the construction of a budget, and the choice of which substantive alternatives to support during the heat of a legislative session are affected by the same kinds of calculations.

In Loomis's view, these strategies are shaped by the influences of "political time," a function of long-term trends, regular cycles, and deadlines: "Nothing so defines politics and policy-making as deadlines" (Loomis 1994, 10). The budget process is embedded with deadlines, and cycles are central to the structure of political life and to its interpretation. From a structural perspective, the regularities of budget and other cycles directly affect how politics and policy-making play out. Budget cycles, revenue estimates, and legislative sessions are of great significance because they establish deadlines for when decisions must be made. Budgeters' actions, therefore, are influenced by such timelines. Chief executives, for example, work within electoral as well as budgeting cycles. The budget cycle is particularly important because budgeting, more than electoral and other cycles, dictates actions, even when everyone involved would prefer delay and avoidance.

Although policy literature tends to focus on *an agenda*, Loomis finds *multiple, competing agendas*. And participants can view the governmental agenda in different ways, especially since Kingdon found that policy communities tend to focus their attention on their own areas, without significant overlap, at least at the national level. "Within the context of state policymaking, such specialization also occurs, but policy communities, to the extent they exist, are smaller and less insular. In most states, a number of key actors—especially those on the governor's staff, within the legislature, and among the corps of lobbyists—operate simultaneously in several policy arenas. Thus, individual networks and interests overlap, so that there may be an emergent consensus on some single, overarching set of agenda items" (Loomis 1994, 46).

The garbage can model has also been applied to budgeting models, both explicitly and implicitly. Budgeting theories resembling the garbage can model focus on the *uncertainty* in budgeting. Gerald Miller (1991, 73) is drawn to a budgeting model resembling the GCM because a decision structure composed of loose coupling and independent streams creates a system that "can retain a greater number of mutations and novel solutions than would be the case with a tightly coupled system." Operating under conditions of ambiguity, "answers" are interpretations of the random interaction of variables, and the random interaction of choice opportunities and participants who want to make decisions. Therefore the decision context affects decision outcomes by influencing the information available and by whom it will be interpreted. From Miller's perspective, "budgets represent simultaneous flows of information through various choice structures. . . . Many solutions . . . swamp the number of problems . . . [and] the number of choice opportunities . . . may vary from time to time" (Miller 1991, 76).

Using an ambiguity theory approach, Miller describes public financial management as loosely coupled with other elements of the organization, and argues that the role of the finance office is that of decision-making, with its output being the interpretation of randomly associated ends and means. The key role of the finance office lies "in its careful attention to the processes that enable communication and marshal competence, content and relevance. The finance officer's most important role may be that of timing: helping focus attention on truly relevant issues at just the right time to gain the power to interpret events important to the organization" (Miller 1991, 78).

Although she does not attribute her real-time budgeting model (RTB) to the idea, Rubin's (1997) model of budgetary politics has many features that parallel the GCM (and by extension the PAS model). Rubin's RTB model begins with the notion that budgeting is not equivalent to politics, but rather involves a particular set of political decisions. It is open to the economic and political environments and must be able to cope with changing exogenous factors. The wide variety of actors with different goals, agendas, and resources only compounds the need for budgeting to be flexible and adaptable to changing circumstances. Such flexibility is provided by a decision-making structure that incorporates five distinct, loosely coupled, decision streams, each with a cluster of decisionmakers and its own "politics of budgeting." A brief review of the five decision streams in the RTB model highlights the GCM's features implicit in the model.

Decision-making in the *revenue stream* is permeated with the politics of persuasion. It answers the question, "Who will pay how much?" The principal constraint for revenue decisions is the technical estimate of the revenue base. The estimate is extremely sensitive to the economic environment. Yet, constraints are also opportunities for policy entrepreneurs (Majone 1989). The major decisions in this cluster concern *whether* and *how* to alter the revenue-base constraints with changes in taxes and tax policy. Efforts to alter the revenue base are constrained by the overall political environment or national mood. Elected officials, especially the governor and legislative leaders, therefore dominate this visible cluster of budget actors.

Some of the broadest political engagements involve decision-making in the *balance stream*. Decisions about budget balance (how it is defined, whether to balance, and how to balance the budget) create the politics of constraints. Fundamentally, it is linked to decisions about the scope and role of government, and we would again expect elected officials in the visible cluster to dominate the discussion. But it is also an interactive process between revenues and expenditures estimates, and for this task both the governor and legislative leaders may rely heavily on the state budget director for critical information and identification of policy alternatives.

Decision-making in the *budget process stream* is concerned with the politics of how to make budget decisions and, especially, who decides. Rubin argues that *who* participates, as individuals and groups, influences budgetary outcomes. Conflict in this stream involves the balance of decision-making power between the separate branches of government (executive versus legislature), and between the citizen taxpayers and the government officials who decide allocations. Who holds hearings, when in the process, and whether they are open to statements by the general public are only a few of the issues here. This argument follows Paul Diesing's (1962) concept of political rationality. Effective political decisions allow society to express the relative social valuations of government programs. Political rationality creates decision-making structures that balance the need for diverse viewpoints to be represented in the social debate with the need to reach some decision after the debate has occurred. Such issues are fundamentally questions about the nature of a democracy and, as such, this decision cluster will be dominated by elected officials in the visible cluster.

Decision-making in the *budget execution stream*, in contrast, is viewed as much more technical in nature and is characterized by the politics of accountability. Important questions in this cluster concern precisely how the budget plan will be followed, what deviations will be allowed, and which policy parameters cannot be violated. The routine nature of this decision stream belies the importance of these decisions for establishing the base budget and budget balance carried forward to the next budget development period. Many states have legislative restrictions on minimum balances and appropriation transfers and also have elaborate procedures for supplementing appropriations running short of funds at year-end. Yet states are increasingly aggregating multiple appropriations into lump-sum appropriations for each agency, giving the agency head greater flexibility to manage agency operations. To the extent that expenditure controls remain on refilling vacant positions and on appropriation transfers, these "technical" decisions are dominated by SBO examiners in their capacity as budget experts and institutional gatekeepers. As we shall see in some states (e.g., Kansas, Georgia, and North Carolina), deft management of budget execution becomes a critical tool that allows the SBO to reallocate the budget to gubernatorial priorities.

Changes in environmental factors often trigger implementation changes, yet budget means (programs and policies) are seldom, if ever, value neutral. Thus, depending upon the scope of changes, rebudgeting may involve considerable policy discussions. Furthermore, significant rebudgeting affects the base budget for the ensuing year, which affects both the expenditure stream and the budget balance stream. Periods of retrenchment budgeting can significantly raise the involvement of elected officials in implementation strategies, but they do not necessarily diminish the examiners' role in the decisions, as we shall see in chapter 8.

Finally, decision-making in the *expenditure stream* is characterized by the politics of choice. The first constraint is the technical estimate of base expenditure demand (the base budget), which is an important role for the SBO staff. Yet the budget base definition is increasingly a political decision itself. There is considerable debate over what constitutes the base budget of the federal government (dollars spent in the previous year or the "baseline" budget), and the base budget definition is increasingly subject to debate in the states as well. The large number and variety of actors involved in this cluster are in keen competition to influence the relative allocation of revenues across competing purposes. The goal of budget actors is to reorder expenditure priorities or preserve the current order of priorities, depending upon the actors' standing in the base budget. In this text, we focus much of our attention on this set of decisions. This stream arguably involves the largest number of decisions, and we will see how the governor and legislature rely on the SBO and its examiners to serve as critical gatekeepers in the expenditure decision process. It is their gatekeeper role that gives the SBO examiners a prominent role in this decision stream.

According to the RTB model, the nonlinear nature of budgeting requires continual decision adjustment in each stream, responding to decisions and information in other streams and changes in the political or economic environment. The streams are semi-autonomous, yet interdependent, because key information links them together. A critical feature of RTB is the interruptibility of cluster decision-making, a feature required by the nonsequential timing and different decision-making intervals in the various clusters. Budget actors are not confined to a single decision locus, but move from one decision to another as needed. If work in one cluster is interrupted because information is missing or circumstances have changed, actors may revisit previous decisions in light of changing environmental conditions, or even leave a cluster temporarily to fetch the necessary information from other clusters. The result is that decision blocks in one stream do not have to interrupt the rest of the clusters.

The Treatment of Time and Timing in Decision Models

The treatment of time as a constraint is much different in the RTB model than in Kingdon's policy agenda setting model, however. According to the PAS model, time is less important than *timing*. In contrast, *time* is a real constraint in the RTB model, as it is in the Loomis description of state policymaking. Loomis (1994, 14) argues that "deadlines affect the policymaking process in at least three distinct, if related, ways. First, many deadlines are imposed by constitutional and legal structures; although such rules of the games are susceptible to change and even manipulation, in the short run they are regarded as fixed by virtually all the relevant actors."

Loomis (14) describes a second set of deadlines that "reflect institutional practices; the executive and legislature set many of their own time limits internally. Internal budget deadlines and legislative process strictures provide frameworks for all involved." Rubin (1997, 302) agrees: "Budgeting has a bottom line and a due date, which distinguishes it from many other political decisions." The budget must be passed at some point, and the budget process as a whole is always working toward that deadline. It is the deadline constraint that creates the predictable budget window of opportunity in the PAS model.

Timing is also important in the RTB model, since the various actors must be able to interrupt the work in their cluster, either to fetch necessary information from other clusters or to revisit previous decisions in light of changing environmental conditions. This is facilitated in part by the fluid participation of actors who move from one decision to another in the RTB model, as needed. For example, a legislator may meet in a committee to discuss an expenditure issue with an agency, then attend a meeting of the rules committee to determine the budget process for a different issue.

Although Rubin notes that budgets have deadlines, the RTB does not explicitly deal with the deadlines and their impact on budgetary decision-making. We submit that the budget process forces a confluence of the budget and policy decision-making streams when the deadlines arrive to pass the budget. As Loomis (1994, 40) observes:

> The coupling of these streams does not happen automatically. Policy entrepreneurs often seek to pull together diverse forces, but success is not guaranteed. Alternatively, many policy items, such as annual budgets, require resolution, even if channeling the problem, policy, and politics streams into a single set of proposals appears impossible. Indeed, the cyclical nature of much policymaking creates deadlines that political actors must react to, thereby forcing the three streams to converge. . . . Required decisions produce a different strategic environment. If budgets must be balanced and public education funded, all within the time limits of a legislative session, tremendous pressures build for resolution, even if large cuts must be made or tax increases enacted.

As deadlines near, the SBO exerts a gravitational force that pulls the streams closer together. The various streams eventually must be integrated fully for a new budget to be approved—if only for two short moments each year. The two points of confluence are the two important deadlines in the executive budget process. The first is the deadline for the executive to submit a budget proposal to the legislature. The second is the final vote on the budget agreement between the executive and legislature (which may constitute a vote to sustain or override an executive veto). In the same moments that the budget is approved, so are the policy decisions that are embedded in the budget. The decision streams of the RTB model immediately disjoin once the executive's policy and budget decisions are announced. Revenue, expenditure, and balance decisions will be reviewed, modified, and remodified. The structure of the legislative budget process will delimit the amount of the conflict surrounding the proposals. Ultimately, the streams must conjoin again for the budget to become law, and most of the chief executive's recommendations will be affirmed.[1]

It is also important to note that the RTB is essentially a macro-level, descriptive model of budgeting, just as Kingdon's model is a macro-level model of the policy agenda setting process. Together, they suggest the constellation of factors that influence the macro-budgeting environment. But this synthesis leaves open the question of how budget decisions are made at the micro (individual) level of budgeting. The Kingdon and Rubin models suggest some of the factors to be considered, but they stop short of suggesting how budget actors finally decide to allocate X dollars to program A and Y dollars to program B. Rubin calls for others to explore the macro-micro–budgeting links further, which we do momentarily.

Synthesis of Change Models

Expanding, extending, and combining the RTB with Kingdon's PAS model of the policy process illustrates the nexus between the budget and policy processes as it has evolved in state government. Several common features are particularly noteworthy. First, both models highlight the nonlinear complexity of budget and policy decision-making; they both use multiple, interdependent streams of decisions to describe budget and policy activities. Second, both describe clusters of actors characterized by fluid participation in various decisions of the budget and policy processes; Kingdon's visible and hidden clusters are compatible with Rubin's sets of actors. Third, both models emphasize feasibility decisions over optimizing decisions. The feasibility in the PAS model includes technical, political, and budgetary feasibility, while the RTB model dissects budgetary feasibility into multiple components. Fourth, the treatment of time and timing in the two models is linked by the "most predictable window of opportunity" in the policy process, the annual budget cycle.

Loomis (1994, 172) likens policy formulation to an improvisational jazz group:

> The performances are loosely structured, often around an old standard, yet all of the players have room to innovate and improvise, both in solos and as a unit. The end product is always unique, yet it progresses along well-established patterns of riffs and harmonies. New members join a group and its sound changes. Its musical products are less formal than laws, but just as well articulated. The jazz group, like the legislature, learns from its past performances. The governor may seek to lead this band, but the syncopated rhythm of a Duke Ellington has given way to the more improvisa-

tional touches of contemporary executives who are encouraged to reinvent government.

The synthesis of these budget and policy process models highlights important features of the role of SBOs in state government. First, the nonlinear nature of budgeting and policy-making suggests that a model of budget rationality should include flexibility in decision sequencing, yet provide some organizing framework by which the interdependent budget and policy factors can be reconciled for decision-making when a budget deadline arrives. Second, the fluid participation of multiple actors highlights the important institutional memory role that the SBO may play in budget and policy analysis. The most fluid participants in the RTB and PAS models are elected officials, including governors. SBO staff members tend to be longer-term actors, and, as an institution, the SBO can maintain systems of institutional memory management that facilitates detailed budget and policy "history." Consequently, governors can depend on the budget examiners for maintaining policy continuity *or* developing effective policy changes in conjunction with budget decisions.

Third, both models highlight feasibility requirements. As we discuss in chapter 3, both models suggest that social, political, and legal feasibility are just as important for examiners as technical and economic feasibility, because they make their decisions in the context of the governor's policies and priorities. They review policy analysis aspects of budget problems to frame their technical and economic analyses.

Fourth, policy decisions can be postponed in the budget process, but the effect is to reify the status quo, and that may mean no program development or no program changes. (In the rare case, it may mean letting a sunset provision on a program take effect.) This last point (the reification of the status quo) is the reason for which Lindblom's incrementalism model argues that most policy changes occur gradually, incrementally, within a given policy arena. There are too many factors and actors that must felicitously combine in a timely manner to make substantial changes in every policy area a common occurrence.

Incrementalism Models

While the PAS model helps explain major changes in public policy, Kingdon acknowledges that most policy changes occur incrementally within a given policy arena. The incrementalist model of decision-making is based on the assumptions that there are multiple decisionmakers facing a variety of often amorphous goals within an explicit time constraint. Lindblom (1975, 162) suggests that the incremental method "is actually the most common method through which public policy decisions, including decisions on taxes and expenditures, are approached." The incremental method is characterized by a preoccupation with only a limited set of policy alternatives that are politically relevant. This usually means the policy is only incrementally different from existing policies, involving analysis of only those aspects of policies that differ from current policy and a view of the impending policy decision as one in a succession of choices.

According to the incremental method, political decisionmakers focus on the marginal values of various social objectives and constraints, and they intermix evaluation and empirical analysis rather than solely conduct an empirical analysis of the consequences of policies for independently determined objectives. In this way incrementalism sidesteps problems posed by disagreement on values because decisionmakers deal directly with policies. No virtue attaches to objectives or values that result from prior discussions and agreements. This is feasible and acceptable because the decisionmaker is tentative about objectives or values, counting on policy choices to lead to fresh perceptions about values. Experiences will teach about values even as the values are pursued, and in the long run, policy choices have as great an influence on objectives as objectives have on policy choices.

Incrementalism manages the complexity inherent in policy analysis by focusing attention only on a small number of all the important relevant values. Lindblom argues that this drastic simplification of complex problems achieved through outright neglect of important consequences of policies is acceptable—*as long as the consequences are not neglected by the policy process itself.*

> If important consequences neglected by one examiner or decision-maker are the concern of another, the policy process has not neglected the consequences. Thus, through the composition of the policy process of multiple actors representing their own interests and predicting and evaluating the consequences of policy actions for their own interests, the policy process itself can be considered rational. . . . [Thus] policy decisions can be rational even if each decision-maker ignores important values, if only the values neglected at one point are attended to at another. (Lindblom 1975, 165–166)

We shall soon argue that SBO examiners fulfill a critical role in the budget and policy processes because they are charged with ensuring that none of the important values and consequences of pending policy alternatives have been neglected.

The theory of budgetary incrementalism (Wildavsky 1964, 1988) that has long dominated budget research is based on these same concepts of "bounded rationality" and policymakers' "muddling through" the policy process to make policy decisions. It has focused on the budget process at large and the final appropriations results (macro-budgeting), providing little information on the individual budgetary decisions within agencies or central budget bureaus (micro-budgeting). Traditional incremental views of the executive budget process assign decisive budgetary decision-making powers to elected legislators and describe the ultimate budget outcomes as products of the political negotiation and logrolling within the legislature and between key committees and subcommittees. Agencies, chief executives, and legislative institutions are assigned roles that they play in the process.

Incrementalism emphasizes the *predictable* aspects of budgeting. A key notion in the theory is ex ante agreement by legislators and chief executives on the budget base, moving the focus of their attention to political resolution of the incremental change to the unified budget. Budget discussions predictably focus on the incremental changes to the base budget, making an agency's budget fairly certain next year: the base plus a little extra. Budgeting is thus viewed as a mode of conflict resolution aimed at ordering whose preferences will prevail in the incremental allocation of society's resources.

This theory of decision-making sought to reduce uncertainty in the process by noting predictable patterns of behavior by expected actors. In the incrementalism model, the budget bureau played a role of treasury guardian, and even as the role was expanded to become a stronger advocate of presidential policies, the bureau normally gave "less weight to advocating presidential programs than to keeping them within bounds, particularly since everyone already expects the agencies to perform the functions of advocacy" (Wildavsky 1988, 92).

Finally, the incrementalism model of budgeting emphasizes the linear aspects of budgeting. The bulk of budget decisions are to approve the base budget and concomitant policy decisions, a powerful linear force over time. Long-term trends may appear linear over time, and immediate changes will usually appear as small, simple extensions of current activities. The incrementalism model has been criticized for several weaknesses, including its inability to cope with entitlements funding and to explain increasing uncertainty in public budgeting in the 1980s and 1990s. In addition, incrementalism has been subject to an increasing number of studies that challenge its methodological, substantive, and normative grounds (e.g., LeLoup and Moreland 1978).

GCM–RTB–Incrementalism Synthesis and Implications

A further synthesis of the incrementalism model with the GCM-based models leads to several important features of SBO budgeting. The RTB model and incrementalism highlight the importance of budget deadlines, which require decisions to be made with the information available. The SBO is at the center of this budget and policy nexus, charged with managing the budget process so that budget deadlines are met and ensuring that budget examiner recommendations meet budget and policy rationality criteria. Whether analyzing incremental changes or substantial policy shifts, the SBO is charged with making effective recommendations that meet budget rationality criteria.

Next, the PAS model highlights that policy-making is the product of decisions made by two distinct groups of actors: a visible cluster (mainly elected officials) and a hidden cluster (including bureaucrats, policy analysts, and academics). Similarly we recognize two distinct sets of decisive decisionmakers to distinguish between macro-budgeting decisions and micro-budgeting decisions. Macro-budgeting involves setting large policy targets for both fiscal and political purposes. These decisions are a product of the negotiations between a visible cluster of legislators and chief executives, and may represent significant shifts in the allocation of budget resources and have long-term consequences for the state. Governors transmit their macro-budgeting decisions to agencies and departments as policy guidelines with the budget instructions. Typical examples would include school finance reform, major highway construction and maintenance initiatives, and major prison construction initiatives.

These macro-budgeting issues consume the bulk of legislative debate and receive much public attention. From the perspective of the total budget proposal, however, the dollars involved in these initiatives will generally represent only a small fraction of total revenues or expenditures. The bulk of the revenue decisions tend to be fixed by previous decisions that determined how and from whom the state will derive its revenue. Incidental revenue changes in the annual budget process might include opening or closing "loopholes" as suggested by lobbyists or the revenue department (respectively).

In this book, we recognize SBO examiners as essential actors who mesh the budget and policy decisions for multiple agency budget problems, and who assist in folding these decisions into a balanced budget proposal that the SBO recommends to the governor (and subsequently the legislature). The two decisive budget deadlines in the executive budget process highlight the critical need for the governor and legislators to have a cadre of stable, dependable budget examiners who can provide the institutional memory and the budget and policy expertise needed to "couple" decisions and still meet the annual (or biennial) budget decision deadlines. Decision deadlines require a mechanism for choosing which issues will receive more attention than others. We shall see how the governor can use the SBO to dominate the budget decision agenda.

We also recognize the centrality of SBOs and examiners as the nexus between macro- and micro-level budgeting. The legislature delegates the vast majority of the expenditure decisions to the governor (Kiewiet 1991; Lauth 1992), who in turn delegates significant decision-making power to the budget staff in the state budget office (Gosling 1985). The budget office is a central player in the hidden cluster of bureaucrats and other policy actors who focus their attention on crafting "solutions" to agency budget and policy problems. It is through the budget office that macro-budgeting decisions are transmitted to agencies, and in the budget office that micro-budgeting decisions about specific agency programs are aligned with the macro-budgeting decisions of elected officials. The budget examiners are charged with translating the macro-level decisions into individual agency budget decisions. With one eye on the policy process and one eye on the budget process, SBO examiners must evaluate how various solutions fit with the prevailing flow of decisions and the preferences of the governor. It is in this combining role that budget examiners also act as the nexus between the policy and budget processes. Landmark legislation or precedent-setting executive decisions can establish new principles that leave the policy arena changed, and the new incremental changes that occur in policy do so from a new point of origin. Even if the immediate effects are not dramatic, the importance of these events "lies in their precedent-setting nature" (Kingdon 1995, 200).

Examiners confirm this garbage can notion of budgeting, indicating strategies that are dependent upon streams colliding at any given time. For example, the following exchange with a Missouri examiner illustrates the environmental scan of political and revenue streams that is common practice for examiners involved in budget preparation:

Q: To what extent did you have cases where you said, "This is dead on arrival" to the director's desk? There is no way I am going to recommend this.
Examiner: That happens occasionally.

Q: Do you ever "go to the wall" for the department, even if you think your recommendation would be dead on arrival?
Examiner: I have done that a few times. I pick my battles.

Q: What distinguishes whether you fight or move on?
Examiner: That sometimes changes during the year, depending upon the revenue forecast. If the revenue looks bad, I may give up on it.

Q: Even if you know that the department really needs it?
Examiner: If I think there is a good chance I can convince my director, and those in the governor's office, that this is a mandatory item and has to be funded, I will go to the wall for it. If there is any doubt about that, and the fiscal situation looks bad, I am not going to spend a lot of time on it.

Many examiners recognize revenue availability as particularly influential on their subsequent activism related to budget recommendations. Along with the consideration of revenue availability or lack thereof, politics and timing come into play. For example, an examiner from North Carolina discusses budget-cutting strategies as dependent on timing:

> It depends on when it is decided that the cut needs to be made. If the cut needs to be made early in the process, I work with the agency and identify what has instigated the cut. If it is later in the process (for example, if continuation budgets come in at a level that takes away from potential expansion and the governor needs to cut back 5 percent to create funds for special initiatives), then we would go ahead with our cut initiative from our office.

The Budget Decision Agenda

The prominent and pivotal role of the state budget office in budgetary communications flows squares with the general characteristics of Kingdon's PAS model. Parallel to his notion of a policy decision agenda, we note the phenomenon of a budgetary decision agenda. *The budgetary decision agenda is the set of issues that policymakers are actively considering for inclusion in the next budget.* In some ways, the budgetary decision agenda is similar to what Barbara Nelson (1984) describes as a diffusion of the formal policy agenda into the popular and professional agendas. The latter is more specific than the popular, since citizens blur issues together. Many issues on the formal agenda may also lack popular appeal. The SBO will be focused largely on the professional agenda. The budget decision agenda may also qualify as an "operational agenda," which gives more shape to the formal agenda— this is the list of immediate items to be addressed on the agendas of the various policy interest networks and policy actors, including the governor, legislature, and specialized bureaucracies (Eyestone 1978).

As with the policy decision agenda, the budgetary decision agenda is set largely by the visible cluster of actors, particularly the governor. And also following the PAS model, the specification of policy alternatives is largely in the hands of the hidden cluster of actors, dominated by examiners in the SBO. The key actors responsible for the coupling of problems and solutions in the predictable budgetary window of opportunity are the SBO examiners. *We consider examiners to have a policy role when their activity involves them in the discussions and decisions regarding state policies in a substantive policy area, as such issues appear on the budgetary decision agenda.* While Kingdon's model highlights the critical role of policy entrepreneurs in forcing a confluence of all three major streams in the policy process, we argue that the budget director plays the corresponding pivotal role in the budget process of further coupling problems and solutions with budgetary politics.

It is not necessary for all budget examiners in an SBO to have a significant policy role. An examiner assigned to the budget of the cosmetology board, for example, would be expected to have little policy content compared to the examiner(s) assigned to the Medicaid budget. Other factors that may affect the level of policy influence an examiner has on state budgeting include the overall degree of policy orientation of the SBO, the position of the policy issue on the decision agenda, the size of the budget request, and the budget office experience of the examiner.

As gatekeepers, examiners' policy activities are concentrated in the budgetary windows of opportunity. The policy alternatives they analyze for inclusion in the budget have already been pruned by the policy-making process—they have cooked and survived in the "policy primeval soup" under the watchful eyes and talents of agency program and budget staffs, as well as assorted interest groups. The examiner's input, as we shall see, adds critical decision ingredients that provide a budgetary "flavor" to the policy soup.

Examiners normally choose their recommendation from among the main alternatives competing for the decision agenda. The alternatives at their disposal await the final evaluations—political and budgetary feasibility. If they pass muster, then the likelihood of being matched to a problem is greatly increased. Ultimately (according to one examiner we interviewed), "you must be able to look at something and know the politics, the governor's agenda, and is it fiscally sound." On the other hand, Gosling (1987) found that in the Wisconsin SBO, examiners were often asked to develop the governor's budget *initiatives*.

As key managers of the budgetary decision agenda, examiners take cues from political leaders as to what problems will be on the agenda, and then sift and hone the alternatives from the policy community to determine which alternative or alternatives will be promoted for consideration by elected officials, particularly the governor. After all, as many SBO examiners told us, "the overriding priority is the governor's agenda." For this reason, other political actors in the decision-making structure are keen to get agreement from the state budget office, thereby surmounting a major obstacle in the policy-making process (Duncombe and Kinney 1987; Mosher 1952; Wildavsky 1988). The examiners' initial position in the process is generally one that receives arguments, making them targets of persuasion. Examiners are subjected to various, and sometimes conflicting, alternatives promoted for the same problem. Nevertheless, the budget director usually wants a recommended alternative and the rationale to show that the recommended alternative satisfies budget feasibility criteria.

For example, when interviewed for this study, the budget director from the Kansas SBO expected that examiner recommendations would be well-rounded and "made on their best analytical judgment about what they know about the agency and the fiscal resources available to the agency and the responsibilities of the agency. Their job is to say: 'Number one would be best for the agency; however, it costs a lot more than we have. Number two, management would opt for this opportunity. Number three is the bare minimum.'" According to the deputy director of another budget office, the examiner is in a sensitive position requiring a heightened awareness about state programs and services. "This job is not only crunching numbers. It involves looking at policy and organizational and financial consequences of policy." Yet another SBO director noted that when recruiting examiners, he is predisposed "not to look at accountants. Our budget office involves a policy function and a budgeting function that requires a thought process about how state programs need to be organized. It is about trying to set priorities. It is not about accounting."

When items are not on the agenda, the examiners are informally delegated residual decision authority by the governor and the legislature, and traditionally, their instinctive response is to say "no." When examiners receive cues that a policy issue is on the budgetary decision agenda, they are critical gatekeepers in the hidden cluster who help determine the set of legitimate alternatives. But in any event, they must persuade elected officials that their recommended policy change is feasible and in accord with the governor's policy focus. We explore how this is done a bit later. At this moment, we explore the unique and powerful gatekeeper positions held by the budget examiners in the SBO.

The SBO as Gatekeeper

The locus of decisive decision-making in the executive budget process of American states is commonly fixed with the legislature and the governor. A significant share of the literature is devoted to the influence of the governors and legislatures on budgetary outcomes (see Abney and Lauth 1985; Anton 1966; Gosling 1991; Lee 1992; Sharkansky 1968b; and Thompson 1987, among others). Governors have been the driving force behind policy decision-making in most states (Clynch and Lauth 1991). With the exception of North Carolina, governors exercise some form of veto power over legislatures. Crafting the executive budget proposal is perhaps one of the most important policy advantages available to governors (Forsythe 1997; Ransone

1982; Sabato 1983). Although legislatures have reasserted their position in the budget process, especially with the development in the late 1970s of professional legislative budget staff (Caiden 1984; Gosling 1985), governors have maintained considerable political and policy clout to enforce their budget policies and priorities.

The high level of attention directed at gubernatorial–legislative budgeting neglects the far greater number of decisions in the budget process made concerning each of the agency and program budgets that comprise the total budget. Big "trade-off" debates at the macro-budgeting level get high profiles, but are few: for example, "education versus highway investments" or "prisons versus Medicaid." The reality behind these vociferous debates on a few decision items is that the vast majority of the budget decision items are incremental or decremental changes to agency budgets: adding or deleting department positions to adjust for changing workloads, capital investments to maintain or expand programs, and new program enhancements to improve program effectiveness. Although the overall budget for the state is established in the process, each agency budget independently must stand able to finance the activities the legislature demands of it. This applies to the small regulatory agencies (e.g., the banking commissioner), large social welfare agencies, and those agencies funded heavily through intergovernmental grants (such as a Department of Community Affairs or a department that administers unemployment compensation). Each of these agency budgets must be evaluated on its own merits as well as within the context of the overall state budget. Those who decide how to address the issues in the agency budgets make the vast bulk of the decisive decisions in the budget process. This is the responsibility delegated to SBO examiners by the governor (and indirectly by the legislature).

The bulk of the budget decisions "made" by governors and legislators are merely affirmations of decisions made earlier in the process, when the agencies' requests are first reviewed. Having delegated responsibility for reviewing requests to examiners in the state budget office, the legislature and governor rely on examiners to determine which requests have merit. The complex factors contributing to each budget decision require significant analytical time, more than the individual legislator or governor can afford. In order to cull the decisions to those with the greatest impact on public policy, the legislature and governor rely on the SBO to act as the gatekeeper in the budget process, in fact, delegating most budget decisions to the SBO. The SBO serves a role of institutional decision gatekeeper for the budget process, and the budget examiners serve as individual gatekeepers with respect to specific policy areas and agency budgets.

A budget director we interviewed who had previously worked as a legislative budget officer in the same state noted that the duties and perspectives were "totally different. The only thing that's similar is you use the same state agencies and the same basic budgets. A legislative fiscal analyst analyzes the budget the governor puts together and makes adjustments to that for what the legislature wants to do." By contrast, "The budget office takes the basic budgets, puts them together into a state budget, taking into account all the issues that must be kept in consideration, like the revenue package, the governor's priorities on some programs, and statutory responsibilities. The budget office builds the budget; a legislative analyst analyzes and makes adjustments to it. It's a very, very different job."

SBO examiners thus have considerable influence on budgetary outcomes, serving the governor as powerful gatekeepers who stem the flow of budgetary requests to the governor and legislators and who increasingly work beyond mere financial analysis to serve the role of policy analyst (Berman 1979; Davis and Ripley 1969; Johnson 1984, 1988, and 1989; LeLoup and Moreland 1978). For example, although subject to review by the governor and legislature, the examiners we interviewed estimated that, on average, 85 percent of their recommendations are affirmed by their governors or budget directors, a proportion corroborated by the SBO managers and budget directors. This is particularly important in light of the evidence that governors have increasingly turned to the examiners in state budget offices for policy analysis in conjunction with their budget analysis (Gosling 1985 and 1987; Thurmaier and Gosling 1997). An examiner in Virginia's SBO describes what is best about the job of the executive examiner:

> There is a fair amount of time that an analyst feels something that very few people in state government ever feel at all. And that is that what we are doing is making a direct impact on the way that state government operates. In this office, we get to decide whether a program should even exist, how it should be changed, where it should be modified.

The budget submitted to the legislature is an expression of the executive's policies. Within the SBO, fiscal and other policy considerations are considered, balanced, and coordinated to put form to the governor's policies. The budget that emerges from this "black box" is the "most important policy-making instrument for assuring responsive and responsible government" (Burkhead and Bringewatt 1977, 1). The budget is formulated through both a top–down and a bottom–up process. Generally, the top–down process sets the fiscal and policy boundaries of the budget and the bottom–up process establishes budget specifics within the boundaries (Bozeman and Straussman 1982). Policies are communicated down to the agencies through the budget instructions distributed at the beginning of the executive budget process (top–down), and the policies are given expression in the flow of decisions on agency requests through the SBO and up to the governor (bottom–up).

The management of this process within the SBO is the responsibility of the budget director. The influence of the SBO often reflects the strength of the relationship between the governor and the budget director. Appointed by the governor, the director is keenly aware of the executive's policy preferences as well as the financial and political "big picture." The governor relies upon the budget director to "define the limits of resources, and to establish within the administration the agenda of economically feasible alternative courses of action to reach agreed upon goals" (Burton 1943, 104).

Flows of Information

Top–Down Flows

There are two components of the top–down streams of information: (1) policy guidelines that indicate the policy priorities and directions of the governor and (2) revenue forecasts that set fiscal parameters. The budget instructions that are transmitted from the governor down to the agencies via the SBO set the stage for meeting critical macro-budgeting objectives. At the federal level, such forecasts and directives are linked to the role the budget will play in affecting the national economy. Given their less direct impact on the national economy, the primary budget concern of state and local governments is attention to the near universal requirement to balance the budget as well as the allocation of resources to finance the governor's policy priorities.

Therefore, budget planning begins with the governor formulating goals and policies in accord with revenue and expenditure forecasts. Working from baseline estimates in June, a former Kansas SBO budget director describes the initial boundary session: "We ask the governor what kind of balance he wants at the end of the year. So you take the revenue, subtract the balance at the end of 1990, and that's what you've got to work with" (as quoted in Loomis 1994, 43). The budget director then adds in capital expenditures and social spending commitments to estimate the budget surplus (or deficit).

The first steps of the executive budget process produce the revenue forecasts. The revenue forecast is an important piece of information for all actors in the executive budget process because it places an upper limit on total planned expenditures and thus helps to determine which and to what extent public programs and services will be funded. The revenue forecast usually is based on current revenue sources; that is, it projects total revenues for the upcoming budget year assuming no changes to current taxes and fees levied by the legislature.[2] The revenue forecast is often combined with a "cost-to-continue" expenditure forecast so that the SBO can determine any budget "gap" between the costs of current service levels and projected revenues. The "gap" analysis permits policymakers to consider the magnitude of revenue and expenditure adjustments that will be required under various economic scenarios (Bahl and Schroeder 1979). This is an example of the interdependency of the revenue, expenditure, and balance streams in the RTB model.

The revenue forecast presented in the budget instructions is an important piece of information in the budget process. The initial revenue forecast is announced, to some degree, as part of the SBO's strategy to curb acquisitive spending by agencies. Accompanying instructions or guidelines usually indicate a tight fiscal situation, although some may treat the forecast as a mere formality. Typically, initial revenue forecasts are refined as more current data become available to the SBO. Meanwhile, other policymakers and policy actors track the actual and projected revenues, which tend to act as constraints on future expenditure claims. Flowing from the top down, the forecast provides fiscal guidance to the examiners as well as the agencies. While it is a rare set of budget instructions that urges agencies to "ask for the moon," depending upon the governor's policy priorities, the policy directive for a particular agency may "open the door" to consideration of larger than average spending increases for certain programs.

The SBO advises departments as to the governor's policies by issuing guidelines in the budget instructions. These policy guidelines may be general or may be tailored to specific agencies. One of the budget director's principal responsibilities is to convey the policies of the governor to other members of the SBO staff and to the agencies. The budget director uses the top–down flows of information in the budget instructions to define the fiscal and policy parameters within which agency budget requests will be considered by SBO staff. The formulation of the guidelines is of considerable importance. The guidelines often include a suggested range of expenditures to match projected revenues and areas in which some special consideration seems to be needed. They identify programs that need particular attention to meet developing problems, areas where there is room for improved efficiency, and programs that may require significant increases or decreases in expenditures—or even the entire elimination of programs because they are no longer required or must be dropped because of fiscal constraints. New programs are often under consideration to meet new needs that have developed. However, an important constraint on policies, especially new programs, is the availability of revenues. The examiner must apply these top–down fiscal and policy cues from the budget director to the analysis of the bottom–

up flow of agency requests. In fact, the SBO director is heavily dependent upon the examiners to manage the bottom–up flow of agency requests to the governor (Anton 1969; Davis and Ripley 1969; Rall 1965).

Bottom–Up Flows

Executive budgets are formed in an iterative process that requires examiners to bring their judgment to bear on thousands of individual decision items. Information streams into the budget process from a multitude of tributaries: agencies, interest groups, legislative representatives, and other interested persons. Important decisions are being made along these tributaries to determine what information finally flows into the agency budget requests. All of these requests, in turn, flow into the SBO where they are held for analysis and recommendation by the examiners. Much of the remainder of this book will explore how the examiners manage the multiple information flows (both top–down and bottom–up) to generate effective budget recommendations to the budget director and governor.

Coupling Macro and Micro Decisions

The first confluence of the budget and policy streams is the period when the SBO examiners must evaluate the budget and policy proposals arriving on their desks at the beginning of the budget-development phase of the budget process. The requirements that policy solutions have budget feasibility means that, de facto, they have become budget decisions. SBO examiners are well placed to monitor the various decision streams in the policy and budget process. Many of the examiners we interviewed support the characterization of the SBO as "where the action is," and offered comments on their environment as illustrative of "a global perspective" or "the big picture." According to one examiner, "If it is something that the agency has to do that affects policy, programs or dollars, then we will look at it."

The powerful role of the SBO examiner is played largely inside the hidden cluster of policy actors, with less accountability to citizens than more visible budgeters, but high accountability to the governor. One examiner explained that "we have exposure without having to put our necks on the chopping block all the time." They are somewhat fluid participants in the process as well, discussing revenues with one set of actors, expenditures with others, balance issues and execution issues with still others. An examiner describes this fluidity: "Budget recommendations flow to the budget director. The decision-making process is very fluid so that decisions can be made and unmade at several different points. My preparation is entirely self-imposed."

At some point during the budget year, budget examiners will likely participate in choice opportunities in each of these streams with each of their assigned agencies. As active participants, they know the other important budgeters, and monitor problem development and evolution. Their links with agency policy actors (including program directors) keep them abreast of solutions in the policy primeval soup. Examiners may participate in evaluations of solutions for other feasibility criteria but their primary role concerns budgetary feasibility. With one eye on the policy process and one eye on the budget process, they evaluate how various solutions fit with the prevailing flow of decisions and the preferences of the governor.

Thomas Lynch (1995) points out that examiners in SBOs are uniquely qualified to pursue policy development and innovation because their allegiance to the governor exposes them to the global perspective (so noted earlier) of state government, yet their contact with line managers focuses examiners' attention on specific program initiatives. Forsythe (1991, 171) observes that examiners "usually have a good idea of which agencies are doing well, which are doing poorly, which agencies are using resources intelligently and efficiently, and which are not."

Kingdon (1995, 139) concludes that policy specialists discard many ideas because they "cannot conceive of any plausible circumstances under which they could be approved by elected politicians and their appointees." Loomis (1994, 82–83) observed the same phenomenon in Kansas policymaking:

> Problems will frequently reach the agenda stage only to go no further. No compelling conditions or energetic policy entrepreneur will force the coupling of a problem to a politically palatable solution. In such an instance, the problem will be dismissed, perhaps to resurface another year. Not every agenda item is ripe for policymaking. In 1989 two major issues fit this category: Washburn University's entrance into the state university system and the legislative pensions question, which had been crucial in several 1988 election races.

Loomis's findings (1994) in his Kansas study concur with Kingdon's argument that some policy ideas are kept alive with hopes that the larger political climate will change, even though the ideas might not be currently in favor. For example, the emergence of the Kansas "highway issue" is particularly interesting. "If converting agenda items into policy outcomes is indeed the coupling of problem, policy, and political forces at an opportune time," Loomis argues, then a 1987 special session of the legislature had been premature. The "highway problem" had not been adequately defined, and "the governor's very specific set of policy solutions was seen as inappropriate. In addition, there was no overriding political reason for most legislators to adopt

Figure 2.1   **The State Budget Office Decisions Nexus**

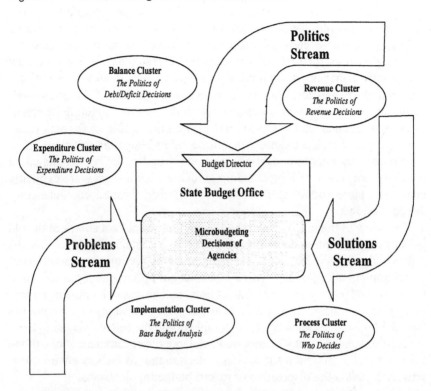

a comprehensive highway policy. But the special session did contribute to increasing interest in the problem. Likewise, it demonstrated that project-specific proposals might well produce more opposition than support" (Loomis 1994, 110). These are the kinds of problems in which the SBO can prove to be a useful policy tool for governors. The issues may be complicated, but they demand solutions—viable, feasible solutions.

Figure 2.1 presents the state budget office situated at the nexus of the policy process, the macro-budgeting process, and the micro-budgeting process. The confluence of these processes explains the tremendous breadth of budgeting that is the examiners' decision domain. As seen in Figure 2.1, the examiners face a seemingly daunting task of aligning and combining the information in the various streams in a way that leads to effective recommendations to the budget director and governor. Their influence is felt throughout the budget and policy process.

Figure 2.1 also highlights the micro/macro relationship in budgeting. Macro-budgeting decisions affect the entire state. Micro-budgeting decisions are made for each agency and each agency program, under the umbrella of macro-budgeting decisions. Although modern governors' macro-budgeting decisions are increasingly bounded by nondiscretionary spending requirements (for example, for social welfare programs, formula-based education programs, Medicaid, earmarked categories like transportation, and mandated spending such as for regional hospitals and corrections), it is through the budget office that nondiscretionary and discretionary policy decisions are transmitted to agencies. The budget forces an alignment of the micro-budgeting decisions of career bureaucrats with the macro-budgeting decisions of elected officials, and the examiners play a critical role in aligning them. The examiners' task is to ensure that these micro-budgeting decisions are in accord with the macro-budgeting decisions, whether the macro-budgeting decisions are recent or long-standing guidelines. Unless they are explicitly changed, macro-budgeting decisions are enforced through continuance of the base budget.

This view of the macro–micro budgeting link should not smack of the old politics-administration dichotomy. It would be a mistake to characterize the micro-budgeting decisions of examiners in the budget office as administratively implementing policy. There is substantial policy-making involved in the micro-budgeting decisions of the examiners. The task of harnessing agency budget developments to support macro-budgeting decisions of the governor (and the legislature) adds layers of complexity to the micro-budgeting decisions of examiners. They cannot make defendable recommendations to the budget director without a substantial understanding of the key environmental variables and the disposition of macro-budgeting decisions.

Development-Phase Decisions

It should be evident from our discussion of the nexus issues in budgeting and public policy that all budget decisions are not the same. Some budget decisions, relatively few, reflect significant shifts in policy as described by Kingdon's PAS model. Others, the majority of decisions, strike the observer as rather mundane. We shall follow Gosling's (1985) typology of three levels of decision items in budget development, and discuss the relative influence of examiners on the different levels of decisions. This is useful later when we discuss budget rationality and examiner roles with respect to their assigned agencies.

The First Decision Level

The bulk of the decisions during budget development are not high-profile decisions. Level-one decisions adjust the base budgets of agencies, and therefore influence quite a bit of spending. The goal of this decision set is to craft the "continuation budget" or the "cost to continue" budget for the agency. This base budget definition corresponds to an allocation that will permit the agency to continue providing the current level of services, given no changes in policy demands or responsibilities. Examiners heavily influence most of these decisions.

The first decision is whether or not to accept the spending allocated for the agency in the current year as the base allocation (base budget) upon which to build the next budget. There are several reasons that this may not be acceptable. First, agencies may have been given "one-time" spending for capital acquisitions or for a pilot program of sorts. This spending may have been explicitly designated as such in the budget bill, and the examiner should be aware of the one-time flag if he or she worked on the agency budget that year. If the examiner is new to the agency assignment in the SBO, this is one of the important things to learn early in the assignment. The team leader and examiner previously responsible for this agency's budget, when available, are good sources for this kind of information. The examiner needs to ensure that the base continuation budget excludes this type of funds in the calculation for next year's funding.

Second, the budget instructions from the budget director may require agencies to submit a reduced-level base budget (at 97 percent or 95 percent of what was allocated in the current fiscal year). In periods of financial stress, this may be used to reduce overall state spending, cutting funds in one agency for reallocation in another agency, which requires an increase. Exceptions will be pressed by each agency, especially smaller ones that feel percentage reductions more readily than larger agencies. The examiner, especially if assigned to small agencies, needs to know the programmatic impact of the cut. In small agencies, the reduction may require cutting a personnel position, especially if reduced budgets become a norm, as they did in the early 1990s. Repeated base budget reductions can also result in reduced positions in larger agencies, although the effect may be less because of greater organizational slack and the ability of larger agencies to reallocate funding and positions more easily than smaller agencies.

The budget instructions that set the reduction level are decided by the budget director in consultation with the governor. Examiners have virtually no input on the reduction level required for budget submissions. However, examiners are delegated responsibility by the budget director to analyze agency budgets for the impact of a reduction level on agency operations. It is with the examiner that the agency must try to gain an ally against a base budget reduction. As we will see in later chapters, examiners become as familiar with their agencies' programs as possible so they can determine the impact of forced base reductions on agency programs. If they ally themselves with the agency, they become advocates for the agency budget in their recommendations to the budget director and governor. Without examiner support, agencies will have a difficult time convincing the budget director or governor to overturn the initial examiner decision to reduce the base budget by some amount.

Even in periods without financial stress, reduced-level budget submissions may be required in budget instructions to force agencies to reveal priorities. This has become a frequent practice in many states, including those in our sample. During the first rounds of these exercises, sometimes called target base budgeting, some agencies tried the "Washington Monument Maneuver": They identified spending for some highly visible program with highly visible political support as a "low priority available for elimination or reduction," knowing full well that the money would not be cut by the legislature, even if the governor would agree to the cut. Several rounds of target budgeting seem to have eliminated most of these episodes, and agencies seem to be taking priority revelation as a routine exercise in state budgeting, at least in our sample states. Still, there are exceptional cases where agencies are said to still fight this exercise, and they seem to be noncabinet agencies; that is, those without allegiance to the governor because they have independent boards or elected state officials as agency heads.

Base budgets are also adjusted for increases on a routine basis. Even if agency budgets are submitted at a reduced base level, the proposed reduction decisions can be rejected and the current budget base will be accepted. Furthermore, base budgets need to account for changes in the cost of delivering services, mainly accounting for commodities inflation costs and any personnel cost increases. The personnel cost increases account for significant spending, but they are highly political in many states. These decisions are sometimes tied to collective bargaining agreements, which means they fall differentially across agencies. The prison guards may bargain successfully for a higher pay increase (affecting the corrections budget) than the engineers or nurses (affecting the transportation or mental health budgets, respectively). Oftentimes, however, the majority of state workers are affected by an overall pay increase decision that raises most agency personnel accounts by the same percentage. Because these decisions involve so much money, however, they are often among the last decisions to be made in the budget, after policy priorities have been met. Examiners have little or no influence on these decisions. The exception is the SBO examiner responsible for personnel statewide. This examiner may advise the budget director and governor on the desirability of reclassification schemes and estimate the costs of various pay increase schemes. Still, this examiner is often advising the governor regarding recommendations from the state's personnel agency. For the average SBO examiner, however, this would not be a decision for them to consider, although they will need to make sure the final salary increase amount is calculated correctly in their final agencies' budgets.

An inflation adjustment for commodities and services is a decision area with more examiner influence. Some states use inflation adjustments estimated specifically for different commodities groups, and these must be applied specifically to programmatic inputs in each agency. The estimated inflation rate for construction materials, for example, concerns the transportation budget more than the social welfare budget. The heating fuel inflation estimates affect the corrections and welfare budgets more than the economic development budget, and so on. Although these inflation rates may vary only slightly from some average, depending upon the agency's program input mix, applying the inflation adjustments incorrectly can amount to significant dollars, for better or for worse! This may be a mundane calculation for the agency and the examiner, but it is not an insignificant one.

The Second Decision Level

The second level of decision items includes minor policy and budget adjustments, often involving a decision to add a personnel position to a program, or to increase capital outlays for major equipment or a building improvement. It can also involve funding for a pilot program that can be an agency's initiative or a governor's initiative. Decisions about increasing agency positions are important and often difficult, especially where governors have run election campaigns on platforms to reduce the number of state government positions. These kinds of decisions are often called budget "enhancements" because they increase or alter the level of program services by an agency. This is a very influential decision area for examiners, because they are highly qualified to advise the budget director and governor regarding the policy and programmatic impacts of these decisions. This decision level often involves the most decisions, since agencies routinely argue for improving and expanding their programs. The examiner's assignment is to analyze the request and decide whether it has intrinsic merit, and whether its merit warrants inclusion in the next budget. The latter half of the decision requires an understanding of the macro-budgeting environment and the standing of the particular request with regard to the policy and budget nexus. It is in this decision level that the examiners are most visible, and for which they are delegated major responsibility.

The Third Decision Level

Level three decisions include the major policy decisions that significantly alter base budgets. Increased property tax relief to homeowners and major restructuring of the school finance formulas are major policy shifts that involve significant budget changes. Although the decision may affect only one agency budget directly (the revenue department or the education department, respectively, in the above example), significant funds spent on such policy initiatives usually represent lost allocations to other agency spending enhancements. Thus, budget directions that specify gubernatorial policy priorities, such as increased property tax relief, may be interpreted by both agencies and examiners as suggesting it will be difficult to get spending increases for other agency budgets, especially if the fiscal climate is not robust. When major policy initiatives are included in the budget development, the SBO examiner assigned to the target agency often identifies and analyzes the feasible alternatives, but often stops short of recommending one alternative above others. Usually the final choice of the governor involves a high degree of political consideration; as we discuss later, the examiner cannot ignore the political factors, but the high political stakes involve risks by the governor, not the examiner.

Our model of budget rationality is most applicable to decisions and recommendations in levels one and two. It applies to the analysis of level three decisions, recognizing that the examiner usually does not make a recommendation at this level. Level three decisions are not routine and their probability for happening is described well by the PAS model. SBO examiners are important players in the decision process, but they are substantially less influential in final decision outcomes than in the other two decision levels. Decisions in levels one and two, adjusting the base budget for increases or decreases and routine enhancements to agency programs, are largely incremental (or decremental) changes. But while the outcomes of these decisions correspond to the outcomes described by the incrementalism of Wildavsky and Lindblom, we shall soon argue that the rationality underlying these judgments does not fit their descriptions at all.

Execution-Phase Decisions

There is also another set of budget decisions that are not generally considered budget-development decisions, and they are not included in Gosling's (1985) typology. These are execution-phase budget decisions, and they affect budget development decisions in several ways. First, periods of fiscal stress can require cutback budgeting, which essentially resets the base budget for the agency. Depending upon the method used, the cutback will be across the board or cuts will be applied to agencies selectively. Examiners in our sample of states were usually experienced with these cutback decisions, having just survived the recessionary budgets of the early 1990s. The major factor influencing how they recommended agency budget cuts was whether they were allowed to work with the agencies or were required to generate the cutback options by themselves, for presentation to the budget director and governor without agency comment. We will include these decisions in our discussions of examiner decision-making in policy-oriented and control-oriented decision contexts.

A second set of budget-execution decisions essentially mixes with decisions defining the agency's base budget. As the current fiscal year nears completion, the development phase has already begun for the next budget. Technical procedures are often used by SBOs to ensure that agencies do not rush to spend remaining allocations before the end of the fiscal year. The conventional wisdom in budgeting is that if an agency does not spend all of its allocation, then its budget will be reduced in the next fiscal year by a corresponding amount. The conundrum is apparent to agency budgeters and SBO examiners alike: if an agency does not need the money, it should not spend it; but if it does not spend as planned and the budget is subsequently reduced, the agency relinquishes organizational slack and the ability to reallocate funds internally to accommodate emerging problems and priorities. Some states, such as Virginia, have experimented with letting agencies "bank" some percentage of unspent funds for future capital outlay spending, especially for information technology enhancements.

From the perspective of the budget director, the amount that agencies collectively do not spend in the current fiscal year is carried forward as funding available for allocations in the next budget year. Especially when the fiscal climate is not robust, this can make or break a governor's policy initiative. Without the carry-forward balance, there may be insufficient new revenues to pay for the governor's policy priorities. So the examiners have a responsibility to make sure that their assigned agencies do not spend lavishly or unnecessarily in the remaining months of the fiscal year solely to "preserve" a base budget allocation. Ultimately, they must balance the needs of the agency programs with the need of the governor to have a sufficient funding pool upon which to build future policy initiatives.

Summary: The Foundations for a Model of Budget Rationality

This chapter lays important groundwork for the development of a model of budget rationality. We have described the important features that characterize the complexity inherent in budgeting in state budget offices. We have noted the important features of timing for policy changes, and also the importance of deadlines in budgeting, which make time itself a premium resource. We have investigated the gatekeeping role of the examiners at the vortex of the policy and budget processes, and how they must bridge the macro-budgeting and micro-budgeting environments.

The forces that move issues to the budget decision agenda are influenced by the factors at play in the policy process. The policy process and the macro-budgeting process are distinct, but inseparable. Budget decisions require resolution because policies and programs require funding, and the funding decision must be made according to deadlines inherent in the budget process. The examiner in the SBO must understand the difference between incremental and nonincremental policy changes, and how those produce incremental and nonincremental changes in agency budgets. The examiner in the SBO needs to know whether the timing is right for an agency proposal, or whether it is not feasible in the current political or fiscal environment.

Finally, we have noted that while examiners exercise their judgments in a critical gatekeeper role, they have uneven influence on the range of decisions made in budgeting. Their influence is weakest for major policy decisions such as school finance reform. Their influence is considerable regarding base budget adjustments and minor to moderate program enhancements. They are delegated considerable discretion when they are placed at the center of the budget and policy nexus. We will explore the implications of their position throughout this book.

The next chapter proposes our budget rationalities model by first assessing traditional considerations of budgetary decision-making, focusing specifically on the inadequacies of the "economic man" when ruminating about budget problems specific to state government agencies. Following explanation of various notions of rationality, we consider the demands of a model of budget rationality that will accommodate the complexity and fluidity characteristic of budget problems. We continue our model development by recognizing Diesing's (1962) typology of decisions and the applicability of decision type to our concept of multiple rationalities. The rest of chapter 3 and then chapter 4 describe the effectiveness and efficiency decisions of the SBO examiner, respectively. We illustrate that considerations of effectiveness encompass social, political, and legal rationalities, while those of efficiency comprise economic and technical rationalities. We conclude chapter 4 by summarizing our multiple rationalities model, explaining how budget problem-framing determines the decision rationality expected of an SBO examiner.

Notes

1. The phenomenon is strongest for state and local governments. It is weakest at the national level, where sharp partisan differences between the legislature and executive can significantly reduce the president's influence on the budget. Aside from these alignments, the impact of the president's recommendation on the final budget passed by Congress is substantial.

2. The forecast is commonly prepared several months prior to the new fiscal year (for further discussion see Bretschneider, Gorr, Grizzle, and Klay 1989; and Lee and Johnson 1998, 86–88).

3

Budget Rationalities: Effectiveness Decisions

Why Propose a Budget Rationalities Model?

The previous chapter explained the foundations of the budget decision agenda, and the role of the SBO and budget examiner regarding such an agenda. To explain the budget decision agenda, we have illustrated the confluence between policy-making theory and budget-making theory. We assessed decision-making theories—in particular, Kingdon's policy agenda setting model, the garbage can model, and Rubin's real time budgeting model—to cull important components that contribute to a multiple rationalities model of budgetary decision-making. We now use this chapter and the next to flesh out an understanding of budgetary rationality, the multifaceted nature of budget problems, and then aspects of problem framing that we believe influence the budgetary decision approach of SBO examiners. We will begin by reviewing current understanding of budgeting in the United States.

We know that there are budget cycles, budget players, predominant revenue sources, finite resources, the usual expenditures, and wish lists for consideration. Much of budgeting is explained by its historical nature, hence traditional reliance on notions of incrementalism. What we have agreed to in the past—policy decisions and funding levels—heavily influences what we will be doing next year, and how much we will spend to do it. In this sense, a relatively small proportion of total spending will be debated openly for citizen and media consumption in the legislative sessions.

The regularity of budgeting sustains this historical nature. Budget cycles, whether annual or biennial, require systematic action on the part of specific budget actors. Chief executives develop a policy agenda, executive budget staff disseminate budget guidelines to agencies, agencies develop spending plans and improvements that the chief executive and his/her staff consider when developing budget recommendations to be submitted to the legislature. Subsequent legislative deliberation ends with an appropriation bill or bills. The session ends and eventually agencies close out one fiscal year and start up another. The cycle begins anew. Concurrently, agencies are involved in budget execution, carrying out legislatively and administratively prescribed activities, and expenditures from the previous fiscal year are being audited.

However, we have noted that modern budgeting has become much more complex than can be adequately explained by economic rationality, traditional incrementalism, or even a strictly political model. State governments provide excellent examples of this changed environment. In fact, states have been at the center of government reform in the United States for at least two decades, serving as laboratories for public policy experiments and taking on complicated activities that serve as models to their counterparts at the federal and local levels.

As we have already argued, we do not believe that this behavior is sufficiently explained from a strictly political or economic perspective. For example, the standard budget process model suggests that the executive branch is responsible for budget development and presentation to the legislature. The legislative branch then deliberates the chief executive's recommendations, supplementing with its own institutional resources (e.g., a legislative budget office). However, as illustrated in the introductory chapter, states represent a variety of circumstances regarding politics and fiscal condition, as well as gubernatorial budget powers and organizational arrangements, making it difficult to distinguish states clearly if all variables are considered together. For example, in North Carolina an advisory committee made up of legislators and executive branch administrators provides input (albeit advisory) during executive budget development. This group, along with analysts from both branches, tours the state and holds hearings to assess agency needs and to hear first-hand how state dollars are spent, often visually reviewing the results of such spending. This offers the chance to consider program efficiency and effectiveness. A historical look at the use of this advisory group reveals that its political influence has waxed and waned, depending upon the political split of the legislative and executive branches. Certainly, we see that, in this case, peeling away the superficial layers of the general model suggests the complexity of the executive branch as it develops a budget proposal.

Is There Such a Thing as Budget Rationality?

This brings us to one of the main questions of this book: Is there such a thing as "budget rationality"? The question begs two more: If budget rationality is a valid construct, (1) what are its characteristics, and (2) how does it compare and contrast with other notions of rationality? The answers to these questions are at the heart of the arguments in this chapter. Our first task is to challenge the notion that budgetary decision-making is synonymous with economic rationality or political rationality. The second important task is to show how a concept of budget rationality built on a framework of multiple rationalities captures the complexity of budget decisions, while also providing decision rules that allow examiners to analyze and simplify budget problems so that they can make credible recommendations to the governor.

Toward a Concept of Budgetary Rationality: The Limits of the ECM

Studies of budgetary decision-making generally make implicit assumptions about the nature of rationality. In particular, they often evaluate budgetary decision-making based on the rationality model found in economics, namely the utilitarian economic actor. Such assumptions have sometimes been made explicit, such as in Herbert Simon's (1947) comparison of "economic man" and "administrative man." Another example is in Lewis's (1952) article that fostered the first wave of performance budgeting based on economic notions of marginal utility analysis. This stylized construct of rationality is often called the synoptic model, since it requires comprehensive analysis and information search steps. We will refer to it as the economic choice model (ECM) of rationality.

The ECM requires the decisionmaker to separate means from ends, gather all pertinent facts, and analyze alternatives to identify the option that maximizes results. Results are usually stated in terms of maximizing a goal of individual utility or preference satisfaction. For example, one decisionmaker chooses butter to maximize rich flavor in the cake, while another chooses applesauce to minimize cholesterol and maximize health. The extension of individual decision-making models to collective actions has spawned the lively discipline of public choice theory, including agency theory, which seeks to analyze all human behavior from the singular perspective of maximizing individual satisfaction, be the actors police department officers or bakers.

But this notion of rationality, at least applied to governmental activities, and particularly to budgeting, is too narrow and problematic (Hogarth and Reder 1987; Elster 1986; Buchanan and Musgrave 1999). As Diesing (1962, 14) notes, the existence of economic rationality is almost universally recognized. The task is rather "to treat it in so specific a way that it does not automatically become identical with all rationality, but can take its place *as one kind of reason among others*." To restrict ourselves to just one type of rationality is to restrict ourselves to a severely limited range of rational actions. If we can treat the rationality underlying economic decisions as only one of several types of rationalities evident in public policy processes, then we can describe the rationalities underlying noneconomic decisions and create a more holistic view of "rational" budget decisions.

The ECM severely limits the scope of rational budget behavior because it ignores a broad range of rationality concepts found in other social science disciplines, including philosophy and psychology. A small sample of the vast literature on rationality in the social sciences is sufficient to suggest the possibilities for a broader notion of budget rationality that is not necessarily synonymous with economic rationality. Robin Hogarth and Melvin Reder (1987) note that although the economics and psychology disciplines are direct descendants of a common body of philosophical ideas, their separate evolutions have led them to quite different interpretations of those ideas, even though they both analyze human behavior. For example, norms are prior to individuals in explanatory order and cannot be reduced to subjective feelings of what to do. There are other social norms besides that of means-ends efficiency. In this sense, norms explain behavior beyond the instrumental concept of rationality inherent in the economic choice model (Elster 1986, 23–24). Budget decisions may be subject to more than one type of social norm. If so, the task is to identify those norms, their underlying rationalities, and the principles that guide those decisions.

R.P. Abelson (1976, 58) points out that social psychologists are leery of the rationality concept, generally because they find them prescriptive, presumptive, and preemptive. Western tradition has a prescriptive concept of rationality that has "ideologized rationality," and the perfection of rational behavior remains an implicit goal. The presumptive concept of rationality suggests that there are limits to practical rationality, and "hidden" social structures that impede personally rational actions (e.g., groupthink). Finally, rationality as a preemptive concept suggests that once we start talking about rationality, we tend to think always in terms of default from a standard—for example, *Why do people not behave rationally?* "Rationality simply may not be a useful descriptive concept when we look carefully at what is going on psychologically" (Abelson 1976, 61).

Abelson's concept of "limited subjective rationality" deviates from notions of objective rationality in important ways. First, one can use reasoning capacity upon a personally distorted picture of reality, or, second, one can apply predictable mental processing rules that do not correspond to the rules of formal logic. Each can also occur together such that "predictable but not necessarily fully logical rules might be applied by the individual to a specifiable but not necessarily accurate picture of the world" (Abelson 1976, 62).

Rationality is also often limited by a tendency of humans to turn a deaf ear to the social influences on behavior.

Work on dissonance theory has led Elliot Aronson (1972) to state that man is not a rational animal but rather a *rationalizing* animal. The actor ends up changing his attitude to provide internal justification for behavior that is prompted by external social pressures. Studies in attribution theory suggest that although individuals tend to seek simple explanations for their own behavior and the behavior of others, they are often unable to arrive at adequately complex explanations.

Percy Cohen (1976) reviews several characterizations of rationality, including those of Max Weber, Vilfredo Pareto, and Talcott Parsons. He compares and contrasts Weber's notions of instrumental and value rationality. Weber's instrumental rationality applies to conduct "when it is determined by expectations of the behaviour of objects, including other humans, which are used as conditions or as means for the attainment of calculated ends. . . . Instrumental rationality requires that the choice of means and the pursuit of one particular end take account not only of whether the particular means achieves the particular end, but also of whether this will permit the achievement of other ends" (Cohen 1976, 133) Accordingly, Weber's value-rationality applies to conduct when either an aesthetic or a moral belief is the basis for action that is valued in its own right, regardless of its prospects of success. An example is giving a gift to someone to convey sentiments, as opposed to the gift's being a means to garner a favor in return (instrumental rationality).

Cohen recognizes that others find rationality to be nearly synonymous with Weber's instrumentality, and that norms and values are seen as providing the bounds within which the actor's choices are made. He then discusses *affectivity*; that is, the need for gratification from actions. Holding that the expression of affectivity usually demands immediate rather than deferred gratification, affectivity becomes something of an obstacle to rationality. Thus, affective neutrality leads to increased rationalization, much as Weber associated impersonality to increased judicial and substantive rationalization.

Quentin Gibson (1976) suggests that the function of reason is not merely to devise means but to reconcile or harmonize ends. "To achieve this, the agent must keep all his relevant ends in mind, he must ensure that his scale of preferences is internally consistent, and then he must work out which ends are in his circumstances capable of joint achievement and which have to be sacrificed. *What he has to achieve in fact is not so much an end as an optimum position, given his scale of preferences* [emphasis added]. Though he may fall short of this in varying degrees, it is what is required for his full rationality" (1976, 120). Gibson goes on to argue that the complexity of rationality should give warning to social scientists who try to ascribe rationality (or irrationality) to study subjects. "For the more complex a problem is, the less likely is it that people will cope with it adequately. . . . Calculable risks [of each alternative] are rarely found in real social situations. And . . . departures from the right answer become progressively more likely with the number and diversity of the hypotheses compared" (Gibson 1976, 121–122).

Geoffrey Mortimore (1976) argues that human rationality can be divided between beliefs that are rational and actions that are rational. The concept of practical rationality applies to rational actions and describes the conditions under which one might observe someone to have practical rationality as a trait. The practically rational man is "concerned to identify considerations which are good and sufficient reasons for choice, [and] his research and deliberative activities will no doubt conform to the requirements of epistemic rationality. However, such activities are performed because he is practically rational, i.e. *because* he has a conception of what count as good and sufficient practical reasons and cares about identifying and acting on such reasons" (Mortimore 1976, 101). Certainly, practical rationality tempered by norms, rules, principles, and standards might be considered as less than rational to some. To the extent "that normative considerations act as rigid barriers to reflection about other considerations and other options, they are non-rational influences. *If, however, they are treated by the agent as simply some amongst his range of relevant considerations* to be taken into account in comparatively assessing options, to be weighed against each other in such assessments, *rationality is unimpaired by the influence of normative considerations*" (1976, 109).

Diesing (1962) establishes a foundation to answer the challenge of normative dominance of the neoclassical economic theory application to decision-making when he argues that economic rationality is but one type of reason found in society. He defines rational action as that which effectively promotes some good, such as efficiency. Rational decision-making is defined in such a way as to make economic rationality just one of several types of reasonings. Both technical efficiency and economic efficiency are strongly held values in the executive budget process, and economizing is a principal function of the executive budget process. But as the government's principal policy document, the budget involves more than efficiency values, and its effectiveness demands more than economic considerations. Public policy also involves social, legal, and political problems. Thus, budget decisions are necessarily policy decisions, and one must analyze the policy facets of the budget decision, with special attention to monetary aspects.

Wildavsky (1964, 84–98) criticized the notion that only economic rationality applied to budgeting, arguing that, at the very least, there was also a political rationality to budgeting. Lindblom (1959) also criticizes the "synoptic" ECM as impossible and therefore invalid in the policy process. He describes a political, incremental choice (PIC) model of decision-making, based on a notion of limited rationality developed by Simon (1957), among others. In fact, Wildavsky (1964) advocates incremental decision-making in the public budgeting arena as quite rational. Nevertheless, budgeting systems have routinely been judged "rational," or not, based on an economic rationality model that by extension limits the range of acceptable budgeting systems to those that are economically rational. Meanwhile, other decision-making models have been posited as rational for public administration—with mixed success.

For example, there have been a few attempts to define a concept of administrative rationality as something beyond Simon's *Administrative Behavior* (1957) and apart from strictly economic or political reasoning. Each has important parallels with the basic principle that there are different types of decisions to make in public policy and administration, and each requires its own reasoning or rationality. John Pfiffner (1960) and Nicholas Nicolaidis (1960) posit an administrative rationality that has multiple standards of validity that constitute several different behavioral norms upon which an administrator decides an issue. Pointing out that the typical administrator faces a "galaxy of decision points" and a "galaxy of information points," the decision-making process is characterized as nonlinear in nature, more a process of fermentation in biochemistry than an assembly line (Pfiffner 1960, 129). The result is that decisionmakers often screen information through conflicting considerations bolstered by their professional knowledge and experience. The administrator cannot rely solely on the economic rationality model because it precludes the influence of other important factors, including politics, power, group dynamics, personality, emotions, and intellect.

While the Pfiffner and Nicolaidis model was oriented to the complexity in administrative decision-making at the individual level, Richard Hartwig (1978) develops an administrative rationality model that focuses on "ideal types" of organizational decision-making. Using Diesing's concepts of multiple rationalities, he argues that the ambiguity concerning administrative responsibility that has resulted from the evolution of the concept through successive schools of administrative thought demonstrates the need for a reformulation of administrative theory. Central to his model is the notion that the activities of complete organizations necessarily involve multiple types of rationality. Hartwig (1978, 16) emphasizes that "two or more modes of rationality may often be relevant to a single organizational decision. When this occurs, the different evaluative criteria may yield conflicting results. For example, a given decision may be socially desirable but economically undesirable. Such a situation requires criteria for deciding between the relevance or degree of relevance of each type of responsibility. . . . Thus we will talk of socially responsible decisions, economically responsible decisions, and so forth."

Demands of a Model of Budget Rationality

Hartwig's use of Diesing's concepts of multiple rationalities has an intuitive appeal for budgeting as well. What public budgeting practitioners require is a general theory of micro-budgeting that views public budgeting as an inherent element of the public policy process and provides a theoretical basis for their decisions. Such a theory of budgeting would embody the virtues of both the PIC and the ECM models within a general framework of the rationalities underlying budget decisions. The successful budget rationality model must meet two fundamental demands. First, its descriptive and predictive features must apply to the individual unit of analysis, in this case the budgeter. The model must explicate the factors that influence the decisions and recommendations of individuals in the budget process. Further, the predictive features of the model must stipulate under *what* conditions examiners will use *which* decision factors and *how*. As a starting point in this book, we build a decision-making model based on the decisions of the examiners in state budget offices. The robustness of the model with respect to other budgeters (in agencies, legislative budget offices, and other levels of government) awaits extension and empirical testing in future research.

The second demand on a model of budget rationality is even more difficult. The model must account for the administrative complexity inherent in the decisions of state budget examiners. The conditionality of examiner decisions, at root, is an issue because examiners in state budget offices are fundamentally linked to policy and program implementation. Two features of administrative complexity stand out. As discussed earlier, state examiners are at the vortex of the macro/micro budgetary processes. The decision calculus of these particular budgeters must account for both macro-budgetary environmental factors, and the micro-budgetary features of the process linked to policy and program implementation. And the attention of SBO examiners is focused on funding policies and programs. Which programs are funded, for how much, and in what manner, are precisely the questions V.O. Key raised more than fifty years ago. As we have seen, the nexus between the budget and policy processes is extensive and intensive.

In the previous chapter we saw how the theory of budgetary incrementalism fails to account for these necessary theoretical elements, and how the policy process model works at the macro-budgeting level, but is inadequate as an explanation for decision-making at the micro-budgeting level. The incrementalism model explains some, but not all, of the necessary factors required above. Incrementalism does not do a good job of explaining agenda changes. There are too many cases of abrupt changes in the agenda. Incrementalism does a much better job of explaining the development of proposals or alternatives or the enactment of changes in small increments. An old policy alternative, known to specialists and discussed and refined at length by policy analysts, can appear and disappear from the policy agenda. Incrementalism is particularly important for understanding the development of alternatives and proposals, while agendas exhibit a good deal of nonincremental change. More specifically, incrementalism does not address the nexus issues of the macro/micro and the budget/policy links.

We also explained that the garbage can model (as modified by Kingdon for the policy process) helps explain policy agenda setting at the macro level but has not been applied at the micro level. The micro-level discussion is restricted to listing criteria for moving a policy alternative out of the "policy primeval soup" to the active decision agenda. Although we learn something about the decision calculus of the policy entrepreneur, the model is noticeably silent on the calculus of other individuals. Aside from noting that the development phase of the budget process is a predictable window of opportunity for policy entrepreneurs, the model has little to say about the nexus of budgeting and policy. It has even less to say about the central budget office and decisions by examiners.

Finally, we briefly argued that the economic choice model of rationality, although a micro-level decision-making model, is an inadequate explanation of budgetary decisions because it does not apply to noneconomic types of problems. Legal problems are not economic problems, for example, and their solutions lie in legal reasoning, not economic reasoning. The ECM has also been attacked frequently as a normative model without any descriptive power. That is, it has an elegant logic that does not fit with the way individuals actually make decisions. Amos Tversky and Daniel Kahneman (1987) use several experiments to convincingly demonstrate that the logic of the economic choice model does not provide an adequate foundation for a descriptive theory of decision-making. They "argue that the deviations of actual behavior from the normative model are too widespread to be ignored, too systematic to be dismissed as random error, and too fundamental to be accommodated by relaxing the normative system. . . . Normative models of choice, which assume invariance of preferences, cannot provide an adequate descriptive account of choice behavior" (Tversky and Kahnerman 1987, 68 and 73).

In sum, the major competing models of budgeting are macro-level models, including RTB and Wildavsky's budgetary incrementalism. The principal paradigms for the micro-budgeting level are the economic choice and the incrementalism models. Yet none of these models provides a satisfactory solution to a budget problem that demands a treatment of the nexus between micro- and macro-budgetary spheres, and the nexus between the budget process and the policy process.

Empirical Support for a Model of Budget Rationality

These theoretical discussions and empirical studies suggest that our model of micro-budgeting decisions must accomplish several goals. First, it must account for multiple criteria used in decisions. Second, it must account for variations across fiscal and political environments. Third, it must account for organizational and technical factors that may temper or otherwise affect the interaction of the decision criteria and the environmental factors. The model we propose is descriptive of micro-budgetary decision-making, taking into account the critical connection these decisions must have with macro-budgeting decisions. It is based on the decisions reached by state budget office examiners, but may be applicable to other budgeting actors as well.[1]

Several experiments and simulation studies suggest that budget decision-makers use multiple criteria to make budgetary decisions (Stedry 1960; Barber 1966; Stewart and Gelberd 1976; Bretschneider, Straussman, and Mullins 1988; McCaffery and Baker 1990; Thurmaier 1992 and 1995a; Willoughby 1993a and 1993b). The first premise of our model is that examiners use multiple types of decisions to compose their budget recommendations. We begin with the axiom (suggested in previous chapters) that budgets are multifaceted problems, with social, political, legal, economic, and technical aspects. In a simplified model, each type of decision can be characterized as addressing either effectiveness (social, political, and legal) or efficiency (economic and technical) problems. Effectiveness decision-making focuses on adjustments to the social, political, and legal aspects of the budget. The enacted budget represents a political agreement about the underlying social values and relative priority of public functions within a legal framework that distinguishes between fundamental social norms and subordinate rules that define rights and responsibilities within the polity. This agreement is reached on a given day in a legislative session when the budget is voted. The resource allocation agreement inherent in the budget is largely static for a year, although subject to modification either through midyear adjustments or in the next budget.

As suggested by Lindblom, Wildavsky, and incrementalist decision theory, most of the base budget agreement will be subjected to only minor discussion and modification in the future. This is because the base budget reflects historical macro-budgeting agreements regarding the proper activities of government, sources and methods of revenue, and relative expenditure priorities among government programs. However, base budgets do change, and some programs increase faster than others, while some programs are diminished or terminated. These modifications are generally the result of micro-budgeting decisions, pursued within the context of the macro-budgeting framework. Primary responsibility for these adjustments falls to the governor's budget staff. The second premise of our model is that responsibility for maintaining the macro-micro nexus requires examiners to understand the macro-budgeting framework, including the governor's perspective on how programs should be modified. The integration of macro- and micro-level decisions is not a simple task for examiners. They must also understand the implications of budget decisions for policy and program implementation by agencies. The third premise of our model is that the degree to which these first two premises are true depends upon the decision contexts of the examiners, as we will explore in chapter 5. That is, we expect a multiple rationalities decision-making approach and a conscious linkage of the macro- and micro-budgetary issues to be most evident in policy-oriented SBOs and least evident in control-oriented SBOs.

It should be clear from our earlier discussion of rationality that a model of budget rationality is not wedded to defining rationality exclusively in the efficiency sense. Rather, the high degree of policy content inherent in state budgeting decisions requires a broader view of budget problems, and consequently a broader range of acceptable methods of reasoning to address the problems. Having described how the multiple actors and environmental factors inherent in budgeting problems yield multifaceted budget problems, the next step toward developing a model of budget rationality is discussing how each facet or problem requires its own process of reasoning, or rationality. An integrated view of budgeting requires a common denominator for analysis, an analytical method that can be applied equally well to the efficiency and effectiveness aspects of budgeting.

Diesing (1962) identifies five types of common decisions and carefully argues that each type of decision requires its own type of reasoning or rationality. He argues that each mode of rationality can be evaluated based on its effectiveness in producing a unique value. Following Karl Mannheim (1940), Diesing argues that effectiveness "refers to the successful production of any kind of value, leaving open and problematic the question of what kinds of value there may be. The efficient achievement of predetermined goals is a special kind of effectiveness. If there are other kinds of value besides goal values, then there are presumably also other kinds of effectiveness or rationality" (Diesing 1962, 3). His typology is easily transformed into a framework that describes the different decisional bases of multifaceted budget decisions and which rationalities take precedence over others. This section develops the multiple-rationalities model by associating each budget facet with a decision type as defined by Diesing.

Applying this framework to budgeting illuminates multiple bases for budget decisions. We begin by restating the axiom that each budget problem is a multifaceted policy problem, with technical, economic, social, legal, and political aspects. We now consider budget analysis as treating each facet as a special type of problem—technical, economic, social, legal, or political. If economic problems require economic decisions, it follows that other types of problems may entail other types of decisions. And if there is such a thing as an economic decision-making process—an economic way of reasoning— then technical, social, legal, or political problems may require their own unique reasoning processes, or rationalities. We argue that effective recommendations and decisions by an examiner must take all these facets into account. Budgetary decisions that neglect consideration of each of the five types of rationalities are less effective. They are less effective because they neglect at least one potentially serious policy constraint. We now discuss the components of our model regarding effectiveness decisions. We consider efficiency decisions in the following chapter, then build a description of a "rational examiner" and their decision-making in SBOs.

Effectiveness Decisions

The first premise of our model recognizes that public budgeting involves both efficiency and effectiveness decisions. The essential quality of effectiveness decisions that distinguishes them from efficiency decisions is that they are characterized by conflicts of values. Thus, effectiveness decisions focus on social relations. Their respective rationalities are fundamental to effectiveness decisions and to the valuation and ordering of social ends. There are three types of effectiveness decisions identified by Diesing: social, political, and legal. These three rationalities produce the antecedent framework for exercising the economic and technical rationalities necessary for budgetary decisions.

Budgeting is a dynamic, not static, process. Throughout the budget year, agencies manage their programs to accomplish assigned goals and objectives with the resources granted in the budget. Programs are expanded, diminished, or otherwise modified to reflect the expectations of the legislature and governor, as specified in the most recent budget. Agencies advocating for program spending try to justify their budget requests as responses to changes in effectiveness demands. The transportation department, for example, may argue that more money is required to satisfy complaints of inadequate signage for highway exits. Or the welfare department may argue that increased funding is required to meet statutory obligations to provide health care to low-income children. Examiners in SBOs cannot propose and defend their recommendations for agency budgets to governors without understanding how the agency request under review alters or conforms to the social raison d'être of the program. Why does the program exist? How has it changed over the years, and why? Which are the most important aspects of the program and which are the least important? How important is this program relative to other programs within the agency?

Each budget request from an agency that proposes a change to the base budget must be assessed relative to the social, political, and legal aspects of the base budget. In important ways, the base budget embodies the fundamental elements of the effectiveness framework for budget analysis. First, it identifies the array of programs the polity has previously agreed to establish and fund. Second, the funding proportions embodied in the allocations for each program signal the relative priority of the programs established in previous political compromises. Third, the budget and associated statutory references codify the legal standing of each program, identifying funding sources and expenditure limits, among other things.

To propose funding for one program and not another is to challenge the standing priorities previously agreed to, or even to increase the scope of government activities to embody a wider array of public programs. Under tight fiscal constraints, increased funding for one program implies decreased funding for another, further challenging previous budgetary agreements. An extended discussion of each effectiveness facet illustrates the decision framework that facilitates the economic and technical analyses of budget requests.

Social Rationality

Howard (1973) observes that budgets emerge from cultural environments. The cultural environment provides the social conditions that the political system seeks to change—or preserve—and to which it must adapt its budget process. The social facet of the budget problem concerns the underlying social rationale for the public policy or program and the social rationale for proposed changes. Rationales for policies and programs range from the simple to the complex, and usually pertain to a social problem. Social problems involve social disintegration and disharmony. These problems are usually addressed in a largely unconscious manner in the daily interactions of social members as they strive to adjust their lives to accommodate differences in values among subgroups and individuals (Diesing 1962, 76–88). Cohen (1976) points out that much social conduct exhibits a "weak rationality" in that many people follow, even semiconsciously, beliefs that are developed and constrained by their individual situations. This finding acknowledges the incomplete information that most people face when they decide on daily activities. Likewise, Amartya Sen (1986, 73–74) remarks that, fundamentally, "the act of choosing is a social act, and an individual's choice is more than merely an expression of personal preferences." The complex interrelationships in society generate behavioral rules and norms that separate, however subtly, individual behavior and welfare.

Diesing (1962) claims that individuals try to reduce conflicts and tensions within roles and between roles by trying to live up to their obligations a little more and finding some accommodation between conflicting obligations. Individuals learn to temper their expectations of roles and to conform in some degree to the expectations others have of them. People substitute more realistic obligations for those that are too severe and are unattainable, and then turn unattainable obligations into ideals. Sen (1986, 79) agrees that behavior is often tempered by what is socially acceptable. For example, behavioral experiments reveal that individuals will act against their own self-interest to conform to a group norm such as a social code. As noted earlier, norms are prior to individuals in explanatory order and cannot be reduced to subjective feelings of what to do.

Examples abound where people abide voluntarily with certain pronouncements even when not in their personal best interest (e.g., recycling programs, carpooling, and voting). James March (1986, 156–158) observes that people "accept a degree of personal and social wisdom in ordinary hypocrisy" because they believe they should do some things even if they are unable or unwilling to act that way in the short run. They make a conscious and important distinction that preferences as beliefs are independent of their immediate action consequences. People may wish not to be prejudiced or not to discriminate, for example, but may find themselves acting in prejudiced or discriminating ways.

Among the several reasons March has enumerated for ambiguous and inconsistent goals and preferences is that people appear to be comfortable with an array of unreconciled sources of legitimate wants. "They maintain a lack of coherence both within and among personal desires, social demands, and moral codes. Though they seek some consistency, they appear to see inconsistency as a normal, and necessary, aspect of the development and clarification of tastes" (March 1986, 156–158). It is no surprise, then, when Howard (1973, 42) observes that problem definition often is not a given at the outset of the budget process, but the nature of the problem is exposed in the process itself. We note that this is contrary to the requirements of the economic choice model, which assumes the principle of preference invariance, or fixed and ordered preferences. We call for balanced budgets in government, but is our own budget balanced?

The important point is that inconsistent, unordered, and unstable preferences are necessary and rational for social integration because they provide individuals with flexibility to accommodate contrasting and conflicting values and preferences held by other individuals with whom they must interact. Individuals can "go along" with a suggestion or action because they lack a strong preference or rigid ordering among several alternatives. Conflict is reduced or prevented precisely because of the flexibility inherent in unstable and inconsistent preferences. Value conflicts that cannot be resolved through unconscious accommodations are thrust into a more visible theater of actions, including discussions regarding peripheral public policies in the policy-making process or the judicial system.

The unconscious actions of adjustment and accommodation promote social integration by forming a common set of values and beliefs that identify roles and expectations, rights and responsibilities commonly accepted for social members (Diesing 1962, 65–69). Socially rational decisions are those that promote greater social integration, because it is social integration that develops and strengthens the attachment of members to common values. The accumulation of effective social decisions produces the core values and beliefs underlying public policies and guides the development of public programs.

The basic trend of social systems is toward greater integration, and we can recognize an underlying continuity to most public policies, that is, a core set of policy principles upon which discrete legislative and administrative actions are based. Agreement on the fundamental policies that arise through social integration permits society to pursue goals through various programs and activities, public and private. Giandomenico Majone (1989) claims that these core values provide continuity through time; their stability and consistency give meaning to actions and expectations that are integral to legislation and administration. An integrated social system is rational because "it is effective in making action possible and meaningful, and the integrative trend in social systems is a trend toward rational social organization" (Majone 1989, 84–85).

Social integration finds expression in such core policies as the provision of police and fire protection services to ensure public and personal safety, the provision of schools to ensure public education, and the provision of water and sewer services to ensure public and personal health. Where social integration is low, such as in the newly democratic countries in Europe, conflict surrounds almost every aspect of public policy, and there are few identifiable core policies. At higher levels of social integration, the conflicts surrounding these policies are concerned with peripheral policy issues, and the existence or rationale for the core policy principle itself is rarely questioned. Although social integration decisions produce a set of core social values and beliefs, there is a large residual of value differences surrounding that core. Majone labels these as peripheral values, and the issues arising from these peripheral differences are the more common subjects of debates in the political process, at least as witnessed in the United States.

Thus, social rationality defines the parameters of social debate by creating its substance—social values. "It is the value system of a culture which determines the extent to which ends can be alternative, which makes some means normative and others neutral, and which allows media of value comparison to develop" (Diesing 1962, 46). It is through this process of social rationality that the parameters for budgetary debate are broadly defined. This corresponds to Rubin's (1997) budget balance decision cluster, where the fundamental question is about the role and scope of government. In short, the products of social rationality are the core and peripheral values of the society that arise from the interaction and interdependence of individuals and groups.

The policy core is largely protected from change because it ensures stability in the society, provides predictability for members, and avoids conflict (Majone 1989). The concept of zero-based budgeting (ZBB) is fundamentally at odds with the notion that core policies should be modified only gradually and with great care. If the public library system is fulfilling a role in the community, then to abolish the service would be to introduce social instability. The notion that one could begin an analysis of the fire department with the question, "Should we abolish it?" is normally nonsensical. Its acceptance signifies *revolution* rather than *evolution*; it suggests that a radical transformation or abandonment of the policy core is under consideration. Therefore, consideration of this alternative should only occur in unusual circumstances, such as a crisis in which there is already social instability, and society must consider measures to restore stability (e.g., municipal bankruptcy).

Likewise, a proposal to severely reduce the fire department's budget or to "privatize" fire-fighting services would likely be unattractive to policy decisionmakers because it might jeopardize the core value of fire safety for every individual in the community. For such an alternative to emerge from the "policy primeval soup" and get a substantial hearing in the policy debate would require the support of a group with substantial economic and political resources. For such a group to identify with such a radical change in core policy would signify that the core values had already begun to change and were continuing to change.

On the other hand, the PAS model illustrates that although significant shifts in public policy are infrequent, they do occur under certain conditions. A central condition is a shift in core values or, rather, a swing in the public mood. Shifts in public sentiment regarding core values are recognized by elected officials and are translated into political activities. A shifting in the nature of a core principle generates actions in the PAS political stream, which begin to redefine the parameters of acceptable policy changes, or what Majone terms the political feasibility frontier.

Political Rationality

Barry Bozeman and Jane Massey (1982) emphasize that policy evaluation is useless if the political environment is not properly accounted for on the part of analysts. Political decisions are often described as the issue of who gets *how much* of *what* in the public policy debates, because the political process allocates social resources in an authoritative way. The goal of the political process is to translate "political values into decisions," and in important ways, budgetary politics is the translation of social values into government actions through the design and implementation of policies and programs (Howard 1973, 140). The focus of attention is normally on the *products* of political debates. Yet *who decides* in political debates is a key determinant of who receives how much of what. In this sense, who gets invited to the negotiating table, how big the table is, and how many sides it has, are important factors determining political outcomes. It is this aspect of political decisions that is most salient to a model of budget rationality.

Political rationality is the rationality of decision-making structures where members of the decision-making group share a common set of beliefs and values and commitment to a course of action to previous decisions. Diesing argues that political problems arise when the decision-making structure of a group or society is threatened with collapse. Their dissolution threatens social decisions and the ability of society to take concerted actions on public issues. Effective decision-making structures need to (1) accommodate a plurality of values, views, and beliefs, and (2) achieve a unified decision through discussion. As these two attributes are progressively embodied in a decision structure, they are increasingly in conflict with each other. As the variety of suggested facts and opinions increases, it is harder to reach agreement. And as the resolution process becomes faster and more certain, it is harder to make the group aware of varied and unusual factors (Diesing 1962, 178).

Political problems are addressed by balancing the need for diverse viewpoints to be represented in the social debate with the need to reach some decision after the debate has occurred. "A decision structure yields improved decisions as it embodies both of these characteristics to a greater degree. First, the greater the variety of the presented facts, values, and norms, and the greater the variety of proposed alternatives a structure is able to produce, the more effective its decisions are likely to be" (Diesing 1962, 177). Decisions are made necessary by problems, and complex problems require complex treatment for adequate resolution.

Effective political decisions are those that preserve or improve the decision-making structure by achieving the required balance of these two forces. The goal of a political decision is to structure the decision process so that an agreement is not only possible but also probable. A budgetary decision process that uses the SBO as a decision-making structure to serve at the nexus of the budget and policy processes, and at the vortex of the macro- and micro-budgeting decision streams, can produce highly effective budget decisions. As explained earlier, the SBO is uniquely situated to reap the benefits of the decision-making skills of the examiners employed in them, especially when they are endowed with a policy orientation toward budgeting.

Budget Process: Decision-Making Structures Associated with
Political Rationality

Three elements appear in a variety of forms in all decision structures. First, there are the people who assume social roles that discuss issues of concern, suggest courses of action, and accept them. The second element is the set of beliefs and values that the members hold in common. Our discussion of social rationality suggests there will be greater agreement with respect to core social values and policies and lesser agreement with respect to peripheral values and policies. These values define the kind of ideas that can be seriously considered for discussion and decision by the group.

The third element of decision-making structures, the current commitments and courses of action already accepted by the group, is particularly relevant to budget analysis. All decisions have to be made in the context of actions and commitments resulting from previous decisions. The adaptation of any new decision to this context of "givens" provides continuity and stability and helps to make vague goals and values more specific. This is the ordinary process of making only incremental changes to the budget, as captured in Wildavsky's incrementalism model. But there is usually discussion about some aspects of the budget base as well because there is ordinarily disagreement among the members of a group as to what its commitments and present actions are. New programs and appropriations will engender some conflict, and this will generally be resolved by a bargaining process that involves the exchange of policy commitments for the continued participation of groups in the society. Base budget appropriations represent decisions resulting from past bargains, and conflict can be avoided by conducting the review in such a way that the past agreement is not reopened for debate. That is, normally only incremental changes to the base are subject to review (Gerwin 1969, 34).

The decision structure is the mechanism for integrating, ordering, and prioritizing the products of social rationality. Political actors bring with them the core values they hold largely in common and more or less unconsciously. Their focus is on the peripheral policies and programs designed to effect the core values. In the United States, for example, there is a core policy principle that we should structure society to promote a decentralized market economy. Yet agreement about how "free" the market should be is much less certain. There are peripheral policies and programs that regulate private enterprises, working conditions, and environmental discharges. These peripheral policies are subject to change because there is a much higher degree of conflict about their necessity and their scope, and various interests will try to change these peripheral policies in some way. Political decisions are reached using problem-solving, persuasion, bargaining, or politicking. In practice, these four processes are usually combined in various ways, with people bargaining on some points, using persuasion on others, and engaging in problem-solving on others (Diesing 1962, 175–176).

Wildavsky (1964, 192) discerns from Diesing's account of political rationality the importance that political actors must place on weighing the political benefits and costs of reaching agreement on a policy objective or policy direction. The political decision is taken to minimize political discord, to achieve a consensus or compromise necessary for pursuing policies and thereby governance. Therefore, in a *purely* political decision:

> Action never is based on the merits of a proposal but always on who makes it and who opposes it. Action should be designed to avoid complete identification with any proposal and any point of view, no matter how good or how popular it might be. The best available proposal should never be accepted just because it is best; it should be deferred, objected to, discussed, until major opposition disappears. Compromise is almost always a rational procedure, even when the compromise is between a good and a bad proposal. (Diesing 1962, 204)

So we find presidents, governors, mayors, city managers, and other central authorities continually forced to persuade others of their views and to reach agreements wherever possible. As Lindblom (1968, 104–105) notes, policy analysis is used to persuade proximate policymakers to realign positions and views. The process pushes the actors toward agreement by reshaping preferences and because "the most active participants recognize the need for agreement." Thus for one governor, a veto is said to represent "a failure of negotiations" (Forsythe 1990).

Choosing Peripheral Policies and Programs

While policy continuity and the stability it brings are desirable for social cohesion, it is also important that policies be responsive to changing conditions in the society and its environment. What gives the policy adaptability is that many peripheral "values, assumptions, methods, goals, and programs are disposable, modifiable, or replaceable by new ones. . . . Thus, the distinction between core and periphery [values] articulates the intuitive notion that not all policy changes are equally significant, nor all programs equally important. The closer some particular activity is to the core, the greater the pull to retain it and the sense of discontinuity when it is abandoned" (Majone 1989, 150–151).

While a society seeks the *ideal* of total integration and harmony, conflict is inevitable between individuals and cultural norms. The unstable and inconsistent qualities of preferences permit and promote social integration because ambiguity allows accommodation of differences, and inconsistency provides greater flexibility for bargaining and negotiating. As people act, they challenge existing preferences and readjust them to fit new conditions. Moral rules of behavior developed through social integration can serve as implicit social contracts and thus provide norms for behavior beyond individual welfare maximization (Sen 1986, 79).

The policy-making process parallels the unconscious process of social integration that produces core values. Because conflict is by nature more visible than harmony, peripheral policies—and changes in them—are also more visible than core principles. Lindblom (1968, 103) notes that in the policy-making process, what is wanted is endlessly reconsidered in light of what is possible or feasible. What is feasible is reconsidered and the possibilities reconstructed in light of what is wanted. The extent to which policies are revised depends partly on the extent to which the initial policy decision settles the ideological and normative issues.

Agreement is paramount for political rationality because the product of the agreement is the expression, stipulation, and articulation of the policies and goals the society desires to achieve. Thus, *"whenever political and nonpolitical problems occur together, the political problem must be solved before one can hope to achieve a lasting solution of the nonpolitical problems"* (Diesing 1962, 230–231, emphasis added). This principle suggests that budget examiners in SBOs must analyze alternatives with respect to what is possible, technically *and* politically. As political problems are paramount over other problems, the question of political feasibility is a paramount policy concern. This suggestion raises issues of political neutrality. A central conflict of budget and other policy analysis is the controversy about how much political issues should—and do—influence budgeters in their deliberations. Edward Lehan (1981) takes it for granted that public administrators share a major role with political leaders in defining common burdens and the need for sharing them. "What distinguishes the better leaders on this point is their skill and success in either building up, or tearing down, as the case may be, the vital popular consensus underlying the scheme of allocations and supporting taxes" (Lehan 1981, 6). We will return to this issue of "neutral competence" in our discussion of the rational analyst.

Political Feasibility Frontier

Rubin (1997) reminds us that a public budget is a purposeful distribution of scarce resources, quite distinct from the quid pro quo transactions of the private marketplace. In most cases, payments (taxes) are separated from goods and services received; costs and benefits are not as easily matched as in the private marketplace. It is precisely this separation of payment from use and enjoyment that brings out the moral and political dimensions of the budget process.

Majone claims that there is a "political feasibility frontier" (Figure 3.1) akin to the "production possibility frontier" in economics.[2] Social conflict is ameliorated when the decision structure permits one group that values policy X less and policy Y more, and another group that values policy X more and policy Y less, to agree on a resource allocation among the two policies that satisfies both groups. The political feasibility frontier represents those combinations of resource allocations for X and Y that can be agreed upon by both groups in the political process.

The political feasibility frontier is not drawn smoothly in Figure 3.1. First, persuasion and compromise may be logical and reasoned, but they are not mathematically elegant. The "art of the possible" can produce agreements among groups with little agreement on ends *if* there is sufficient agreement on means that accomplish several ends. Second, means are seldom, if ever, value-neutral. As such, a change in allocation may be characterized as a lurch from one point to another, rather than a smooth change from point *b* to *c*.

A society may stand behind the frontier at point *a* where there is potential for spending more on both X and Y. This represents the base budget; the current allocation is tenable but potentially subject to review and change.

Figure 3.1   **Political Feasibility Frontier**

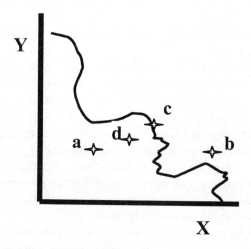

Source: Adapted from Majone (1989), p. 78.

Although a technical or economic analysis of a budget problem might suggest *b* as a policy change, reallocating money from *Y* to increase *X*, the solution is not a viable option because it is outside the political feasibility frontier. A political group with sufficient political resources is able to oppose an increased allocation for *X* without an increased allocation for *Y.* However, the contending groups might be able to agree on point *c*, representing an increase in resources for both *X* and *Y.* Program *X* may receive substantially more of an increase than *Y*, but there is no reallocation from *Y* to fund an increase in *X.* Alternatively, *d* may represent another politically viable option. There is still a slight increase in funding for *Y* but the increase in *X* is less than under options *b* or *c*.

What determines the frontier? Who is allowed at the table to negotiate the budget, and what are participants' relative strengths? How does the examiner know where the current frontier is? In the search for effective policy alternatives, the "creative analyst must be able to maintain a dialectic tension between the practicable and the ideal—between probing the limits of public policy and trying to extend the boundaries of what is politically possible" (Majone 1989, 70). The frontier may change in ways otherwise not thought possible, with new compromises forged on such highly controversial issues as abortion. In Wisconsin, for example, an elected official put himself in the middle of two vocal groups on each side of this issue and, by meeting the concerns of each group, was able to get them to agree on a program to reduce teenage pregnancies. It did not alter either group's fundamental positions on abortion, but it did allow the initiation of a new program that allocated more resources to stopping pregnancies, thereby (theoretically) lowering the demand for abortions in the first place—an approach on which both sides could agree.

The key to integrating political feasibility into policy analysis is that political judgment must be introduced at the appropriate time (Majone 1989). Examiners and other policy specialists take their political feasibility cues from the visible cluster of political actors. Kingdon's stochastic "window of opportunity" designates the moment when changes in the political or problem streams of the policy process permit the coupling of perceived problems to program alternatives that have survived the "policy primeval soup" in a political context where public opinion pressures the government for action. The budget cycle is a predictable "window of opportunity" opening on a regular basis, with the same possibilities.

The analyst can search for the feasibility frontier with reference to an elected boss, an unelected boss, and elected bodies such as legislatures or councils. These people are most keenly aware of the current status and shifting positions of the political feasibility frontier, and they are also the active participants in that process. Logrolling, bargaining, vote swapping, and other methods of exchange underlying the dynamics of politics are all mechanisms for reexamining values and reaching agreement on the ordering of priorities. The primary characteristic of the political feasibility frontier is the dynamic set of possible compromises and other agreements that will permit policy to be set and executed. Although the examiners and other actors in the hidden cluster are primarily observers of political exchange rather than negotiators, the political exchange issue and its impacts are no less salient to their policy analyses.

The Politics of Substantive Policy Areas

The politics of a particular substantive policy area may also constrain the available solutions to the budget problem. James Wilson (1974) enriches Theodore Lowi's (1964) policy arenas scheme by arguing that the ability to modify policies and programs, or reach political compromises, is greatly affected by how the costs and benefits of a particular program are distributed. Wilson (1974, 332) asserts, "Policy changes can be crudely classified on the basis of whether the cost and benefits are widely distributed or narrowly concentrated from the point of view of those who bear the costs or enjoy the benefits." There is little modification possible for programs in which widely distributed benefits are perceived to exceed widely distributed costs, except to increase benefits. On the other hand, if benefits are concentrated but costs are dispersed, such as veterans' benefits and agricultural subsidies, the costs can be dramatized and the beneficiaries painted as vested selfish interests, thereby calling into question the motives of those officials who support the program(s).

Conflict thus surrounds programs that benefit one well-defined group but impose costs on another well-defined group, such as the former regulation by the Interstate Commerce Commission of freight charges for trucks versus railroads. These programs are continuously subjected to revisions, interpretations, and efforts to repeal the initial policy. Policy changes in these programs will generally occur only as the result of negotiations among the associations or by changing the political balance of power among them. "The former involves a tedious process of mediation, the latter an effort to change the partisan or ideological coloration of the appropriate regulatory commission, congressional committee, or administrative bureau. This is very difficult to do . . . and will be fought every step of the way by the organized opponents" (Wilson 1974, 335–336). Intellectual factors also have to be taken into account in order to explain the direction of new policy. Even policies driven by selfish economic or political interests are still justified to the public with some appeal to its merits. Changes in policies and policy environments often subject the implicit policy rationale, especially previously unnoticed or unexamined policy assumptions, to critical review (Majone 1989, 149).

William Niskanen (1986) observes that most proposed changes to policy occur within small groups such as bureaus and subcommittees. He argues that policy advisors have a dominant influence on the design of proposed policy changes within their respective groups. But this influence is constrained by reviewing officials, including other policy advisors who also have strong influences on policies. According to the PAS model, these actors are in the hidden cluster where most policy alternatives are developed.

The credibility that arises from a high degree of professionalism increases the influence of these actors in a program. They may be able to sustain arguments favoring a policy or program that is currently beyond the political feasibility frontier until an opportune moment, as Niskanen (1986) argues the Council of Economic Advisors did with respect to free trade and deregulatory policy. Kingdon makes a similar example out of the health-care reform debate of the 1980s and 1990s. This approach to changing the political feasibility frontier is possible when the profession is in wide agreement regarding a particular position. But when the professionals are divided, Niskanen claims that they serve the interests of politicians they are advising. Examiners need to be able to speak their policy language to evaluate credibility and gauge professional consensus about the options in order to provide effective recommendations to the governor. Substantial change will require change in law.

Legal Rationality

The social values produced by integrative decisions are codified as laws in the political process. Legal problems arise when different individuals or groups have conflicting interpretations of these laws. The legal "realist" approach to legal reasoning recognizes that no two situations are exactly the same, and therefore discretion will always exist. From this view, precision in law is impossible, the law is often a compromise, and the result is conflicting values in a single law creating a wide area for discretion.[3] Legal decisions address these problems by the public and impartial application of the laws according to legal principles. Effective legal decisions settle disputes regarding the rights and responsibilities of legal individuals (including corporations) by producing a clear and exact assignment of resources and obligations among the disputing parties.

The budget process effectively transforms public spending into value allocation instruments that are binding on all covered parties (Osigweh 1986). Examiners do not generally make formal legal decisions; instead their application of legal rationality to budgeting is usually preliminary and indirect. Budget solutions are constrained first by laws governing the budget process; second, by laws that define program responsibilities; third by restrictions from "rights-based budgeting"; and, finally, by contractual obligations between an agency and other levels of government, nonprofit organizations, and private firms and individuals. Some of these constraints are more formidable than others. Constitutions (as written and interpreted) are fundamental laws that define decision structures and outline areas of core policy agreements with respect to such values as property and civil rights (among others). Statutory laws direct and control policies and programs. Public budgets are statutory laws that allocate public funds to policies and programs. Legally, an appropriations act establishes the right of an agency to spend public funds, as specified in the law, and sets a limit on such spending.

Budgets are windows of opportunity to change current policies and programs by amending existing statutes and ordinances. A typical legal facet of a budget problem concerns limitations and mandates associated with intergovernmental grants. The federal block grant to states for welfare reform set minimum "maintenance of effort" (MOE) spending requirements. The significant drop in cash assistance caseloads has given many states a growing surplus of funds within the program accounts. Unfortunately for states, they cannot reduce their state funding below the minimum MOE. Furthermore, federal grant restrictions specify how funds can be used. Examiners with the welfare assignment in an SBO need to understand the grant limitations in order to evaluate budget proposals from the state welfare agency and others (e.g., legislators) who would alter the program's current budget allocation. An economically rational solution, such as reallocating funds from the welfare program to prisons, may not be a viable option because it is constrained by the legal aspect of the budget problem.

Another example of a more restrictive problem of legal rationality concerns a state's corrections budget. Many states have had courts rule that prison or jail conditions are inadequate, violating the federal constitutional prohibition against cruel and unusual punishment. A court does not usually order a state to build a bigger or better prison, but this is often a consequence of the legal decision (Straussman and Thurmaier 1989). Such decisions may also have impacts on the operating budgets of prisons, including staffing requirements, heating and cooling costs, provision of medical care, and so on.

Another area of rights-based budgeting with impacts on state budgets has been public school finance. Court decisions in this area have often held that state constitutions require some formula of state aid to equalize educational opportunities across school districts. Debates about the formula are often hotly contested political battles, but the legal decree remains one of the defining parameters. Whatever the budget solution, it must protect the rights of students and fulfill the obligations of the state as defined by the court decision.

The growing use of contractual services with nongovernmental providers is a new source of legal rationality within budgeting. There are volumes of court decisions regarding expectations and obligations in contracts (torts). When an agency considers contracting to a nonprofit group for foster care program management, it becomes imperative for decisionmakers (including examiners) to understand the liabilities, incentives, and penalties imbedded in the contracts. Depending on how the contract is written, it may preclude certain funding mechanisms or permit increased agency flexibility in program funding and expenditures. Understanding the legal context of the program permits the examiner to decide whether the requested change in program expenditure conflicts with, or conforms to, the legal constraints on the program.

For purposes of budgeting, legal decisions are usually subordinate to political decisions, and sometimes even tangential to the budget problem. The common legal facets of a budget problem are whether the authorizing statute for the agency permits the activity proposed for funding, or whether a particular revenue source or appropriation can be used for a certain agency activity. The examiner may analyze how a statutory law would need to change to facilitate a change in an agency budget. Whether it is tangential or central to the budget problem, budget analysis is incomplete without acknowledging and studying the legal facet of the budget problem.

Summary: Conclusions About Effectiveness Decisions

Effectiveness decision-making is concerned with problems characterized by conflicts of values, including community and group conflicts. Rights and responsibilities, values and beliefs attached to social roles, and the other factors involved in these kinds of problems are not understandable in terms of neutral means or alternative ends. These types of problems therefore cannot be dealt with using the means-ends reasoning of economic decisions. Furthermore, operative goals are not predetermined in these situations in the way that is required for economic decisions. When solving problems of value conflict, any immediate goal is subject to change as the solution proceeds. Values and perceptions are adjusted or otherwise modified to produce some kind of resolution, harmony, or equilibrium.

Social problems occur when social integration is threatened during the interaction of two or more individuals. Social decisions follow the rational principle that conflicts in values should be avoided through accommodation of differences in preferences and mutual adjustments of values. Unfixed, unordered, and inconsistent preferences enable each member to be somewhat flexible in his or her responses to contrary or conflicting values in others. Where there is agreement, social integration allows for public policy formation and program development, as core social values and priorities are identified and articulated in the political process.

When accommodation or adjustment is not possible, resolving value conflicts and establishing social priorities require conscious actions of negotiating, bargaining, and other tactics that will enable the polity to reach agreement on a course of action. Politically rational decisions support social integration by effectively making social decisions and actions possible, and they proceed according to the principles of discussion and decision in the political sphere. Political rationality follows the principle that the best decisions are produced when the two conflicting requirements of a decision-making structure (a plurality of viewpoints and the ability to reach a unified agreement) are embodied in it to the greatest degree possible. Ambiguous goals and preferences leave room for flexible responses to conflicts. This process involves conscious deliberations in the political process and supplements and corrects the largely unconscious process of social integration. Political rationality is paramount over other types of rationality because social action is made possible by decisions, and the assurance of decisions is the task of political rationality. Without political feasibility, decisions—and thereby social actions—are impossible.

The legal order developed from the political process codifies established social ends and enforces the fundamental rules that govern the actions, rights, and responsibilities of social members. Legal problems occur when there is a doubt about one's status or conflicts over who has claim to certain resources. Legal problems are resolved by following the rational principle of clarifying the rights and responsibilities of each entity associated with the circumstances, including which resources are available to which persons, according to the legal order. Legal rationality produces rules that clarify what each person can and cannot do, and what is expected of him or her. Legally rational decisions support social integration by effectively settling disputes when other means have failed.

Together, the principles of order embodied in legal, political, and social rationalities produce social integration and social decisions that enable social actions. However, the identification of social ends is irrelevant if they cannot be met. If the society is unable to satisfy the needs expressed by its members, conflict will increase and social disintegration will ensue. Thus, expressed social ends need to be satisfied through an efficient mechanism for allocating society's resources. Moreover, social integration will be enhanced to the extent that the social resources are used to satisfy as many desires as possible. Economic rationality fulfills this function, supported with technical rationality. We explore efficiency decisions in the following chapter.

Notes

1. See Willoughby and Finn (1996), who have extended this research to legislative budget analysts.
2. For a standard treatment, see Musgrave and Musgrave (1980, 63–73).
3. For the legal realist perspective, see Frank (1930 and 1949). Our thanks to Chuck Epp for helpful guidance on this issue.

4

Budget Rationalities: Efficiency Decisions

The Efficiency/Effectiveness Cleavage

The previous chapter defined our concept of a multiple rationalities model of budgetary decision-making. We explained that multifaceted problems require multiple rationalities that we categorize as encompassing both effectiveness decisions and efficiency decisions. We then discussed the social, political, and legal rationalities inherent in effectiveness decisions. This chapter continues to lay the foundation for our model by explaining efficiency decisions. Not surprisingly, the examiners' oldest and most fundamental role vis-à-vis the public budget is to squeeze efficiency out of agency operations. They are always looking for the most efficient way to deliver public services. Realistically, the bulk of agency requests are relatively minor changes to programs, such as adding a position or increasing a contractual services agreement. And departments commonly invoke efficiency as well as effectiveness goals as the rationale for these requests.

The efficiency/effectiveness cleavage of budget decisions explicitly acknowledges that economic and technical decision-making are different from social, political, and legal decision-making in important ways. Effectiveness rationalities establish the social ends to which the technical and economic decisions are oriented. And while many of the characteristics of effectiveness decisions are different from economic decisions, there is a symbiotic relationship between the two types of decisions. Whereas effectiveness decisions focus on solving conflicts in the values that frame and identify the social ends, efficiency decisions focus on subordinating means to maximize fixed and given ends. Whereas the goal of effectiveness decisions is characterized as social integration, the goal of efficiency decisions is characterized as maximizing utility or satisfaction. Whereas the effectiveness focus is on the ends themselves, the efficiency focus is on the means-ends relationship.

Economic and technical decisionmaking must have, ex ante, specified goals and objectives with some degree of priority ordering.[1] Economic and technical rationalities link means to ends, but cannot specify the ends. The ends in the executive budget process are specified by effectiveness decisions. Thus efficiency decisions are bounded, or are dependent upon, effectiveness decisions. In important ways, effectiveness decisions frame the context in which efficiency decisions are made.

Wildavsky's (1978) argument that economic and technical calculations are ineffectual or undesirable because they increase budgetary conflict is misplaced because he focused on the macro level where "deals" are cut crudely and not with the precision needed to implement the policies and programs born of social rationality. Enhancements to the economic and technical calculus of budgeting have been adopted in bits and pieces over the decades with good reason (Rubin 1990). Ceteris paribus, if budget examiners can work *with* departments to increase economic and technical efficiencies, these decisions need not increase budgetary conflict.

The ceteris paribus condition is critical. Examiners employ technical and economic rationalities when effectiveness decisions have established the proper framework. Not all means are value-neutral, and their use to increase technical efficiency may be proscribed by social, political or legal imperatives. Within the framework established by effectiveness decisions, however, examiners are encouraged by their traditional "guardian" role to apply economic and technical reasoning to increase operational efficiency.

Efficiency Decisions

Economic Rationality

In very important respects, budget problems resemble the classic economic problem: a scarcity of the common means necessary to maximize the achievement of multiple, alternative ends. By common means we intend things such as money, time, and labor, as well as techniques and organization. By alternative ends we mean to include some "good" that is essentially quantifiable and that will satisfy individual preferences, such as the production of cars and trucks.

The classic economic decisionmaker is an individual consumer or producer in the economy. An economic decision is required to determine how to allocate the scarce common resources available to the individual (including time, land, energy, capital) to achieve multiple ends that will yield satisfaction to the individual. The logic of an economic decision is explicated in the economic doctrine of marginal utility (Diesing 1962, 20):

> Goals demand achievement, but not all of them can be achieved because there is a scarcity of means. If some goals must be sacrificed, they should be the least important ones; or if partial achievement is possible, the most important parts of each goal should be achieved. This requires a detailed measurement of the comparative importance of each goal and each part of a goal. The available means should also be measured carefully so that just the right amount can be assigned to each end—not too much and not too little. When means are being assigned, the most important goal or part of a goal should receive the first assignment, then other goals in order of decreasing importance, until the means are used up. The use to which the last means is assigned should not be less important than any remaining disallowed use; this is the marginal utility principle.

The public budget is a focal point of economic rationalization because it is the point at which the alternative ends of the government are subjected to comparison and allocation with common means: money and the program inputs it buys. Given a variety of alternative ends for achieving a given goal, economizing (rational economic allocation) will allocate the given resources among the alternative ends so as to maximize achievement of the goal. There are several types of economic decisions in budgeting. At one level, decisions allocate resources *across agencies*; this is the level addressed by Verne Lewis and other advocates of increased economic rationality in budgeting. For example, suppose that the state wanted to train unemployed and poor citizens so that they could get jobs. Several agencies could provide alternative job training programs, including the vocational school system, the welfare department, the labor department, the university system, and private-sector organizations. The problem facing the examiner responsible for recommending the budget allocation for such a program would be how to allocate money across the agencies to get the most and "best" job training for the amount of money available.

At another level, decisions allocate resources across programs *within an agency.* For example, a state department of economic development may consider budget reallocations from the bureau of "smokestack chasers" (state representatives who visit firms in other states to entice them to locate or relocate plants in their state) to the bureau with international trade offices for export promotion or foreign investment. This type of decision receives far less attention from legislators, but occurs more frequently than allocations across agencies.[2] Absent political cues regarding an agency's budget, the examiner will consider agency suggestions that may internally reallocate funds among programs to more effectively accomplish agency objectives. The marginal utility analysis inherent in such decisions is usually based on some agency evidence that the suggested options are also technically efficient. Before recommending how to allocate money across the agencies, or within an agency, the examiner would likely want evidence regarding how efficient each particular program would be in achieving the given goal, which is a problem of technical rationality.

Technical Rationality

The efficiency quest for which SBOs are famous, and for which examiners are infamous in the eyes of agencies, is evident in the technical reasoning examiners apply to budget problems. Technical rationality can be confused with economic rationality because both make up elements of the economic choice approach to analysis. The two are not the same. Technical rationality concerns the efficient achievement of a single goal and is an efficiency of production, where raw materials enter the system and are transformed into product in a specialized system designed to avoid waste (Diesing 1962, 236). Technical efficiency is the maximum achievement of a specified end with given resources. This type of decision allocates resources across alternative inputs to maximize output within a single process or program. Economic rationality, in contrast, is the allocation of resources across multiple means to maximize achievement of multiple and alternative ends. Kingdon (1995) argues that policy alternatives cannot leave the policy primeval soup unless they are technically feasible. This type of decision is a common decision for program managers in an agency.

Technical rationality is the decision process behind performance budgeting, for example. Management tools such as productivity analysis, unit cost analysis, and workload analysis are related to the concept of maximizing output for a given input, or minimizing inputs for a given output level. Consider the process of administering unemployment compensation to individuals throughout the state. The goal is to disperse checks as efficiently as possible. Technical efficiency is gained by refining the steps in the disbursement (production) process—computer programming, physical human processing, delivery to the post office, and so forth—to achieve the goal at least cost..This approach results in the most effective application of scarce resources (tax dollars) in the production process.

Many of the changes to budget procedures in recent decades have been to improve the ability of examiners to analyze agency productivity and effectiveness. Renewed emphasis on productivity analyses and performance measurements was enhanced by the introduction and proliferation of microcomputers in budget offices (Botner 1985 and 1987; Poister and Streib 1989). Technological advances and the reorientation of budget offices away from accounting control activities have increased the degree to which examiners are conducting analyses of productivity and program effectiveness (Lee 1991). Even if macro- budgetary parameters for an agency are static in a given budget year, the examiner will work to identify program expenditure savings that can be reallocated by the budget director to higher-priority activities.

Agencies often use workload measures to justify position and funding increases in their budgets. A state securities commissioner, for example, may request another securities examiner position for the office, citing an increase in the new securities issued per securities examiner. The efficiency analysis begins with the examiner asking whether that means the examiner is overworked or simply reaching "full" capacity (otherwise labeled "improved efficiency" or "improved productivity"). Yet leaving the analysis at this question alone is incomplete budget analysis. An effective budget decision requires more information. What is the impact of not adding another examiner? Does that lessen scrutiny of new securities issued to citizens in the state? What, in turn, is the impact of lessened scrutiny? Is there reason to believe it will lead to increased securities fraud? How much? How much is too much? Is the prevention of securities fraud the reason the program exists in the first place, or is there another purpose more central to the securities agency's mission?

To focus only on the workload measure, ignoring the end (possibly fraud prevention), may yield no increase in positions for the securities office. But once the program goal (end) is considered, the analysis of the workload has a new context for analysis. The technical decision is actually concerned with the process of examinations, whether filings and examinations would be faster if electronically conducted, whether a central typing pool for certificates would be faster or slower than the current process, whether the system for ultimate review by the securities commissioner is efficient. The complete budget analysis incorporates the technical decision with the related effectiveness decisions: What is a socially "acceptable" level of securities fraud, what are the legal obligations and requirements for fraud detection and prevention, does the securities industry oppose or embrace increased securities review by the office? Effective budget decisions cannot ignore the effectiveness facets of this seemingly technical question of a securities position.

The Limitations of Efficiency Decisions

The economic choice model is most noted for its strong normative grounding, and the logic that individuals should maximize utility has spawned an immense literature. A thorough treatment is problematic because, as March (1986, 147) explains, there is currently no "single, widely accepted, precise behavioral theory of choice." One could spend pages reviewing the specific assumptions behind game theories, preference revelation techniques, and other aspects of what John Harsanyi (1986) collectively labels "utility theory."[3] There is no doubt that economic and technical rationalities are especially evident in certain budgeting decisions where the central purpose is the allocation of scarce social resources to achieve alternative ends. The goal associated with economic and technical rationalities is often stated simply as efficiency. But there is an important distinction between the concept of efficiency in each case. Economic rationality provides an order of measurement and comparison of the values behind the achievement of multiple ends, or goals. *The essential prerequisite of economic rationality is that multiple ends have been specified and valued.* Economic rationality then provides a principle for the measurement and comparison of the values. Economic decisions and economically rational organizations embody the efficiency principle to maximize marginal utility. Economic calculation requires that a variety of simultaneously held goals (or ends) be specified so that their relative importance can be compared and available resources be rationally allocated according to the principle of marginal utility.

Technical decisions embody the efficiency principle to maximize the output/input ratio. Consequently, as Diesing (1962, 12) explains, "whenever a person has an end, he ought to be technically rational in achieving it. The technical norm does not apply to decisions about ends. . . . Nor does it apply to situations in which one is prevented from formulating a clear goal." Thus, the ECM in both cases upholds the social norm of means-ends efficiency. It prescribes that the examiner should allocate resources toward a single end so as to maximize achievement of the goal at least cost. And the examiner should allocate resources toward alternative ends so as to maximize achievement of the most important end first, the next most important second, and so on, because that will maximize the effectiveness of the last unit of resource allocated to the economic problem.

There are important limits to technical and economic rationality that are central to the debate in budget theory. The first limitation is that technical and economic rationalities require that ends be designated and ordered before either rationality can be invoked. Simply stated, the theories of economic decisions are only relevant when people and society know what they want and what resources they have available (Diesing 1962, 95–96). Whether maximizing the benefit/cost ratio or maximizing cost-effectiveness, technical rationality subjects the means-end relationship to evaluation. Different means are evaluated with respect to a given goal. The principal limitation of economic rationality with respect to social allocation problems is that ends are often *not* comparable and the valuation of them can be very imprecise. Under such conditions, economic allocation cannot proceed efficiently, if at all.

The second limitation (which follows from the first) is that the designation and valuation of social ends is quintessentially the product of effectiveness decision-making and the rationalities underlying effectiveness decisions. Health care and space exploration may both be socially desirable, but the relative valuation is imprecise, and the preference order is not fixed. The varying amounts of dollars allocated across functional categories in a typical state budget (e.g., education, natural resources, human resources) will not reflect the precision implied by marginal utility calculations. Rather, it involves a complex set of factors—efficiency and effectiveness—that results in a temporary (typically one year) social allocation of resources (the annual budget).

To some extent, this limitation also applies to means. Staff hours worked or jobs created are not value-neutral means to increased economic development in a community. Cities want to use economic development programs to attract "good jobs" at "good wages." Thus, few cities will try to lure polluting firms to the tax base. A city commissioner may oppose tax abatements to lure a liquor warehouse to the city on moral grounds. Decisions to allocate money to economic development programs will therefore include some effectiveness valuation of the means used to spur economic development. Finally, norms are prior to individuals, and there are other norms besides that of means-ends efficiency. As such, the efficiency rationalities alone cannot provide a satisfactory descriptive model of budgetary decision-making; they require the complementary effectiveness rationalities.

The Rationalities Framework

The SBO budget examiner, as an integrated member of society, may instinctively or intuitively recognize the social value of a police force. Unless directly ordered to do so, she will *not* conduct a full-scale base budget analysis because she recognizes that there is a high degree of consensus in the society that there should be a police force. Rather, the examiner will focus attention on areas of public policy conflict, the peripheral programs and policies that comprise the public safety program. Whereas core policy goals are largely the product of unconscious decisions, the peripheral program objectives are the product of active policy debate. On the other hand, the consensus read in public policy formulation "does not normally mean that agreement must be reached among a majority of all citizens. Rather, consensus typically means obtaining a majority among the vocal participants who are taking part in the process of deciding a particular issue" (Howard 1973, 32, fn. 6). Consequently, it is critical to know the politics of the "issue" rather than politics generally. A section manager we interviewed from the Virginia SBO regularly holds discussion sessions with analysts to take political "soundings" on an issue:

> What normally happens, something will come into the budget office or, let's say it's an area for downsizing something, and either they'll have the idea or I'll have the idea, and we'll just sit and we'll kinda play it around for half an hour maybe, just talk about it and talk about the politics of it, talk about how we would do it, what the reaction of the advocacy group would be, what the reaction of the agency would be, and *whether or not it feels good.*

The sometimes acrimonious debate and fierce partisan struggle that accompanies public budgeting illuminates the process of making adjustments to peripheral and core values. "Struggles over budgets simply mean that the boundaries of a community's conscience are open for redefinition. Each new budget sets service levels and tax levies which define those social, economic and political interests which are deemed worthy of a recognition as 'common' burdens" (Lehan 1981, 6).

Moreover, neither policies nor decision-making structures are static concepts. They are constantly changing to fit the new power alliances and other environmental conditions. It is impossible for the examiners and other policy analysts to "freeze the action" in order to have current goals and their current ranking presented for use as a dependent variable in some econometric equation. They must be constantly probing the political feasibility frontier to determine what is possible this year, this month, today! And they must watch how the frontier is shifting to enable—or preclude—policy alternatives tomorrow, next month, or next year.

Consequently, the base budget is also subject to review and modifications. If the governor's goal is to decrease state expenditures, the examiner's job is to respond with recommendations that abide this approach. If the governor emphasizes increased expenditures in one policy area at the expense of others, the examiner's job is to respond in kind. Cloaked with technical and professional expertise and "objectivity," examiners have great influence over the policy agenda. Diehard advocates of a particular policy such as environmental regulation (or deregulation) can bide their time until a policy window of opportunity opens. Then their task is to convince the budget examiner, among others, to recommend the policy change. Success at this point also depends on the quality of the relationship between the examiner and the agency policy and budget staff.

This description of political reasoning in micro-budgeting diverges from the incrementalist view of budgetary politics. In our model, the examiner's focus is not restricted to incremental changes to the budget base. Nor is the examiner's reaction predicted by the acquisitiveness of the agency. Political rationality is essential to the policy process because it is essential to the expression and articulation of core and peripheral policy values and goals— and to the ordering of those values and goals. These are essential prerequisites for economic rationality.

Effective budget rationality requires an effective SBO decision-making structure. In the policy-oriented SBO, examiners gather alternative views from the agency as well as those arising from their own investigations. They may have a gubernatorial imperative to consider if the budget problem fits within one of the governor's policy priorities. The examiner's task is to find the feasible alternative that allows a budget decision to be made with respect to this budget problem. This task often will require negotiations with the agency, especially as they consider the feasibility of policy implementation.

The complex relationships between the different rationalities is very apparent when one tries to use any singular view of rationality to explain, much less predict, the behavior of a budget examiner or policy analyst facing a particular policy problem. Instead of defining and redefining actions to fit a single view of "rationality," we have described a framework for placing different types of actions within the appropriate context to evaluate whether it is rational. By viewing rational decisions or actions as those that are effective in producing some good or value, we have identified five different types of rationality at work in society.

When a problem is technical in nature, it requires technical rationality to reach a decision. An end has been given, means are available but scarce, and the task is to refine the production process or technique in such a way as to maximize the output/input ratio. It is the basic means-end relationship that is most commonly associated with the value of efficiency. When a problem is a social one, however, the value involved is not efficiency and the techniques are not readily amenable to a means-ends relationship because neither means nor ends are value-neutral. Social problems require social rationality for a solution. Integrative decisions require accommodation and adjustments to values in order to reduce conflicts. Immediate goals are temporal in that they may be sacrificed to avoid tension and social instability. This process is played in two arenas, with the unconscious one producing core policy values and the conscious (and visible) one producing peripheral policy values. Political decisions are improved when the conflicting factors of a plurality of viewpoints and the capacity to reach agreements are present to the greatest degree possible in a decision-making structure, a politically rational solution.

Multiple Rationalities at Work

But these straightforward examples are not usually the kind that are encountered by examiners. Rather, they face multifaceted problems involving multiple rationalities. These problems cannot be solved by making purely economic decisions because the solutions prescribed by economic efficiency criteria generally have social implications. Nor can the decisions be purely social in character because of the resource-scarcity problems inherent in public budget decisions. The problems that are mainly economic in character can be approached primarily with the application of the appropriate efficiency rationality, keeping in mind the need to avoid aggravating social, legal, and political problems with the recommended solution. Problems that are mainly social, legal, or political in character can be approached primarily with the application of the appropriate effectiveness rationality, keeping in mind that if the solution requires resources, there must be a method for gaining their allocation from competing demands. While a given problem may be dominated by one or two types of decisions and their rationalities, the other types of rationalities will likely also be present.

Yet, the complexity of budget problems, replete with multiple facets and multiple rationalities, suggests a decision comprehensiveness that is unattainable according to many scholars (Simon, Lindblom, and Wildavsky, among others). The problem of comprehensive analysis has dogged budget reformers for decades—the failure of Planning, Programming and Budgeting Systems (PPBS) is only the most cited example of the "impossibility" of comprehensive budget analysis (Wildavsky 1969). We suggest the possibilities for solving the comprehensiveness problem below.

Certainly comprehensiveness must be addressed. However, criticism of unattainable comprehensiveness leveled by Wildavsky (1964) against PPBS and other reforms are not valid for the model of micro-budgeting we are developing here. First, Wildavsky argued that elected officials shunned comprehensive review of budget problems because it unnecessarily raised policy conflicts. This was especially true of the base budget, which signified the set of past policy conflicts that had been resolved in earlier budget conflicts, and were best left untouched. Second, Wildavsky's focus was on the ability of elected officials (executive and legislative) to conduct comprehensive analysis within the limited amount of time they were able to devote to budgeting. His point was that they had many other competing interests, and time was not available for exhaustive consideration of alternatives. While his first argument may have been true in an era of ever-increasing revenues, we have observed in the 1980s and 1990s that the base budget is no longer sacrosanct, especially in periods of fiscal stress. Moreover, as we will explain more fully in chapter 5, the policy-oriented SBO is an arena where policy conflict is not shunned (it may even be encouraged), and comprehensive budget and policy analysis is not threatening to key decisionmakers.

Wildavsky's focus on elected officials is also not germane to our micro-budgeting model. Our focus is mainly on unelected decisionmakers working in a state budget office. Comprehensive decisions-making is not only permitted, it is *demanded* of SBO examiners. Comprehensiveness is possible due to the flexibility and luxury of the complete budget cycle, which permits effectiveness analysis first, and then efficiency analysis. While legislators and governors have many other duties in addition to the state budget, budgeting is the full-time occupation of examiners. At the national level, Bureau of the Budget's (now OMB) Director Smith (Wildavsky 1964, 188) observed, "Though we compile and enact the budget once a year, all those concerned with budget preparation, budget legislation, and budget execution can and should use their heads each day of the year and each hour of the day. We must learn to think of the budget not as an incomprehensible book but as a living process of democratic policy formation and policy execution."

Research on local government budgeting suggests that the execution phase of the budget cycle is used extensively for budget analysis. The intensive development period should actually be viewed as the end of the budget cycle rather than the beginning. It is the culmination of the analysis of agency budgets rather than the beginning. The execution phase analysis is essential to the ability of analysts to conduct comprehensive budget analysis in the short development period. Moreover, using the full budget cycle, local budget examiners were shown to be able to address budget problems as multi-faceted issues, and they used multiple rationalities to think about agency budget issues and to develop their budget recommendations to the budget director and chief executive (Thurmaier 1995b).

We observe a parallel process at the state level. The task of budget comprehensiveness is delegated by legislators and governors to SBO staff precisely because it is their year-round task in the process of governance. Examiners devote their full attention to the budgets of the agencies, to the budget presented to the legislature by the governor, and to the budget process itself. Examiners conduct budget analysis over a twelve-month budget year, not just intensively for three to five months. It is what gives their recommendations the weight of decisive decisions, because they have had the opportunity to conduct a comprehensive analysis through the various problem representations. The ability of examiners to conduct year-round, comprehensive analysis will be apparent in chapter 6 and chapter 7, when we follow two examiners through their decision-making activities during a budget year.

Problem Framing: Simplifying Decision Rules to Reduce Complexity

But *which* aspect of a budget and policy problem should receive *what* emphasis in the examiner's analysis and recommendation? What principle (or principles) guides decisions of examiners who face budget problems where the facets are so nearly equal in importance as to require a blend of efficiency and effectiveness rationalities? A systematic analysis of a budget problem cannot simply accept objectives as immutably given and then proceed to seek the most effective or efficient means of achieving these objectives. The decision-making process is too complex. Both objectives and means, and their influence on the other, must be considered in these situations (Schultze 1968, 64–65).

The mechanisms used to weight and blend the multiple rationalities depends on several factors, including the degree of discretion allowed the examiner in the decision-making process. As we shall see in chapter 6, examiners in policy-oriented SBOs exercise broad discretion both in their analyses and their recommendations. We illustrate in chapter 7 that examiners in control-oriented SBOs lack this broad discretion in their analyses and, in fact, often do not craft budget recommendations at all. Consequently, the principles developed below mainly apply to conditions under which the examiners exercise discretion in a policy-oriented SBO.

The implication of a multiple rationalities approach for examiners in a policy-oriented SBO is clear. Examiners are making policy decisions in their analyses, even though they are constrained in their search for alternatives by the social and political environments, including how well the political process has articulated policy values and consequent social objectives. They are also constrained by various types of legal parameters. Because means and ends are so intertwined, as Lindblom suggests, effective analysis of budget problems requires a constant analytical interaction between objectives and means. "Analysis of specific objectives and alternative policy action clarifies initial value judgments leading to revised value judgments which in turn guide further analysis" (Schultze 1968, 65–66). Lindblom developed his model of decisionary incrementalism by combining this interaction requirement with assumptions of limited cognition. Yet we already have found this approach unsatisfactory as a description of examiner decision-making.

The Rational Analyst and Budget Rationality

Rather than resigning ourselves to the limitations of a rational analyst based on decision-making models of limited cognition, let us develop the model of an ideal-type "rational analyst" as *an examiner who exercises a high degree of budget rationality in his or her decision-making in the SBO*. The test of rationality for examiner decision-making rests on two components: the validity of the recommendation analysis, and the reliability and credibility of the examiner. The examiner is deemed to exercise budget rationality if she or he is able to apply multiple rationalities to an agency request, and then craft an effective recommendation to the budget director and governor. *An effective recommendation is defined as one that has a high probability of being accepted with little or no changes by the budget director or governor.* The probability of the budget director and governor accepting the examiner's recommendation is a function of the recommendation's validity and the examiner's credibility and reliability. *A valid recommendation does not violate the rationality of any facet of the budget problem at hand.* The requirement of the examiner's reliability and credibility implies the governor can expect some degree of consistent delivery of valid examiner recommendations.

The rational analyst has two major tasks when transforming budget analysis into a budget recommendation. First, the analyst faces the dilemma of simplifying decision-making to a manageable range of activity. This critical step means selecting the range of policy options and alternatives that are to be analyzed for recommendations. Screening out "silly" options is easy; focusing energy on a select few is more difficult (Fessler and Kettl 1996). The second dilemma facing the rational analyst is how to frame the alternatives for the target audience (the budget director or governor), including the degree to which the examiner asserts his or her own values on the selection of alternatives "deserving" analysis and recommendations, while also anticipating the alternatives preferred by the budget director or governor. We shall address each of these dilemmas in more detail by applying cognitive process research on problem representation to finish building our multiple rationalities decision-making framework.

Budget Problem Representation: Framing Decisions

Research in cognitive processes of decision behavior has found substantial evidence that the choice of solution is dependent on how individuals frame the problem at hand (Wallsten 1980; Tversky and Kahneman 1981; Kahneman and Tversky 1979 and 1984; Singer and Hudson 1992; and Forrester and Adams 1997). The term *decision frame* refers to the decisionmaker's conception of the acts, outcomes, and contingencies associated with a particular choice. "The frame that a decision maker adopts is controlled partly by the formulation of the problem and partly by the norms, habits, and personal characteristics of the decision maker" (Tversky and Kahneman 1981, 453).

When conflicting values are relevant to a particular issue, how one responds to an elicitation of personally held preferences and values will vary in part with the manner in which the question is posed.

Baruch Fischhoff et al. (1980) have demonstrated that "how problems are posed, questions are phrased, and responses are elicited can have substantial impact on judgments that supposedly express people's true values." This supports Diesing's understanding of the instability inherent in social values. An existing view toward a particular value-laden issue (e.g., a state lottery) may be destroyed; or a new perspective may be created where none existed before. Even one's general perspective (e.g., on gambling) and understanding of the issue to be considered can change. The priming or evocation of one perspective will tend to suppress the ability or willingness to recall or use an alternative perspective.

Alternative framing is similar to the changing perspectives one gains from viewing the same object from different positions, as in the perceived change in relative heights of two mountains as one changes position relative to them. The perspective metaphor highlights two aspects of the psychology of choice that are important for the policy-making process. First, decisionmakers facing a defined decision problem might have a different solution preference if they have a different framing of the same problem. Second, these same decisionmakers are normally unaware of alternative frames and therefore unaware of the relative attractiveness of alternatives that may be apparent from viewing the problem from other frames (Tversky and Kahneman 1981, 456).

To understand the role of problem-framing in examiner recommendations, it is useful to recall our discussion of the policy process where issues begin to move to the decision agenda when conditions are identified as problems. Sometimes this occurs due to a crisis of some kind, but usually it happens slowly, with data collected, analyzed, and presented in a variety of ways to elected officials and the general public to convince them that a condition has become a problem. For example, malnutrition in elementary children is demonstrated to cause them to perform poorly in schools. The subsequently adopted solution is a breakfast program at schools so that these children have a healthy start to the school day.

While Kingdon did not dwell on how problem definition occurs (except to say that this is one of the tasks performed by interest groups, academics, and others engaged in policy analysis), other scholars have focused more attention on this area of agenda formation. David Rochefort and Roger Cobb (1994) present a range of case studies that illustrate the importance of problem representation to the debate on public policy issues in the United States. "Societal characteristics and cultural values converge with existing structural and political conditions to create the contexts within which political actors jockey to promote competing problem definitions and formulate public policy. These conflicts, in turn, influence dominant values and policy processes" (Rochefort and Cobb 1994, 200).

Deborah Stone (1989) argues that causal argument is at the heart of political problem definition. Conditions become problems through the strategic portrayal of causal stories. Effective causal arguments attribute a bad condition to human behavior rather than nature, fate, or accident. Policy advocates try to push the interpretation of a bad condition out of the realm of accident and into the realm of human control. This creates a burden of reform, since someone is responsible, which in turn leads to policies and programs to attack the human behavior problem with human behavior modification. Causal theories have a strong normative component that links suffering with an identifiable agent. This permits criticism of existing social conditions and relationships. By defining victims and agents, policy actors can realign political coalitions for reform. Although political actors increasingly use probabilistic rather than mechanistic notions of cause, problem definition is also constrained by law and science that have their own ways of arbitrating disputes.

Denise Scheberle (1994) illustrates the influence of causal stories and problem framing with radon and asbestos issues. A common attribute of these problem identifications is that the identifiers must frame the condition (which may have existed for quite some time, as is the case with child malnutrition and radon) as a problem in need of attention. How the condition is framed determines how successfully it is transformed into a problem.

One of the principal functions of discussion in the policy-making process is to reframe, recombine, and reconsider problems and alternatives until the actors involved can agree on a response to an identified problem, or problems. This is the principal function of the "policy primeval soup" in Kingdon's (1995) policy agenda-setting model. A "condition" becomes a "problem" or several "problems." An incomprehensible number of alternatives are reduced to only a few. When the process is finished, the plurality of views will remain, but at a minimum, there will be a consensus on a few principal alternatives that should be on the decision agenda.

Similarly, William Jacoby (1999) extends issue-framing research to government spending, and demonstrates that the seemingly contradictory positions of the American public toward government spending are due to the issue frames in which their opinions are elicited. Political actors, he argues, recognize the limits on public attentiveness, and use relatively simple frames for political issues. "Issues arise from complex problems that are separate and remote from the direct experiences of most American citizens. Therefore, information about these problems must be communicated to and at least partially interpreted for the public, before an issue can truly be said to exist in the first place" (Jacoby 1999, 14). The interested parties on a given issue do not provide exactly the same information to their respective constituencies. Instead, "they differentially interpret the causes, nature, and consequences of social problems, a process that is usually facilitated by the very complexity of the problems themselves. But this is the essence of the issue framing process" (Jacoby 1999, 14).

Jacoby systematically compares citizen opinions on several policy issues when they are presented in a general issue frame (support for government spending) versus an issue-specific, government-spending frame (e.g., spending on the poor or disabled or for veterans). He expected to find that varying the frame of an issue between general and specific presentations would affect the salience of different psychological components within the opinion formation process. Issue statements that are framed in general terms highlight the symbolic nature of political conflict, and encourage reactions based upon long-term predispositions and emotional orientations. A specific issue frame encourages connections between governmental policy and particular segments of American society, and reactions to the issue are affected, at least partly, by citizens' feelings about the target group. Using public opinion data, he finds that "differing frames produce widespread changes in the ways that people respond to a single issue, with systematically lower support for government spending in the general presentation, and greater support in the specific frame. Thus, issue framing effects appear at the individual level; they do not merely affect the aggregate contours of public opinion" (Jacoby 1999, 3 and 12).

Jacoby's research has important implications for understanding policy decisions, and it is particularly useful to extend his argument to parallels in the way budget recommendations are crafted by examiners in the SBO. Of particular interest to us is Jacoby's point that:

> Issue framing effects operate by differentially influencing the causal factors that underlie overt responses to an issue. In other words, a particular interpretation of a social or political problem (i.e., an issue frame) activates certain types of thinking among the people who are exposed to that interpretation. Differently framed presentations of a single issue may vary the salience and accessibility of the concerns that individuals bring to bear on their responses to that issue. Or, they may simply affect the importance of the separate elements within a person's belief system and their immediate relevance to a particular issue. (1999, 8)

A compounding influence of framing on budget director and gubernatorial decisions is that research evidence suggests that value judgments of decisionmakers are often poorly defined or formulated by the subject. Fischhoff et al. (1980) demonstrate that elicitation procedures can be major influences on *shaping* values, and attitudes towards values, in decision-making. This is particularly true when the value judgment may have been heretofore inchoate. To a large extent, the budget examiner developing a recommendation for the governor plays a role similar to the elicitor in the experiments that seek to determine a subject's values and value preferences. Under circumstances where people do not know, or have difficulty apprais-ing, what they want, "how problems are posed, questions are phrased, and responses are elicited can have substantial impact on judgments that suppos-edly express people's true values" (Fischhoff et al., 117–18). Ambiguity in expressed preferences is inevitable—questions posed and methods used to pose them may have a large effect on elicited responses. Elected officials, including governors, rely on general issue framing in their campaigns. Their specialty is generalizing issues. Examiners, on the other hand, routinely must deal with specific policy issues arising from agency budget problems and their budget requests. As we shall see momentarily, they tend to use specific issue framing when recommending an alternative budget decision. The im-plications for SBO budgeting are startling: even how the examiner asks the budget director or governor a question can influence the elicited value ex-pression!

A Wisconsin budget office examiner once began a budget briefing for the governor on the tourism budget with the question, "Governor, pick a num-ber: How much do you want to spend on tourism promotion?" The governor then struck his fist on the briefing table, turned to the secretary of the eco-nomic development department (who also happened to be the lieutenant gov-ernor), and began to vigorously express his unhappiness that the department had submitted a budget request to increase the tourism promotion budget by about 300 percent. The question elicited a gubernatorial response that indi-cated the "team player" was not abiding by the governor's policy priorities and that the funds for a large tourism budget increase would have to come from somewhere. The governor was unwilling to make the reallocation based on the politics of which constituency wanted the budget increase versus other constituencies that wanted other spending. Later in the briefing, the exam-iner framed another decision item as an economic allocation choice between spending funds for tourism welcome centers versus spending funds for the overall state advertising promotion budget. The conversation with the gov-ernor focused on a marginal utility analysis of which program would yield the most effective promotion.

On the other hand, lest we conjure an image of governors at the mercy of examiners, Tversky and Kahneman explain that people are most likely to

Figure 4.1   **Value Preference Intensity of a Typical Agency Program**

Weak   Strong

Governor   Program
                                                             Manager

have clear value preferences for issues that are familiar, simple, and directly experienced. For a governor, these may be the issues that formed his or her campaign platform and for which the governor has become well versed in the surrounding controversies (and choices). Each of these properties (familiarity, simplicity, and direct experience) is associated with opportunities for trial-and-error learning, particularly such as may be summarized in readily applicable rules or homilies. "Those rules provide stereotypic, readily justifiable responses to future questions of values. When adopted by individuals, they may be seen as habits; when adopted by groups, they constitute traditions. . . . They are often derived and formulated to be coherent with a wider body of beliefs and values. And, they are readily applicable, both because of their simplicity and because the individual has had practice in working through their implications for various situations" (Kahneman and Tversky 1984, 118).

Successful governors have relatively few policy priorities, and may be relatively indifferent to the countless other policy tradeoffs inherent in budget decisions. They stake their claim to a few issues upon which they hold strong value positions, and on which they will be less willing to change their positions under the pressure of budget development than on issues on which they do not see their political future is dependent and which they perceive have little or no political risk. To the extent that these low salience issues are moved to the budgetary decision agenda by other budgetary actors, the governors may hold weak or transitory positions.

Figure 4.1 illustrates a scale of value preference intensity, such that governors hold weak and vague value preferences on most issues but relatively strong value preferences on a few key policy priorities. Agency program managers, on the other hand, hold the strongest value preferences for their programs. For the typical agency program, then, the program manager holds the strongest value preference while the governor holds the weakest value preference. In between are the SBO examiners who hold a larger number of stronger value preferences because (1) they deal with multiple programs and their attached, underlying values, and (2) they are also delegated by the governor to broadly imbue budget decisions with values of efficiency and economy.

So, what happens when the examiner believes the agency request deserves funding but has doubts about whether a positive recommendation will receive affirmation by the budget director and governor? It depends. Budget problems, like many decisions, are a choice between retaining the status quo and accepting an alternative that is advantageous in some respects and disadvantageous in others. Tversky and Kahneman argue that the status quo normally defines the reference level for all the attributes evaluated in a decision comparison. The advantages of alternative options are evaluated as gains and their disadvantages as losses. "Because losses loom larger than gains, the decision maker will be biased in favor of retaining the status quo" (Kahneman and Tversky 1984, 348). This is often the type of problem examiners present to budget directors and governors, and it helps explain the status quo bias in budgeting and, to some degree, provides an alternative explanation for what we observe as the incremental bias in budgeting.

Given a relatively fixed resource constraint in every state budget, almost every budget request, if granted, represents a policy loss in the sense of opportunity costs. The $250,000 per year spent on a trade office in Singapore cannot be spent to capitalize a loan fund in a small business incubator. Granting a new position in the tourism office may represent a lost opportunity to grant a new position in the Department of Aging, especially if the governor's priorities include limiting the growth in government positions. If governors are focused on their policy priorities in budget development, every addition to the budget outside the priority area diminishes the amount of money available for priorities, and can be viewed as a loss by the governor.

Examiners understand gubernatorial priorities. They understand that if their agency issue or request is not on the priorities list, it is unlikely to receive gubernatorial attention, and the decision-making bias of the governor —and the SBO bias—is toward the status quo. The status quo position is preferred because it normally does not change policy, increase spending, or increase the risk of policy conflict (and thus political conflict). Since the governor wants to save political conflicts (and political capital) for policy priorities, the inclination of the governor and his or her chief assistants (especially the budget director) is to decide against an agency request. The decision for the examiner is whether to try to convince the budget director and the governor to support the request, however improbable an affirmation may be, or to accept the status quo bias in this case and deny the agency request. This is an important dynamic, since governors are ambivalent to most issues that are brought to them.

Tversky and Kahneman's research results suggest that if the examiner wants to gain approval from the budget director or governor, then the policy "loss" must be reframed as a policy "cost to a gain" for the governor. Their research demonstrates that it is possible to reframe a loss as a cost necessary to obtain a gain, and thereby increase the acceptability of the loss. In a series of experiments that parallel insurance purchases, they and others found that individuals were unwilling to accept a known loss of money when they could gamble to lose less money. However, when the same information is reframed such that the known loss is relabeled as a cost to achieve the equivalent gain, the same individuals were much more likely to accept the known loss. Consider the two problems used in their experiment, which were separated by a short filler problem (Kahneman and Tversky 1984, 349):

> Problem 10: Would you accept a gamble that offers a 10 percent chance to win $95 and a 90 percent chance to lose $5?
>
> Problem 11: Would you pay $5 to participate in a lottery that offers a 10 percent chance to win $100 and a 90 percent chance to win nothing?

Although the outcomes of each problem are exactly equivalent, almost a third of the subjects agreed to problem 11 when they refused problem 10.

There are interesting implications for examiner recommendations. Examiners may reframe a request as a cost to achieve a gubernatorial policy priority. If the governor's priority is economic development, then the examiner may try to reframe the Department of Aging position request in terms of economic development. If that is not credible, it may be rejected by the examiner and not recommended to the governor. A more likely scenario for priority framing, however, is that the *agency* will try to frame its request in terms of a fit with gubernatorial priorities. For example, a new position for the securities commissioner may be framed as an economic development initiative. The examiner may analyze the request and reframe it in other terms. But managing risk aversion is a tricky feat, as this examiner detailed:

> When money's tight, you know a lot of new things aren't going to happen, particularly because the reluctance to trade in something old, that's too big a risk to take. Too often, what the legislature will do is they'll take away an old program, this $150,000 we've been spending for this. It's been around for twenty-five years, really isn't serving what it should be. We'd like to take that money and start this new thing. That's taking a risk. Because the legislature will probably take your money, they won't give you your new thing. You'll just have lost. It's a losing game. And that's happened enough that people are very cautious about that. But I think it's good to bring up new stuff if for no other reason than you may be greasing the wheel. And, hell, we grease the wheel all the time with the legislature. The governor does that with recommendations realizing that's not going to happen this year, but gets the discussion started, greases the wheel.

The Credibility of the Issue Framer

Examiners must be seen as credible sources if they are to be allowed by governors and budget directors to frame budgetary problems. Experimental results demonstrate that the perceived credibility of the source conditions the framing effects: "only certain types of speakers can use a frame to influence another's opinion" (Druckman 1999, 8). A credible speaker possesses two attributes. First, the target audience must believe the speaker possesses knowledge about which considerations are actually relevant to the pending decision. Second, the target audience must believe the speaker can be trusted to reveal what he or she knows. The SBO examiners meet Druckman's criteria for being credible speakers who can frame issues for others.

Examiners in this field study were asked about the extent to which they anticipated the reaction of the budget director or governor when they were deciding *whether* to, and *how* to, analyze an agency request. The responses are remarkably similar across states and across levels of experience within an office. About 80 percent of the examiners (excluding section managers) indicate that they anticipate the reaction of the budget director, and to a lesser extent the governor, when they choose which issues to analyze and how to fashion their recommendations. The anticipation was unanimous among examiners in Wisconsin, Georgia, Virginia, and North Carolina; ranged from 89 to 78 percent in Kansas, Iowa, and Missouri; and fell to 64 percent in Minnesota, 52 percent in Illinois, and only 33 percent in Alabama. We note that the last group (Illinois and Alabama) is found to be primarily control-oriented SBOs while the first group (particularly Wisconsin, Georgia, and Virginia) exhibited strong-policy orientations. (We discuss this more fully in chapter 5.) The grouping pattern does not change when the section managers are included in the analysis, and the differences between the states in both cross-tabulations are statistically significant at the 0.05 level.

Most examiners we interviewed could (and would) cite requests that they perceived to be DOA (dead on arrival) from the perspective of the budget director or governor, yet examiners would try to "sell it" to the budget director anyway. The decision to push an alternative or drop it was influenced by political and economic factors. This examiner's response is typical:

> I think you have to pick which battles you're going to participate in. So, yes, there are some cases where I knew that something may be dead on arrival, but I'm going to try to convince them [the budget director and governor] otherwise, to see if maybe some consideration, or a part of a proposal, or if a study may be agreed to, or something along those lines. I think a lot of times it depends on judgment, what the atmosphere is. If

we're in a period where budgets are slightly increasing, you tend to push more than in times where we've lost revenue and budgets are tight; you tend to recommend less things.

Most section managers in policy-oriented SBOs expressed reluctance to "weed out" recommendations.[4] Rather, they are there to push for better analysis and to help anticipate the budget director's or governor's questions so the examiner is ready to respond to their presumed concerns. Section managers generally supported their examiners who felt strongly about an issue (whether supporting or opposing an agency request) and tried to help the examiner make the best case for the position, even if the manager viewed it as DOA or had a contrary position. A Missouri SBO section manager characterized the job this way:

> I've never told somebody to drop something. If it's an issue that somebody feels strongly about or they have a different perspective about, that's part of the function of providing the best technical advice that you can provide. There can be strong differences of opinion about how to approach something. The best way to make sure the budget director and governor and governor's staff know how they ought to solve the issue is to get as many different opinions and facts as they can get. So I'd be hurting the governor, the taxpayer, my customers, if I were to stifle creativity or different thoughts about how to approach things.

On the other hand, Illinois's section managers were more willing to weed out analysts' recommendations and issues before they reached the budget director:

> Part of my job is to weed out [pause] . . . I think analysts should be sort of pure; they should just look at the facts, present the facts, and let the policy-level people make those decisions. I guess I see myself as a person that would look at the facts, look at the details, take into consideration what policy decisions are out there, what direction the administration will likely go, and then present the information in that particular way. I think then at the [budget] director's level she has even more of a policy twist to her particular recommendations. So I think as it goes up the ladder that the bias on maybe what's presented is based more on what the goals of the administration are.

Examiners in Alabama's budget office, another SBO with a predominant control orientation, reiterated this type of behavior and chain of command regarding policy initiative:

> We put together worksheets and sit down with the agency head with questions and policy issues. Then we sit down with [the budget director] and [deputy director] and they take it from there to the finance director and the governor.

The framing of budget requests in terms of their policy implications illuminates one of the ways in which policy-oriented examiners must work at the macro-budgeting level, at the nexus of the budget and policy processes. Problem-framing and representation also works simultaneously at the micro-budgeting level in examiner analysis. As Howard (1973, 161) suggests, "Analysis is not a technique so much as it is a way of looking at problems, a frame of mind, a disposition, or an attitude." Problem-framing is central to budget analysis just as it is to the policy-making process. Budget controversies arise when budget problems are only viewed partially, for example with a political frame or an economic frame but not both. Agencies have a vested interest in framing their budget requests in ways that augment the resources they desire to more effectively achieve their goals.[5] Rational budgeting requires "rational partisans, advocates who are informed of the potential consequences of their positions and their possible alternatives" (Howard 1973, 161). Analysis must be applied strategically, with administrators and political leaders, including the governor, deciding which opportunities will be exploited.

A Multidimensional View of the Budget Problem

As we suggested earlier, each agency budget request represents a budget problem for the examiner. In keeping with a multidimensional view of budget problems, it may help to think of a pentagonal carousel that can spin on its central axis. As seen in Figure 4.2, each side of the pentagon represents a problem frame. At the center is a fixed set of all possible alternative budget solutions. The solution set is fixed and unique to the particular problem at hand at any point in time, and thus the position of the solution set with respect to the different problem frames depends on the problem at hand. Viewing the solution set through alternative problem frames reveals a variety of solution perspectives. Much as one "sees" new aspects of a Dalí painting by viewing it from different angles and in different lights, the examiner "sees" new aspects of budget solutions by applying different problem frames to the budget problem at hand.

There are three consequences that follow from this framework. First, the examiner must look through a problem frame to "see" the solution set. The solution set of feasible alternatives must be feasible with respect to some

Figure 4.2   **Budget Problem Framing with Multiple Rationalities**

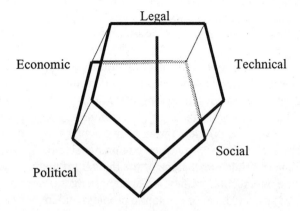

criterion, such as political feasibility or technical feasibility. For example, the social problem frame examines the social feasibility of the proposed solution, determined by criteria relevant to social rationality: Does the proposed solution promote social integration or social conflict? The technical problem frame examines the technical feasibility of the proposed solution, judged by criteria relevant to technical rationality: Does the proposed solution increase or decrease technical efficiency? The other problem frames have corresponding effects.

A second consequence of this multiple framework is that the examiner cannot fully appreciate the full solution set unless he or she has looked at it through all five problem frames. Each frame presents the solution set from a different angle (or perspective), identifying alternatives that are feasible when the budget problem is framed this way. Simultaneously, it identifies alternatives that are not feasible when the rationality of that frame is applied to the budget problem. The systematic exposure of the solution set to the multiple frames effectively eliminates certain proposals from consideration because they violate one or another of the decision rationalities. For example, an agency proposal to relocate a trade office from Singapore to Nanking may meet the technical feasibility criterion, but it may violate political feasibility because the governor is philosophically opposed to the Chinese government.

Finally, solutions are only evaluated by SBO examiners with respect to a budget problem on the budget decision agenda. The examiners deal with a relatively small set of problems, usually when they appear as budget requests. However, they also must address budget problems as they arise during budget implementation. In the course of their discussions with agencies throughout the year, they help identify alternatives for future consideration, and they also may even participate in problem definition activities with their agency officials. For example, effective policy entrepreneurs use the media to help frame their problem and possible solutions to the public to encourage support for their initiative.

Problem-framing is at once a means of simplifying decision-making and a means to permit comprehensive and integrated analysis of the multiple facets of budget problems. Framing simplifies decision-making by narrowing the set of feasible options: the type of reasoning to apply to the problem follows from viewing the problem through a particular frame. A synthesis of the multiple framed analyses provides a comprehensive perspective and appreciation of the multiple dimensions of the budget problem.

There can be intersecting frames. An agency budget officer may frame a budget problem as a technical or economic problem and identify a particular set of alternative solutions. Yet an elected legislator may view the same problem through the political frame and identify another set of alternative solutions. Some solutions will be included in both sets (e.g., more money for consultants), while others will not (e.g., an extra position). In terms of set theory, there is some intersection of the political and technical solution sets (Figure 4.3). Similarly, the agency client group may view the problem through a social frame and identify another range of solutions, a subset of which will be in the intersection of the political and technical frames. On the other hand, the legal counsel for the agency may view the problem through a legal frame and see no legal problem, and therefore no solution set, at least as it is framed at this moment. Circumstances may change and legal issues arise such that another viewing of the budget problem through the legal frame would identify a legal problem and alternative solutions.

The multidimensional quality of budget problems cannot be appreciated, nor the consequences of each dimension evaluated, without a holistic approach. Consequently, budget rationality demands that examiners use a process of multiple problem-framing to view budget problems holistically. Examiners need to identify the gain/loss characteristics of a budget request in more than economic terms, because value preferences are inherent in the decision. Framing a problem in one way draws upon a different type of reasoning than if it is framed another way. Viewing the budget problem at hand through the series of problem frames is antecedent to analyzing budget problems using multiple rationalities. The goal of the rational analyst is to define the set of budget alternatives that are feasible from the perspective of multiple problem frames and then recommend an alternative to the governor.

Framed as a social problem, the analysis of an agency budget request (the budget problem) follows reasoning that examines social expectations and

Figure 4.3   **Subset of Alternatives Feasible Politically and Technically**

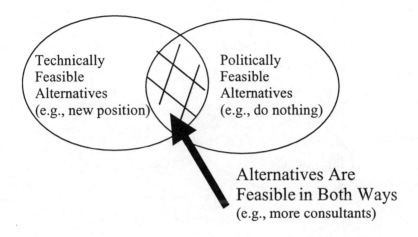

obligations to determine the social rationality underlying the existence of the public program. Christopher Bosso (1994) notes that debates over public problems invariably are framed in terms of whether proposals are constitutional more than whether they are "good" or "right." "This legal construct has no small bearing on what kinds of problems are or are not considered within the legitimate purview of government" (Bosso 1994, 193). The request may raise questions of whether the agency activity represents a proper role for government (Area A in Figure 4.4). When a problem is defined as a constitutional question, it is effectively taken (perhaps temporarily) out of more openly political realms (Area B in Figure 4.4).

The rational analyst who confronts this situation when viewing a budget problem through the legal frame proceeds on the basis of legal rationality to determine the available solution set. A similar process applies to the budget problem viewed through the political, economic, and technical frames. A full appraisal of the budget problem results from a multifaceted approach to its solution set. The process reduces the solution set of acceptable (feasible) recommendations to only a few (the shaded area of Figure 4.4). These are the alternatives not precluded by any single rationality.

The order in which a particular examiner may apply the different frames may vary depending upon the examiner's individual biases, professional experience, and educational background. These characteristics will filter out potential alternatives even before the analyst views the budget problem

Figure 4.4   **Identifying the Subset of Feasible Alternatives from a Multiple Rationalities Decision Framework**

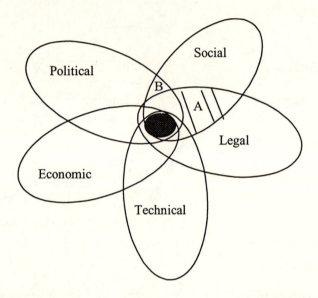

through any given frame identified above (Tversky and Kahneman 1984). It is possible then, even likely, that two examiners looking through the same frame at the solution set initially will not identify an identical set of budget solutions. However, the process by which examiners discuss their analyses and develop recommendations with their supervisors and the budget director acts to counter an individual's bias and permits a relatively full range of solution alternatives to be identified and discussed within the budget office. This may account for findings that senior examiners sometimes make decisions differently than junior examiners (Willoughby 1993a; Thurmaier 1995a).

Summary: Complex Problems Require Complex Analysis

It is worth noting that the nexus of the policy and budget processes will be most evident in the social, political, and legal frames. These frames focus on the effectiveness rationalities, those that create the public policies and programs from the array and interplay of social values. As we have noted, governors often campaign on only a few issues, and these become their policy priorities during their term of office. It is very important for examiners to respond to the governor's imperatives and to develop alternatives that reflect the governor's values and perspective while also meeting the multiple rationalities criteria, including efficiency values. In a parallel way, governors tend to focus attention only on selected issues for any given budget, delegating decisions on the bulk of the budget to the budget director and his or her staff. On the other hand, governors may convey a general attitude or approach toward governing that examiners must transmit and translate to agencies for their budget preparations. Seasoned examiners are aware of the governor's approach, receiving political cues from the governor that indicate support or opposition to current programs, and programmatic changes that the governor desires. It is this understanding of the governor's goals and objectives that shape their own approach to agency budget requests, and highlights their responsiveness to macro-budgeting issues and the policy process.

Yet, there are a great many policy issues that will not be of concern to the governor, at least as a policy priority. These issues likely are not imbued with a gubernatorial imperative when the examiner reviews them in the context of agency budget requests. Still, such issues may have important long-term policy consequences for the state. Governors rely on the examiners to ferret these issues out of the mass of budget request decision items, to bring to their attention those items most in need of the governor's personal attention. Consequently, attention is directed to changes in program, which in turn emphasizes incremental changes in programs and policies rather than raising questions about fundamental changes. The disposition of these issues dominates the examiners' decision workload. The bulk of the micro-budgeting decisions in a budget process are the hundreds of individual decisions made by the various budget actors regarding the sometimes mundane issues that do not attract the media spotlights or the attention of elected officials. They are nevertheless essential to the functioning of state government.

Howard (1973) observes that budgeters are action-oriented, open to the politics of issues and flexible in their time horizons, so they mesh well with elected officials' needs. Examiner analysis can take a long-run view, while politics tends to be short-run. If examiners incorporate the long-run view into their recommendation, it may consist of a phased implementation of a program or policy, accommodating the political reality while projecting long-term strategic thinking and planning with the agency bureaucracy in mind, who will remain for implementation after the politicians are gone. The historical role of SBOs as the delegated arm of the governor surfaces with respect to managerial oversight of agencies. Yet the perspective is more of a concern for policy implementation oversight rather than strictly a management oversight role. Political evaluations are a pass-fail test in legislatures. Administrative evaluations are concerned with the quality of the decision process, the quality of the data and planning process, the efficiency and effectiveness of the program implementation, and the external validity of program practices.

The conventional wisdom about budget rationality is that it is X part political and Y part economic, with too much of the former and too little of the latter. Budget reforms have generally aimed at increasing the amount of economic rationality in budget decisions, while defenders of incrementalism have highlighted political rationality as the essential ingredient in budgetary decision-making. To the extent that economic rationality has been recognized in budgetary decision-making, it has the flavor of budget-maximizing bureaucrats using public funds to maximize their own utilities. These approaches focus too narrowly on one type of rationality or another. Budget decisions are neither exclusively economic nor political in their rationality.

Budget problems analyzed in the context of the budget as a policy document require a multiple-rationalities decision-making approach. Each of the five facets posited above is present to lesser or greater degrees depending upon the actual budget problem. For ease of explanation and analysis, we have divided them into effectiveness and efficiency facets. Effectiveness facets include social, political, and legal aspects of budget problems. Efficiency facets include the economic and technical aspects. Each facet of a budget problem requires a different way of thinking, a different rationality. Economic rationality is inappropriate for legal problems, just as political rationality is inappropriate for technical problems. A full treatment of an agency budget problem requires a full range of rationalities for both efficiency and effectiveness.

Budget examiners shape and emphasize budget issues, and in so doing, they "take on the often unrecognized moral responsibility of defining for other people the reality of what is occurring in various state programs," a somewhat metaphysical role (Howard 1973, 279). The result is not a "yes" man role for the examiner. The array of alternatives and arguments presented to the budget director and governor by the rational analyst is more complex. Gubernatorial imperatives eliminate some alternatives, but governors may still get arguments urging them to accept an alternative anyway. This is partly due to the examiners' having a long-term and "neutral" partisan perspective, in contrast to the elected official's partisan and relatively short-term perspective. In addition, examiners are well aware of the power to initiate change, power that can rival that found in agencies.

Kahneman and Tversky (1984) demonstrate that the way in which the governor evaluates a request is susceptible to problem formulation effects because the value function is nonlinear and people tend to evaluate options in relation to the reference point that is suggested or implied by the statement of the problem. In general, the agency's base budget serves as the decision reference point and the examiners frame the cost-loss evaluation based on the agency request option. Alternatively, examiners can set an alternative reference point upon which governors and budget directors make decisions. This situation would arise, for example, when a court order requires an administrative response to prison overcrowding or unequal school financing systems. But it may also arise when an examiner has experienced an agency problem first hand, for example through a site visit to a state historical site or a crowded income tax processing room with inadequate ventilation. The examiner may accept the mandatory nature of a budget change and set the reference point for the budget directors and governor as the agency's request, developing alternatives that provide a gain/cost/loss analysis for the budget director and governor.

The nonlinear nature of budgeting and policy-making suggests that a model of budget rationality should include flexibility in decision sequencing, yet provide some organizing framework by which the interdependent budget and policy factors can be reconciled for decision-making when a budget deadline arrives. This condition is met by framing the budget problem in social, political, and legal, as well as economic and technical, terms. There are parallels with Kingdon's checklist of feasibility criteria applied to a policy solution before it can emerge from the policy primeval soup. Kingdon's (1995, 138) criteria include technical feasibility, value acceptability within the policy community, tolerable cost, anticipated public acquiescence, and a reasonable chance for receptivity among elected decisionmakers.

In the following chapter we assess SBO context and orientation in our sample states. Then, we apply our model of micro-budgeting under two different conditions that we found present in states we visited. Chapter 6 follows a rational analyst through a year of budgeting in a policy-oriented SBO. The subsequent chapter follows a rational analyst through the same year in a control-oriented SBO. The contrast between the complexities in their decision-making is clear, and has important implications for the role of examiners in SBOs. Therefore, we examine the changing roles of SBO examiners in chapter 8 before drawing conclusions from our study in the final chapter.

Notes

1. We will not enter the problematic discussion of single-peaked preferences and other problems with identifying "public" priorities here. It is enough for present purposes and our theory development at this stage to identify "some degree" of priority ordering, even if it is dynamic over time for the same set of goals.
2. A standard tool for this type of economic analysis is a benefit-cost decision-making process. Using this tool, the analyst considers each alternative, identifying and quantifying the benefits and costs and yielding some ratio that is compared with the ratios of the alternatives. The difficulties with this methodology are well known, and include problems quantifying intangible costs and benefits, and problems of applying the appropriate discount rate and time frame to estimate the benefits and costs.

Under the best of circumstances, the benefit-cost analysis allows one to identify the alternative with the highest ratio of benefits to costs. Yet even its strongest advocates acknowledge it should not be the sole criterion for making a budget decision.

3. Harsanyi (1986) attempts to broaden the theory of rational behavior using his "utility theory" (individual maximizing behavior), game theory (behavior of two or more interacting rational individuals), and ethics (the theory of rational moral judgments). The Elster (1986) volume provides a good overview of the various aspects of "rational-choice" theory.

4. We refer to section managers as responsible for a budget review division within their budget office; these managers may be called team leaders, budget supervisors, or section leaders or some other title within their SBO. They are responsible for the activities of the examiners in their section that review budgets for a specific grouping of agencies, such as education, economic development, or general government.

5. See Niskanen (1971) and subsequent agency theory literature. Yet they do so without the budget-maximizing traits described in agency theory.

5

Budget Office Orientations and Decision Contexts

A Typology of Budget Office Decision Contexts

In previous chapters we described the environment of state budget offices and assessed the characteristics of our sample SBOs according to economic, fiscal, political, and organizational factors. Next, we deciphered the budget problem that confronts the SBO examiner. In doing so, we synthesized the GCM, RTB, and PAS models of decision-making to provide the foundation for our multiple rationalities model of budgetary decision-making. In chapters 3 and 4 we distinguished these rationalities, explaining problem framing and the angles—social, legal, political, economic, and technical—through which an examiner can view the budget problem. Now, we will describe in much more detail the decision context within which examiners function. Examiners from the SBOs we visited will describe in their own words the orientation of their office, be it more strongly control or policy in focus. Then, in the next two chapters we shadow, through one budget cycle, prototypes of examiners found in SBOs of one orientation and the other. Finally, in chapter 8, we are able to assess the influence of distinct SBO orientation and context on the budget rationalities that examiners depend upon when making budget decisions as well as the roles they adhere to when involved in various decision tasks throughout the budget cycle.

We know that not all SBOs can be characterized as serving the governor in the capacity of a policy tool. In his seminal 1966 article, Allen Schick suggested there were at least three central budget office orientations: control, management, and planning. The analysis of these orientations suggests that each orientation represents a decision context in which examiners may approach budgeting problems with a particular viewpoint, and playing a particular role. For example, a control orientation may emphasize forcing agencies to cut expenditures and restricting their abilities to internally reallocate funds; a management orientation may emphasize forcing agencies to improve management practices; a planning orientation may emphasize helping agencies forecast and build multiyear program plans.

However, thirty years later, Schick's (1997) analysis of current budget reforms in Organization for Economic Cooperation and Development (OECD) nations, including the United States, identified a new *policy* orientation for central budget offices. In the policy-oriented central budget office, "budgeting shifts from items of expenditure to policy changes" (Schick 1997, 5). The policy-oriented central budget office encourages departments to initiate trade-offs among their programs—within prescribed constraints—and the trade-off becomes the main decision unit in budgeting.

Shelly Tomkin's (1998) study of the federal Office of Management and Budget (OMB) supports the argument that budgeting in that central budget office has evolved from an orientation emphasizing budgeting as a controlling mechanism to budgeting as a policy mechanism, although the latter seems to be somewhat episodic. Tomkin describes how the changing orientations of OMB have affected the roles played by the examiners staffed there, particularly regarding the question of how politicized examiners have become over the years. Discussions by James Davis and Randall Ripley (1969), Hugh Heclo (1975), and Bruce Johnson (1984 and 1989) also contribute to our knowledge of examiners in the national budget office. These analyses suggest that decision-making by OMB budget examiners has changed over the years, especially with respect to their discretion in budgetary and policy-making decisions. These findings illustrate that OMB examiners exercise considerable influence over the ability of agencies to obtain their budget requests.

Such research findings about budgeting at the federal level of government are consonant with a series of state budgeting studies suggesting that a growing number of SBOs have relinquished some or most of their traditional control orientation in favor of more active management and policy analysis foci. Seventeen of the state budget directors responding to a survey by Schick (1971, 174) preferred that their offices be regarded as "policy staffs" and seven regarded their offices as "management assistance operations"; none listed "control over expenditures." Schick (1971, 174) points out that "budgeters view themselves as policymakers and want to eschew a financial control role."

When Gosling (1987) examined the orientations of SBOs in three midwestern states, he found that while Iowa maintained a control orientation, Wisconsin had evolved to a policy orientation and Minnesota was in transition to a policy orientation. In part, these differences were seen as a reflection of the governor's desire to use the budget as a policy tool. The Minnesota governor recruited his budget director from the Wisconsin budget office to reorient the Minnesota office to the policy orientation emphasized in Wisconsin. Thurmaier and Gosling (1997) revisited the three states nearly ten years later and found the transition to a policy orientation nearly complete. In fact, the Iowa office had moved decisively from a control to a policy orientation as part of a general reorganization of Iowa government in the mid-1980s. The association of the governor's policy agenda with the development and execution of the budgets in these states was firmly in place in the mid-1990s. The analysis of the SBO policy orientation suggests that this orientation may require examiners working with agencies to align programmatic activities and budgetary priorities with the policy preferences and priorities of the governor. Thurmaier and Gosling found little evidence that these states had any significant management or planning orientation, however.

Gubernatorial Activism and Policy Influence

The results from our field study support the concept that state budget office orientations can be arrayed along a control-policy continuum. SBOs on one end of the continuum have a strong *policy orientation*. They are closely tied to the governor's policy agenda; their mission is to manage the development of the state budget so that the governor's priorities receive the highest attention. In these states, the SBO is a powerful tool through which the governor can draft budget proposals that implement his or her policy agenda, whatever his or her partisan stripe.

On the other end of the continuum we find a few SBOs that retain a *control orientation*. They are technical accounting shops where the examiners are far removed from the policy issues and debates that surround the governor. The SBOs in these states are not expected to exhibit much policy activity because the institution, as well as the individual budget examiner, serve mainly as instruments of financial accountability and control. While formal budgeting powers are consistently viewed as a governor's most powerful policy tools (Bernick 1979; Ransone 1982; Sharkansky 1968a and 1968b), some governors are more active than others in policy formation. For example, in some control-oriented states, governors may not have a history of activist policy agendas. In such cases, the governor has little need of a policy-oriented SBO to draft proposals or redirect state operations according to his or her vision.

In between these models are SBOs with a *weak policy orientation*. Examiners in SBOs with a weak policy orientation are cognizant of a role in which they work to pursue the governor's agenda, yet their policy orientation is weaker because they can find it challenging to discern the governor's agenda and priorities (Thurmaier and Gosling 1997). The policy orientation may be weak for several reasons. A few states historically have activist governors, but they may or may not choose to use the SBO to craft budgets that implement their policy agendas. In such cases, the SBO's policy role may be intermittently supplanted by a governor's personal policy staff—a cadre of advisors immediately surrounding the governor and serving as intermediaries between the budget staff and the governor. The SBOs in these states may alternatively emphasize the management aspects of budgeting identified in Schick's 1966 description.

In other states, the governor's policy power may be constrained by the state's political culture. Besides the constitutional basis of power and partisan alignments with the legislature, "the customs and traditions of the state . . . over a long period of time, seem to set the tone of state government . . . make the governor more powerful than he would appear . . . while in others they seem to limit the governor's powers." (Thurmaier and Gosling 1997, 85). Further, "the governor's idea of his proper function is also significant," especially in which duties receive the most emphasis (Ransone 1982, 85). Governors possessing significant formal powers are seen as relying on them for success, while those with weaker powers have to rely on their informal powers, especially the power to muster popular support. In addition, a longer term with unlimited succession yields a stronger position for a governor than a limited term, such as two or four years only. Sharkansky (1968a and 1968b) found governors with succession power had greater budgetary process influence than those without it. Whether implicit or explicit, the tie between budgetary and policy power is evident.

The degree to which examiners find the governor's policy priorities and agenda a salient or remote factor influencing their analysis and recommendations on agency budget requests may be described as the "policy distance" between the examiners and the governor (and his or her policy staff). Policy analysis services for the governor require a pool of budget examiners who can conduct policy analysis, a budget director who views their role as policy analysts rooted in budgetary realities, and an organizational structure that facilitates regular and abundant communications between the budget examiners, the budget director, and the governor's office. We find that the more directly examiners are linked into—and responsible for—expediting the governor's policy agenda, the more likely they are to view the office as having a policy orientation, and the more likely the governor's agenda will influence their budget recommendations. This orientation is at least partially influenced by the manner in which the governor communicates his or her agenda to examiners within the office.

SBO Orientations

Midwestern States

We first explored the types of budget orientations found in our field study of the six Midwest SBOs. The budget office staff was queried to determine the presence of any of the four orientations suggested by Schick (1966) and subsequent studies: control, management, planning, and policy. The results suggest that it may be simpler to envision a "more control"–"more policy" continuum of orientations.

In the course of the interviews for the Midwest SBOs, examiners were asked the degree to which their budget offices were oriented toward the control, management, planning, or policy aspects of budgeting. Table 5.1 presents their responses by state. The total number of responses exceeds the number of examiners because many subjects identify more than a single orientation. This is consistent with Schick's (1966, 1973, and 1997) argument that while the primary orientation shifts over time, the multiple purposes of budgeting ensure the continued presence of each aspect, especially expenditure control, which is at the root of budgeting.

The number of unique responses and the total number of respondents to the question are presented for each state. About 71 percent of the subjects (77 of 108) in the sample characterize their budget office as having a policy orientation. The policy orientation is the modal response in five of the six states. A policy orientation is also the modal category among the unique responses, with 34 of 108 respondents identifying only a policy orientation for their office. The strongest policy responses are found in Iowa and Wisconsin, where 100 percent of the staffs identify the budget office as having a policy orientation. The lowest response for a policy orientation is found in Illinois, where only 29 percent of the staff identify it as an office orientation.

The Midwest budget staffs seldom (19 percent) cite the management orientation, describing it as mainly involving macro-management-level interagency coordination. They generally characterize micro-management activity as providing technical assistance to the smallest agencies, usually at the agency's own request. As seen in Table 5.1, there were two unique responses indicating an SBO had a management orientation; both are from the Kansas budget office (KSBO), one from an examiner and the other from a section manager.

The 19 percent of staff who note a planning orientation are largely drawn from the budget directors and section managers who see this perspective as rather unique to their levels in the budget office and their responsibility for financial management planning for the entire state. Only 5 percent of the

Table 5.1

Distribution of Orientation Responses in Midwest State Budget Offices

SBO Orientations	Iowa	Illinois	Kansas	Minnesota	Missouri	Wisconsin	Unique Responses	Total Responses
Numbers of responses (n = 163)								
Control	2	23	3	1	2	13	15	44
Management	0	5	4	2	8	2	2	21
Planning	3	6	0	3	7	2	5	21
Policy	11	8	13	16	11	18	34	77
Total responses	16	42	20	22	28	35	56	163
SBO staff (n = 108)	11	28	17	19	15	18		
As a percentage of SBO staff (n = 108)								
Control	18	82	18	5	13	72		40
Management	0	18	24	11	53	11		19
Planning	27	21	0	16	47	11		19
Policy	100	29	76	84	73	100		71
Total responses	100	100	100	100	100	100		100

Note: The number of responses to each question varied. For example, only 18 responses were recorded for this question in Wisconsin.

respondents provide a unique response for a planning orientation, and none of the Kansas staff note this orientation at all.

Only 15 of the 108 examiners (16 percent) identify their budget office as having a unique control orientation. Illinois (14 examiners) and Kansas (1 examiner) are the only states where control is identified as the exclusive orientation of the budget office. Of those who identify control and another orientation for the office, 17 also mentioned a policy orientation. A control orientation is the modal category in only one Midwest budget office, Illinois (ILSBO), with 82 percent of the Illinois responses.

The other SBO with a significant share of control responses is in Wisconsin (WISBO), where two-thirds of the staff cite control as an important emphasis of the budget office. However, they mentioned this as a secondary orientation, and all of the examiners who identified control as an orientation in Wisconsin also identified a policy orientation. Aside from the Illinois, Kansas, and Wisconsin responses, only five other examiners view control as a budget office orientation. Almost every examiner in Iowa and Minnesota report that their office is moving away from a control orientation and toward something else (usually a policy one). The Iowa state budget office (IASBO) and the Minnesota state budget office (MNSBO) have almost identical responses. They have much less affiliation with the control orientation than WISBO, but share a strong policy grounding.

In striking contrast, the ILSBO is solidly grounded in the control orientation, with few responses in the policy orientation. In fact, not one ILSBO examiner identified policy as the unique ILSBO orientation. It shares the same response weighting in planning as Iowa and Minnesota, and the same share in management as Minnesota.

The Missouri state budget office (MOSBO) has the most diverse orientation. Although it is strongly grounded in a policy orientation, it also displays substantial planning and management responses. In fact, Missouri respondents provided a third of the total planning responses in the sample (Table 5.1), and a third of the total management responses in the sample. Still, the modal response in Missouri (73 percent) is a policy orientation. A senior Missouri examiner even argues that MOSBO examiners should no longer be called "budget and planning" analysts:

> It would be fairer to call our analysts "budget and policy" analysts. We do not engage in planning in the sense of preparing a planning document that then sits on a shelf somewhere. When I first came to Budget and Planning, we had forty folks appropriated to Budget and Planning, we had federal funds, and the planning and budgeting functions had relatively recently been merged, and planning documents were prepared on a variety of top-

ics. But that is not something that takes place anymore. It's much more policy oriented. What does the governor want to accomplish with the budget or with legislative initiative?

Only two Missouri examiners mentioned control, and in both cases they view the Missouri office as having multiple orientations, including policy. None of the Missouri examiners viewed management as an exclusive orientation of the office.[1]

Thirty years after Schick's initial presentation, we observe that few of the Midwest offices maintain a control or management emphasis, but that most are strongly grounded in a new policy orientation. However, with the exception of the Iowa and Kansas SBOs, all of the states have some responses in each orientation. Overall, of the 163 total responses by the 108 staff in the Midwest budget offices, about 27 percent identify a control orientation while 47 percent identify a policy orientation, with only 13 percent identifying management and 13 percent planning.

Figure 5.1 is a schematic presentation of the different orientations of the Midwest budget offices, based on the distribution of responses by the 108 budget staff. (The Wisconsin and Illinois ovals are shaded to help clarify the figure and because they are highlighted in the following discussion.) The background is a matrix representing Schick's original three orientations of budgeting (*control*, *management*, and *planning*), and an extension that includes a *policy* orientation in the fourth quadrant. The orientations are arranged clockwise in the extended evolutionary pattern. Each office is represented as an oval that indicates the multimodal response categories to the question about office orientation. Although somewhat inexact, the ovals are positioned roughly proportional to the various orientations noted by respondents. The ovular shape captures the overlapping traits of the polymorphic (and polyphasic) nature of SBO orientations. The width is indicative of the proportion of multiple responses to the orientation question. As such, the ovals are not precise representations of a quantitative algorithm; rather they are an attempt to sketch the responses in a graphical format that captures the principal emphasis in a particular office, while recognizing multiple functions of an SBO at any given point in time.

There are several notable features in the orientation patterns. First, the figure affirms the conventional wisdom that state budgeting is predominantly policy oriented *or* control oriented. Most of the states are anchored in the policy quadrant; the important exception is ILSBO. The WISBO has a fatter profile and straddles both the control and policy orientations, reflecting the large number of multiple responses for each. Still, the figure captures WISBO's strong policy orientation, prominent in budgeting literature for some time.

Figure 5.1   **A Schematic Presentation of SBO Orientation Patterns in Six Midwestern States**

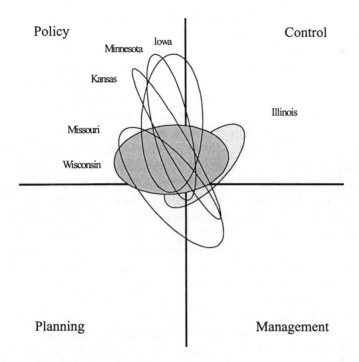

The diverse SBO orientations can be divided roughly into those that are primarily policy oriented and those that are primarily control oriented. The policy-oriented SBOs represent a decision context in which the SBO is dedicated to aligning the state budgets with the governor's policy priorities. The control-oriented SBOs represent a decision context in which the emphasis of the office is on controlling agency spending and not on the governor's policy agenda. Policy is thus the primary orientation of most of the Midwest SBOs. Let us explore these orientations more carefully, beginning with ILSBO, which exhibits a strong control orientation.

Control Orientation

Illinois. Illinois's distinct control orientation is an interesting case. While it has previously enjoyed a national reputation as a strong policy-oriented office, it was definitely a control-oriented office when we interviewed examiners in 1994. Examiners in the Illinois budget office (ILSBO) were most likely to view their function as one of controlling agencies and serving as technical number crunches. It is something of a paradox, since the ILSBO examiners are not civil servants and technically are housed within the Office of the Governor. The ILSBO examiners repeatedly spoke of their lack of policy input into budget decisions and their isolation from the governor's policy development. To the extent that they were involved in program or policy analyses, communications with the governor's policy staff were highly formalized and strictly channeled through the "front office" (budget director) and the division managers (first line supervisors). ILSBO examiners were not only isolated from the politics of budget issues, they rarely were given enough of the "big picture" to have a policy context in which they could evaluate a department's request for alignment with the governor's priorities.

The budget director stated that she wanted to develop the budget in cooperation with the agencies. She wanted the agency budget "agreement" concluded at the lowest level of the budget office, that is, with the examiner. Consequently, she wanted the examiner to know the agency as well as the agency director so he/she would be able to understand what the agency "needs" and what it "must have." There was a discussion process that was often characterized as "negotiations with the agency" between the examiner, the ILSBO section manager, and agency fiscal staff. Yet the examiner rarely had contact with an agency head. Such contact might occur only when the examiner, section manager, and agency fiscal staff met as staff for a "minisummit" of the ILSBO director and the agency head to finalize the agency budget.

The minisummit was the point at which the agency budget must be settled for inclusion in the governor's budget. Most issues in the agency budget should have been resolved at this stage, but some issues may remain. The issue was what the level of the agency budget would be, and this was driven by the components that cumulate to "the number." The agency argues that this item should be included or that program should be expanded, with the resultant "number." The examiner may agree or disagree with the components and thus "the number"; the goal of the process was to agree on "the number." There was no explicit decision request list that was reviewed by the examiner and upon which the examiner makes a recommendation. Yet there was a high degree of line control in ILSBO budgeting, and the examiner could argue against charges to a line for specific items, such as more personal computers in the electronic data processing line or new furniture in the property line. The examiners also tracked expenditures by line and needed to consent to transfers between lines (up to 2 percent). While vetoes of transfers were apparently rare, the threat was there and the agencies knew it.

The office had lost positions in recent years (fifteen full-time equivalents) as its share of the governor's campaign to reduce the number of state employees. The consequence for the office was greatly increased workloads and a focus on the technical aspects of budgeting, with little time and no encouragement from the "front office" to take a greater role in policy analyses related to their assigned agencies and programs. The budget director wanted to develop performance measures for agency programs as a way to increase the degree to which state programs were subject to policy analysis. Yet the examiners saw this as increased technical workloads rather than increased policy analysis.

Weak Policy Model

Several Midwest states were in transition, decidedly moving away from a control orientation toward a policy orientation. Some states were evolving more quickly than others, with weaker and stronger policy emphases reflecting the degree of transition. The evidence from these states indicates that the relatively unfettered flow of information between the examiners and the governor's policy staff is essential to well-grounded and well-rounded budget analysis, even as both groups recognize each other's unique perspectives.

Minnesota. The MNSBO was still working through the transition from a control to a policy orientation that Gosling reported in 1987. Although a majority of the examiners report that policy analysis was one of the primary roles of the office, seasoned veterans on the staff tend to maintain a control orientation and do not hesitate to characterize their examiner role as "antagonist" at times. There have been several Minnesota budget directors since the reorientation to policy analysis began in the mid-1980s. Each of them had maintained the momentum to ease the office out of its role of controlling agencies, including reassigning examiners to conduct policy as well as fiscal analyses of their agency budgets and programs. Intrinsic to the reorientation efforts was a title change for examiners, from "budget controllers" to "executive budget officers" (EBOs). As one veteran examiner explained, controllers "thought less of governor's policy. . . . That was up at a higher level. Policy didn't quite get down to the controller level. You carried out policy but you weren't forming policy. Today there's a lot more forming policy."

Veteran examiners have seen the very nature of the examiners' job change. According to one:

> I would say back in those days, it was probably more important to know state operations than it was to have budget analysis skills. If an agency

> needed to know about the computer statewide operation for payroll, you
> were expected to be knowledgeable about that. . . . If you go back probably
> the last four years they were hiring a lot of [new examiners] out of the
> Humphrey Institute, strictly for budget analysis. They didn't care what they
> knew about agency operations. They were strictly analytical experts.

Yet the orientation of the office was unclear to new examiners: "My read
of the agency is that we haven't clearly defined that role, that there's some
people at the EBO level who are there just because of the policy orientation
and that's all they want to do. There are others who are much more into
accounting and financial structure side. At the senior level there's sort of
mixed signals as to whether we're policy oriented or process oriented. When
you put those all together, I'd say it's unclear."

The budget director argued that the examiners' assignments in the office
reflected their strengths; some were more process oriented while others were
good policy analysts. The budget director agreed with her staff that the examiners were delegated a great deal of budget decision authority, with the
director and her immediate assistants focusing on the larger issues that interest the governor. As one examiner noted, when "the governor is distant, we're
pretty much free to put the budget together ourselves. We work with one of
his staff."

Despite the fact that the examiners rarely briefed the governor directly on
budget issues, there was a constant flow of information between the governor's
staff and the budget office staff. The lines of communication need not flow
through the budget director and section managers, although they were kept
apprised of events from both the governor's staff and their own. The Minnesota office was still searching for the right control-policy "balance," as one
experienced examiner put it. Most would agree it may take a few more years.

Missouri. The Missouri budget office (MOSBO) has been moving away from
a control orientation toward a stronger policy orientation in recent years.
There were still "old control laws" to be administered, but the budget office
had tried to keep from using its legal stick in favor of helping the departments find alternative ways to accomplish the same ends. The governor's
policy staff had a direct line to the budget staff, and the budget director did
not act as a political screen. The Missouri budget director wanted examiners
to understand that the budget operates in a political environment, that when
they make a recommendation, it has political implications, and they must be
able to make their case within that context. In his view, if the examiner is to
be an effective advocate for a department's needs, she or he needs to anticipate the reaction of the audience (the budget director, governor, or policy

staff) and take that into account in their presentation. They should not hesitate to strongly present their case, but it might be prefaced with "I know you have been inclined to alternative A, but here's why I think you should consider alternative B."

The policy orientation was stronger in some examiners than others, depending upon their assignments and tenure. Quite a few said, "I work for the governor," while some would *never* work for the governor because "the governor is political" and they were not, and they instead work for the budget office, and the budget office works for the governor. A few said they work for the departments or they work for the taxpayers. This did not surprise the budget director; the office was in a transition toward a stronger policy role, and an orientation toward trying to be more cooperative and helpful to departments. It would take time before all the examiners were comfortable with the new orientation.

Strong Policy Model

By far, the most policy-oriented offices in the midwestern states of our study were Iowa, Kansas, and Wisconsin. Examiners in Kansas and Wisconsin enjoyed a very direct relationship to the governor that allowed them a certain independence and proactive approach to budget recommendation strategies. They briefed the governor on major budget items in their agencies and felt a closer tie to the governor and his or her policies. The Iowa examiners rarely, if ever, briefed the governor personally, yet they provided a comprehensive array of policy services to the governor.

Wisconsin. The WISBO had a clear policy orientation because that is what the governor really wanted out of the budget office, according to the budget director. There was some aspect of controlling in the budget process, especially when it came to denying perennial requests by agencies to increase the number of positions. But that controlling discussion, he argued, was relevant in the policy context of the request: Is this something the state should be doing? And, if so, should it be doing it the way the agency is suggesting? Some departments had more policy content in their budgets than others (K-12 education versus banking regulation), but policy was the overriding concern of the Wisconsin budget office.

Examiners engaged in a relatively unchanneled and unrestricted flow of policy discussions in the Wisconsin office. The WISBO budget director encouraged a close working relationship between the governor's policy staff and the budget office counterparts. They have different perspectives, he noted, but neither can do their job well without knowing what the other is thinking.

The governor's policy staff is more political and less detailed than the budget staff, for example. Yet, the examiners need to "factor in" the governor's policy "orientation" without letting it overwhelm their analyses. If the governor is inclined toward one alternative and the examiner disagrees, he or she must be prepared to say, "I think this is a bad idea," and then explain why. The governor wanted to hear the arguments on most issues. The budget director's job was to ensure that the examiner's analyses include alternatives that interest the governor.

WISBO examiners understood the subtlety required in discerning the governor's priorities and orientation. One examiner noted that keeping track of the governor's views is a constant process:

> You just kind of keep feelers out all the time. What is the feedback you're getting from the decisionmakers? What are the things they seem interested in? What do they bring up at meetings? And just file those away either literally or mentally to go back to periodically and say: What can we do here as we do the budget bills, as separate legislation comes through? Does this address our priorities? Is this doing something bad to their priority items?

Wisconsin's policy orientation is long-standing, dating from the mid-1960s when it adopted and adapted PPB for state budgeting (Axelrod 1995). There were no signs that the Wisconsin idea of budgeting was changing anytime soon.

Kansas. The KSBO had evolved from a control orientation to a management and policy orientation. The trend was instituted with a change in budget directors in the early 1980s, and the transition was promoted by subsequent governors of both political parties. The budget director noted that the examiners exercised very little control over daily management activities within agencies. Most agencies had a single appropriation and most were permitted to transfer among major line items as necessary. The evolution from a control to a policy orientation had also resulted in a significant turnover in examiners. Only one member of the analytical staff had been in the office before the evolution began more than ten years earlier.

The budget director promoted a constant flow of information between the governor's office and the budget office. These conversations were essential for examiners to conduct good analysis and make good budget recommendations for the governor. As the KSBO director explained: "I shouldn't be surprised by anything that they put in their analysis and none of it should be a surprise to the governor. That's called communication."

The KSBO examiners also stayed aware of the political aspects of their budget issues. Although these examiners personally briefed the governor on their budget recommendations, they were professional civil servants and, as such, keenly aware that they were not the governor's political staff. The examiners relied heavily on the director for political cues that identified the governor's priorities for the ensuing budget. Their charge from the director was to conduct analysis so they could make recommendations that were technically and managerially sound. Their emphasis was less on efficiency and more on effectiveness. The priority placed on effectiveness required them to understand the role of the agency and the rationale for its various programs and activities. At the same time, there was a prevailing sense that the budget staff works for the governor, even though the budget director was the boss. As a KSBO examiner noted:

> I don't see us as a control mechanism right now. I think that to an extent we are a bit of a management-oriented agency, and I think that we do assist in policy development and implementation. Not direct-line authority in that the governor doesn't come down to the director and say, "You will tell all the agencies to do this." It's not that sort of thing. But we help to implement policies through our discussions with the agencies and the development of the budgets and focusing the efforts of the agencies and their budgets toward particular areas or away from particular areas. . . .
>
> The agency is continually asking for advice. When they are thinking of proposing something, they'll call and say, we were looking at this sort of a thing, what do you think? That gives us the opening if the word has come to us that we are to discourage or encourage something or another, that gives us the opportunity to indicate that a particular program at this point in time could be very difficult to achieve, or that the likelihood of getting money for a new program that would add staff to the state would not be likely to receive any money. Those sorts of things, to kind of either discourage something or encourage it. That's usually the opening. It's usually initiated with the agency. They are looking for some direction and that's the opportunity for us to do that.

It is interesting that no examiner from this SBO indicates a planning orientation. Rather than evolve sequentially from control to management to planning to policy, this budget office seems to skip over planning altogether. That is, examiners leave strategic planning and direction to others (the governor). However, these examiners provide crucial support for advancing an overall "scheme," that is, the governor's agenda, through their discouragement and encouragement to agencies.

Iowa. One of the most striking findings of our field study was how much the Iowa SBO (IASBO) had changed its orientation in recent years. Gosling's (1987) study of the office in the mid-1980s revealed an office with a strong control orientation. The Iowa Department of Management (DOM), like many of its counterparts in other states, is a very powerful department in the state, especially since it houses the state budget office. It can play "the heavy" when it comes to controlling state agencies, and in the past it had played the role well.

The budget office transformation had been part of an overhaul of budgeting in Iowa. In the previous few years, there had been a concerted and sustained effort to change the atmosphere surrounding the budget process in a way that had also transformed the examiners' relationships with their agencies as well. Whereas previously they saw themselves as agency antagonists fulfilling the DOM's controlling mission, now a majority of the examiners considered their role to be advocates for agency needs, fulfilling the new DOM mission of acting as a facilitator in the budget process.

The result was a greater sharing of information flowing up and down the tiers of government, and a "realistic" array of budget requests from departments. As one of the more experienced examiners noted, the environment and process changes had given examiners a new sense of "ownership" of many of the budget requests that arrive on their desks: "And so from the sense that what they put together is doable or reasonable . . . it's easier to support."

Part of the facilitating function was being more closely tuned to the governor's priorities, something that had been elusive in the past, when information flows were more restrictive. A veteran of the office noted:

> I try and think about how the governor's going to respond to a particular recommendation, try and think of how the public would respond to a certain recommendation if the governor were to include that in his budget. . . . If there's an issue that I don't feel real strongly about, that I think the governor's just going to say "no" to, most of the time I won't recommend it. . . . On the other hand, there have been times that even though I knew the governor or budget director would not agree with it, I made that recommendation to the governor and [successfully] backed it up with the reasons why I felt it shouldn't be done that way.

The same pair of statements could be heard from many of the examiners, and there were many indicators that the transition under way in Iowa was headed toward an even stronger policy and "facilitating" direction.

Southern States

As noted in the introductory chapter, in some cases not all questions were asked of examiners in every interview, usually because of the natural flow of discussion on the part of those interviewed, or given the time constraints. Specific to the southern states, examiners were asked the first two parts of question 21; however, only the deputy director or budget director was asked directly about the orientation of the budget office. Thus, to provide comparable data regarding budget office orientations of the southern states with those of the Midwest, a content analysis of responses to questions 21 and 22, as well as questions 10 through 17, of the interview protocol was conducted of each examiner's transcript. The first two parts of question 21 ask examiners if they feel that they influence state spending, and then state policy, usually with a follow-up if the response was affirmative of "In what way?" Question 22 asks about important qualities that an examiner should have in order to be successful working in their SBO. Questions 10 through 17 regard examiners' relationships with other budget players in their state's budget process when involved in activities related to putting together agency budget recommendations. Responses to this series of questions provide many opportunities for examiners to outline how they approach their work, the factors most important to them when assessing agency requests, their consideration of other budget players in their budget process, as well as their interpretation of their SBO's orientation and their specific role in the budget process.

The content analysis of transcripts from the southern states therefore involved looking for words and comments by examiners of their activities regarding typical control functions, like checking expenditure reports, in addition to looking for their mention of the word "control" as an important function of their work. Examiners were scored as expressing a management orientation when they relayed as part of their activities involvement with agency and program operations, personnel, and administration. Any discussion of planning, multiyear assessment, and tactical activities was coded as planning, and examiners who noted that development or influence of policy and/or those who mentioned substantive policy analysis and/or its promotion as part of their work were coded as having a policy orientation.

Table 5.2 illustrates that the SBOs in southern states fall along a continuum of orientations like the midwestern states, from a classic control function to an active policy function. Overall however, the southern states are quite distinct from those of the Midwest. For example, the control function reigns as a primary orientation of these offices (73 percent of total responses indicate this orientation), with policy occupying secondary status (40 percent of total responses). The control orientation is the modal category for Alabama and South Carolina, and almost bimodal with a policy orientation in Georgia and Virginia. Modal orientation for North Carolina is management, perhaps explained in part by the state's attention to program budgeting in the past. Interestingly, the management function remains quite strong in these SBOs with 37 percent of total responses indicating this orientation. This may be due to governors' renewed emphasis on department-level performance accountability, given the trend of performance-based budgeting reforms initiated in most states during the early to mid-1990s (Melkers and Willoughby 1998). While the control and policy orientations "trade places" between SBOs in the Midwest and South, and the management orientation is much stronger in the southern SBOs, results in Table 5.2 show that the planning function is slightly less important to most of the SBOs examined in the South. Except for Georgia's SBO, planning is not a significant function of the budget offices in the South.

Figure 5.2 provides the schematic presentation of the different orientations of the southern budget offices, based on the distribution of responses of the seventy-three budget staff. The background and representations are defined the same as those illustrated earlier in Figure 5.1 that represent the orientations of SBOs in the Midwest. Again, the ovals have been drawn roughly proportional to the orientations indicated by respondents. The Virginia and Alabama ovals are shaded to highlight differences noted below.

It is interesting to compare features of these orientation patterns with those of the Midwest SBOs. First, most of the southern SBOs studied here have not "evolved" into a policy orientation, although Virginia and Georgia come closest to a policy and control orientation illustrated earlier by Wisconsin and Iowa, respectively. In the southern SBOs, unlike those examined in the Midwest, the control orientation remains strong, although all budget offices except Alabama do reach into the policy quadrant, some significantly more than others. Also, these patterns illustrate that a management orientation figures more prominently in budget offices in the South as compared to those in the Midwest. Overall, Figure 5.2 seems to represent the process of budget office orientation evolution (at least in the South) by illustrating states that have made little, if any, change from a strictly control orientation to those that have evolved, albeit however partially, into a policy orientation. Unlike the conclusion drawn regarding Midwest SBOs where policy is the primary orientation, there is not a primary orientation that can be generally ascribed to these southern SBOs. We now explore the orientations of the southern SBOs more carefully, beginning with Alabama and South Carolina, the SBOs in this region with strong control orientations.

Table 5.2

Distribution of Orientation Responses in Southern State Budget Offices

SBO Orientations	Alabama	Georgia	North Carolina	South Carolina	Virginia	Unique Responses	Total Responses
Numbers of responses (n = 120)							
Control	8	13	6	13	14	18	54
Management	3	7	8	4	5	3	27
Planning	0	9	2	0	1	1	12
Policy	0	11	3	1	15	4	30
Total responses	11	40	19	18	35	26	123
SBO staff (n = 73)	8	18	12	14	21		
As a percentage of SBO staff (n = 73)							
Control	100	71	46	93	67		44
Management	38	41	62	29	23		22
Planning	0	47	15	0	5		10
Policy	0	59	23	7	71		24
Total responses	100	100	100	100	100		100

Note: All percentages have been rounded up.

Figure 5.2   **A Schematic Presentation of SBO Orientation Patterns in Five Southern States**

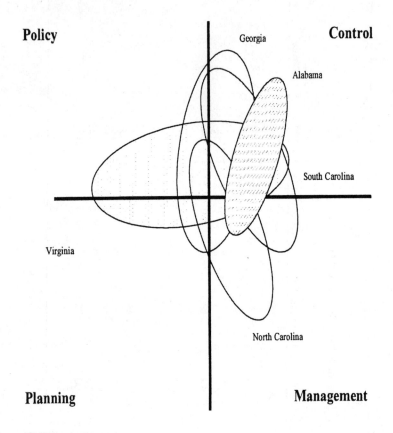

Control Orientation

Forsythe's remark regarding underutilization of the policy capacity of budget offices may be on target regarding Alabama and South Carolina as well as Illinois, all states that have a distinct control orientation. The low allegiance to the governor and his policy priorities is understandable, given the isolation of the budget staff from the policy process.

Alabama. Examiners in Alabama's Executive Budget Office (ALSBO) were inhibited by legislation, management, and lack of revenues in their ability to break out of a traditional control and management orientation. Most examiners considered budget execution to be a primary day-to-day activity. One examiner pointed out that "the Budget Management Act spells out what we are to do, just administer the budget once it is passed. We are not so much involved in recommendations." Another described somewhat of a regression in the role of the examiner in the ALSBO: "We used to do a tremendous amount of legislation analysis. Now, we are back to administration and what the governor wants."

No examiner from this office heard about gubernatorial priorities directly from the governor. One examiner emphasized, "We don't have that much contact with the finance director. We don't have any contact with the governor." At the time of the study, the governor communicated a broad framework of budget priorities to the finance director, who filtered them down to the state budget officer, who then communicated directly with examiners. Agency heads meet separately with the finance director to discuss spending requests. Examiners said that recent leadership changes (a new budget director and a new head of the Department of Finance) made information difficult both to receive and interpret.

Interestingly, the newly placed budget director expressed the desire to push examiners beyond the simple, yet historical accounting orientation. According to the budget director:

> The mindset of the staff is not what I want it to be. We are operating under a budget law of 1975 with a focus on compliance, and not recognizing what I call budget analysis. The program budget in law is not in reality. The budget request is built from line item by program. The law affords immense flexibility to agencies.

Examiners concurred with the director, acknowledging that he "would like us to do more, get more involved. Traditionally, however, we haven't had the staff to be so involved." The office had lost several positions in recent years, and at the time of the study, examiners in shifts were completing the duties of a full-time clerical position. It is hard to analyze policy if you are answering the telephones.

South Carolina. The South Carolina budget office (SCSBO) was in transition as part of a major reorganization of state government. Legislation from the 1993 session established a cabinet form of government, the first executive budget in the state's history, limits on new revenue, and a year-end surplus fund. The reorganization was expected to radically change the relationship between the governor and the examiners who historically had been located in the Budget and Control Board (BCB), a joint body of legislative and executive branch officials, including the governor. Beginning the following year, the governor sent out the budget call information that the

BCB used to send out to agencies. Examiners were now providing spending recommendations to the governor's staff. One examiner suggested, "With reorganization, we have greater accountability as we serve at the pleasure of the governor."

Like the ALSBO examiners, none from SCSBO claimed to receive information directly from the governor about his priorities. Rather, they were likely to receive information from their section manager about budget priorities as relayed from the governor's staff. The governor still consulted with the comptroller general and the treasurer for information in developing a budget proposal.

It is instructive, however, that these examiners portrayed themselves as more policy oriented than did those in Alabama or Illinois. Examiners influenced spending by making recommendations that affected funding. "An examiner must identify a problem area, develop solutions, and explore options available to agencies," claimed one. The important point is that most emphasized their role as a conduit of information among numerous players in the budget process. One examiner summarized the role of examiners within this office as "logistic rather than activist." For example, one examiner claimed, "Analysts [in our office] influence state spending by providing support to the governor and legislative staff." While their divided allegiance was not surprising, given the location of the office within the BCB, these examiners anticipated some transition in orientation, given the newly implemented executive budget system.

Transition (Weak Policy) Model

North Carolina. Examiners in North Carolina's Office of State Budget and Management (NCSBO) expressed a much clearer interpretation of their governor's agenda and their role than either ALSBO or SCSBO examiners. According to one, "you have to know what kinds of things the governor is looking for." Examiners in this state commonly received their information about the governor's priorities indirectly from the senior deputy state budget officer, a thirty-year veteran of the budget office. The comfort level of these examiners in terms of their understanding and interpretation of the governor's priorities was due in part to the longevity of most examiners within the office (average years of service in this office was approximately nineteen years, the highest among the states) and to the fact that the current governor had returned to serve a third term as governor, having served two consecutive terms from 1977 to 1985. The stability from this routine enhanced information flows: "Our senior deputy state budget officer meets with the administration and they let us know," acknowledged one examiner.

Budget analysis in North Carolina oscillates between a continuation budget (in odd years) and an expansion budget (in even years). Some examiners explained that the difference between the two budgets (and subsequently in examiners' preparation and deliberation of each type) lay in accounting decisions (for continuation budgets) versus programmatic or policy decisions (for expansion budgets). That is not to say, however, that the governor's wishes were irrelevant during development of the continuation budget. As one examiner warned, "Even with revenue growth, you may have to go back and cut continuation, depending on the governor's agenda."

Expansion budget items, along with salary increases and capital items, were funded with money left over once the continuation budget had been fully funded. The governor identifies no more than ten expansion budget priorities, and departments also present requests for priority items. The examiners analyze and develop options for department items that have merit and discuss them with their section supervisors. Then the supervisors meet with the senior deputy state budget officer and together they develop an overall budget package. While examiners' recommendations for continuation budgets may "sail through" the legislature, the decisions about the expansion budgets "are made higher up." In general, however, NCSBO examiners seemed at ease with the role they played. Claimed one, "The analyst provides objectivity to the governor, helping in his development and execution of the budget."

Although the policy role of this office was not as strong as in other states, examiner activities went beyond a strict control function. In part, the policy "weakness" of this office can be related to the weakness of the governor vis-à-vis the legislature, since the governor does not have a veto power. The transition in the NCSBO was supported by internal office changes. Several very long-term examiners were on the verge of retiring from the SBO, opening up the possibility for bringing in new examiners with a policy orientation. The senior deputy state budget officer also explained that the office was implementing a team approach in which examiners would work across sections to gain expertise in more than one policy area.

Strong Policy Model

By far, the most policy-oriented offices in the southern states are Georgia and Virginia. Examiners in Georgia enjoyed a very direct relationship to the governor that allowed them a certain independence and proactive approach to budget recommendation strategies. They may brief the governor on major budget items in their agencies and feel a close tie to the governor and his or her policies. The Virginia examiners rarely, if ever, brief the governor in person, yet they provide a comprehensive array of policy services to the governor.

Georgia. Of the southern states we surveyed, Georgia's Office of Planning and Budget (GASBO) houses some of the most policy-oriented examiners. When asked, "To the extent that you make recommendations, do you anticipate reaction to your recommendation from the governor?" one representative examiner responded,

> You find an angle and try to make the governor see it. You have to develop a tactic, a strategic plan. The governor is very vocal. He is much more willing to get in the nitty gritty with questions about programs than the previous one.

GASBO examiners may have had a stronger policy orientation than those in the other southern states studied because of the direct relationship they maintained with the governor. When asked how they gained a sense of his budget priorities, one examiner casually said, "I pick up some when I meet with the governor." Another elaborated, "The governor's priorities come through in speeches, meetings, sometimes the media, press releases, and through the director of OPB." Other avenues that examiners mentioned for learning of gubernatorial priorities included the governor's platform (published quarterly) via the deputy budget director or section managers.

Much like examiners in North Carolina, Georgia's examiners recognized a distinction between their development of continuation and improvement budgets. Stated an examiner, "For continuation, I provide recommendations. For improvements, I present options and show benefits and cons of all options."

And, similar to NCSBO examiners, these examiners did not seem concerned about the bifurcated nature of their job, at once analytical and political. On the one hand, the examiner must be objective. "It's not good to be seen as too subjective. You have a piece and you need to show how it fits into the big picture," claimed an examiner. Said another, "The analyst should be neutral. Justify the need and I will support it." Alternatively, examiners recognized their allegiance to the governor. One examiner explained that "our job is to get money for the governor. The agency's job is to get money for themselves."

Most of the GASBO examiners embraced a balanced role between policy activist and program examiner. As one examiner warned, "You must be prepared to make your case. You must make a good case for new spending or know that the governor likes it." Georgia's examiners portrayed budgeting as an art: "The job is not only crunching numbers. It involves looking at policy and the organizational and financial consequences of policy. It is gratifying to know that you were there at the start and pushed it forward to program start."

Virginia. Examiners in Virginia's Department of Planning and Budget (VASBO) had a clear sense of their mission and the priorities of their governor. Their role was to see that the governor's policies were implemented. As one examiner explained, "We serve the governor and his agenda." To fulfill that mission, examiners "have to learn how to budget within the governor's agenda and limited funds, accounting for mandates and compliance items." One examiner stated that, "to his credit, this governor has made his agenda clear." Examiners in this state usually received information about gubernatorial priorities from "guidance memoranda" or from the budget director via section managers. Different from the GASBO examiner, no VASBO examiners claimed to receive information directly from the governor.

On the other hand, like their Georgia counterparts, Virginia's examiners had a clear sense of their strength and influence. "Collectively, analysts make a difference in state policy and spending because we shape decisions, alternatives, and choices," claimed one. Much of their influence can be attributed to the wide array of services they provided the governor. The budget office operated as "a one-stop shop. We do legislative impact, executive legislation, fiscal legislation, review regulation, budget execution and control, and budget development." The breadth of activities that examiners were involved in speaks to the analytical abilities necessary to conduct duties effectively.

These examiners also portrayed budgeting as an art. According to one examiner, "I like the creativity and innovative aspects of the job, the politics. To see how something is going to play. Getting something through the legislature is an art." Another offered, "I like reading about the impact of my recommendation the next day in the paper. Examiners [in this office] can be more proactive and influence state policy." The policy orientation of the office was strong, despite the fact that the examiners did not brief the governor directly; nor did it seem to have been affected by the loss of several examiner positions over the past few years.

Policy Distances in State Budgeting

Our research about the policy roles in the eleven state budget offices that we visited suggests a wide range of SBO *policy distances* across these states. The policy distance between SBO examiners and a governor is a fruitful device for characterizing the decision context in which these examiners conduct state budgeting. We now turn our attention to several factors that contribute to policy distance and thus influence the decision context of SBOs.

Several factors may affect the policy distance between the examiners and their governor. The distance may be a function of the degree to which examiners personally brief the governor on their budget recommendations, and their professional and educational backgrounds. The policy distance, in turn, may also influence the degree to which the examiners anticipate the reactions of their budget director to their budget recommendations, and the degree to which examiner recommendations are accepted by the budget director and governor.

Policy Consonance and Priorities

A governor's policy function is not clearly delineated within his staff in most states, partly because the natural or inherent blending of politics and policy means policy staff is largely political staff. Governors also may rely on department heads for policy preparation. The National Governors Association (as cited in Ransone 1982, 113) notes the need for a "perspective keeper" to keep the governor from being isolated by a "yes men" staff. The "perspective keeper" can be a spouse, a friend, or "others who are not seeking any public office or further political advancement."

This role can be filled by SBO staff with respect to budget and policy issues. This closely fits the self-identified role of WISBO and other examiners in policy-oriented SBOs. They were not afraid to "tell it like it is," even if the governor is out front on an issue with a questionable "policy" position. A senior WISBO examiner explains:

> There can be areas where one would disagree with the position one thinks the governor is moving in, on policy and technical grounds. So it's not a personal, it's not like I'm, deep in my soul, I'm pro choice or pro life, if we take the abortion issue, or whatever. But there's certain issues on policy grounds that one thinks the governor is perhaps heading down a path that's not the best path. And in briefings with the governor you make the best arguments, say, here's what I think the weaknesses are.
>
> If the governor says, "I think you've got a good point, we're going to modify it," great. If the governor says, "No, we're still going to do it my way," at least I think we presented him the best information. And we're in an enviable position in that regard because the governor's staff are beholden, and this is regardless of the administration, are beholden to the governor. They're his appointees, so I think they have to operate a little more cautiously.

> I think we're in a position, being civil servants, and also having a longer view, there's sort of a history in the budget office, that there's always people around that have twenty years' experience here, that we're in the position that we can tell the governor things that perhaps his own staff would be reluctant to say.
>
> We can take it. If the governor would tell one of us we're dead wrong and we don't understand the politics of the situation, that's fine because it doesn't affect our careers that much. So I think we're in a good position, that we can be more truthful with the governor and I think that that puts us in a good position.

Still, examiners in a policy-oriented SBO usually are sensitive and responsive to the governor's policy direction and are criticized only infrequently for making recommendations that are unpopular with the governor. In the end, examiners in policy-oriented SBOs are not free to navigate the policy-budget nexus based solely on their own attitudes and values. Instead, they analyze the multitude of budget requests they receive with a gubernatorial imperative: the final budget and policy decisions must be consonant with the governor's policies and priorities. The sensitive judgment required of policy-oriented examiners incorporates the budgetary politics of the issue, even while maintaining standards of neutral competence. "One must have the discernment to avoid stretching a good principle to its breaking point," advises Paul Veillette (1981, 67).

Working for the Governor

There is a stark contrast in the briefing practices between the states, as seen in Table 5.3. In Wisconsin, Kansas, and Georgia, nearly all of the staff (examiners and section managers) brief the governor often. The practice is less frequent in Iowa and Missouri, although 77 percent and 71 percent (respectively) brief the governor often or sometimes. The other six states present nearly the opposite case. Even the section managers rarely brief the governor. Typically they are meeting with the governors' policy staffs. Contacts with the governor in these states are limited to the budget director and "front office" staff. We note that three of the six are control-oriented SBOs, and only VASBO is characterized as a strong policy state. Viewed another way, none of the control-oriented SBOs have the practice of using budget examiners to brief the governor.

Interviews with the staff in the Wisconsin budget office reveal that briefing the governor is a key ingredient to ensure that examiners know the governor's viewpoints. Briefing the governor is part of learning the ropes in

Table 5.3

Frequency of Gubernatorial Briefings by State

Frequency of Governor's Briefings	State											
	GA	WI	KS	IA	MO	IL	SC	NC	MN	VA	AL	Total
None		1*	1*		3	22	12	9	11	16	4	79
% within state		5.6	7.7		23.1	81.5	92.3	81.8	78.6	76.2	57.1	49.1
Rarely				2		2	1	1	2	5	3	16
% within state				28.6		7.4	7.7	9.1	14.3	23.8	42.9	9.9
Sometimes				2	6	2		1	1			12
% within state				28.6	46.2	7.4		9.1	7.1			7.5
Often	17	17	12	3	4	1						54
% within state	100	94.4	92.3	42.9	30.8	3.7						33.5
Total	17	18	13	7	13	27	13	11	14	21	7	161
% within state	100	100	100	100	100	100	100	100	100	100	100	100
Examiner N	17	18	16	9	14	27	13	11	18	21	7	171

*The KSBO and WISBO examiners who had no briefing experience had just been hired. Both expected they soon would brief their governor.

the budget office. It is how examiners learn the governor's parameters, and then how they learn to develop well-thought-out options within those parameters. The budget director encouraged new examiners to sit through other briefings with the governor because it is to their "benefit to sit there and listen to the rest of the analysts brief. That's how you help get a feel."

The Wisconsin staff was quite clear about their partisan political neutrality and their distinction from the governor's partisan policy staff. Yet they valued the frequent interactions with the governor in various briefings and meetings because it kept them informed of his policies and priorities. At the same time, they were comfortable enough in their relationship with the governor to present arguments that they "knew" he might not agree with. That is their job, and they were strongly encouraged to present their independent and objective analyses of their assigned agencies and issues.

The Iowa and Missouri experiences with briefing the governors were much weaker, depending upon the governor. Although the current governors had more frequent interactions with the examiners, previous governors in both states had secluded themselves from the budget staff, preferring that examiners brief the governor's chief of staff instead. Although they currently attended the budget briefings and the monthly progress meetings, the Iowa and Missouri examiners were less often participants and more likely observers. During the final stages of the budget cycle, the usual practice in Iowa was for the budget director and the director of management to present the budget office recommendations to the governor, and the examiners attended the briefing to answer detailed questions. Certain examiners, especially senior staff, sometimes personally briefed the governor. The Missouri examiners spoke in terms of the governor's "office" and not the "governor." As in Iowa, they sat in the budget briefing meetings with the governor, but tended to act as information specialists for the discussions, participating when specific or technical information was required.

MOSBO examiners' investment in the meetings was much smaller than their Wisconsin counterparts. They were prepared to answer questions, and sometimes would make a presentation, but that was the exception rather than the rule. Still, this contact allowed them to listen to the governor express his views and concerns, and observe the politics of his inner circle. It gave them a foundation and context for their negotiations with their assigned agencies. This description from a MOSBO examiner is typical of both Missouri and Iowa:

> It just went like, "Well, Robert, you prepared this memo, I'm going up at 1 o'clock, why don't you come up in case there's any questions." I was very glad to see that, because I had no problem taking responsibility for my

work, but it also gave me the option. The governor's chief of staff or someone else said, "Well, what if we do this?" I had already looked at that
option and we could tell them immediately instead of spending three days
going back and forth trying to set up meetings.

Finding out the governor's position on an issue was more difficult for
examiners in other states, due in part to the absence of personal contact with
the current governor. Although located in the Office of the Governor, the
Illinois staff surprisingly was far removed from the governor's briefings.
They saw the governor personally only when he stopped by the office to
thank them for their budget work after the budget was passed. A former
ILSBO examiner (now working in a different SBO) described the weakness
of this system:

> The problem I saw in the Illinois Budget Office is the analyst who was
> supposed to be monitoring the legislation and tracking it had no im-
> pact or recommendations they could make to people of importance. I
> would brief my division director, who would brief the deputy director,
> who would talk to the budget director, who might talk to the governor's
> senior staff on whether they should do something. It became very frus-
> trating at times because you've done the analysis, you've prepared
> this, but you're not there, you don't hear the context in which the ques-
> tions are asked. So a lot of times I think there's miscommunications as
> you go up and down that chain. . . . Unless things have changed in the
> last two years, that's where Illinois is kind of inefficient. They've got
> some communications going up and down the ladder.

This point reemphasizes the control orientation of ILSBO and its examiners; they were most likely to view their function as one of controlling
agencies and serving as technical number crunchers. The ILSBO examiners
repeatedly spoke of their lack of policy input into budget decisions and their
isolation from the governor's policy development. As might be expected
from a strong control orientation, there was a high degree of line control in
ILSBO budgeting. The examiner could argue against charges to a line and
needed to consent to transfers between lines. While vetoes of transfers were
apparently rare, the "threat is there and agencies know it." To the extent that
they were involved in program or policy analyses, communications with the
governor's policy staff were highly formalized and strictly channeled through
the "front office" (budget director) and the division chiefs (first line supervisors).

ILSBO examiners were not only isolated from the politics of budget issues, they rarely were given enough of the "big picture" to have a policy context in which they could evaluate a department's request for alignment with the governor's priorities. The policy distance between the governor and the examiners partly may reflect the political culture of Illinois, famous for the power of patronage in job selection and performance. Although the budget office is technically within the Office of the Governor, examiners seemed to gain their positions through merit competition, perhaps reflecting a desire to maintain a group of technical budget experts with "neutral competency."

The ALSBO examiners are at least as distant as ILSBO examiners from the governor and his policies, as evidenced by one examiner who claimed not to know the governor's policies, even after working under said governor for a year! As another ALSBO examiner explained, "I do not have any contact with the governor." She described how "mostly what we are expected to do is dictated to us through the budget officer. . . . During the budget hearings we have with the governor's office, it's just mainly probably directed more by the finance director. We don't, [and] I personally do not have, much contact with the finance director himself." The contrast between the WISBO examiners at one end, and the ALSBO and ILSBO examiners at the other end, points to the utility of examiner briefings as a means for giving the examiners insight into the governor's agenda and policy priorities. Governors who wish to infuse budget development with policy analysis may need to spend more time with the examiners, at a minimum having them in the room for policy discussions surrounding the budget decision agenda.

Nurturing a Policy Orientation

Examiners were asked to distinguish between their boss and whom they "work for." Such a distinction draws a line between organizational or personnel links versus allegiance. Presumably, examiners' indication of who they work for correlates with their relationship to the governor, be it distant or close. Table 5.4 presents the degree to which the examiners and section managers felt they "work for" the governor as opposed to "citizens" (or the state), their immediate supervisor, or the budget director. We see that there is significant variation in perceptions of whom the examiners work for. The states are ordered from left to right by the percentage who "work for" the governor. Working for the governor is the modal category in six of the eleven states. Of the remaining five states, Alabama, Illinois, and South Carolina are control-oriented states. "My supervisor" is the modal response for ILSBO and GASBO examiners, while the budget director is the modal response for Alabama and South Carolina examiners.

Table 5.4

For Whom Do You Work? By State, Only Examiners and Section Managers

	Virginia	Wisconsin	North Carolina	Iowa	Missouri	Kansas	Illinois	Georgia	South Carolina	Minnesota	Alabama	Total
Governor	11 65%	9 64%	4 57%	5 56%	7 50%	6 46%	9 35%	3 23%	2 17%	1 6%		57 38%
Finance director		3 30%		2 22.2%			2 9%			7 40%	1 14%	15 11%
Budget director	1 6%	1 7%		2 22%	4 29%	5 38%	4 15%	2 15%	7 58%	2 12%	5 71%	33 22%
My supervisor	2 12%		1 14%		2 14%		11 42%	6 46%	2 17%	4 24%	1 14%	29 19%
Citizens or the state	3 18%	1 7%	2 29%		1 7%	2 15%		2 15%	1 8%	3 18%		15 10%
Total	17 100%	14 100%	7 100%	9 100%	14 100%	13 100%	26 100%	13 100%	12 100%	17 100%	7 100%	149 100%

Note: Counts exclude budget directors and secretary of administration positions.

The utility of briefings in nurturing a policy orientation is supported by correlation analysis of examiners that indicates that frequency of gubernatorial briefings is positively correlated with a "work for" the governor affiliation (rho = 0.315) and a policy orientation of the budget office (rho = 0.437).[2] Working for the governor is also positively correlated with the policy orientation of the budget office (rho = 0.165).[3] Such correspondence of frequently briefing the governor, taking a policy-oriented approach to budgeting, and working for the governor achieves perhaps its greatest expression in the WISBO examiner who matter-of-factly stated, "I would say I work for the governor. I don't think there's really any other answer to that because truly we are here to be a tool for the governor. A tool meaning we assist the governor in developing his own positions and then help to explain those positions or present those positions once those decisions are made."

Table 5.5 presents the correspondence between the frequency of briefing the governor and a belief that the examiner works for the governor or someone else in the budgeting hierarchy. The top half of the table includes all budgeting staff who responded to the two questions, while the bottom half tallies only the responses for examiners.

In both parts of the table, there is definite correspondence between briefing frequency and affiliation with the governor. Of the forty-three staff who never brief the governor, only 21 percent feel they work for the governor. Of the forty-eight staff who brief the governor often, 54 percent feel they work for the governor. The pattern holds when we examine only the responses of the examiners as well. Viewing the table slightly differently, we observe that of the twenty-seven examiners who feel they work for the governor, 48 percent of them (13/27) *often* brief the governor. Moreover, of the twenty-two examiners who feel they work for their supervisor, 64 percent (14/22) *never* brief the governor.

Measured in terms of examiners' affiliation with the governor, the Minnesota and Alabama staffs had the most distant relationship. Only 6 percent of the Minnesota examiners—and none of the Alabama examiners—agreed that they "work for" the governor (as distinct from their boss, their immediate supervisor). A senior Minnesota examiner noted that the relationship with the governors had changed over time. Under a previous governor, "there were meetings over in the mansion, over in his office in the capitol, we were pretty much almost all on a first-name basis. We were there, we were expected to be the person that did the briefing, made the recommendation, go through the budget." But things were much different under the current governor:

> There used to be kind of this iteration where we'd work up our recommendations, we'd take them to our boss, we'd reach some agreement, then

Table 5.5

For Whom Do You Work? By Frequency of Governor's Briefings

All Budget Staff	None	Rarely	Sometimes	Often	Total
Governor	9	1	8	26	44
	21%	9%	73%	54%	38.9%
Finance/Adm	7		1	5	13
dept director	16%		9%	10%	11.5%
Budget director	9	6		9	24
	21%	55%		19%	21.2%
Supervisor	14	3	2	4	23
	33%	27%	18%	8%	20.4%
Citizens/State	4	1		4	9
	9%	9%		8%	8.0%
Total	43	11	11	48	113
	100%	100%	100%	100%	100%

Examiners Only	None	Rarely	Sometimes	Often	Total
Governor	9		5	13	27
	21%		63%	43%	32.1%
Finance/Adm	7		1	3	11
dept director	17%		13%	10%	13.1%
Budget director	8	2		6	16
	19%	50%		20%	19.0%
Supervisor	14	2	2	4	22
	33%	50%	25%	13%	26.2%
Citizens/State	4			4	8
	10%			13%	9.5%
Total	42	4	8	30	84
	100%	100%	100%	100%	100%

we'd go to the budget director and then from there to the commissioner, and when the commissioner agreed to them, then that's the finance position and we'd take the finance position to the governor. It just seems like in this case the governor is interested in some large issues but it just doesn't happen to be in my area. So he's sort of distant. So we're pretty much free to put the budget together ourselves. We work with one of his staff.

Similarly, an NCSBO examiner admitted that he "generally" knows "what kinds of things [the governor] is looking for and we have some broad idea of the kinds of things that are going to be looked at favorably. In some sense that helps us in our decision-making." NCSBO examiners find out what is on the governor's agenda through the budget director, when he meets "with the staff or the administrators" to "keep them abreast of the situation."

The GASBO experience does not conform to the general patterns developed here. While all the GASBO examiners consistently brief the governor on their budget recommendations, only 20 percent felt they worked for the governor, compared to 40 percent who worked for their immediate supervisor, their boss. One explanation is that the GASBO budget teams were very close-knit and examiners depended on the section manager to prepare them for the briefings with the governor. Although they had allegiance to the governor's policy agenda, they understood that their best chance of getting affirmation of their recommendations was by first working through or with the section manager. However, section managers played much the same role in other budget offices, such as in WISBO, without apparently weakening the affiliation with the governor. A second explanation for the weaker allegiance of the GASBO examiners to the governor is that they had a weaker sense of the GASBO as a policy-oriented SBO. Only 59 percent of the examiners saw the office as policy oriented, while 71 percent perceived a control orientation. More telling, perhaps, is that over 40 percent perceived a management orientation, which is focused more on agency problems and less on the governor's policy agenda.

This provides an interesting counterpoint to examiners in VASBO, who were policy oriented and had a well-developed understanding that they were tasked to support the governor's policy agenda as they crafted their budget recommendations. Yet VASBO stands apart from the other policy-oriented SBOs with respect to gubernatorial briefing practices, as very few examiners ever briefed the governor, and even then it was rarely. The VASBO and GASBO exceptions suggest there may be alternative methods of orienting examiners toward budget analysis with a view to the governor's priorities.

Affirmation Rates of Examiners

Table 5.6 presents the mean affirmation rates of examiner recommendations, as estimated by different supervisory levels. The states are ordered from left to right according to the budget directors' estimate of the percentage of examiner recommendations that are generally affirmed by the budget director during the budget development process. The estimates for the last three states (North Carolina, Virginia, and Alabama) are presented for information only, because they are based on so few observations, and because there is no confirmatory estimate by the budget directors in those states.[4] The ILSBO staff estimates are included in the table, although a confirmatory estimate from the budget director is missing due to interview time constraints. Estimates by budget directors range from 95 percent of examiner recommendations in Wisconsin to 87 percent of recommendations in Missouri. The estimates by the budget directors support the rather high estimates of the examiners themselves, which range from 91 percent in Kansas to 80 percent in Iowa.

Table 5.6

Mean Affirmation Rates by Supervisor Level

		Wisconsin	Kansas	Minnesota	Iowa	Georgia	Missouri	Illinois	North Carolina	Virginia	Alabama	Total
Examiner	Mean	90	91	87	80	90	84	79	100	95	90	86
	N	8	8	10	7	12	5	16	1	3	1	71
Section manager	Mean	90	91	63		90	93	76	95	90	85	85
	N	2	4	2		1	4	4	1	1	1	20
Budget director	Mean	95	90	90	88**	85	80					87
	N	1	1	1	2	1	1					6
Total	Mean	90	91	83	82	90	87	79	98	94	88	86
	N	11	13	13	9	14	10	20	2	4	2	98

Note: Some budget directors were not asked the question, given the time constraints. There are no SCSBO responses to this question.
**The IASBO value is the average of the Department of Management director and the budget director. IASBO has no manager level.
ANOVA F test for affirmation rates by states is significant ($p \leq 0.002$).

The WISBO budget director noted that the examiners' recommendations on minor policy issues (less than $0.5 million and one to two positions) were affirmed about 95 to 98 percent of the time in later stages of the process. The overall success rate is about 90 percent when major policy issues are included. On major policy issues such as school financing or property tax relief, the budget office will more often present a range of alternatives to the governor, but even then, the governor usually asks the examiner for a recommendation.

The lowest estimate of affirmation rates is given by the MNSBO section managers, who estimate as few as 63 percent of the examiners' recommendations were accepted by the budget director. The low average is influenced by the fact that only two of the section managers were responding to this question—one estimate of affirmation rate was 50 percent, another was 75 percent. Other estimates by section managers are consistent with those of the examiners and budget directors. The overall average for the examiners and their supervisors is 86 percent. This analysis supports earlier evidence that examiners have a substantial impact on the final shape of the budget.

The analysis of affirmation rates provides further evidence of how a closer relationship with the governor influences the perspectives (and perhaps decision-making) of budget examiners. Higher affirmation rates of examiner recommendations are positively correlated with more frequent briefings of the governor (rho = 0.233), and a policy-oriented SBO (rho = 0.326). Correlation analysis also suggests that examiners are less inclined to anticipate the budget director's and governor's reactions if they perceive they work for their supervisor instead of the governor (rho = 0.288) and are more inclined to anticipate the reactions of the budget director and governor when they brief the governor more frequently (rho = 0.394).[5]

The strongest policy orientations and roles seem related to the degree to which the examiners have a personal affiliation with the governor. The exception here is MNSBO, where the examiners identify the policy orientation in spite of little affiliation with the current governor. The senior staff recalled closer relationships with previous governors and the affirmation rates may have been higher in previous years, although we did not pursue that line of inquiry.

The KSBO interviews indicated that the high level of communication between the governor and the examiners resulted in a high level of the examiners' recommendations being affirmed by the budget director and the governor. The KSBO director estimated she affirmed as high as 100 percent of a seasoned examiner's recommendations.

> For the average analyst who's got some level of experience . . . I probably affirm a very, very high percentage, probably 85–90 percent, maybe even

higher than that. . . . [For] an older analyst who knows the agency really well, has worked with the governor, and has some perspective on the total picture of revenue and those types of things, the rate could be virtually 100 percent.

Most GASBO examiners claimed that their recommendations were usually approved by both the director and the governor (typically 90 percent of the time). While their approval level on improvements was sometimes drastically diminished (ranging from 25 to 80 percent of the time), examiners still felt they influenced policy and spending through their packaging and presentation of options. One examiner suggested that approval from above on improvement budgets depended on "how well you can sell a particular project."

In stark contrast, the ILSBO case illustrates the importance of the governor's affiliation with the examiners as a factor influencing their role perceptions. ILSBO examiners perceived a role substantially different from their Midwest counterparts in a context that harkens back to Schick's control orientation of the 1920s through the 1950s, and the OMB examiners under director Stockman in the early 1980s. Isolated from the governor and his policy development, they were conduits and technicians, unable to see the big picture the way their counterparts did in the other states. The lack of gubernatorial contact seemed to reinforce a resistance to a stronger alignment with the governor's policies and priorities.

Patterns of Communication Flow in SBOs

Although there are important exceptions to the patterns we have analyzed above, it is often helpful to characterize patterns graphically to highlight the important features. Figures 5.3, 5.4, and 5.5 model three flows of information among the governor, budget director, and budget examiners that correspond to three degrees of policy distance between governors and budget examiners. The thickness of the lines indicates the intensity and frequency of communication flows between sets of actors. Figure 5.3 reflects the rigid and hierarchical communication flows of states with a long policy distance between the governor and the budget examiners, as found in Alabama, Illinois, and South Carolina. The strongest information flows are up and down the bureaucratic structure, with some steady links between the examiners and the budget director, and the budget director and the governor. Section managers occasionally brief the governor's policy staff (dashed lines), but the communication generally flows through the budget director first. The examiners know little about the governor's positions because of the large policy distance between the examiners and the governor, learning only what

Figure 5.3   **Large Policy Distance (Strong Control) Model**

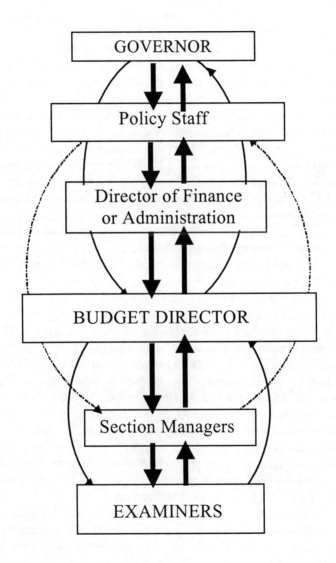

is filtered to them in the process. These states exhibit a strong control orientation to budgeting.

Figure 5.4 presents a picture of budget office communication flows in states with an intermediate policy distance that yields a relatively weak policy role for the budget office. We note that the governor is separated from the policy staff in this model, indicating that the governor only occasionally has direct communications with examiners. More often, the policy staff is linked directly to examiners. Only occasionally will the budget examiners brief the governor on an issue. The links between the budget director and the governor, and the budget director and the examiners, are still the strongest lines of communication. The section managers also have a more formal link to the policy staff and may sometimes brief the governor on key budget issues. The section managers are likely to play a larger connecting and conduit role between examiners and other actors, including the budget director. States in our sample with this communication framework include Virginia, North Carolina, Minnesota, and Iowa.

Figure 5.5 represents communication flows in states with a short policy distance, where examiners are directly linked to the governor, although their strongest link is with the budget director. States in this setting have examiners directly briefing the governor on key budget issues and receiving direct feedback from the governor on policy views and agendas, yielding a strong policy orientation. The main flow of information is between the governor and budget director, and the budget director and examiners. In this model, the governor's policy staff is nearly indistinguishable from the governor in terms of communication flows, with examiners and policy staff directly communicating on a regular basis. The secretary of administration may be involved in the discussions and decisions, but the influence varies with the appointee and their relationship to the governor relative to the relationship between the budget director and the governor. Budget section managers (team leaders, principal examiners) play a technical assistance role for examiners more than they serve as a political and policy screen between the examiners and other actors. Wisconsin, Kansas, and Georgia exhibit the strong policy orientation that is characteristic of this system.

These three models capture the increasingly complex relationships between the principal executive budget actors as the policy distance shortens between the examiners and governors. The shorter policy distance is characteristic of a stronger policy orientation, while the longer distance is characteristic of a stronger control-oriented SBO. VASBO and GASBO do not conform precisely to the models, although the models are reasonably robust with respect to the other states in our field study sample. As we proceed to analyze the complexity of state budgeting in subsequent chapters, we find it

Figure 5.4   **Intermediate Policy Distance (Weak Policy) Model**

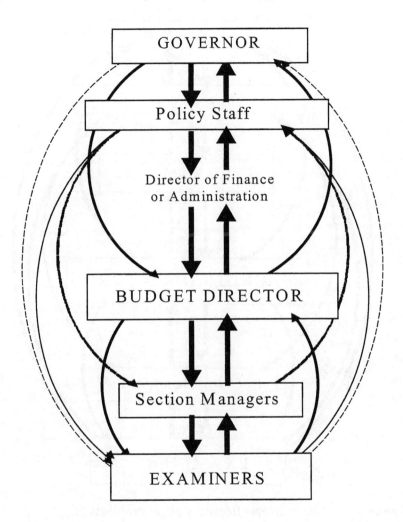

useful to condense the strong and weak policy models into one group. The reader is alerted to the result that the category of policy-oriented SBO includes a range of policy orientation. However, we find that the contrast between the control-oriented SBOs and the policy-oriented SBOs provides substantial variation in state budgeting, and allows us ample opportunity to model the influence of decision contexts on examiner decision-making and budgetary roles.

Figure 5.5   **Short Policy Distance (Strong Policy) Model**

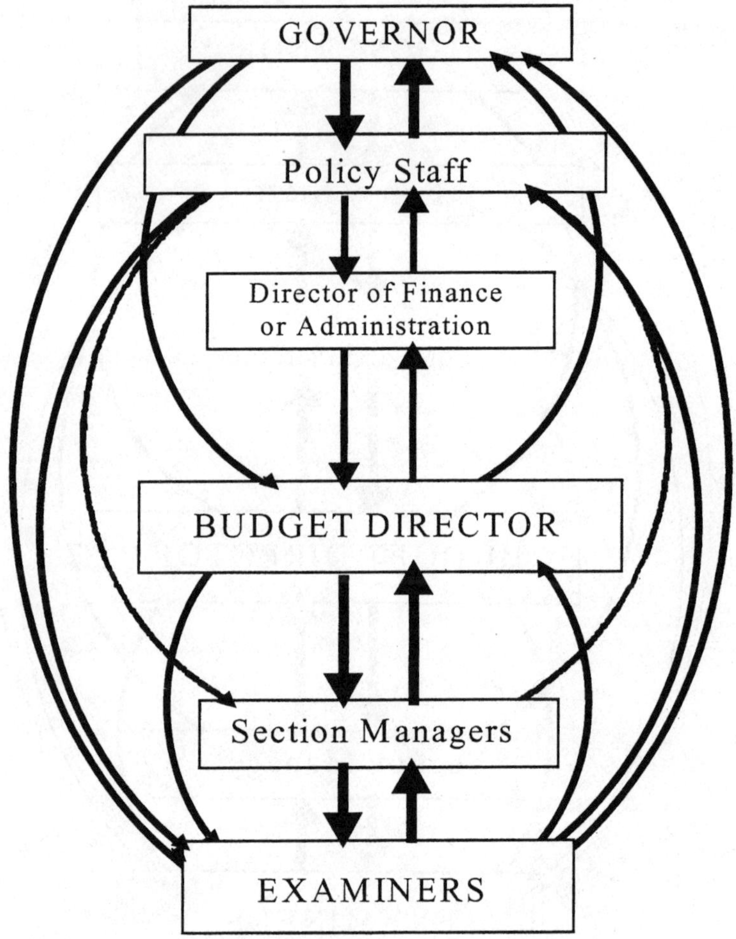

Summary: Policy Problems Become Budget Problems in a Decision Context

State budget offices act as the vortex through which the various policy and budget decision streams must flow. The problems, solutions, and politics of the policy issues embedded in agency budget requests flow together with the decisions about revenues, expenditures, budget balances, budget process, and budget execution. It is therefore no surprise that problematic preferences are intrinsic characteristics of public budgeting because problems are ambiguous and capricious, solutions have chameleon qualities, and the politics of an issue depends on who is politicking. The notion of fluid participation across decisions is appealing because we have learned that *who* is budgeting *when* matters for budgetary outcomes. Budget decision technology had been unclear because neither Kingdon's PAS model, Rubin's RTB model, nor incrementalism copes with the joint linear and nonlinear aspects in public budgeting.

We want to explore *how* SBO decisions are made in a state budget office. Our central question in this book is what decision-making is required of examiners who make budget and policy recommendations. A typology of state budget office decision contexts is an important step in the construction of a budget rationality model in two important ways. First, it explicitly recognizes that there are multiple decision contexts for budget decisions, a step beyond the narrow micro-budgeting literature to date. Second, it suggests that we might expect to find different kinds of decision-making in different decision contexts. If decision contexts are more complex in some state budget offices than others, we might expect that examiners' decision-making will be more complex in those offices than in others. Furthermore, examiners facing more complexity in decision-making may also play different roles with respect to their agencies than examiners engaged in less complex decision-making.

The fluid participation and unclear technology that arise in the decision vortex of the SBO present the examiner with budget problems that appear ill-structured and complex. Budget problems appear poorly structured partly because they are multifaceted. Expanding upon OMB director Smith's list, one can posit at least five facets of budget problems: social, legal, political, economic, and technical. A micro-budgeting decision-making model must account for this complexity. We have suggested that the answer lies in a model of multiple rationalities applied to budgetary decision-making in the SBO.

The notion of multiple decision streams of various types in a GCM framework is very compatible with our evidence that examiners use a multiple-rationalities approach to micro-budgeting decisions. Budget problems analyzed in the context of the budget as a policy document are far too complex to be reduced to mere political or economic problems. Budget decisions require a multiple-rationalities approach. Each of the five facets posited above is present to a lesser or greater degree, depending upon the actual budget problem. Each facet of a budget problem requires a different way of thinking, a different rationality. Economic rationality is inappropriate for legal problems, just as political rationality is inappropriate for technical problems. As explained in chapters 3 and 4, a full treatment of an agency budget problem, therefore, requires a full range of rationalities—fiscal and nonfiscal.

Chapters 6 and 7 create two archetype SBOs in which we explore the differences in budgetary decision-making by examiners in two different decision contexts: a policy-oriented SBO and a control-oriented SBO. We will follow the decision-making by two archetype examiners: Mary, an examiner who works in a policy orientation, and Robert, who works in a control orientation. We will show that decision-making within a control orientation is rather limited to the technical and legal aspects of budget problems, whereas decision-making in a policy-oriented SBO is more complex. The latter encompasses the technical and legal facets of budgeting, but also includes the social, political, and economic facets of budgeting. We shall see how the anatomy of the different decision-making processes affects the types of recommendations the prototypical examiners develop in the executive budget process.

Notes

1. For a detailed study of the MOSBO transition, see Michael Connelly (1981). His dissertation includes extensive coverage of the conflicts and resolutions involved in the planning and budgeting functions in MOSBO.
2. Correlations are statistically significant at $p \leq 0.01$ or better.
3. Correlation is statistically significant at $p \leq 0.05$ or better.
4. SCSBO was omitted from the table because the question regarding recommendation affirmation rates was not asked of any SCSBO staff.
5. These correlations are significant at $p \leq 0.05$.

6

The Anatomy of a
Policy-Oriented Budget
Recommendation

Shadowing the SBO Examiner

This chapter and the next describe decision-making throughout the year in the life of two archetypal examiners. This chapter focuses on an examiner in a policy-oriented SBO, while the next chapter focuses on an examiner in a control-oriented SBO. To simplify these descriptions and to make them more easily comparable, we assume that our archetype offices are engaged in an executive budget process modeled in Figure 6.1, with a fiscal year that runs from July 1 to June 30. This means that the budget calendar roughly falls in three areas. The new budget is signed by the governor and implemented on July 1, beginning the *execution phase* of the budget cycle; the adopted budget is implemented throughout the next twelve months, until June 30. The period leading up to early October is called the *predevelopment phase* (Schick 1983); it marks the period when the agencies are preparing their budget requests for submission to the SBO and when the SBO examiners are conducting their predevelopment analysis. From early October until about mid-January is the intensive *budget development phase* of the budget cycle. This is the period when the SBO examiners are analyzing the submitted agency requests and SBO recommendations are forwarded to the governor, who sometimes modifies them, and then the governor's budget proposal is submitted to the legislature for approval, on or about February 1. The *legislative phase* that follows lasts until the veto override session (if there is one) is finished and the new budget is signed into law. The discussion and analysis in this chapter increase our understanding of the decision-making by

Figure 6.1   **The Budget Process**

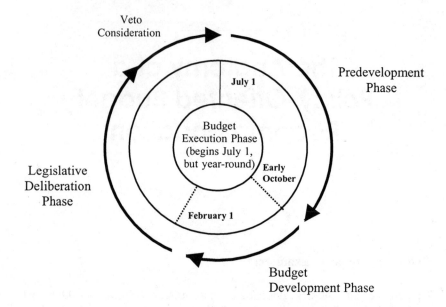

policy-oriented examiners as they develop the governor's budget recommendations to the legislature through the *predevelopment* and *development* phases of the budget process. The chapter concludes with a brief discussion of examiner roles in the legislative phase.

The Task of the Policy-Oriented SBO

As we discussed in previous chapters, governors have been the driving force behind policy decision-making in most states. We have noted that crafting the executive budget proposal is perhaps one of the most important policy advantages available to governors, and in some states, the governor uses the SBO as a powerful tool to draft budget proposals that implement his or her policy agenda. As we discussed in chapter 5, some states have developed reputations for strong policy-oriented SBOs that meet the needs of their activist governors, whatever their partisan stripe. Other states, however, have a history of governors whose agendas may not be activist at all. In such states, the governor has little need of a policy-oriented SBO to draft proposals or redirect state operations according to the governor's vision. Finally, we have seen that in a few states with historically activist governors, some governors choose to use the SBO to craft budgets to implement their policy agendas, while others do not. In these states, the SBO's policy role may be weaker because it is intermittently supplanted by the governor's personal policy staff, who serve as intermediaries between the SBO examiners and the governor.

The variety of policy roles for SBOs suggests that there is a wide range of SBO policy distances across the states, even in states with activist governors. In chapter 5 we used the variation in policy distance to distinguish our sample states. We suggested that our sample states fall into one of three sections along a policy-control orientation continuum. The strong policy-oriented states are Georgia, Iowa, Kansas, Virginia, and Wisconsin. Weaker policy orientations are found in Minnesota, Missouri, and North Carolina. States with a strong control orientation include Alabama, Illinois, and South Carolina. This chapter most accurately describes decision-making activities in strong policy-oriented SBOs, although we believe it is pertinent to a large extent for the weaker policy orientations as well. Decision-making in control-oriented SBOs is described in the next chapter.

A distinguishing characteristic of an SBO with a strong policy orientation is that there is a very short policy distance between the SBO and the governor. The policy-oriented SBO is at the nexus of policy analysis and budget analysis in the state's budget process. By this we mean that the examiners in the SBO have a general assignment to analyze budget proposals for the extent to which they are in accord with the governor's policy agenda, and to *develop alternatives* to agency budget requests that better serve the governor's policy preferences. Sometimes they are even called upon to develop initiatives outside of the agency requests because, as one examiner reminds us, "sometimes the governor may have some of his own ideas that may not have been included in the agency request." Gosling suggests that a primary characteristic of a policy-oriented office is that policy development provides a "unifying focus," anchoring decisions about the role and responsibilities of the examiners with respect to the budget process. The staff in a policy-oriented SBO is encouraged to "review policy alternatives in response to agency requests . . . and initiate policy proposals where no agency request has been made" (Gosling 1987, 64). In this book, we consider examiners to have a policy role *when their activity involves them in the substantive discussions and decisions regarding state policies affecting their assigned agencies as such issues appear on the budgetary decision agenda.*

Palumbo (1995, 8–9) describes public policy as a moving target that must be "inferred from the series of intended actions and behaviors" of the agencies and officials involved in making the policy. The complexity of the wide variety of issues, large and small, that comprise public policy demands a concomitant complexity in the way examiners approach a given policy problem. In the context of the annual executive budget process, policy analysis requires early identification of policy issues by examiners so that issues can be prioritized and studied as budget problems in preparation for the next budget. Policy problems become budget problems because they need funding in the next budget.

Jon Yunker (1990, 97), a former state budget director in Oregon, argues that the value of having examiners involved in policy decisions "is the broad objectivity they can provide." The examiner is responsible for ensuring that the governor's policy staff members are aware of all the interested parties in a decision, and the alternatives available to the governor. Moreover, heeding the adage that "one makes dust or eats it," Yunker argues that the SBO needs to be "out front of most of the major issues, and to be a major player within the executive branch and in the dealings between the executive and legislative branches" if it is to have a meaningful contribution to state government (p. 101). He adds that the examiner in a policy-oriented office is given the "responsibility to research issues completely, identify the options, and recommend a course of action," including a rationale for the recommendation (p. 100). Consequently, issue identification is routinized from the first weeks that most examiners begin their new jobs in the policy-oriented SBO. These examiners' responsibilities include monitoring the budget execution of their agencies and analyzing their agencies' budget requests. There is also an explicit responsibility to advise the governor on the size and composition of the next agency budgets. Let us now "observe" how a new examiner, Mary, learns how to make budget recommendations in a policy-oriented SBO.

Predevelopment-Phase Analysis

One of the central lines of inquiry in our field interviews was eliciting a description of how examiners begin to think about their agency budgets in the first weeks on the new agency assignment. The responses of examiners in policy-oriented SBOs suggest that they begin with effectiveness analyses of agency programs during the predevelopment phase, building a framework for analyzing the efficiency aspects of the agency budget requests when they are submitted to the SBO during the budget development phase of the budget cycle. Their descriptions identify the three types of effectiveness thinking we have discussed in the previous chapter: social, political, and legal reasoning. These are used to build a framework for thinking about the economic and technical facets (efficiency rationalities) of agency budget problems. The following sections follow Mary's progression of thinking from the beginning of a new agency assignment to her budget recommendations crafted for the budget director, and ultimately the governor.

The policy-oriented budget cycle begins with the execution phase of the budget process (July 1), not in the budget development phase. This period is generally characterized as the "slow period" of the budget cycle, but this is the point when examiners begin their analysis of the agency budgets that will be submitted to the governor and the legislature, either because they are newly hired examiners or because they are seasoned examiners who receive new agency assignments. Moreover, the prime time for starting new examiners in many SBOs is in June or July, at the beginning of the *predevelopment* phase of budgeting. According to the MOSBO budget director, the best time to start an examiner is "probably at the beginning of the process, probably early summer so they have some time to get around and maybe do some site visits, but then see the budget requests come in, analyze the requests, track it through the General Assembly, see the bills come." After learning the locations of the coffee machine and copy machine, the new examiner is usually assigned responsibility for a set of state agencies (and their budgets).

As our new examiner, Mary, begins her assignment, there are a host of questions racing through her head. What do these agencies do? Why are they doing that? How do they do it? How much money does it take to run the agencies' programs? Are costs going up or down in the last few years? Are they effective in their mission? Are they efficient in their operations? What changes do they want to make to their programs and who will care if they do? How do I learn what the governor thinks about these programs and changes?

The scope of these questions reflects the multiple facets of budget problems and fall into the two broad categories of underlying effectiveness and efficiency questions. The underlying effectiveness questions incorporate the social, legal, and political aspects of agency operations and budgets. What is the underlying social rationale for an agency and its programs? What degree of political support do the programs enjoy from the governor, the legislature, and the other policy actors? What is the legal authority (and legal constraints) upon which the agency operates? The underlying efficiency questions are not entirely financial, but emphasize the monetary aspects of the policies and programs of each agency. Are agency programs allocated funds according to marginal utility analysis and are they operated with technical efficiency?

Overall, the new examiners we interviewed expressed a sense of being overwhelmed by the numbers of questions and piles of potential information. An IASBO examiner reported he spent his first couple of weeks on the job "confused. [The agency] uses a very extensive indirect cost system. I spend a lot of time trying to understand implications of the budget decisions that were made in the [agency]. If you made the decision to cut this program, which was 100 percent General Fund, why do they end up losing addendum funds? It's just the way they use their indirect costs, but it took a while to understand that." Since most SBOs we studied have no formal training program for new examiners, it is no wonder that a VASBO examiner spoke for many when he said, "It's pretty much a sink or swim environment around here when you first come to work for them. You either have to be bold and ask questions or you walk around in a daze."

Yunker explains that examiners are expected to become experts in their assignment areas. "This requires spending a great deal of time meeting with senior agency staff and program managers, and visiting both state and state-funded programs" (1990, 100). A senior VASBO examiner could not agree more: "I think knowing the operations of the agency are most helpful [for analysis], and then having some educational background on a particular issue. So you know, in [VASBO] we laughingly say we become experts on whatever issue is on the table, because I think a good knowledge base on whatever issue you're reviewing is helpful, so you can identify alternatives."

During the intensive legislative phase of the budget cycle, there is no time to wait for agency answers or to develop a response to a hot issue. The examiner is expected to fill the information gap quickly and accurately. Getting up to speed, according to many examiners, is "just a hodgepodge" of activities. One GASBO examiner recalled, "I read anything in the files, performance audits or any management review studies. I went through anything. . . . When I first started, we had a pretty good library of performance audits, financial audits, and management review studies."

Fortunately, the "slow season" of the summer provides time for the examiner to ask the "big questions" and learn all about the assigned agencies. During these few months, Mary needs to explore the social, legal, and political aspects of her agencies' programs, identify the policy issues embedded in proposals to change these programs, and determine consonance or dissonance with the governor's policy agenda and policy priorities. She may not know this when she begins the process, but she will learn quickly, and be guided and aided by her supervisor and fellow examiners. A VASBO examiner agreed that colleagues are great resources. "What I needed them more for was the concept of state budgeting . . . just understanding how you budget and how you work . . . asking a lot of questions, not being afraid to go to others for help, finding out where the resources were."

The examiner who previously held the assignment can be a critical resource for an examiner when learning about a new agency assignment. A WISBO examiner had many questions for his predecessor:

> For example, right now the department is coming in with a request to unfreeze a position. We froze it when it became vacant. As they reallocated people around, they created another position federally, and so we froze the

position. Reallocation, now they want to unfreeze that position. So I've asked him, why did you freeze this originally? What was your intention? What kind of conversations did you have with them when this action was taken? What are their expectations as you would see them? For the school aids, I ask him technical questions that still come up. Or questions where people ask, why did the governor do this in the biennial budget bill? Implications of things that didn't go into effect right away, people start to focus on these later on. So I ask him, what was the tone of the briefings? Do you recall the governor's intent here? Just trying to understand why things were done.

Relationships between examiners are largely informal and, for the most part, are important sources of help for the new examiner in the SBO, or even to a senior examiner new to an assignment. That is good, since there are many reasons to ask for help as the new examiner learns how to craft a budget recommendation.

Social Facets of Budget Problems

Budget directors in policy-oriented SBOs require a healthy dose of social rationality in examiner recommendations. The KSBO budget director argued that it is not possible to participate in the budget discussion with the budget director or governor without a clear understanding of the program's purpose and activities: "When somebody talks about closing Winfield State Hospital, what are they talking about? If they're talking about correctional facilities and overcrowding, what is a minimum versus a maximum correctional facility?" Eliminating a program to save money is not a common examiner practice for good reason, she added: "Most programs have got some basic level of service and constituency that they're responsible to, and unless that clientele list or whatever has been eliminated, it's probably premature in most cases for the examiner to be recommending it [for elimination]."

The examiners in the policy-oriented SBOs described a search for the social rationale behind the agency to meet the social rationality requirements. The very first task of a examiner, either new to the office or new to an agency assignment, is to learn the purpose for the agency itself (and each of its programs and activities), how the agency operates, and who operates it. Al Kliman (1990, 112) argues that a budget process that is designed to reflect the policies of the top decisionmaker begins with the major policy decisions in which the examiner asks the big questions: "Who are we?" and "What are our goals?" Framing their agency budget as a social rationality problem, the most important questions they ask are: "Why do you do that?" and "Why do you do it that way?"

The policy-oriented examiner immediately begins predevelopment analysis by gathering basic information on what each assigned agency does. On that first day of the new assignment, the examiner often faces an office full of old budgets, old budget requests, files of past issue papers, and a To Do list left over from the examiner who last had the assignment. This pile of papers, in reality, is a gold mine of background information that is vital to a better understanding of the agencies, particularly the old budgets for each agency, and any issue papers that have been written about the agency (especially in the last budget session). This gold mine will help the examiner discover the social purpose underlying the agency programs for which budgets will be requested.

Most state budgets today use a basic program budget framework, and the narrative descriptions about programs provide general information on what each does. The old budgets provide the examiner with some key information. First, they place the agency's budget in the context of state operations. Is it a large budget or a small one? Is it complex, with several programs, subprograms, and program elements? Or is it relatively simple, with one or two programs? An experienced GASBO examiner begins each new assignment by looking "at any historical financial data . . . becoming very familiar with their legislation, with their enabling legislation. I always try to start there first and then just whatever you can read in terms of their programs. The reading consisted of narrative and financial" information.

In many states, issue papers cue the examiner about which issues are new, which are perennial, and which are "hot" topics and likely to be on the forthcoming budget decision agenda. Issue papers identify histories of agency problems and delineate the alternatives that were considered, including which were rejected for what reasons. The general flavor of the issue paper indicates to the examiner whether the agency is under scrutiny by decisionmakers or whether it is quietly doing its job. As such, it tells Mary how much work she can expect to devote to the agency assignment. This VASBO examiner relied on issue units for key information on her agency:

> What we're currently doing, and I think you have to do this each year, is identify what the major issues are going to be for budget development. And a lot of that sometimes is generated through the governor's agenda, what he wants. For example, Governor Allen has stated that he wants a cap on tuition to try to keep tuition at the level of inflation. Well, knowing that, one big issue that we are going through the session is how are we going to do this. So what we do now is issue papers and try and identify some of the big issues that we're gonna have and how we're gonna fund it. And maybe laying out alternatives, in some cases not laying out alternatives, just rais-

ing the issue, trying to get some sense of direction. And we're doing this independently of what the agencies come in with, their specific needs. . . .

We're looking at it more in the global sense. These are the issues for higher ed and how are we gonna attack it. In some cases they're the same every year as far as the tuition fees, but it may not be the same this year. We used to be formula driven, so we had to amend the formula-type of thing. Now we've got to adopt a whole new policy. We've got to think of new ways of funding higher ed and that kind of stuff. Although the process may be the same, the issues change, and that's where we are now, really trying to identify what our main issues are going to be and how to fund those particular issues.

Budgets are anything if not dynamic, and issues are constantly changing. The fortunes of agencies and their initiatives ebb and flow with the changing currents of the policy streams. Consequently, the issues described in the issue papers and past budgets may or may not be valid concerns for the next budget round. The best source for what is likely to be on the agency's budget agenda is the agency's management team.

Therefore, one of Mary's first tasks is a meeting with the agency head and his or her management team. These initial meetings serve multiple purposes. First, they are important for establishing personal relationships between the agency and SBO actors. These relationships need to be strong enough to withstand the stress and pressures of the intensive budget development phase. Agencies report that the quality of their relationship with the SBO examiner is one measure of their budget success (Duncombe and Kinney 1986). Likewise, examiners also stress the importance of a relationship with agency staff built on trusting in one another to do the best job they can, playing the budget roles they are assigned, and having a free flow of information back and forth between the SBO and the agency.

A VASBO examiner stressed the importance of a professional working relationship with assigned agencies:

> Well, it's important. I feel it's important to work in an open environment. And that is no surprise to agencies. We are very dependent upon agencies for accurate information. An agency could make our job absolutely miserable if they choose not to cooperate. It has always been my commitment to agencies that "I'll be as open as I can with you, with what I'm going to recommend, as long as you don't take that knowledge and go and try to lobby outside of our relationship, lobby with the secretary or lobby with the governor or particularly lobby with adversary groups with regard to the approach."

I don't want to be in a situation where I recommend something and it turns out that I didn't have full knowledge of the issue for you, and the agency had to come in and say that they didn't know about this, and here I am sitting here with egg on my face publicly because I got a bad recommendation out there, and I've got to either back down or else try somehow to save face and dig in.

We can always differ over the issue but we shouldn't differ over the facts, and I need to have all the facts in order to [pause]. There's an old saying that everyone's entitled to their own opinion, but no one is entitled to their own facts. And, as I mentioned earlier, I'm totally dependent upon the agencies and making sure that I have all the facts is important and that's why I try not to operate in a very closed-door atmosphere.

A WISBO examiner stated, "For most of my agencies I have a good relationship with them. One I do not and they are a totally different story. Like with the [agency], when I need something, they get it for me; when they need something, I get it for them immediately. It's a lot of back and forth, give and take. I help them out, they help me out, and we have a really good working relationship." The problematic agency in this case was a noncabinet agency, and the agency chair "has had a long-standing problem with the budget office." This was usually the situation in other states as well. In another case, a KSBO examiner also had experience with an agency where "we're not on the best of terms."

Q: So how does that affect the way you handle their budget?
Examiner: Well, I think it's probably a disadvantage to them. Some agencies I can call them up and ask them any question any time of day and they'll be responsive, they'll immediately tell me this is the way it is, this is why we've asked for it this way. That agency I may not even bother to call them because (1) they won't respond, and (2) I don't know if what they'll tell me will actually be true or not. So I may make decisions on what I recommend to the governor that may not be as good a decision and I may cut their budget and maybe they should get a higher amount, so I'll just go with what they recommend. I think she views this office as we're trying to micro-manage her agency and she doesn't see any need for that. It's not necessary in her mind. She reports to the commission, she doesn't report to the governor. The commission has sort of taken a very hands-off approach to administering the agency, so she pretty much has free rein.

A KSBO section manager noted that examiners work hard to develop healthy, respectful relationships with agencies: "I try to get my folks to make sure they develop a positive attitude with the agency that allows them to be respected and allows them to obtain information because the agency knows it's to their advantage to keep the analyst well informed, but yet doesn't get in bed with him. I respect you but I don't love you, that kind of deal."

Another important role of the initial meetings with the agency management team is early identification of agency budget priorities. Which of the issues from last year remain on their budget agenda? What are the emerging problems that require attention? What proposals are they discussing to put in their next budget request? These discussions are tentative in nature, and often the agency is also probing Mary for reactions that may indicate the budgetary feasibility of any particular option. A WISBO examiner recalled an agency head briefing of this sort:

> Now at this point [the agency] is asking some questions: "We want to look at developing certain standards for equipment. We want to have your thoughts." Clearly we can't give guarantees about anything, but we can give our comments. So I think this is really a time where they can kind of feel out where we're going, and kind of thus, ultimately, where the governor may be going with certain things.

Another examiner agreed:

> I think one of the things we do here is provide a sounding board for the governor or for the [budget] director as well as for the agency head. So when [the agency heads] think of ideas, they'll frequently call and say, "Well, I was thinking of doing this. We've got a pool of attorneys over here and it seems like we've got plenty of legal assistants, but we're really short on somebody over here to do this task. I was thinking of taking one of these positions, because this person has left, and move it over here, and change it, and maybe we'll hire this type of person." So we'll sit and talk about that sort of thing. Kind of restructuring workload or restructuring personnel to reflect a change that's occurred in the workload. They like to bounce those ideas off us. Gives us an opportunity to bounce them off the director.

As a new examiner, Mary may not have a good idea of this yet, but meeting the agency management team raises her awareness and helps her start learning about the multiple facets of the policy problem and building an analysis framework in which the forthcoming budget request will be evaluated as a budget problem.

For an IASBO examiner, meeting the agency management team "helped me understand more what they were asking for and how it programmatically, and facility-wise, related. Again, I'm one of those who just hates this idea, well, they got so much last year, let's incrementally boost them 2.5 percent. I just think that's so dumb." A GASBO examiner echoed the value of speaking with the agency management team when she gets a new agency assignment: "I ask if there's anything that I would need to know before I get their budget submissions in September; and then we talk about those items, those highlighted areas; and then their budgets come in September, and by that time I'm a little aware of what to expect because we've talked about it, hopefully, at our visits."

While the agency management team may have a sense of overall agency priorities, mission, and upcoming issues, Mary needs to probe more deeply into the operations of the agency. Examiners in policy-oriented SBOs are encouraged by budget directors to "get out of the office" and take site visits to agency operations. The IASBO budget director wanted her analysts "over in the agencies . . . working with program people . . . out on field trips. I go to institutions in the summer. I've spent time with troopers in cars doing night patrol. I went to DOT garages. I went to parks and lakes under construction. And that's what I expected them to do, to get out."

What does she think the examiners get out of the site visits?

> I think they can see what everyone talks about for seven or eight months out of the year. They can actually visualize the high-profile areas. People know you care, that you really do care what's going on out there, that you don't sit over here in the golden dome and make decisions without knowing, and that you have a genuine interest in learning. It's hard for me to believe that someone can sit there and make decisions about some place they've never seen. That's why I got out and that's why I wanted my people to get out.

Thus the welfare examiner may visit a client intake site, a job training class, or an elderly meal site. The parks examiner may tour the state parks and historic sites. The examiners described the purpose in much the same way as the IASBO budget director: the principal task is to determine "how it really works" and "to get a feeling" for the way the agency operates. For many examiners, site visits are essential for "putting a face" on the dollars requested in the budget. The parks examiner can then recall walking the trail blocked by fallen trees and washed out bridges to help evaluate a request to increase funds for parks maintenance. The welfare examiner can understand the request for more intake workers, recalling the long queues and interviews with exhausted welfare staff at the end of a long day at the intake site.

The examiners' quest is to understand the expectations and obligations at play between the agency and its clientele. They pursue the public interest in the agency, and they seek the public's interest in the programs and activities, as revealed by this examiner:

> My principal analyst at the time . . . took me around to the agencies that were local and introduced me to the secretary or the agency director, met the budget staff. . . . Also set up a few agency visits, particularly for the hospitals, to go out on the road and actually tour the hospital and meet the superintendent and budget people . . . to just get a better understanding of what the agency does and how it operates, meet the people I'd be dealing with over the phone. I thought that was important to meet them face to face and hear a little bit more about their perceptions of what it is they were doing and what their problems were and what they thought they needed from a budgetary aspect. . . .
>
> We talked a lot about what it was they were doing for clients with mental retardation hospitals. Generally what the plans were. At that time they were, I think, just initiating a plan to downsize the hospitals and get more of the patients out into the community settings. So it was talking to the program people about the treatment and the prospects for getting individuals out into the community. On the agricultural side, I went out with some of the inspectors to get a better understanding for what they did on a day-to-day basis.

The understanding of what agencies' programs do is the first step in understanding what their priorities are as they develop their budgets. The search for the social rationality underlying agency activities provides a broad context in which examiners can identify the relative priorities in an agency. A KSBO examiner emphasized the link between site visits and understanding the social rationality underlying agency programs:

> The main thing you're looking for at this point: What are their goals and objectives? What are they trying to accomplish? What was the legislative intent? You get a hold of the Legislative Research documents. What are they supposed to be doing? What's not occurring? Why? . . . You understand why they're requesting some of the very strange things that do show up from time to time, whether it be tradition, or custom, or there's a real need. The programs or the courts have ordered it. In my case, [something] had been mandated; things have changed a lot since '88 when the courts stepped in.

A GASBO examiner revealed a similar rationale while looking for "the angle" that made sense with respect to the governor's perspective:

The most important thing for me is to actually go to the department, talk to the people who are in charge of the programs, and then go out and do my site visits, those are two of the most important. You can read all the material you want to and that still doesn't give you a handle on how they're managing the program or give you a sense for a confidence level of, you know, what are they doing at the lower levels. And also those meetings that you have, especially in a large agency like we have, with their management team of what's going on, what's your problems, what do you see your needs are, those type meetings are really invaluable.

This last budget cycle we had some problems in our hospitals and I couldn't get a handle on it and finally called this big meeting of the department and brought in hospital superintendents, nurses, psychologists, and other people, budget people from the other hospitals and sat down and talked out what the problems were in personnel and staffing over at the hospitals. What was going on that was causing all this *and it came to light and really gave me better angle to explain it to the governor and his staff why we were asking for the money to put in personal services in the hospitals, cause the other angle I had—reading the material and looking at it—just really didn't make sense.*

The operative rule is "seeing is believing." Without exception, examiners reported that seeing the museum, the prison, the roads, the highway patrol "beat," and other facilities and activities in person made it much easier to understand the numbers that appeared on paper as budget requests. According to policy-oriented examiners, the agency personnel, with few exceptions, understand how important it is to show the examiners their operations. Many of the examiners meet with someone from each level and division of the agencies, from the department secretary to the street-level bureaucrat:

You've got to visit the place before you can have an idea of the seriousness of the problem. As far as just a general agency . . . you can't go into a physical plant and say they've got a fat budget or a thin budget. They might try to give you that impression that they're thin, but it's hard to get any strong evidence of that. . . .

I just get an idea where priorities are. Well, first of all, you have to get an idea of the base program . . . how they're staffed. . . . You actually talk to line and staff people about how stressed out they are, or whatever, and you'll get an impression of those kinds of needs they have [in their program]. When you do your budget review, you'll remember that, how much the shrinkage is impacting them, things like that.

Seeing how things are related may take several visits to the agency, suggested this IASBO examiner: "The first time I went around, the tours were a lot more like they would take a legislator on, the 50-cent stock kind of tour. The next time I went out and visited, I wanted to see their problems, not their nice things. The nice things aren't what you worry about at budget time. It's the problem things. But I really thought it was necessary to get out."

Policy-oriented examiners consistently displayed a solid understanding of the social rationality underlying agency programs, as suggested by this exchange with a KSBO examiner:

> Q: Why do we have Public Broadcasting?
> Examiner: Basically at one time there was a great emphasis that we can use public broadcasting to go out to smaller communities, smaller cities, schools. Basically the intent was to send it out to the schools where the small schools could have the same expertise in their teachers as the larger schools. I guess it didn't evolve into that, it evolved into basically just another station. I guess there's some contention whether there is a need for public broadcast, especially with the 100-plus channels you can get on some satellites and TV stations.

As Mary gathers background information on the social facets of her agencies' budget problems, she is actually building a personal database that she can use in later phases of budgeting to analyze budget requests and develop alternatives to agency proposals and gubernatorial initiatives. But the underlying social rationale for programs comprises only one facet of budget problems. Our new examiner also needs to learn and understand the political facets of agency budget problems.

Political Facets of Budget Problems

The second component of the new examiner's predevelopment analysis is gaining an understanding of the politics of each agency's budget. Agency programs do not exist without political support. The agency's political history can be learned by reading the issue papers and through the discussions with agency personnel. In any given budget year, most programs have a low political profile. But a few programs are at the center of political controversies, prominently featured on the budget and policy decision agendas. Some issues are perennial because they involve important social value conflicts, such as welfare reform or education finance. The examiner quickly learns *who* supports *which* agency programs, both within and outside the agency.

It is useful to acknowledge two levels of budgetary "politics" at work in agency budget development. There is the "obvious politics" of exchange and power brokering by legislative and executive political leaders, and the less visible, less dramatic, behind-the-scenes problem-solving that characterizes everyday governance. It is this "other politics" that most influences examiners, although they also must be cognizant of the "obvious politics" when their agency program is controversial.

Social and political facets are closely related, but distinct. Whereas the social rationality involves thinking about *why* a program activity is funded in the budget, political rationality is framed by thinking about the *relative value* of a particular program or activity to the agency's mission. In Majone's (1989, 150–153) terms, the task is to identify which programs are associated with core values, and how far the peripheral programs are from core values. For example, how important is it that grain elevators are inspected—relative to inspecting slaughterhouses? Examiners search for the underlying priorities the agency places on its programs and activities so that they have some way of allocating scarce funds to the most important activities. The primary sources for this information are the agency personnel, especially the department head. The initial discussions with the agency management team can reveal the depth of commitment they feel for a given program. This is usually the principal area of discussion between the examiner and the agency head, since the latter is generally not involved in the technical aspects of the agency budget. One of the KSBO examiners noted that:

> On most agencies, we do get a fairly good feel for which [programs] they consider most important. You get that mostly from talking to the secretary or the head of the agency, especially during the summer. You talk to each division head and they think their division's most important, so that's why you need to talk to the top guy, to really get a feel for what they feel is most important. Also . . . what the head of the agency feels is most important, the governor may not feel is most important.

Understanding the agency's priorities in this vein is helpful, but incomplete. A richer picture of program politics emerges from discussions with the program personnel and street-level bureaucrats. Field office visits can reveal that policy issues being pushed by the top management on behalf of program staff are sometimes surprising to the program managers. A senior examiner finds that "Sometimes it's kind of interesting what a person at the middle level or maybe slightly below thinks they need as compared with what the budget says they do. Sometimes more, sometimes less. Quite often less. But you also have to take into account that if I'm responsible for something and I'm managing it, I'm going to show you how good I do."

Discussions with program managers can reveal interesting rationales, as noted by a WISBO examiner:

As opposed to just dealing strictly with the [agency] budget office people, go out and meet the program people, the people that don't see or talk to budget analysts except maybe once or twice a year. . . . It serves a couple purposes. I can see what they're thinking about, and in a lot of cases [they are] not so concerned about managing the information for the budget office. They'll tell you what they think the problem is.

Case in point . . . I was out at one of the program offices one time, an [agency] southern district office and we were talking about some subjects. I can't remember what it was, but the conversation turned to the need that this district director had for emergency equipment for his people to respond to spills. It turned out that his point was that he didn't want his people responding to spills. He did not see his staff as a first responder in an emergency type of situation. He felt that was the duty of emergency [services] and the fire department and the sheriff's department or something. He didn't really want the equipment because that would imply that he had to get out there as soon as a gas truck tips over, he had to have one of his guys out there sloshing up gas. It turns out that the [agency's] budget comes through, lo and behold, as you requested [the agency's] budget for emergency equipment for all their district offices, many thousands of dollars. And I'm thinking back to what the guy at the district office had told me, that this is not the role that those people play. So you start to pick up information, that things just don't fit.

An examiner in another state still goes on site visits even though he has had the Corrections Department for "umpteen years":

You bet. It's not static out there. I still go out with the increase in prison population, with the new construction out there. I still think it is valuable to go out and visit the sites. There's new people. To me if there's a new business manager, the best way to meet that business manager and sit down and get to know that business manager is at his/her facility. Not saying, hey, by the way, the next time you come to [the capitol], stop in, I'd like to see you for a while. I think it's a lot better psychologically and otherwise to meet the person there. If there's a new superintendent, if they built 200 more beds out there, I want to see them.

Understanding agency priorities is fundamentally an exercise in political rationality. Underlying the relative value of a program is the axiom that a program's value varies across individuals and their collective interests. Agency programs are crafted to serve various constituencies, and the first step in understanding the political facets of a program is determining who supports (and opposes) the program. Budget rationality in the policy-oriented SBO requires a degree of sensitivity to the political feasibility of a proposed budget solution, especially with respect to the governor's position on a particular program.

Most examiners indicated that a routine part of early budget analysis is identifying policy issues with the agencies during discussions with the management team, and then reporting back to the budget director through informal discussions to get a reaction. Is this a direction the governor wants to go? Should I spend more time or less time working on this issue? It is important for the examiner to get feedback early. As an IASBO examiner explained, "It isn't so much early on that I go in with dollar amounts because I may not even have their actual budget presented. I tell them what I think are going to be issue areas." In addition to the examiner getting an initial reaction from the budget director, the early information also helps the budget director begin to see the emerging picture of what the major and minor spending initiatives will be in the agency requests, how this jibes with the governor's policy priorities, and where the budget director can quietly and effectively "put the brakes" on a particular initiative.

The political portrait is even richer after accounting for the legislative support for a particular program. Programs that the agency considers to be a low priority can be described to the examiner as impossible to eliminate because they are legislative mandates and their elimination will be opposed in the legislature. On the other hand, when elections change the composition or majority status of the legislature, or install a new governor in office, there is a fresh window of opportunity to resurrect the push to eliminate such programs (Kingdon 1995). This examiner's example echoes other experiences:

> I've had the situation where a governor didn't want to cut it and you get to the next governor and the governor says, "Don't they have such and such program in there?" And you say, "Yeah."
>
> "Couldn't we do without that?" And you say, why didn't I bring that up? There are a lot of changes that take place because the governors will differ so much. Sometimes you've got to bring those items back to be revisited.

This next examiner's story of dealing with the complications of legislative mandates is compounded by intergovernmental grant regulations, but is not unique:

> We took the money out of the [agency's] budget and then the legislature refused to remove the mandate, so now we do have to find that budget— they have to get it from someone else in the department or they have to get the legislative mandate removed again.

The budget [people] didn't talk to the program people. . . . I'm not sure whether they could have known it, but the bill to remove the legislative mandate almost went through and two days before the deadline for legislative committee action to report out, the director of the regional office of the Federal Home Administration sent a letter to the relevant people on the legislature or something saying that a criterion for awarding money, loans (mostly development grants and loans in rural areas and small towns) was that the technical assistance provided by the [state agency] to their wastewater treatment program, the sewage program. . . . One of the criteria was that they would get technical assistance from the [state agency] because they can be sure the engineering was done well. And so they said they would remove all this grant and loan money if [the state] canceled this program, which is the program that had been offered up and sacrificed through budget cut. Well, at that time they were totally caught out of the blue, they didn't know that the federal government was using this program as a criterion and they didn't know that there would be an impact and they didn't know whether other states were in the same situation, whether this particular administrator was being arbitrary or what.

But they found that the requirement was not federal law and it wasn't in the federal reg, it was just an informal guideline that they use, like underwriters do when they are giving you a mortgage loan or something like that. And so now they've engaged in a real big nationwide survey of all the forty-eight contiguous states and they found out that, yes, indeed, this is the policy in every other state. So now they're gonna go to the secretary and to [the state budget office] and say, "Here's our recommendation, here's our report, we know what the other states are doing, we've been able to cut the program down to this amount." They're gonna have to give us this money and they're also trying to see whether they can get some federal [money] that right now goes for [another state agency], but which is eligible for funding this program and whether they can do that. But, I don't think they're going to.

So anytime when everybody is being asked to cut, they're gotta get this money back for the state with this $26 million in loans and grants, and I don't think that the administration wants to risk that. I don't know if we could have avoided that because I certainly would have no way of knowing that—only the program people would have and I don't know whether they could have, because it had not become an issue before.

But anyway, we're now at the point where we're gonna be asked to make some more cuts, and I don't know enough about the programs to find a place where I think we can cut which doesn't risk federal money, because the general fund monies need to be matched and [yet it] is not a legislative mandate. Because, I mean, I've gone through and figured—I know where there is a little money that is not a legislative mandate, but it's mixed in with activities that our legislature mandates and there is no way to tease it out because of the way we budget. And it's connected to the fact that the way we budget is not the way they do things out in the district. So I don't know what we're gonna do about that, I just hope to God we don't have to cut anything more out of that agency because I don't know where to cut.

New decision agenda items are more difficult to analyze because they lack the rich history of the recurrent items. Just as with the recurrent items, however, the political question pertains to the governor's agenda. Is the new item fostered by the governor's agenda? Is it a campaign promise? Such a political imperative moves it to the forefront of the budget decision agenda and requires careful work by the examiner. Sometimes the initiative comes directly from the governor and his or her policy staff, directing the SBO to develop a program (Gosling 1985 and 1987). This is more often the case when agencies are not part of the governor's cabinet. A good example is K–12 education, which is often directed by an elected official or board. Such independence from the governor may promote two separate education policy agendas, and the SBO is dedicated to developing the governor's version.

A senior WISBO examiner argued that "with noncabinet agencies . . . the analyst actually has more flexibility in terms of coming up with budget initiatives . . . we're less constrained by what the priorities of the agency are." He contrasted his work with a noncabinet agency with that of a gubernatorial appointee, such as the secretary of health and social services. If that agency head says, "I want my big push this year to be prenatal care, I really want to emphasize that and have a big initiative on prenatal care for low income people," then the examiner for that agency may be "more reactive to the agency's priorities and have to recognize that the secretary of the agency is a direct appointee of the governor." By contrast, this examiner developed initiatives independently from the noncabinet agency: "To give an example in this last budget adjustment bill, the governor said, 'I think we need to get more school aid to districts with low spending, low property value districts,' and asked us to put together a formula to do that. So we did that and that was totally independent of the [state agency]. We didn't discuss it with them."

Yet, political pressure points are not the principal concern of the examiner in a policy-oriented office—unless the pressure comes from the governor. Interest groups may pressure the agency for new programs or decision items, but unless it is part of the governor's agenda, the interest group pressure is unlikely to influence the examiner's analysis and recommendation. Policy-oriented examiners are generally well protected from the partisan political struggles in the legislature and between the legislature and the governor.

And anything overtly partisan is usually channeled through the budget director's office, an unwritten policy that is understood and respected by legislators. Still, policy-oriented examiners usually are *not* insulated from the "other politics" of budget problems, that is, the general support and opposition to a particular program or problem. In some offices (e.g., WISBO and MOSBO), the budget directors actually encourage examiners to converse directly with political interest group lobbyists to learn about their views on particular issues and programs.

One of the more difficult tasks for a new examiner is to discern the distinction between *politics* and *policy*. The governor's "obvious politics" is viewed as the arena in which the governor counts his or her political friends and enemies generally, and on any particular issue. Governors form alliances with legislative leaders and various interest groups as part of their campaigns. Rewarding them during the administration with budget allocations for favored programs is often cited by examiners as a reason for their recommendations not being accepted by the governor. In state budgeting, "obvious politics" tends to trump other kinds of rationality, and the governor holds all the trump cards when seated at the briefing table with the SBO staff. As a VASBO examiner points out, "There are some cases where the governor has said 'no,' even though the secretary may have said 'yes,' and everyone along the road has said 'yes.' . . . Or we may have said 'no' and the governor may say 'yes' because of some particular issue that may be a burning issue or interest of the governor."

Still, examiners scrupulously try to avoid any hint of partisanship. That would diminish their credibility as an institution and as individual examiners. That said, a policy-oriented SBO serves the governor and the governor's policy agenda. Devotion to the governor's policy agenda and issues is accepted as the institutional role of the SBO. The governor's policies permeate SBO thinking and analysis, and are inherently linked to the "other politics" of agency programs.

At the intersection of the governor's policies, the governor's politics, and the SBO is the budget director. Examiners need to be cognizant of the political environment in which the agency and its programs operate; but knowing it and allowing that to alter a recommendation on a decision item is another matter. There is a need for balance and common sense. Paul Appleby (1957, 157), former budget director of New York, observes that "most of our decisions stand up because we have learned how to make sensible decisions." As a GASBO examiner acknowledged, "I don't always agree with the political machinery, but I recognize that I work in a political machinery."

The state budget director has the primary responsibility for maintaining the necessary balance. While policy-oriented examiners should present "technically solid management recommendations, not necessarily worrying about political ramifications," the KSBO director thought, "They should be aware of those things." This particularly included the support for, or opposition to, the program articulated by the governor.

Q: How often do you get a recommendation from an analyst that has a recommendation to do something which is political suicide or would create intense political conflict? Do you see those kinds of recommendations coming up very often?

KSBO Budget Director: Good analysis will lead to good solid recommendations. The people who work here are not politicians, capital P or small p. They're analysts, they're trained professionals, and they view their jobs that way and they take them very seriously and responsibly. So rarely do I see any kind of recommendation like that. Sometimes I may interpret the recommendation that way and highlight, not suicide necessarily, but perhaps just a little hotter button than what you want to push. But that's a decision typically the governor makes. In my opinion, it's part of my job to bring up those issues without making that decision for her. She makes those decisions on her own. I know from working with [a former governor], that's exactly how he did it, too. This office's job is not to be a political advisor to governors. It's to provide professional staff work and staff support on the budget, and that's how we try to do our job.

The governor's immediate staff, sometimes called the governor's policy staff, also serves as a buffer between the raw politics of an issue and the public policy analysis of the examiners. In effect, the budget director often acts in the capacity of another member of the governor's policy staff. The policy staff members do not serve as objective evaluators of policy issues; they can rely on the examiners for that. Instead, they are actively engaged in discussions with interest groups, legislators, and the governor on the "obvious politics" of an issue, while simultaneously discussing the public policy merits of the issue with the SBO examiners. The degree to which budgetary politics are channeled through the budget director varies across the states. Nevertheless, examiners actively engaged in such discussions easily absorb some degree of the issue's politics as they revise and refine alternatives for the governor and his or her policy staff.

At one end of the spectrum of policy-politics interaction is WISBO, as illustrated by this conversation with the WISBO budget director:

Director: One of the things that I'll say to analysts when they start, and to policy people when they start, is "get a very good relationship with each other." The way I look at it, our analysts should be constantly talking to the policy analysts who are their counterparts to have feedback going back and forth. If a policy analyst is going to talk to a legislator, they're going to have to know the substantive background before they go in and make political commitments. They'd better call up and ask, what are the facts here before I go in and have to deal with this person, so I can respond and so I don't commit to something that is going to cause a problem.

Q: So you don't see that the flow from the governor's office to the budget staff should go through you?

Director: No. And I emphasize that to people, that I don't think it logistically can go through me. Just, the bottleneck would be too tremendous. They have to be talking directly. And on the other end, it can't go through the governor's chief of staff, or even the policy director. When things get moving, it's got to go analyst to analyst, or things will—or we just won't be able to keep up with things.

Q: So in that sense, does that imply that, and I think you said this earlier but I just want to double check, that it really is imperative that the analyst understand the governor's politics on this issue, even though somehow they're supposed to still develop sound public policy recommendations?

Director: Yeah. That's the way they'll learn what the governor's politics are and that's the way the governor's analysts will learn in-depth what the policy implications are. The policy analysts and the budget analysts have to have two somewhat different perspectives, but they both have to know the other person's perspective if they're doing a good job. Yeah . . . if a policy analyst calls one of our analysts and says, for political reasons or because he was talking to a mayor or a legislator or whatever, "The governor is interested, thinks he might want to do this, this, and this," I don't want our analyst to automatically say, "OK, I'm going to recommend doing that." But I want them to say, "Here are all the policy factors and I recognize that somebody you talked to has a certain perspective and this is why it either should be or we should not go along with what they want, or we can take it into account to this extent in our recommendation," or whatever. And similarly the policy staff isn't always going to buy what we say on policy grounds because of political factors, but you've got to know, and you've got to have the policy staff and the budget analysts working very hard to talk to each other so they're in a process of learning what all those factors are. I think we've really had a pretty good relationship here, and I say that as strongly as I can to both new analysts here and the new policy people when I see them starting in the governor's office.

Q: So in that sense, the politics of a particular issue, at least the governor's politics of a particular issue, definitely are part of the parameters of the budget recommendations?

Director: Yes. And again, not to say that that's necessarily going to mandate our recommendation, but it's going to be taken into account as we understand the issues so that we know that that's out there.

Q: In the sense that it kind of eliminates alternatives?

Director: Yeah, and if you don't know what he's thinking, you're going to waste time because you're going to go in and develop something in a vacuum, you're going to make a recommendation and somebody's going to say, "Yeah, but these ten legislators and these five cities would blow up if that happens, gee, I guess we'd better think about that." You've got to know that as you go through the process.

Similarly, the MOSBO budget director shunned a "filtering role," and would like to see more interaction between his budget staff and the governor's policy staff. Still, the section manager may occasionally run interference for an examiner who feels uncomfortable answering a pointed question at a hearing about "why the governor did this or why the governor did that, or if a reporter calls on the telephone and wants information that the analyst is not comfortable giving out, they will usually refer the calls to [the section manager], or they'll say, hold on, I'll get my section head or the division director and he can address those questions."

The policy-politics interaction in KSBO was at the other end of the spectrum from WISBO. The KSBO budget director agreed that developing budget recommendations is "an ongoing process that requires a lot of conversations between a whole lot of people." Yet she was more inclined to regulate the exchange between the examiners and governor's policy staff. Her frequent involvement in the development of budget recommendations facilitated her informal policy for KSBO, that "analysts should not personally be attached to anything, in my opinion. I think they should be viewed as professional staff who are doing a job. Anything that's political or controversial should be coming through this office, not theirs."

The degree to which an agency program enjoys political support and is a priority for the agency and its clientele is an important factor in the budget problem for many examiners. As an activity loses support, it is more susceptible to funding reductions. As one examiner noted, he tried to "think about how the governor's going to respond to a particular recommendation," and tried to "think of how the public would respond to a certain recommendation if the governor were to include that in his budget." Gauging the governor's support was a factor in his recommendation. "If there's an issue that I don't feel real strongly about, that I think the governor's just going to say no to, most of the time I won't recommend it."

The general politics of a budget problem are known through religiously scanning the media (many offices get daily newspapers and maintain an extensive library of professional periodicals), attending public hearings held by the agency or legislative committees, or discussions with citizens. Budgeting is not exclusively politics at the examiner level; on the other hand, it cannot be excluded either. The policy-oriented examiner needs to strike a balance such that the politics are not ignored but do not become the basis for a budget recommendation. "Their recommendation should say this is the best way to do it," according to one director, who continued, "Factors to consider may be the Farm Bureau has stood against this on a variety of other occasions and the legislature's voted on it three times and never passed it."

At a minimum, although it may not dominate the analysis, political rationality is an important element of a defensible recommendation:

> Examiner: Historically they don't like to cut programs around here, they don't like to cut people, they don't like to have layoffs. Neither the governor nor the legislature wants any headlines to say we're cutting some programs. So I may recommend cutting some programs, but while I'm writing it up, I know it's not going to go.
>
> Q: How often do you anticipate the response of the budget director to your options, when you're sitting at your desk here and working on recommendations?
> Examiner: I think I like to anticipate them all the time because I like to know if I write this, what's her response going to be? OK, she's going to hate it. Why? Then I'll have a response to focus on. Still as far as what I put in my recommendation, no, it's not going to be politically based. Even *if I know the political argument going into it, maybe that would just help me make my logical argument better.* I've done this before, I would recommend this for such and such reasons, and then at the end I'd put a sentence like the governor's shown her priorities to be such and such, or the governor probably won't like this recommendation because of such and such. Just to let the budget director know that I'm not crazy.

Other examiners, especially senior examiners, acknowledged a larger role for political rationality in their recommendations:

> Q: Were there political cues or something you picked up that said the governor basically has an orientation toward [a program]?

Senior Examiner: I can think of one where I thought, as a fairly new analyst, I could make a pretty radical proposal, save quite a bit of money, and still have a good [program]. I made that proposal and was told that that wasn't practical because even though it made sense relative to space utilization and staff utilization and even program operation, it meant that probably the agency couldn't reduce as many positions as the recommendation called for without laying somebody off. I was told we couldn't do that, and I was told as an alternative to go back in and just take out those positions that were vacant. . . .

But I did not make the proposal as radical the next time I made it, which was about three to four years later, as I did the first time, because I knew. The rules were basically the same four years later, as far as vacancies and things, same budget director, same governor, same players pretty much on our side, so I didn't bother with that. But I did make sure everybody realized that this was modest compared to what could have been done. So, yeah, that experience changed it, but it didn't really change what I thought could be done. It did change my recommendation. It did.

Possibly the most difficult facet of the examiner's analysis is political rationality. Examiners are professional civil servants and are keenly aware that they are not the governor's political policy staff. At the same time, there is a prevailing sense that the budget staff works for the governor, even though the budget director is the boss. Examiners rely heavily on the director for political cues about what the governor's priorities are for the ensuing budget. For example, an examiner working on a politically volatile hospital closure noted that "the political promises have to come directly from [the budget director]." Constant communication between examiners, supervisors, the director, and the governor are the key to ensuring that examiners do not recommend options that are totally unacceptable to the governor based on political reasons. The KSBO director noted:

I shouldn't be surprised by anything that they put in their analysis and none of it should be a surprise to the governor. That's called communication. We've certainly got a small enough staff here that, despite the fact I get pretty busy sometimes and it's tough to get one-on-one meetings with analysts, it's still not impossible. . . . There should be no surprises in there at all. . . . It's an ongoing process that requires a lot of conversations between a whole lot of people, governor's office with this office, this office with the staff, principals have to get in the middle of that, the agencies get in the middle of it. There's just a whole lot of conversation that goes on in order to do good analysis and good budget recommendations for the governor.

Examiners have little direct contact with citizen and advocacy groups, except through public hearings held by legislative committees. Most indicated they care about what citizens think about the agency programs, but rely on the agency to indicate citizen dissatisfaction (or other feelings). From their perspective, citizens have two ways of influencing policy: directly through the agency and its programs, or indirectly through their legislative representative. When agencies respond to citizen pressures, the examiners are receptive to evidence that citizens are demanding improvements or changes. However, as this examiner notes, they do not forget that their primary source of political direction comes from the governor: "A big part of our purpose here is to develop a budget that the governor will feel competent in presenting to the legislature. So things that we recommend need to be in tune with what [the governor] wants to accomplish."

Legal Facets of Budget Problems

The policy-oriented examiners also think about the legal facets of programs and activities for which funding is requested. James Fessler and Donald Kettl (1996) note that the most basic distinction between the public and private spheres in the United States is that public-sector agencies can only act in a manner authorized under the law, while private-sector actors can act in any manner unless prohibited by law. If the law does not provide for the agency activity, it lacks a basis for public funding. Examiners do not have to be lawyers or have actual legal training (although some may have law degrees), but they have to understand how laws apply to their agencies' activities. Fundamentally, state statutes codify the political agreements reached in legislative sessions, so examiners need to understand the legal thinking behind the issue—and may need to apply legal rationality to a budget problem. There are four primary sources of legal information for the examiner: enabling statutes, administrative code, court cases, and intergovernmental regulations. Occasionally, examiners may even find themselves referencing constitutional documents, especially state constitutions, because constitutional clauses stipulate higher order rights and obligations that influence why the law is the way it is.

Reviewing past state budgets will often lead the examiner to the state statutes, the legal source of authority for the agency to conduct its programs. Enabling statutes authorize agencies to conduct activities within specified parameters. Consequently, although the practice varies widely across the states, budget bills before the legislature often contain "statutory language" creating and authorizing a new program (or a change in a program) to be funded in the budget. Yet program implementation problems may result from enabling legislation consisting of vague and sometimes contradictory goals.

When an agency's mission is broadly defined, it is the agency's budget that becomes the de facto constraint on the number of programs and activities that implement the statutory mission statement.

Specification of agency activities and goals is also found in the state's administrative code. Complex operations such as Medicaid and other welfare programs may entail many pages of regulations. As a new examiner, Mary cannot be expected to read and digest all of the rules pertaining to her assigned agencies, but it certainly behooves her to initially skim the relevant chapters to become familiar with the structure of the code in the event that she will need to use them to determine if an agency request is authorized by the code, or a particular proposal is otherwise restricted by the code. An MNSBO examiner goes to the statutes "when there's a particular problem. If we're required to sign off on a document that is questionable, I may refer to the statutes at that point" to look for authorization and constraints.

Some examiners will learn in issue papers, or from agency personnel, that the basis for a certain agency activity lies in a lawsuit and court order mandating that the state do X or Y. The corrections and education assignments are prime areas for such cases, mandating minimum dietary requirements or a certain type of grant formula to distribute (or redistribute) funding for K–12 education. Unless they have a law degree, examiners are unlikely to attempt to analyze the court ruling. However, understanding the basic intent of the ruling is essential, and the examiner may need to consult the SBO's legal counsel or some other source to help interpret a case to evaluate whether an agency proposal violates a court order. The exchange below illustrates the linkage between the social and legal facets of budgeting:

> Q: If someone came to you and said, why do we have the Indigent's Defense, can't we just eliminate this, could you tell them why it exists?
> Examiner: Basically it's required by the Constitution; not so much the state, it's the federal Constitution. If you're charged with a crime, you'll have your defense provided for you if you can't afford one. The state supposedly can do it cheaper. The state could push it off to the counties and say the counties have to do it. Somebody has to do it, and the state figures they can do it cheaper than pushing it down to the county level.

Intergovernmental regulations dominate some agency activities more than others. Where there is significant federal-state cooperation, the examiner will find the state agency constrained by grant contracts, cross-cutting federal requirements and other complicating rules. Many federal programs require matching state funds, and there are myriad rules pertaining to what qualifies as matching and what does not. When the examiner suggests cutting some aspect of a program to reallocate funds elsewhere, the change cannot conflict with the grant restrictions unless the state is willing to forgo the federal funds. In that case, cutting state funds to save money for other priorities can ultimately cost the total budget more than will be saved in a particular program. Some examiners "live almost in a federal world when you're looking at their budget. With Department of Human Resources, it's learning their relationship with the federal laws and regulations in the U.S. Department of Labor. Their budget is 82 percent taken up with the unemployment insurance program, which is a mandated program by the federal government."

New decision items also occur because a new federal mandate or a radical change in a state-federal program may require a substantial restructuring of agency programs. The recent changes in federal welfare programs had required substantial work in rethinking and restructuring state welfare activities and budgets. New priorities on childcare and transportation have prompted development of programs to purchase cars for workfare recipients and for increased subsidies to childcare providers. Each of these is forcing changes in state social welfare budget allocations. Yet federal rules can restrict the allocation of funds to one aspect of the problem or another. Recall the extended quote from the VASBO analyst regarding legislative mandates. The state legislative mandate problem was compounded by federal rules tied to the program!

It is imperative that the policy-oriented examiner be able to recognize a legal issue as it arises in the context of a budget request or a policy initiative from the governor. The legal facets of budget problems tend to be constraints to budgetary change, but as Majone (1989) explains, many policy constraints can also be opportunities for change, depending on the political feasibility.

The legal issues underlying the agency budgets are both constraints and opportunities that arise during the annual budget development phase, as this examiner made clear:

> I was asking, why do you do it this way, why do you do it that way? I learned a lot. One reason they did it this way is because this is what the federal government funded them. They gave them a particular software program and a particular piece of equipment. That's how come they're doing it that way, because that's what they got. And so that gives you a little bit of insight into how that agency operates. A lot of it is dictated by the sources, the rules they get from the federal government. . . . If Uncle Sam pays the bill, he makes the rules.

Legal issues can also affect a sense of budgetary priorities. This is particularly true in agencies involved with intergovernmental funding (such as unemployment compensation) or involved with significant judicial constraints (such as corrections). One examiner reported pressure from a previous budget director "to drive down general fund costs and substitute federal discretionary funding and squeeze the agencies." Another examiner reported:

> Take, for example, a piece of equipment that's being requested. If that piece of equipment is related to maintaining a federal grant or maintaining compliance with a court order, that's a higher priority than one that's necessary to meet a program objective that the governor has set forth. That's of higher priority than one where the agency's been waiting for it for three years.

As gubernatorial priorities change (perhaps with a new governor or a new term), proposed program changes (in budget requests) may conflict with previously codified agreements, or conflict with more fundamentally established rules such as the Constitution or court orders. Most examiners said their need to apply legal rationality to budget decisions is generally issue driven, arising as specific problems need clarification and reframing. In one particular case, an examiner worked on the budget for the National Guard, which had been out helping flood victims:

> Their budget has been highly, highly costly this year to them. They had an appropriation for this type of disaster relief, which was expended, like, the first three days of rain. So they went through and determined that they were going to need some additional funding. I went back into the statutes to see what the responsibilities of the adjutant general were, how it relates to flooding, what responsibilities and what legalities they have to flooding, and in particular—with [the governor] trying to establish counties as state disaster counties to make them eligible for federal aid—what responsibilities the adjutant general's office has to obtain that federal aid, because all the federal aid money ultimately goes through the adjutant general's budget.

The most frequent use of legal documents reported by policy-oriented examiners was to find the statutory purpose for an agency, and the authority by which it conducted certain activities. Although they do not exercise legal reasoning to a degree resembling a lawyer, examiners do acquire a sense of how statutes are constructed, what connotations certain words have in a legal argument, and how to interpret the statutes (at least to some degree). It is rare that an examiner delves into the legalities of a particular budget problem so intensely that he or she is deeply engaged in legal rationality (determining specific legal rights and responsibilities in detail). On the other hand, as legal facets to budget problems arise, they exercise their legal knowledge to address budget problems.

The Effectiveness Framework and Efficiency Rationalities

The social-political-legal (SPL) analysis Mary learns to conduct in the predevelopment phase is used to frame the context in which budget requests for her agency programs will be evaluated as budget problems. An examination of the social aspects provides the foundations of why the program exists at all. The political facets are examined to map friends and foes of various programs and gain understanding of how the political actors salient to a given program will support one type of program change and oppose another. The legal facets are examined to rule out alternative program ideas which conflict with intergovernmental and other legal problems.

As a policy-oriented examiner, Mary needs to understand the SPL decision framework before she can examine the actual budget requests submitted to her later in the budget process. She will not have time to glean this understanding then, so it is to her advantage to use the "slow" execution phase of the budget cycle to learn these aspects of her agencies' budget problems. The predevelopment effectiveness analyses have outlined the social, political, and legal facets of agency programs and problems. The SPL facets of agency budgets are particularly salient with respect to the governor's policy agenda and priorities. The governor's preferences provide the examiners with political imperatives that guide the overall budget process as well as their individual analyses of agency budget requests.

Underlying the SPL analysis is a concern for policy implementation. Howard (1973, 117) acknowledges that program implementation—budget execution—has always been a central concern of state budgeting, and state examiners, much more than federal (OMB) examiners, have a long-standing responsibility to monitor program effectiveness for the governor. Budgeting literature suggests that policies are created at least as much during implementation as they are in legislative votes. Examiners in policy-oriented SBOs have integrated their implementation analysis of programs with their budget request analysis. Their visits with program managers and field officers provide them with keen insights into how policies are being shaped at the street level. They can evaluate whether the budget is progressing in consonance or dissonance with the governor's agenda and policies. They need to connect implementation problems in the field with the next round of budget development to continuously shape and reshape state policies as directed by the governor and approved or modified by the legislature.

The examiners are able to blend responsiveness to gubernatorial perspectives with the demands of program implementation. This MOSBO examiner tried to anticipate the governor's reaction to her recommendation, at least "a little bit."

> I tried at least this year, for sure [with] the new governor; I tried to look at some of his position papers on what he felt strongly for, and was trying to push some of those through more than things that he really didn't. His big thing was consolidation of FTEs, making government more productive. So if there were things like some new computer equipment that might eliminate three people, that was something more that I would think about recommending. Or finding out more information on it and was more versed so I could discuss it and try to convince them, or let them know, that this was a good idea.

Examiners need not be involved in managing the state agency to serve in this analytical capacity. The nature of the budget process in the policy-oriented SBOs helps focus attention on areas that need analysis throughout the cycle. First, the initial forays of the examiner to the agency heads for discussions about agency priorities and problems establishes an analysis agenda that focuses the examiner on only a few issues for the next budget development phase. Field visits help the examiner frame the problem in non-economic terms, providing the conditionalities for the technical and economic analyses that await the budget development period. Second, the agency's priorities list and agenda are reconciled with the governor's early in the process, via soundings from the budget director and cues the examiner has picked up from the governor through previous briefings and other sources. Third, as the development phase begins, the constant dialogue between the examiner and his or her supervisor, the budget director, and the governor's policy staff effectively integrates the agency-specific decisions with the overall budget decisions. The latter begin to crystallize around budget balance decisions as the sum of agency requests is juxtaposed with the latest revenue estimates and political estimates of the feasibility and desirability of raising revenues in some manner.

Policy implementation is that part of the policy-making process during which politicians, bureaucrats, private interest groups, and the public at large vie for control over the direction of a program. The policy-oriented examiners are well aware that directives are adapted to the circumstances of each organization area, creating a discretionary gap between the directive from the top and the policy directive as implemented. Examiners are important sources of bottom-up flows of information on program effectiveness. Sometimes street-level bureaucrats disagree with directed policy, perhaps because they see it as unrealistic, perhaps because it upsets established routines. In any case, it is hard for the legislature and courts to sanction agencies. In part, this is due to the problematical measurement of successful implementation. It is hard to measure success *or* failure.

We can view policy analysis as a way of filtering decision items to focus on priorities and important issues, exposing and highlighting the underlying values and decision criteria, explaining why one alternative is preferred over another. The feasibility of specific proposals from agencies for budgetary changes must be gauged by consonance with the governor's policy priorities as well as by technical and economic efficiency criteria.

One policy-oriented examiner made the point clearly:

> If a new initiative is going to be funded, it has to have a solid grounding in policy and politics, no matter if the state has money to burn (which it never has). If a program doesn't make sense and/or doesn't have any political support, the chances of it being included in the budget are not that great. I think we take all those things into account. Obviously, one can override all the rest. Even in a year of really tight fiscal constraints, a new initiative might get funded based on other considerations. And vice versa.

As the policy-oriented examiners approach the end of the predevelopment phase of the budget cycle, about the beginning of September, they are able to construct an SPL framework in which they will analyze the effectiveness of impending budget requests due from their assigned agencies. When these arrive on their desks in early October, the examiners have a short period to analyze the requests with respect to both efficiency rationalities *and* effectiveness rationalities.

Next, we discuss decision-making in the *development phase* of the budget cycle, which coincides with the agencies' submitting their official budget requests to the SBO for review. The traditional task of examiners is technical efficiency analysis of agency budget requests during the budget development phase. The policy-oriented examiners use two types of thinking about efficiency problems to complete their budget analyses. They use technical rationality to think about ways in which agencies can maximize their input/output ratio, that is, technical efficiency. They use economic rationality, characterized by marginal utility analysis, to think about how to allocate the scarce dollars allotted for the agency budget in such a way as to maximize overall effectiveness of agency activities. The effectiveness analyses conducted in the execution phase of the budget cycle are essential for economic rationality to be valid. Marginal utility analysis does not order the agency's program priorities for the examiner. The examiner takes his or her understanding of the agency's priorities, gained through the effectiveness rationalities, and uses them as a framework for the economic rationality that they can now apply to the agency budget.

Development-Phase Analysis

The old budgets Mary reviews during her first week on the job provide some key information for the technical and economic decisions that need to be made with respect to an agency budget request. Most importantly, they place the agency's budget in context regarding size and complexity regarding funding and funding sources. Understanding funding structures is important. For if funds are to be reallocated, diminished, or augmented for some reason, the examiner needs to know what is financially feasible, and needs to know where there is money to reallocate.

The recessionary periods of the early 1990s produced a new emphasis on scrutiny of agency base budgets. In this regard, examiners are increasingly likely to analyze each program to determine how much slack is available for capture and use in the next budget. After all, money saved in the current fiscal year is available as cash balance carried into the next. It is a technique that MNSBO examiners used:

> When we put the budget together, we have to start with a very low level of detailed information and do a lot of manipulation of that and other things. One of the issues is always base adjustments for the budgets, and you have to understand pretty clearly what the agency's done in their budget in order to determine whether you're going to agree or not agree with the way they do their base adjustments, especially when you're not generally providing any more money to the agency. The real budget decisions get made in the base adjustment, even though that's something that usually doesn't go up to the higher levels. That's sometimes where the real money is. It doesn't always surface. There's a variety of ways to manipulate the money in your budget to increase your base and that's something you need to be aware of.

The largest potential savings area is personnel expenditures. It is also a primary area for reallocating program resources to increase allocative efficiency. Recall the examiner previously quoted who discussed reallocating positions with his agency, "restructuring workload or restructuring personnel to reflect a change that's occurred in the workload." The ability of an SBO to capture money left at the end of a year due to vacant positions is a key tool in enlarging the balance carried forward. In severe fiscal stress periods, freezing positions is a tried and true technique for saving money. Once a position is vacated, the SBO can refuse permission for the agency to fill the position. Exceptions to the freeze are routed through the SBO and granted by the budget director. The rationale for maintaining the position can also be opened to review for the next budget. Positions that have remained vacant for more than a year may be "taken" and reallocated to another program or agency. Even though this may actually involve no savings to the state's "bottom line," it represents a real opportunity for the governor to redirect budgetary resources—and increase allocative (economic) efficiency.

Questions regarding vacant positions and the dreaded "position freeze" highlight important issues of the technical efficiency of agency programs. Position management focuses attention on technical efficiency issues such as program staffing and workloads. Related efficiency issues include capital/labor substitution in programs, and whether agency procedures are efficient. Current attention in these areas focuses on reengineering programs and total quality management initiatives.

Technical Rationality

The objective of technical rationality is technical efficiency: to maximize the service provided by an agency with the minimum amount of dollars necessary to support the activity. Technical rationality is very quantitative in the sense of input and output measures. Examiners view budget problems through the technical frame by thinking about efficiency largely in terms of workloads and productivity indicators. The prisoners-per-guard and prisoners-per-cell ratios cannot quantitatively measure the quality of life or the stress levels of guards in an overcrowded prison. The examiner uses the implementation phase of the budget cycle to physically "see" program outcomes and activities. Examiners who tour the facilities gain an understanding of what the quantitative ratios mean, and use this information as they think about their recommendations. A Department of Corrections budget serves as an example:

> Q: A couple of prisons have invited you into the process?
> Examiner: They'll be discussing it with you when you're there. All the sudden you've got the financial officer and the accountant and the warden and the deputy wardens and they're all wanting to know what's the status of this, how much are we going to get this year? Are we going to have to close a facility?. . . . I say, well, send me the research material.
>   They want us to implement a central kitchen facility. Sounds like a big deal, right, for nine prisons. It's a $5 million project. Take the kitchen staff out, make it run. Well, the first thing, they told me it was coming. I asked

for all the research they've done. You start going through that, there's no hard numbers. Fine. They're doing a study presently, they took me out when they went to visit some facilities that actually have this in place.

The principal efficiency measure that requires technical rationality is an evaluation of workload data that are often generated by agencies to support budget requests. The examiner must decide whether the agency's technical framing of the problem as increased workload (for example) is a sign of increased productivity or a sign of service-level stress that will eventually cause political pressures (i.e., problems) for the governor. Once again, the chief means for the examiner to evaluate the workload evidence is by drawing on his or her experiences during the agency visit, when he or she could see the strain on equipment, or the piles in the in-baskets of the licensing bureau staff.

One examiner spoke of evaluating a state hospital, and arguing that "this could be closed because there aren't enough people there to operate it, enough to keep it efficiently running. (So far it's never gone anywhere.)" Another examiner spoke of negotiating with the agency on decision items in terms of technical efficiency issues as subordinate to effectiveness rationalities, but definitely an important consideration:

> If it's something that I think is a nifty little thing, then I will say, convince me. That means take me out and show me a particular problem you've got or give me the information to back it up. Show me that if you make this change, this is going to increase your efficiency to do this or something. When we get to that point, it's usually because they've convinced me that I should do this.

An MNSBO examiner noted that "just because it's a natural resources program, that doesn't mean that it's efficient or effective. I think that there are many of us out there who are questioning whether the approach is just to continue applying resources to some of these programs and policies as they have in the past without ever circling back and sort of reevaluating how things are done."

In addition to analyzing the requests for validity and reliability in terms of technical efficiency, these policy-oriented examiners also *evaluate* the agency request and develop alternatives that they determine better fit the governor's agenda. Policy-oriented examiners cannot ignore technical efficiency analysis; they are responsible for verifying the technical accuracy of the agency requests. More importantly, though, they move beyond this analysis to a policy evaluation of the requests. The expansion of the budget analysis to a policy analysis enables the policy-oriented examiners to conduct an economic efficiency analysis for the governor.

Economic Rationality

How funds have been distributed across agency programs in past budgets is an important indicator of the relative importance of each agency program. In effect, they record the political agreements on budgetary priorities when the budget was passed into law. They suggest that small programs with one or two staff are not as important to the agency mission as a program with fifty staff, for example. On the other hand, larger pools of funds and larger programs are also seen as more likely to have organizational slack, and thus less likely to feel the impact of a lost position or a minor cut in funding.

Allocative (economic) efficiency requires the "capacity to establish priorities within the budget, including the capacity to shift resources from old priorities to new ones, or from less to more productive uses, in correspondence with the government's objectives" (Schick 1997). Given a sense of agency and gubernatorial priorities, examiners think about whether the proposed agency budget requests will maximize the effectiveness of the agency. The problem is framed by consideration of which (if any) of the requests competing for additional budget dollars will help the agency accomplish the goals and priorities established in current law, or stipulated as new initiatives of the governor.

Examiners conduct economic analysis during the budget development phase. Mary, our policy-oriented examiner, is equipped to evaluate the economic efficiency of a budget request because she has previously developed the analytical framework in which she conducts the economic efficiency analysis. Before she begins this type of thinking, she has thought about the role of the agency and the rationale behind the various programs and activities, determined agency priorities (even when the agency could not or would not explicitly state them), and learned about the budgetary fiscal climate from the budget director. Economic efficiency is measured in terms of marginal utility. The marginal utility analysis for an agency budget requires a set of ordered preferences by which the available funds can be allocated to the highest-priority program first, the remaining funds to the next highest priority, and so on. The last dollar appropriated to the agency budget should be allocated to the highest priority program in need of funding. The primary value of the effectiveness framework (the SPL analysis) established in the *predevelopment* phase is a solid understanding of agency priorities. In addition, Mary has also developed an understanding of how the programs work so that she can craft alternative means of achieving program goals.

A senior examiner describes the shift in thinking that begins the development phase of analysis: "When you're making that first or second or third visit out to the agency just to understand what they're doing and how they're trying to meet their objectives, I think numbers are probably secondary." But once agency budgets are submitted to the SBO, "I think at that point in time, the numbers come more into account." Discussions with agencies change:

> Now the things you've seen and talked about that didn't have numbers assigned to them, now they do. You're also probably talking at a higher level. You may not go back to that lower-level manager again. You may, but you probably won't because you know what your background is. Now you're sitting down and you're talking to the people that do know the numbers and do know how the numbers fit with the goals and objectives, and what's going on in the field. OK, here we are, and you talk about the alternatives and how they work.

Although there is only a short amount of time available, the examiners are able to evaluate the merits of an agency request comprehensively because much of the evaluation was done prior to the request's actually being submitted to the state budget office. The examiner looks at the past budget documents and briefing papers and cannot make any sense of them until after a visit to the agency and discussions with the personnel who can explain the context for the request. The statements of policy-oriented examiners, such as this one, support the contention that economic rationality requires a framework wherein alternatives are ranked in terms of priority: "Basically on my recommendations . . . I used a lot of information off my agency visits and the reading that I'd done about them."

Understanding the effectiveness (SPL) aspects of the affected agency program spawns ideas for alternative means for the agency to accomplish the objectives laid out in its budget request. It is difficult to develop policy alternatives without a solid understanding of what happens now, and why it happens that way. Instead of simply deciding "yes" or "no" with respect to a program request, Mary is responsible for developing alternative program changes, or alternative funding levels that will accomplish the agency's goals—consonant with the governor's policy agenda. Once the examiner learns from discussions with the budget director or section manager that the agency request will be recommended by the SBO, then the focus of work is on refining the agency proposal, or developing the most efficient and effective alternative, as illustrated by an example from a VASBO examiner:

> So, let's say, the finance secretary says, "yes, we must go with this [system] but we need to fund it in the most economical and efficient manner."

So even though I know the final result is we're going to fund, I need to . . . ensure that we're funding it for the least amount of dollars. In addition, my recommendation may also be—it was in this particular case—alternative financing because of instead of putting the appropriation in the agency itself, because there were certain costs that we weren't sure about, I suggested that we put it in central appropriations because in Virginia we have that avenue. And then out of the agency-incurred actual costs, then we transfer that money to the agency. It adds more paperwork on me and more responsibility, but it also give the budget agency greater control over the actual dollars being spent. Good example, we funded the [approved system] for $3.5 million. The actual contract was less at $2.9, so we were able to save $600,000 in central appropriations and not in the agency's budget having to take it back out. So that alternative appropriation financing also gave us greater control over the dollars being spent.

If the agency initiative is not a policy concern of the governor, Mary's most likely response will be to deny the request completely. As one GASBO examiner remarked, "If I am going to go out on a limb for something, it has got to be required by law and/or it has got to be a benefit." And a colleague echoed, "You must be prepared to make your case. They can undress you pretty quickly. You must make a good case for new spending or know that the governor likes it." The SBO mission is to find money for the governor's policy agenda; if that coincides with the agency agenda, so much the better for the agency. If not, then the agency request will die for lack of executive support. Rarely, such requests get resurrected in the legislative phase, yet would still face gubernatorial veto.

Crafting the Examiner's Recommendation

The end of the development phase of the executive budget process is marked by the presentation of the governor's budget to the legislature. Thus far, we have observed how the examiners use the *predevelopment* phase of the budget cycle to gather critical background information on their agencies' programs. We have observed the types of information the policy-oriented examiners have collected, and how those affect the type of analyses they conduct on the budget requests they receive in the *development phase* of the budget cycle. The examiners reported that their development phase budget reviews relied heavily on the effectiveness analyses conducted during the execution phase. It is the composite picture, assembled one frame at a time that permits the examiner to provide the budget director and the governor with comprehensive budget analysis during the intensive budget review stage.

The penultimate step in the budget development phase is crafting and presenting the SBO budget recommendations to the governor. The governor has the right to change any recommendation made by an examiner, and freely does so if it is deemed appropriate. Yet a very high proportion of recommendations from examiners in policy-oriented SBOs are accepted by governors for inclusion in their budget proposals to the legislatures, so it behooves us to better understand how these recommendations are crafted.

Our policy-oriented examiner, Mary, has known throughout the executive budget process that she is responsible for crafting effective budget recommendations to the governor. An effective recommendation is one for which she has thoroughly examined the agency's budget request, and she can comfortably outline the feasible alternatives and argue in favor of one policy alternative over another, and which therefore has a high probability of being affirmed by the governor. "If I make a recommendation, I want that recommendation to be valid," remarked a KSBO examiner who spoke for many colleagues in the policy-oriented SBOs. In order to get to that step in the process, the recommendation of the policy-oriented examiner must be feasible with respect to the multiple facets of the budget problem. Each facet has its own underlying rationality that cannot be violated without serious consequences. In effect, the decision rules for evaluating budget requests involves an extensive checklist that ensures that the examiner accounts for the multiple effectiveness and efficiency decision criteria.

Consider this discussion with a WISBO examiner:

> When I have an issue come in front of me, the first thing to do is understand the issue, every little detail about it. So I do that. Then I try and see what's the problem here. Perfect example: the deficit in the [special fund]. [The agency] wanted to increase [certain] fees, which means industry pays more money per ton. . . . I sat there and thought this is really kind of hodgepodge policy-making because there are a lot of things we could alter in this formula to generate additional money. I don't particularly know if, in the budget adjustment bill, if that's one we should jump into right now. Also, it's an election year for the governor. He doesn't want to have to charge industry anymore. So even though they balance about the same, I didn't think it was good public policy to be manipulating this formula in a two-day span when there are a lot of, you know, you could tax more pollutants, you could tax above 4,000 tons.
>
> There were a lot of different options we could have looked at. . . . After collecting all the information I needed, I realized that those were different options I came up with. . . . The agency submitted their request and said, "We have this deficit, and we can either do nothing, do alternative #1 or

alternative #2." And I think alternative #1 was basically a fee increase with some expenditure reductions.

Q: So in addition to the options [the agency] outlined, you came up with several other options?
Examiner: Right. The options I came up with were reducing quite a bit more and throwing [the agency] into somewhat of a noncompliance with the [federal] Act. But we could pick it up in the next biennium. . . . *I knew that an option wasn't increasing the fees, politically.* So I had to come up with something that didn't increase fees. Outside of that, I just had to figure out a way to try and adhere as much as possible to the [federal law] *so we wouldn't be sanctioned*, while at the same time presenting something that the governor would want to recommend. And I knew that was not a fee increase. So that's how I came up with the different [alternatives].

This passage demonstrates a search for feasible alternatives, considering a variety of constraints. First, the examiner cannot approve a request or develop an alternative that modifies or eliminates a program with social backing in ways that violate the underlying social rationality of the program, for example, environmental protection.

Second, the politics of an agency or a specific program (e.g., industrial emissions controls) limit the number of alternatives that are politically feasible. Agency proposals and examiner alternatives that detract from the (sometimes ill-defined) majority consensus about the role of the state are unlikely to receive support in the governor's office or in the legislature. Understanding which interest groups (including their legislative spokespersons) support and oppose agency programs and program changes is helpful in guiding the examiner's decision about which issues will demand more time and analysis.

More importantly, the examiner needs to find out where the issue stands with respect to the governor's policy agenda. If the issue is important to the governor, then it is useful to know the governor's general perspective so that at least one of the alternatives crafted for his or her consideration is likely to be acceptable. This is not to rule out presenting alternatives that the examiner believes to be "good public policy" even if it is intuitively counter to the governor's political leanings. As a VASBO section manager noted, good analytical skills in an examiner mean that it "is not so much two minus one is one and what does that mean, it's more to sit back, look at something, know what the governor's priorities are, what some of the political priorities are, keeping in your mind—you know, that the budget should be prudent and fiscally sound and to weigh all these things and be able to make a sound recommendation based on that."

Majone (1989) describes evidence, argument, and persuasion as important factors in policy decisions. The experienced examiner can go into a
briefing with the governor prepared to argue a position she knows will not
be the governor's first choice. The governor is free to reject the advice, always. But it is quite another matter for the examiner to brief the governor on
an issue and recommend an alternative without knowing that the governor
has publicly taken the exact opposite position. Veillette (1981, 67) observes,
"Only infrequently have budget examiners been criticized for making unpopular recommendations." Criticism is prevented by careful arguments that
anticipate gubernatorial priorities. As a senior VASBO examiner explained:

> Everything comes up to a peak, and it has to meet the governor's agenda
> items. We have to anticipate what the governor's gonna say on a given
> item and a lot of the analysis that we do is try and anticipate what the
> governor would do if he were in my shoes at this point. I mean we don't
> want to go across the street with a bunch of stuff where he just throws it
> back in our face and says, "This hasn't anything, but nothing, to do with
> my agenda, or anything that I'm interested in." My opinion doesn't make
> any difference. . . . Part of my job is knowing what his agenda is and what
> he is going to say, what he will likely say when I give an issue. That way
> we go across the street and say, "Here's this issue and here's what we think
> and this is the reason why we think it" from the standpoint [that] it meets
> all the little points that he would be interested in.

Third, legal constraints required the WISBO examiner to think about the
state's responsibility to comply with the federal law, and some alternatives
offered more concordance than others. Programs cannot easily be modified
or eliminated in ways that conflict with statutory or constitutional provi-
sions. The legal rationality underlying programs details rights and obligations of program participants. Changes that alter these aspects of a program
(such as jeopardizing a state-match requirement for a federal grant, or reducing
funding for foreign trade office services) require a change in legislation, or regulatory code or a contract between the state and a service provider. A VASBO
examiner described another case of trouble when legal rationality is violated:

> I misinterpreted—I didn't read some legislation carefully so I told the powers
> that be that we could make money off the user fees, that in reality we
> couldn't. I mean, we had the authority to, but there weren't enough clients
> or users that we could have charged to make the money, because I failed to
> focus in on one little word that I knew better, but I missed. So we had to go
> to the General Assembly and ask for $400,000 in general funds so as to
> make up for the difference.

There was another lesson in this event for the VASBO examiner. The mistake made at that time was that "we were not allowed to converse with the agencies about what we were thinking about doing, in which my lesson was from that: *if there is something you know, that is controversial or you're not certain about, you need to approach the agencies* . . . communicate informally and off the record to run things by them." Even if the examiner were not permitted to tell the agency what she was doing, "you could still get the feedback."

The SPL framework is a useful heuristic for ruling out certain alternatives, and the policy-oriented examiner learns to be adept at influencing "the direction of agencies' policies." As this extended quote from an examiner indicates, there is much discretion involved:

> We try to, we can send messages subtly or not so subtly, [that the] policy direction that the agency's pursuing is acceptable or not. We can telegraph if you're going to do that, don't expect any extra money in the budget, that's not going to be looked upon favorably. Or that something else will be looked upon very favorably. We can kind of push on the string, so to speak. Case in point. For years there's been complaints about the wastewater permitting system [the agency] uses. Anybody that discharges wastewater anywhere, water in the state, which is municipalities, wastewater treatment plants, large corporations, whatever, has to have a permit. [The agency] has a tremendous backlog of permits. In some cases permits can be over a couple years because they claim they don't have the staff to issue the permits and it's a very complicated, time-consuming process. And it bothers everybody, permitees, municipalities, corporations complain because they're left in limbo because they have to operate under an outdated permit. [The agency] complains because they don't get the full revenues. Environmentalists complain because the environmental regulations aren't enforced strictly enough.
>
> Just on the last budget [the agency] came in and said, look, we need a whole bunch more staff, 10 to 15 people, and a lot more money, and that's just to make a dent in it. We really need like 200 more people if we really want to fix this problem. Well, we looked at that. Again, *the governor's position was that we weren't going to add staff. So we looked for an alternative.* So from a control point, this was very easy. We're going to control this, we're just not going to allow you any more staff. *But then on a policy perspective, we could look at it and say here's a problem that needs to be solved, how can we do this?*
>
> What we ended up doing is putting money in the budget for a study, which is fairly uncommon, and then I talked to [the agency], talked to some other people from [an agency program], they suggested the concept

of reengineering an operation which is a management buzzword in the private sector firms now, but just basically start from scratch and look at the process, see what needs to be done and how it should be done, just to see if all the stuff they're doing with the permitting process is necessary. And I had a kind of a gut feeling that it wasn't. A lot of it was just bureaucratics [sic] that's been there for 100 years.

    Well, we couldn't direct this. What we did was we said there's no more positions, here's funding for a study, figure an alternative out. And then after the budget was signed and the money was there, we went over and said, "Look, you hire a consultant that is experienced in this reengineering concept." We actually gave them two names that [the SBO] people had worked with, said call these people up and have them come up and make a proposal. And they did and the agency accepted that and they're in the middle now of a consultancy to review the entire permitting process, with the idea that they will be able to eliminate a lot of the things they did and still issue the permits that are acceptable to the federal government to protect the environment without spending so much staff time. I think it's going to work out. . . .

The issue as framed by the agency is a technical problem of too few staff to process permits. This framing is rejected by the examiner, who recognizes that a "technical" solution hits political problem constraints. Yet the social rationality underlying the problem, "environmental protection is important," conflicts with the political problem of municipalities and businesses being harmed by an inefficient process. The examiner must seek a solution that resolves the social and political rationalities at work in the program and does not violate other constraints. The recommended option, accepted by the governor and legislature, is a different technical solution (a management study) presumably leading to management reforms.

The IASBO budget director urged her examiners to guide agencies in framing their requests in the best possible way to the governor. In her view, the SBO knew "more about what the climate is and what's going to be accepted. And you may or may not know the direction the governor's going, but if you could help people not waste time on developing something that you know is not going to go, or if you need this little twist, or nuance, to it in the beginning, that's what you should be doing. I think that was our role to do that, to provide guidance to agencies." Framing the budget problem would appear to involve subtle judgments that require the examiner to know the macro-micro nexus for the current budget year, the governor's inclinations generally (or specifically to the issue at hand), and a thorough knowledge of agency needs and a belief that the request is justified.

The requirement in most states of a balanced budget frames another set of feasibility criteria for evaluating a budget request or alternative proposal relative to economic rationality. Marginal utility analysis is an effective method for allocating limited funds to current and proposed programs. Given a set of agency and gubernatorial priorities, the examiner must ensure that the top priorities receive first assignment of available revenues. Programs that rank lower on the priorities list may receive no additional funding. Funding for some lower ranking programs may be cut in order to free funds for higher priority programs. Starving a high-priority program to boost funds in a low-priority program violates the economic rationality underlying the agency's (and the state's) budget.

Simplifying Decision Rules

There are several methods for simplifying the process of matching priorities and funding. First, examiners work mainly on the margins of programs. Which is to say, most changes in programs are incremental, and changes to highest priority programs are considered first. Lower-ranking programs receive consideration only as available revenues permit. Second, budget directors can target allocations for a program area, leaving the development of the details to the examiner and the agency. Thus, $10 million may be initially allocated by the budget director to welfare reform enhancements, and the examiner and agency will develop alternative scenarios and recommendations on which of the long list of agency requests fit the policy agenda within the fiscal target.

The top-down flow of information about the governor's policy agenda frames the effectiveness analysis that is crucial for framing the subsequent technical and economic choices awaiting evaluation of the agency budget requests. Similarly, the bottom-up flow of information about the agency request and SBO alternatives must place the funding proposals in the context of the governor's policy agenda. Cuts are justified in terms of low policy priorities while funding increases enable high policy priorities. The vast majority of programs in the middle are largely left untouched, unable to argue for increases because they are not a gubernatorial priority, but relatively unscarred by base budget cuts because they are not the lowest priority among agency programs.

In effect, as a policy-oriented examiner, Mary considers each agency request as a multifaceted budget problem. As she considers each of the budget problem's facets, she is able to identify alternatives that are not feasible because they violate a rationality inherent in some facet of the problem. As the analysis proceeds through the social, legal, political, technical, and economic facets of the request, the policy-oriented examiner is able to narrow the set of viable policy alternatives to only a few. Ceteris paribus, she will search from among the remaining alternatives to recommend the option that maximizes the governor's policy objectives at the least cost. But if this option violates a legal constraint, for example, the examiner must recommend another option or suggest how the legal constraint should be removed to accommodate her first choice alternative.

A critical component of the comprehensiveness of examiners' recommendations is a continuing dialogue among staff inside the budget office. The examiner uses these conversations to test nascent alternatives with the senior examiner and budget director to determine the fuzzy bounds of "acceptability" with respect to potential recommendations. Senior examiners learn that:

> You bounce your general concept of what your review's going to do off of [the budget director and senior examiner] before you ever start putting the numbers together in complete detail. Or you've started doing it, you know where you're heading, you've set your goal with what you want to accomplish with your analysis, so you go to them and say, here's what I'm thinking of doing. I think I can close these three wards at this institution. We can use that staff to strengthen other areas. We'll save money here and here and we'll do a better job. Does that sound right to you?
>
> Or, I'm proposing a radical solution because we're really tight on the money and we can drop fifty positions if we really want to, but ten of them may require layoffs. Do you want to go that far? Here's why I think we can do that. And here's another alternative. . . . [Then] they say we can't afford to do that, why don't you go back and look at your alternative B which isn't so drastic. So I go back and try that and write the paper and bring it up to [the budget director].

Most policy-oriented examiners report a continuous dialogue with agencies as well. An IASBO examiner reported a particularly close working relationship with one of his agencies:

> About a month ago, [his agency] had a full day retreat kind of thing. . . . I spent a full day, was involved with the division administrators, the department head, deputy, and two other key people. It was very informative. I guess I felt good about it in the sense that they let me sit in on it and have input and thanked me for coming and said I was even helpful in raising issues. And sometimes on those retreat kind of things a department's going to get primarily focused on the things that they want and that they want to do. As somebody told me, it was helpful having the gentle reminders of the reality checks, that they aren't the only department in the world, not everything they want is necessarily a priority of the executive branch or the

legislative branch, and there is a limitation on dollars, and gentle remind-
ers of "what is your highest priority?"

Some of the VASBO examiners also seem to be particularly involved in
exploring new initiatives and options with their assigned agency. This VASBO
examiner was involved in research on a new tax collection system:

> Well, a good example is that the Department of Taxation. . . . I deal directly
> with the secretary a lot and we were looking at a private sector [firm] in
> this particular system. And so I was invited by the secretary to fly up to
> New York with a group of people to look at a private-sector enhanced
> collection system. And money committee staff on the legislative side also
> went. . . . And we saw it in operation. We talked to the people that had
> implemented it, to the vendor. We talked to the people who were operating
> it and we are trying to see the shortcomings as well as the enhancement
> and the positive aspects of it, to come back and communicate that so that
> we might avoid the pitfalls that other people have. The system is now cur-
> rently operational in Virginia.

While each story of a budget recommendation that the examiners related
was unique, there were also common threads in their approaches to making
budget decisions. For the policy-oriented examiners, effective recommendations to the budget director and governor mean that their analysis of the
agency budget problems must be as comprehensive as possible. Acceptable
recommendations lie within the bounds of an alternatives solution set where the
potential alternatives are judged for feasibility from multiple perspectives.

Gosling views problem representation as a critical element of persuasive
policy arguments in budget recommendations. He cites the example that "a
recommendation that defines a budgetary issue largely as a problem of inequity and evaluates budgetary options in terms of the extent to which they
improve equity will not go far in swaying a decisionmaker who sees the
problem not in terms of inequity but as an issue of inefficiency" (1997, 37).
Consequently, he argues, "when preferred options are not premised on shared
criteria of evaluation, the analyst faces the considerable challenge of per-
suading the client that the [analyst's] way of viewing the problem and weighing alternatives is better than the [client's]." A WISBO examiner shared this
experience with many examiners in other states:

> Both [the Department of Administration head] and the governor have par-
> ticular feelings about certain issues, certain initiatives and certain agen-
> cies. [An agency] is not well liked in the legislature and/or in the executive
> branch. So generally anything that you have to deal with [in the agency],

you know that you're going to have to overcome that initial negative reaction, even if what you're talking about is positive. The minute you say [to the agency], you've already got two strikes and you've got to overcome it just because of prior feelings and prior perceptions. So, yes, you certainly have to keep that in mind. I try to distinguish, keep that as a secondary issue. I think our job first of all is to give every request a thorough review regardless of whose views on the matter may be. But once you've done that, I think we would be foolish if we didn't take into consideration that the governor doesn't like [the agency], and if you're going to go in there with a proposal to recommend whatever, you better damn well know that because you're going to have a harder sell, you're going to have a harder presentation.

A KSBO examiner experienced the phenomenon somewhat differently:

When we're putting together a budget for the governor and if the governor says I have to reduce my budget, but the governor's already indicated this particular item I'm not willing to part with, then to come up and recommend that same item again really wouldn't make sense. It might get me technically to where I need to be. I might have been given a target with an agency and say you need to pull their numbers into this area or our budget's going to get overspent. In order to get into that target area, I may have to make a cut. But to select a cut that the governor's already said she doesn't want. . . .

There is a third principle that guides the crafting of recommendations by many examiners. Whereas policy analysis can take a long-run view, politics tends to be short-run. When analysts incorporate this factor into their recommendations, it may consist of a phased implementation of a program or policy, accommodating the political reality while projecting long-term strategic thinking and planning with the agency bureaucracy in mind, who will remain for implementation after the politicians are gone (Howard 1973, 140). This long-term perspective is often cited as the reason many analysts will recommend a certain option even though they presume it will not be acceptable to the budget director or governor. At a minimum, they want to put the issue on the table so that it will have a stronger probability of acceptance in the next budget round, as this IASBO examiner reported:

If I feel strongly enough about it, I will still recommend it. Based on the information I have, if I feel it's a very valid point, I don't want to sound too soft and squishy or anything like that, but if it absolutely is an essential service or something that would benefit Iowans, I'll make a recommendation.

Q: Knowing that it's going to be denied?
Examiner: Just so that in future years, just to make the point known, say we've got a real problem here and if we can't solve it this year because of finances, I understand that. But this is something that probably won't go away.

A similar long-run view was recounted by this MNSBO examiner: "No, I'll send it through. It has to get on the table. It happens many times on items like [certain] fees won't be paid for, we will not have any contingency accounts, and I'll send it anyway because it needs the attention. It's an item that I feel that we're not facing up to. Get on board and maybe hopefully other departments have the same problem. They usually do."

Briefing the Governor

One of the distinguishing characteristics between SBOs of strong policy orientations versus those of a weaker policy orientation is related to the character of the governor's briefings on SBO budget recommendations. The policy distance in strong policy-oriented SBOs is short largely because the examiners personally brief the governor. This is the case in GASBO, KSBO, and WISBO. In the other states (IASBO, MNSBO, MOSBO, and VASBO), the examiners personally brief the governor only occasionally. In VASBO, most examiners never seem to brief the governor, or even sit in meetings with the governor on any kind of regular basis.

Why should this make such a difference in the character of budget recommendations? As we explored in chapter 5, the contrast in the affiliations of examiners with the governor's agenda in the two types of SBOs is striking. In GASBO, KSBO, and WISBO, a personal interaction with the governor seems to have a strong influence on the ability—and willingness—of examiners to heed political imperatives from the governor or the governor's policy staff. Examiners who at least sit in the budget briefings and occasionally contribute detailed information, as in MOSBO and IASBO, feel stronger ties to the administration's agenda. But the affiliation is weaker, and not nearly as uniform among the examiners in other states. MNSBO and VASBO had similar briefing routines when we interviewed the SBO staffs, but MNSBO has a previous history of examiners regularly briefing governors, and the governor at the time (Governor Carlson) had broken that tradition. Very few VASBO examiners, in contrast, could ever recall briefing the governor on budget recommendations, and only a very few had even sat in meetings with the governor. A closer look into the briefing practices reveals the influence the briefing (or no briefing) context has on the way examiners craft their recommendations.

The briefing routine in GASBO, KSBO, and WISBO is very similar to this description offered by a GASBO examiner. "There's usually about a half dozen or more people in the room, including the governor, budget director, deputy budget director (occasionally), the section manager, the examiner, and one or more members of the governor's policy staff. The focus of the briefing is often directed by the budget director. For example, the budget director might say, '[The governor doesn't] want to hear about that, talk about this.'"

> I was toward the end and I think I did two or three of my agencies all at once; maybe I had a total of five minutes. . . . *You don't have much time to spend with the governor. . . .*
>
> Well, you go in, we did these notebook pages and what they are is budget highlights, and you pull them out of the budget requests, and you go through and you do a request column and then you do a recommendation column and when you're finished with all this . . . you have a governor's recommendation [column], and it changes.
>
> But, you know you'll have one through ten or one through five or whatever. And you'll have: this is what [the agency] is asking for in personal services . . . or you've got a bunch of improvements. So, you go in and you say whatever the agency and what page it's on and . . . he'll have a complete notebook with all the agencies that we do (and we're constantly revising those during meetings before meeting with the governor).
>
> But I was actually surprised. *He was very personable, and if he wants to know something, he'll ask you.* Like last year I think I was trying to recommend some money for solid waste loans, which is a really big issue as far as the state getting involved in making loans to local government to build landfills, you know that's always in the paper. *Well, he just came right out and said, well, I want to know what other states are doing about this. Find out for me if you don't know off the top of your head. I couldn't just say, well, no one knows really. . . .*

What is striking about this and similar examiner stories of briefings is that even though they have very little actual face-to-face contact with the governor, it is enough to establish a personal relationship between the governor and the examiner. This GASBO examiner found the governor surprisingly "personable," and they had a professional conversation on a personal level: "If you don't know off the top of your head." This particular examiner was quite nervous about the first briefing with the governor; such nervousness takes a long time to dissipate, if it ever does.

In MOSBO, "the budget director does most of the talking when it comes to briefing the governor." But the analysts are usually there to answer questions about specific items. "If there are items that we don't have a formal decision on yet with the governor, the analyst is always there to answer questions. So when it comes to just trying to give an overview so the governor understands the entire budget, the budget director does that. The specifics, the analyst does." This "on call" status—in contrast to the "at the table, on the line" status of GASBO, KSBO, and WISBO—results in a longer policy distance between the governor and examiners, and a weaker affiliation with the governor's agenda and priorities. As this MOSBO examiner explained:

> So we occasionally brief the governor, but . . . I don't interact with the governor. I don't interact with the commissioner [of administration], except we will brief [him] on the budget toward the end of the cycle and [he] will make their recommendations, "yes" for this program, "no" for this program, based on their administration's priorities. We will make recommendations on legislation to them, but all of that has been independently. . . . No thought is given, at least by me, as to what they want. It's just what I believe is good government and this is what the numbers will support. If they don't like it, that's fine.

The occasional nature of the briefings had a similar affect on this MOSBO examiner:

> I really think we are a separate agency. I mean, [the budget director] works for . . . the [administration department] head. I think we are a step aside, a step away from it. I don't think I work more for the governor than any other state employee. Although I work with them a lot, his staff. I don't work with the governor. . . .
> I may have [briefed the governor] once or twice, but the governors have different styles. I may have once or twice been up there with the governor himself. Probably more in the short time this governor's been here, probably more with him.

This last point is key to explaining the new policy orientation of the MOSBO, but also the larger policy distance between the governor and examiners. The previous experience with governors by MOSBO examiners was much more detached than at the time of our interviews. The new MOSBO budget director had moved the MOSBO orientation decisively away from control toward policy, and part of that change was a closer relationship between the governor and the examiners. The effect of the change apparently takes time to permeate the various aspects of examiner decision-making. The examiners understood the new policy orientation of MOSBO, and they seemed to have a better understanding of the governor's priorities. Yet they did not have the same consistent experience of being "at the table" with the governors to present and defend their budget recommendations.

The MOSBO story is similar to the MNSBO situation, although somewhat reversed. In Minnesota, the previous MNSBO experience was a tradition of a shorter policy distance to the governors. Yet the governor at the time we interviewed them was much more distant and the MNSBO examiners rarely saw him, much less met him at the briefing table. As a senior MNSBO examiner explained:

> [The briefing routine] changed a lot over the various terms. The first ones, yes, I spent a lot of time over in his office in the Capitol, and I enjoyed that part of it. We were pretty much almost all on a first name basis. There were meetings over in the mansion, worked closely with the staff, when Wendy Anderson was governor.
>
> Again, [with Governor Perpich we] worked very closely with the staff, almost on a daily basis. The governor not so much, but we were there, we were expected to be the person that did the briefing, made the recommendation, go through the budget.
>
> Q: You don't do that now with the current governor?
> Examiner: No, it seems like we make a lot of the recommendations and decisions here. There might be a certain level where I'll, depending on the issue I guess, I'll work with [the deputy budget director], we'll make a recommendation to go to [the budget director], maybe even [the finance commissioner]. We don't do things the way we used to do here.

Once again we see that the distance between the examiner and the governor "frees" the examiners "*to put the budget together ourselves.*" Translation: The examiners do not feel a strong policy imperative from the governor because he is "distant." This allows them to craft recommendations based on their perception of "good public policy" that may be in contrast to the governor's perception.

A core issue for Mary's decision-making is the problem of balancing or integrating the competing values of efficiency (both technical and allocative [economic] efficiencies) and political responsiveness to the gubernatorial imperative. Where an imperative is absent, the governor has no (known) preference on the budget issue and alternatives. In this case Mary can focus on efficiency values, relying on the effectiveness rationalities to frame the priorities of competing programs within an agency and across agencies. Knowledge of the relative priority of an agency request comes from initial feedback from the budget director and from what the examiner learns about her other assigned agencies. When the governor has a known preference, the examiner tries to craft alternatives that provide the governor with an acceptable option to meet his/her preferences. Often the recommended alternative may not perfectly match the governor's preferences, but is weighted to the efficiency values. Yet it is not unreasonable (in most cases) to foresee the possibility of the governor's being convinced by the examiner's argument that the recommended option meets efficiency values *and* is politically feasible from the governor's perspective.

Such balancing acts mean that examiners are often willing to "go to the wall" for an agency request, even if they expect a denial by the budget director and governor. In other cases, it means they will push to cut a particular program, or for a specific programmatic cut, even if the governor supports the program or finds it politically unfeasible. In these cases the examiner strives to put the option on the table, at least to give the governor the chance to accept the political risks associated with such cuts. Paul Nutt's (1999, 343) study "found that knowledge about the merits of alternatives helps in dealing with controversial decisions. Analysis was far more effective . . . when it provided carefully constructed argument for such decisions."

Two factors combine to raise the likelihood that the governor will accept the examiner's recommendation. First, examiners are inclined to put only "reasonable" options on the decision table for the governor. For a MNSBO examiner, "It just sort of forms sort of a first level of analysis. I call it the laugh test. Sometimes things get just so convoluted that it's the laugh test, you look at it and you think about it for a second, and if I was walking off the street and I looked at this, I'd say, 'Are you crazy?' That's sort of where I start [my analysis] from."

Second, the integrity the examiner has with the governor (and the budget director) increases the governor's level of trust that the recommended option is feasible in a political sense, as well as "good public policy." This exchange with an IASBO examiner illustrates the balancing act:

> If you do too much of bringing out stuff that you know isn't going to happen, I think you lose some personal credibility. I think you should do some of it, but if you do an awful lot of it, I think you lose some personal credibility [with the] budget director, whoever. Like I say, over the years I've dealt a lot with the governor's office and I think it even can happen more there. As I was told one time when I was trying to support some major maintenance stuff, "major maintenance never got anybody any votes." Damn true. One of those political realities. I don't view my job, although I've certainly learned politics and push-pull kind of stuff, I don't particularly view it as my job to make political decisions. I view my job as to make rational, business, program decisions.

Q: But you're aware of the politics?
Examiner: Oh, yeah.

Q: But it doesn't influence your decision at all?
Examiner: I try to not have it influence my initial decisions. After that first round of discussions within the department, within the liaison staff, the governor's office that's assigned to a particular agency and so on.

Q: So once you're informed of the reality of the politics, then . . .
Examiner: Then there's a problem here and I'll say, yeah, I know. Rationally, this is when I think the decision is. But I know how this is going to be perceived by the House.

The credibility of the option is bolstered by a short policy distance between the governor and examiners, and constant communication between the examiners, the section managers, the budget director, and the governor's policy staff. These multiple conversations induce efforts by the examiner to find an option that accomplishes the "good public policy" objective and also meets the political imperative of the governor. Examiners are not always compelled to seek the option that integrates political responsiveness with efficiency values.

I try, at least personally, to avoid the politics of an issue. But at the same time, I try to look at what's acceptable to the governor. The politics of, I can't think of a good example right now. If there's a program that the governor just dislikes for whatever good, bad, or whatever, he just dislikes a program. That's not so much politics, although that may be what he dislikes in it. But if I know that, that's going to influence the alternative that I come to. That's not going to stop me from sometimes, if I can't find an alternative that will provide good public policy and be acceptable to the governor, then I'll just come up with whatever's good policy. He's going to do what he wants.

A MNSBO examiner with a 60 percent affirmation rate of recommendations was indifferent to gubernatorial concerns when briefing the budget director:

So it's been going into briefings and saying a few words about a particular item and then having the budget director with the numbers saying yes or no, usually based on some completely different criteria sometimes than the merits of a particular project. But I don't have any problem going in and recommending something I think should go even if I don't think it will because it's sort of, it's their decision and if it's a bad decision, then it's their decision, too.

Q: As you're making this recommendation whether it's thumbs up or thumbs down, do you have a sense of whether the budget director is going to accept or reject your recommendation even as you make it?
Examiner: Sometimes I do, sometimes I don't.

Over multiple interviews we tried to capture the essence of the decision to "go to the wall" for an agency request versus the "don't waste my time" decision to reject the agency request (i.e., recommend no funding). A WISBO examiner captures the decision best:

I remember making this case to the governor, one of those cases where I was arguing, myself and my old team leader, were arguing with the governor on an issue where we felt strongly on a particular policy basis that something should be done. He was being lobbied very heavily on a political basis to do something different. And I finally said to the governor, "You know we'd argued the one case," and he said, "Well, come back to me," which is basically his way of saying, "I'm not going to make a decision. Come back and bring me more information." So we did. And I finally said to him, "Governor, what I learned a long time ago is you argue, fight with the boss as long as you want, until he makes a decision, then you shut up." I said, "One more time, this is what I think we should do, this is why I think we should do it." And he says, "Well, we're not going to do it." I said OK and we went on. I think that's kind of the key. I will argue a position when I think it's right, until, as long as I can, until he makes a decision.

A GASBO examiner reported a similar experience, noting that the budget office was having to respond to a dramatic increase in requests from the governor's office, much more than the last two governors:

I tried last year, I made a recommendation to the governor that we fund overtime for the law enforcement agents in the Georgia Bureau of Investigation and Public Safety. Public Safety was not my agency at the time but since then it's been given to me and he recommended, he argued that two step increases would be sufficient and he says, "Don't you think that every agency will be asking for overtime?" And I said, "No, governor, this has been requested for many years and it's kind of hard to, when you have an agent on a project, to take him off because he's gotta work so many hours." And he, well, I didn't win, of course. However, the legislature turned around and put the money in the budget. That was the last one I could recall. It's hard to fight with Governor Miller.

Perhaps one of the most interesting stories about examiner persistence over time, and over political obstacles, is from this GASBO examiner:

> I did the secretary of state's budget for years and attached to that darn thing was Rhodes Hall here on Peachtree Street. Back in the '30s or whatever, the furniture person [Mr.] Rhodes gave that thing to the state under a limited deed which said we couldn't sell it, we couldn't make money off of it. We had to use it for historical purposes, and then it was a state archives until this building was built. . . . The state used it and then the state abandoned it.
>
> By the time I took over that budget, the family was concerned about it, the historical association was concerned about it. The state owned it. It has some sort of architectural value. When I took over that budget and when I went to Rhodes Hall, there were major big holes in the roof, the foundation was falling, it was a crumbling mess, and it was under our ownership. This thing was just falling apart. There were birds. The family really didn't want it back. The trust for historical preservation wanted to run it but they didn't want to have to fix it up.
>
> I fought year after year and finally we were able to back it. My general philosophy was that the state should bring that thing back up, the shell should be enclosed, it should have a roof, it should have a foundation, it should have windows and all the windows—it should have electricity and it should have heating and air and then we should walk away from it and let the trust and the family do what they wanted to do with it. That was a fight. Clark Stevens was the head of it. I do remember the last time and I had to do that every year. We broke it up, we would do bits and pieces. Clark hated it. The governor was not very interested in it, but it was just this personal thing. I just felt that the state had an obligation to do a minimum and then let somebody else who cared about it take over, but it fell apart under our ownership.
>
> I do recall the last time that I did that Rhodes Hall, I always saved it for the end. We were sitting there with the governor, it was Joe Frank Harris, and I said, "Now I would just like to say a few words about Rhodes Hall," and Clark Stevens jumped up and said, "I think there is a reporter, I have to go talk to her" and he went out. I had to talk to the governor about Rhodes Hall and do whatever little piece they were going to do that year. An analyst was sitting out there waiting to meet with the governor, and he said Clark came out of that office saying, "I hate Rhodes Hall, I hate Rhodes Hall." I knew it. I had to deal with it.

This amusing story highlights the long-term perspective of examiners, and how their persistence is a valuable tool. The examiner also credited the staff in the secretary of state's office for helping get the project done, if only in bits and pieces, arguing that "the best combination is if you do your job and the agency takes responsibility for their job, and if you can get it together, that is the best of all possible worlds. It is hard for the agency to do much with the governor if their analyst is not interested and it is really hard for an analyst over here to do much if the agency doesn't hold up their end."

One of the most representative discussions of the decision to "go to the wall" for an agency request or to label a request "dead on arrival" is this succinct discussion with an IASBO examiner:

Q: So what decides whether you're going to go to the wall or whether you're going to say dead on arrival, don't bother?

Examiner: The initial phases of preparing it and talking with the department. If it's something that I think is a nifty little thing, then I will say convince me. That means take me out and show me a particular problem you've got or give me the information to back it up. Show me that if you make this change that this is going to increase your efficiency to do this or something. When we get to that point, it's usually because they've convinced me that I should do this.

Q: Once they've convinced you, OK, I can see it, but it's dead on arrival. Have you gotten to such cases?

Examiner: Those are tough ones. I'm trying to think of a specific example of one of those. I know I had one in DOT last year and I can't remember off the top of my head what it was. I want to say it had to do with increasing the number of highway maintenance workers that we had. They come back and say every year that our efficiency ratings on our highways are down, this is what the standard is, and we need to have X number more people, X number more dollars in maintenance to do this. I have run into that since I've had them and I get the same thing from people who make the decisions, [secretary of administration] on up the line to the governor's office. They just don't believe it. They say they're not as bad as they say and they do this every year because they want to have more people and stuff. I finally told them I can't go to bat for you on that year after year after year because I'm not the one that you've got to convince. Now you've got to convince them up there. Until I see a change in something up there, I think there are more important issues in DOT that I can help you with than that one. The director of the department's aware of that.

Q: Yet you'd do this for the maintenance garage. Even though it's fruitless. What determines whether you do one or the other? Why do you go for the maintenance garages year after year but you don't go for the increase in the maintenance staff?

Examiner: Keep in mind I don't have a problem with the budget director or the governor on reducing the number of maintenance garages. I do have a problem with them increasing the amount of moneys we do put out on maintenance.

Q: So when you get clear political cues from the governor and budget director that they're not interested, then you just say to the department director, go convince them and then we're in business. But don't waste my time.
Examiner: That pretty well covers it.

Ultimately, budget rationality in a policy-oriented SBO means that the examiner seeks to craft an effective recommendation, that is, an option the governor could reasonably expect to affirm, given a proper argument supported by credible evidence. This is why policy distance becomes so critical. If the examiner does not personally make the argument to the governor, the examiner loses control of the argument, and thus loses the ability to inject in the discussion with the governor the additional evidence stored in the mind (but not necessarily on the briefing paper) that guides the discussion with the governor. Those examiners who personally brief the governor consistently reveal the give-and-take nature of the briefing discussions and the importance of being prepared to answer all of the governor's questions. That is the reason for the "prebriefing" with the budget directors and deputy budget directors in several offices. These "mock briefings" attempt to simulate the governor's briefing and anticipate his or her questions. "You always have to be prepared to answer questions," remarked a GASBO examiner. "You should always be ready to know that item and you have to anticipate the questions and any additional questions you may have." In the GASBO prebriefings, the deputy budget director "would ask these very detailed questions that, you know, he would keep asking questions until you couldn't answer them . . . to make sure that you [pause] . . . Sometimes he wanted to know, sometimes he was testing you to make sure that you knew. You know, after I got to know him better and had been here longer, I'd start saying, "Do you know this or are you testing me?"
The WISBO regimen also includes prebriefings where examiners practice with the section manager, then the examiner and section manager practice with the budget director and the deputy budget director. A WISBO examiner could "only remember [the budget director] changing one thing. Then that cluster of people goes into [the secretary of administration], then you add [the secretary of administration] and then we all go over to the governor's office. So it's four times I do a briefing for a single agency." The

WISBO budget director notes, "It's a three-stage process, but both the secretary and governor tend to want to have as much as possible run by them, so at both stages we tend not to remove too much. So it's more a matter of at both stages making sure we're presenting things as clearly and as completely as possible, as opposed to weeding out decision items."

Even for level three decision items, those with highly charged political issues such as school finance, where the examiners have the least influence on actual decisions, and where the SBO may not recommend a specific option, the governor may solicit the examiner's opinion on a specific alternative. "Even if we don't recommend something," the WISBO budget director observed that the governor wants to know the examiner's best judgment. He would "often look at an analyst or team leader and say, well, so and so, what do you recommend? Or if it's a particularly thorny issue, he'll go around the room and ask everybody, analyst, team leader, me, [the secretary of administration], policy staff, what does everybody think?" Of course, the examiner can only proffer the advice if present at the table!

In SBOs with longer policy distances from the governor, where the examiner is not at the briefing table, it is harder to "see" the governor's perspective and the examiner is consequently less likely to feel a gubernatorial imperative in crafting a recommendation. In VASBO, for example, even if an examiner knew the governor did not support a program, he "would still make a recommendation if the issue were the correct or a sound policy issue, but the layers that are above me, between me and the governor, they would probably clean that out and say the governor doesn't support that issue." Consequently, " my recommendation wouldn't even be heard or seen by the governor in that case because that is what their job is, to clean out the things. The governor will basically provide guidance to [the layers] about the things he's interested in. And they would then clean out the pieces that aren't important to him and say the governor is not interested in this issue. You've made a good case that makes sense, but this is not an issue the governor wants to support."

As this examiner noted, the section managers in VASBO have a significant "weeding out" role. The VASBO section managers pay more attention to the politics of an issue than the examiners, and while crafting their recommendations, the VASBO examiners were consequently more inclined to anticipate the questions of the managers than of the governor. One manager knew "there have been cases where the analyst makes recommendations that are devoid of politics or what the political reactions would be. . . . Advocacy groups, consumers may come off the wall. And so your recommendation may be shot down even though marginally it makes sense and will save money, will be shot down simply because the governor, the staff, the secretaries do not want the political [problem]." Although this manager thought "it's incumbent on the analyst to identify the potential political impacts or consequences for those recommendations," he also thought it was incumbent upon the analyst to make recommendations, even if they were politically "insensitive." According to the manager, the key was learning to anticipate the questions of the manager or budget director:

> I think that if you've been around your manager, you've been around long enough, you can anticipate the types of questions he or she will ask and I just think you get a real good feeling for that, and the same way with working the cabinet secretary or a director. I think a good analyst, we won't be aware of what the consequences of certain recommendations are.

And in MNSBO, it was not common for the examiners to anticipate either the budget director or the governor. As one examiner explained, "Number one, I was not aware of what [the budget director's] expectations or preferences would be. The second was from the first day or days that we were here, it was made known to us that our job as budget officers is to again present clear and objective analysis and not to worry about the politics of a particular question." This was not interpreted by him as a prohibition "from commenting on a particularly obvious, or at least what to me, given my knowledge of the issue . . . [if] there's a feeling of hazard in making one decision or another, I might comment on that. But it's not my job to worry about that aspect of it." Still, this examiner did not believe he "can escape thinking in that way. But there was a clear direction from [the budget director] and from [the secretary of administration] that our job is to present clear and objective analysis so that they can make decisions. And I would have no idea what the governor's expectations would be."

Working on a recent supplemental budget bill, this examiner was not involved in the entire decision process for his budget issues and "didn't make any clear recommendations one way or the other." For his analysis, he "rated stuff either as A—clearly deficiency or emergency, B—kind of borderline, or C—clearly not, can wait until next session. Then it was up to the team leader to carry it on past that process. . . . I didn't have any direct conversations" with the MNSBO budget director or governor. At the team meeting he presented his ratings, and at a later departmentwide meeting with the budget director there was an iterative process of oral arguments from a tracking sheet listing all of the requests that had been submitted. "Then [the budget director] just sort of rated, 'Well, that's an A, write that one up' or whatever. So there were several that from [the budget director's] direction at that meeting I wrote up, but in the end were axed and didn't travel further. And again,

I don't know if that was [the budget director's] decision or the governor's decision. But they just didn't go further."

As we shall see in the next chapter, the policy distance between governors and examiners has major consequences for the type of decision-making practiced by examiners in SBOs. While examiners in policy-oriented SBOs are induced to draw on multiple rationalities to craft recommendations that pass multiple feasibility tests, examiners in control-oriented SBOs feel no such pressure and consequently have a much simpler decision-making process.

When the governor is indifferent to a policy area, and there is no gubernatorial imperative, the examiner's influence over the recommendation is even higher. A GASBO examiner observed that "occasionally [the governor] will ask about some specific thing or will express an interest in one particular type of program over another, but not very frequently because I think that our area, probably in education, he does it a lot because education is his thing, education and crime are the thing. But I think health and human services issues are just not a priority for him, so he doesn't really, I don't want to say take an interest in because I know he does, but it just isn't a priority, something he almost really just relies on our judgment."

Control in Policy-Oriented SBOs

Even the strongest policy-oriented SBO cannot relinquish all aspects of a control orientation in budgeting (Schick 1966). There remains the need to make sure that agencies do not exceed the budgetary appropriations approved by the legislature. Although the cases may be rare, it is important that they maintain some degree of vigilance in this regard. As this examiner's story exhibits, the end of the fiscal year bears watching:

> We had one of the smaller departments come in and say they were going to run out of money. It was probably in February or March. The smaller departments don't have the same leeway that the larger departments do as far as budgeting is concerned. So we said OK. It's going to be around $4,000–$5,000. OK, but try to deal with [the budget director] and me, try to deal with what you've got, let us know, and we'll talk about what we need to do. So this person thought that that meant free rein and went out and bought a fax machine or something that she really felt she needed badly. But she was going out and overspending their budget intentionally. Because we had said we may be able to find $4,000–$5,000 for her, she went off and blew $15,000–$18,000 based on OK, you can do a transfer. [The budget director] made a phone call and read the [state law] to her and told her that she was [personally liable]. . . .

The transfer was only for things that you'd already budgeted. In fact, she wanted $5,000 and we only wanted to give her $3,000 because we thought she could work a little closer. Oh, she didn't get any of that money, those things. They had to stop orders. That's happened and she called and read her the code and said you are personally liable. We can take you to court. You are overspending your budget. That's the first time in eight years that I'd ever had to do that. Very first time. Generally the people that I work with, and I think generally state government, they really try to do, I mean, they're maybe going to spend it down to the last penny, but they're not going to do anything that's going to cause them [legal trouble].

A Note About Legislative-Phase Analysis

The legislative phase of the budget cycle is not a time for examiners to relax. There is much to do. In the legislature, "budget-making is a political process, conducted in a political arena for political advantage. The legislature, like the budget, will reflect the integrating forces in a government that produce something that may be called city or state or national policy. The legislature, like the budget, will also reflect partisan interests and sectional interests. The budget is a periodic readjustment and reconciliation of these numerous and conflicting influences" (Burkhead 1956, 307).

Examiners in a policy-oriented SBO usually have responsibility for analyzing the fiscal impacts of the numerous bills that are introduced by legislators during this period. In several states, the legislature meets for only 90 to 120 days (or even less) and the agenda includes approving a budget and any other business. In the latter, legislators can author bills that would effectively amend the governor's budget proposal to accomplish something that the SBO may have rejected as an agency service improvement. The improvement item can be offered as an amendment to the governor's budget proposal (with an anticipated low probability of success) or it can be offered as a separate bill that accomplishes the same thing, with perhaps a higher chance of success. Each of these bills will likely have a fiscal impact, and thus the SBO is keen to assess the impact so that the governor and legislative leaders know it.

Bill analysis for the SBO examiner is thus couched in terms of "fiscal impact statements" or "fiscal notes," but it requires the same analysis as an agency budget request. "Technically it's two different functions," argued a WISBO examiner, "but it's the same type of recommendation. There's an issue. We do a bill analysis for separate bills. If it's a budget issue, if it's a budget bill that the governor's introduced, then we do the policy analysis on each individual decision item. The idea is the same. We make policy decisions about the desirability of the legislator's bill or amendment."

Summary: A Decision Process with Multiple Rationalities

Examiners in the policy-oriented SBO conduct budget analysis twelve months a year. It is neither exclusively technical analysis nor exclusively political analysis. Instead, policy-oriented examiners rely on different approaches to agency budget problems, depending upon which facet of a problem is most in need of attention, which phase of the budget cycle they are operating in, and whether they have received cues or directives that the particular issue is or is not a priority of the governor in the current budget cycle. When fiscal constraints are relaxed, marginal utility analysis may suggest allocating additional funds to one agency program while holding the other programs at current service levels. During periods of fiscal stress, it may require reallocating funds from an agency activity that is a low priority to a program that is a higher priority, one that is more "essential" to the agency's mission. Keeping the governor's goals and priorities in mind, the examiners recommend the budget options that are consistent with good management (technical rationality), available resources (economic rationality), legal constraints (legal rationality), political forces to which the governor is sensitive or willing to respond (political rationality), and the rationale for the agency activity and the purpose that it serves the state (social rationality). The examiners ultimately craft their recommendations as the governor's recommendations, and they reflect their best judgment as to the decision the governor should make to promote good management practices in the state government. In the next chapter we examine the budget decisions of an examiner in a control-oriented SBO. In this case we will witness the effects of an SBO orientation that constrains the multiple rationalities approach to budgetary decision-making.

7

The Anatomy of a
Control-Oriented Budget
Recommendation

The Task of the Control-Oriented Office

We turn now to a control-oriented budget office, one in which we expect the role of the budget examiner to be quite different from his counterpart in a policy-oriented office. At the very least we expect the policy role of the examiner to be muted in a control shop. And we expect that the conduct of policy analysis is not as frequent, if it exists at all. It is much less likely that the budget examiner of a control-oriented budget office is occupied with *developing* initiatives "that better serve the governor's policy preferences." Rather, in a control-oriented budget office, examiners concentrate on "control and service to agencies" primarily through budget execution activities.

These examiners do review and analyze budgets to support the executive budget recommendation. However, this is just one aspect of mostly control-oriented tasks that they perform year round. More predominant is their work of checking, monitoring, and reconciling expenditures during budget execution in order to make sure that agencies function from a legal and technical perspective. Such a focus involves constant contact with agencies. Essentially, the budget office is the first called by agencies if they have any questions related to anything in the budget or the appropriation act(s). According to one examiner, "A lot of [our work] is simply information dissemination to agencies about what happened during the session because a lot of them don't know anything except what they read in the paper." Even in the "off season" there is the closeout of the fiscal year in which examiners assist agencies, in some cases with a daily monitoring of the revenue situation to figure out whether or not supplemental appropriations get funded.

In this chapter we will see that in a control-oriented SBO the concentration on the minutia of budgeting day-to-day detracts from examiners' abilities to pursue and research policy initiatives specific to their agencies and important to the governor. On an even more fundamental level, these examiners are hampered in their search to understand the political facets of their agencies' budget problems. An SCSBO examiner clearly delineates the job of the control-oriented examiner: "We don't tackle major problems, we leave that to others—the governor, the legislature. We check the numbers, we can verify the numbers, [and] we can ask the agencies for justifications."

In some respects, the modern examiner in any SBO is a victim of his position as information and oversight provider. According to an examiner from the Illinois budget office, "There are too many other demands on the [ILSBO] analysts." In the case of examiners in a control-oriented budget office, policy decisions are left to those more closely associated with the chief executive, like gubernatorial policy staff. We will find, in fact, that the politics is left to others in a control shop primarily because the role of the examiner is restricted to development and communication of fiscal analyses associated with agencies and their programs and activities.

As noted in the previous chapter, a distinguishing characteristic of a policy-oriented SBO is the short policy distance between the SBO and the governor. This distance is substantially greater in an SBO with a focus on control and accountability and thus a concentration on budget execution over budget development. Not surprisingly, we find that in Alabama and South Carolina, two states with control-oriented SBOs, the budget offices are located outside of the governor's office, organizationally. The ALSBO, which we label a "weak control" SBO, is a division within the state's Department of Finance. At the time of the study, policy distance was also exacerbated with the hiring of a new director of finance and new budget director. Further, at the time of this study, Alabama was in an election year and so examiners anticipated a potential (and subsequent) change in administration. With many unknowns, budget examiners in the ALSBO were isolated from the governor organizationally, and in a position of waiting on relationships to be determined by the recently placed directors of both the Department of Finance and the executive budget office.

The SCSBO provides another example of an SBO distanced from the governor organizationally, and exhibiting an environment disadvantageous to budget examiners in terms of taking on a policy role. Previously within the Finance Division of the Budget and Control Board (BCB), the SCSBO was originally headed by the state auditor. This historical foundation in accounting may speak to the focus on control of agency spending that lingers to this day. (Similarly, in Alabama, the budget director technically oversees the comptroller and the Purchasing and Risk Management divisions.) At the time of this research, the SCSBO was operating under a newly legislated executive budget system.[1] And, like the examiners in Alabama, these men and women were uncertain about their role given an impending gubernatorial election. Essentially, uncertainty about the future role of the budget office vis-à-vis the governor's policy staff regarding budget development relegated budget examiners in this office to a traditional control orientation.

One caveat of the SCSBO involves examiners' policy analysis activities with regard to legislative staff. While only one of the fourteen examiners interviewed from this office indicated a policy orientation of the budget office, ten of fourteen (71 percent) did express that they engage in policy analysis, primarily for purposes of communication to legislative staff. We will explore this relationship more carefully in the next chapter, which focuses on budget examiner roles. However, by virtue of their considered influence with the legislature due to the office's organizational location in the BCB, we label South Carolina's SBO "strong control" in orientation.

It is also worth mentioning that of the budget offices included in this study, the Alabama and South Carolina SBOs are two of the smallest in terms of examiners employed. The ALSBO is smallest of all states in this study, and South Carolina's budget office was similar in size to the IASBO and the MOSBO.

The Illinois budget office, another control-oriented SBO, is much different organizationally from the ALSBO and the SCSBO. The only Midwest state to exhibit the predominant control orientation (Wisconsin's SBO exhibits a control orientation as well, but in conjunction with a policy one), Illinois's SBO is located within the Office of the Governor. Yet this office did not reflect a policy orientation, despite the organizational proximity to the governor. We do notice that at the time of our research, this state exhibited some fiscal stress (confirmed in interviews by the ILSBO budget examiners) that certainly contributes to a focus on expenditure control on the part of the budget office. Assessment of the financial indicators presented for each state in the first chapter further reflects Illinois's financial capacity in 1994: general fund revenues and expenditures per capita fall below the national average in that year and debt per capita is the highest of all states included in this study in the same year. Interviews with examiners in the ILSBO in fact suggest a change in orientation of the office over time, moving from a stronger policy focus to one predominantly concerned with the details of budget monitoring and execution. One examiner provides perhaps the clearest statement of this backslide to a control orientation for the ILSBO:

> My understanding from talking with people who've been here for a while is that the bureau is much more involved in the day-to-day operations of

the agencies than it was before. So there's a lot more quick turnaround assignments. You monitor on an ongoing basis spending over at the agency and if they're running into problems according to your projections, then you check with them and you see what's going on. You monitor if there's anything going on with new initiatives. As far as in the past, my understanding is that the bureau did a lot more long-term thinking and did a lot more, [was] much more knowledgeable about the programs of the agency. Now because we are doing projection of personal services and monitoring of legislation and writing these bill comments and all that, you really work to get to know a program. You have to really put in a lot of extra effort. Your activities are more at the surface level. You don't have to work with knowing how a program works and what it's supposed to do.

We suggest that Illinois had in fact "regressed" to a control orientation when we visited the office, and for this reason we label the SBO as "temporal control."

Just as we shadowed Mary in a policy-oriented budget office, we will now follow John, a newly hired budget examiner, as he begins working in a control-oriented SBO. We base our understanding of the roles and rationalities of John during a typical budget cycle on data collected in interviews with examiners in the ALSBO, SCSBO, and ILSBO—each characterized as SBOs strongly focused on control over and above management and policy development and analysis. How does John become familiar with the agencies and spending to which he has been assigned? Specifically, where does he go for information about his agencies, their activities and past spending patterns? Do his relationships with agency staff, his colleagues in the budget office, and the governor vary from those exhibited by Mary? Are his search strategies for information about the social, political, and legal facets of his agencies' budgets different from that characteristic of examiners in a policy-oriented office? We will explore these questions in the following sections.

Predevelopment-Phase Analysis

Social and Legal Facets of Budget Problems

Like Mary, John finds that there is no formal education as far as budgeting work goes. That is, John can expect to be thrown into the fire, requiring that he ask a number of questions related to his assignments such as: What has spending by this agency been like in the past? What has the spending been for? What legislation exists regarding this agency and its functions? John is interested in the history of the agency and its spending, as well as technical issues related to the recent budget year. And, like Mary, John is confused and overwhelmed as he is "handed" his first budgets to analyze. Novice examiners know little about state government, as revealed by the examiner who "didn't even know [the legislature] existed, to tell you the truth, other than parking became horrendous when they were here." Another repeated Mary's sentiments, "I didn't really understand what was going on. We worked on getting the budget documents put together and collated. It probably took me a couple of years to learn [what was going on]." Still another examiner recalled, "It was kind of, here are your agencies. I was petrified. I'd never seen the budget requests that are done by the higher heads, you know, the institutions of higher learning. I was not familiar with their forms, the terminology, or anything and had to do quite a bit of reading to get up to speed on that."

John's indoctrination period into the control-oriented SBO is similar to Mary's in that it is also advantageous to the control-oriented SBO to have budget examiners come on board during the "slow period," just prior to budget development. In the ILSBO, one examiner explained that the budget director, among others, typically recruited for new examiners when the General Assembly started up. The budget office then might expect the flock of newly minted graduate students to arrive for work by midsummer. This allows the budget examiner to gain some grounding in the activities and operations of the budget office as well as begin to learn about the agencies for which he is responsible. According to one ALSBO budget examiner, "I had the summer, two or three months, to kind of sit here and study stuff and get my footing on track so I'd know what to do."

Like Mary, many of John's initial questions are answered by reading past budgets, historical analyses, issue papers, and particularly state and federal code, essentially digging into the gold mine of documents that Mary uses to become familiar with her agencies. One ALSBO examiner talked of beginning her job by reading the statutes that affect the budget office itself, "the Budget Management Act, reading to find out what exactly my responsibilities were as far as the home office was concerned." Inevitably, John must ferret out statutes related to the agencies to which he is assigned. For example, an examiner from Illinois stated, "One of the first things I did was go and look at the enabling legislation for each of my agencies, the liquor control act, the horse racing act. [They tell] what gave [agencies] the authority, what the director had the power to do, if there was any dedicated revenue sources. . . . I found that to be valuable at least in terms of just getting a general ideal about the scope of what the agencies are engaged in." Broadly speaking, John consults enabling legislation to understand the purpose of the agency or the social rationale for why the agency exists. One examiner found that "statutes show me what responsibilities the agencies had." Reading code is "a good way to familiarize yourself with a program or why a fund was developed or what the legislative intent of [the agency and its programs] is," stated another.

Yet the examiner in a control-oriented SBO studies the social rationale of his assigned agencies with a more focused approach than he would in the policy-oriented SBO. Not only is the budget examiner looking at statutes for legislative intent (the "why" behind agency existence), he is particularly interested in determining what the state *requires* of that agency, that is, what the agency is *mandated* to conduct or accomplish. An examiner from the ILSBO, for example, is "looking at whatever programs that they've got, see if there's anything that has entitlements. For Public Health, there are three programs that had a quasi-entitlement thing, so looking at whether or not we should fund that." An ALSBO budget examiner illustrated a legal stance when approaching the budget director regarding an agency's spending request by stating, "If we don't fund this, we will be in violation." Further, reviewing code is particularly important in fiscally tight times because, as one budget examiner noted, "we cannot cut mandated programs."

Examiners learn a lot more than social rationale from reading statutes. With a primary orientation of control, these examiners are concerned with revenue sources as well as expenditure categories. Stated clearly by one examiner, "Our involvement is with the funding of the statutory requirements of the agencies in terms of funding, what kind of money they get, what the statutory requirements of their money [are]. Do they just keep the money? Do they have to give it to the general fund and the general fund pays them to run their agency?" Another questioned, "Are monies earmarked to support the activities of my agencies?" The answers to these questions will vary with changes to legislation. Thus, staying on top of the legal grounds for agency existence and activities is vital to the examiner in a control-oriented budget office.

Budget examiners in a control-oriented budget office rarely stray very far from a fiscal or accountability focus regarding where money comes from and for what it is to be spent. One of the first things John will do is dig deep into available databases, including any spreadsheets with past and present budget numbers for assigned agencies. Analyzing cash flow and reconciling with budget law are primary aspects of examiner activity during this phase of budget process. According to an examiner with the ILSBO, "You have to analyze the cash flow for each fund. When I was doing that, I went to the statutes to see, to get some detail about the funds, like the sources of receipts. It specifies in there for many of the funds, the state funds, what are the sources of receipts, and if there's any detail in there about transfers that go out to the general revenue fund. That gives you an idea of what the cash flow is for that particular fund."

Traditional guardianship surfaces with another examiner's explanation regarding the use of statutes throughout the budget process to understand agencies and their budgets. The examiner talked of continually referring back to statutes as a check against agency prerogative, in order to "track down what the agency is telling me. They say it's supposed to be this way, or the program has to be set up a certain way. It's mostly a background issue. There hasn't been anything that's come up where you would have significant reason to doubt the agency, but you just always have to make sure that somebody's interpretation isn't way off." To a certain extent, frequent referral to statutes helps the examiner maintain an objective view (healthy skepticism) about agency needs and desires. The great deal of contact that examiners have with agencies during execution "to help make the budget work" provides ample time for examiners to become principal advocates for spending by their agencies. Yet other factors inhibit this opportunity and few examiners in control-oriented SBOs are seen as advocates for the agencies.

Finally, these budget examiners point out that later in the budget cycle they often look back to existing statutes when new legislation affecting their agencies is introduced during the legislative session. "Usually when we do bill comments on pending legislation and usually when a bill's trying to change a particular program or add or whatever, you generally go look at the statutes to see how this would impact [your] agency." Although the focus on details and reconciliation in budget execution provides examiners with insight about the social rationale behind their agencies and programs, we will see that such activity detracts from the examiners' ability to seek out the political rationale behind budget problems. That is, it is difficult for examiners in control-oriented budget offices to determine the priorities of other budget actors. Therefore they are hindered in their ability to contribute to policy development, initiation, and promotion.

Other materials John can expect to consult for background information on agencies include administrative rules, procurement and personnel code that could impact agency operations, letters that the treasurer or comptroller has sent to the budget office, and old budgets. Generally budget examiners find administrative code more descriptive than statutes. Claimed one budget examiner, "they have more policy descriptions than state law, they are easier to understand." In Alabama, examiners spend a predominant amount of their time reviewing agency operations plans during the execution phase. As does reference to law, this provides the examiner an opportunity to focus on the legal and social rationales behind their agencies. Claimed one ALSBO examiner, "We work with agencies every single day, maybe not every agency every day, but every single day on something or other doing an [operations] plan." Stated another:

First thing I had to deal with [upon entering the job] was appropriation and that's what I walked into. So I at least had a span of time, about eight months, to talk to the accountants with the various agencies and get a feel for [it]. Let me backtrack a little bit. We have [an] operations plan process at the beginning of the year. We load what's called an operations plan the agencies send in to us, and it's broken down into quarters, and all that does is that's a plan that shows how they are going to spend their money that they receive through the appropriation process. So, in going through that process with those two agencies particularly, I was able to talk to their accountants. I had a better feel for the agencies by the time the budgets rolled around.

While John wades through the mounds of papers provided on his agencies to become familiar with the legal, financial, and social facets behind their budgets and budget problems, he is also touching base with other examiners regarding general questions about budget verbiage and process, as well as specific questions regarding his agencies. Disclosed one examiner who admitted knowing nothing about her state's budget process upon being hired, "I went to another analyst and asked, 'What does this mean? How do I find out about this?'" Asking questions is a vital means for examiners to cull information in order to clearly assess both their role and the issues related to their agencies. Next we look at John's introduction to agency personnel and the flow of communication between him and the agency that is characteristic of examiners housed in a control-oriented budget office.

Talking with Agency Personnel

Perhaps especially in a control-oriented budget office, where examiners are likely to interact with agency staff frequently throughout the year for checking purposes, examiners recognize the importance of establishing and maintaining good relationships with agency personnel. In the ALSBO, section managers try to get new analysts to meet with the agencies. "It's important that they know who they are," offered a section manager, "the agencies know who we are and we know the individuals we deal with on the phone on a day-to-day basis. It just makes for an easier working relationship." On entering the budget office, John can expect to be passed a list of agency contacts or a list of the agency budget people with whom he should establish face-to-face contact in his first year on the job. Probably his section manager will help with introductions for the first meeting with each agency contact. John will meet face-to-face with some of these folks frequently over the next year or so; some he will be in contact with primarily by telephone; others he may check with only periodically, for example when assessing quarterly expenditure reports. The number and type of meetings that John will have with agency personnel depends on several variables, including how large and complex the agency's budget is, what budget problems the agency encounters (particularly throughout budget execution), and the visibility of the issues that circle around the agency's programs and activities. According to one examiner, who and how often you meet depends on the department and program. "[You] listen to a few agencies that get a lot of money. The rest is by phone or working on paperwork through mail and phone. Like Mental Health, there's something going on all the time. We are constantly talking to the directors or budget people."

We find that John's accessibility to agency personnel will not be as extensive as Mary's. Typically, the examiner will meet with the agency budget or fiscal officer "or whoever they had assigned from their agency to be the contact with the budget office," claimed one examiner. Budget examiners in the Alabama and South Carolina budget offices spoke less frequently than those from the ILSBO of meetings with agency heads and program directors. The ALSBO and SCSBO budget examiners characterized such meetings as pro forma at the beginning of an assignment, with subsequent contact maintained predominantly by telephone to budget and finance staff of agencies. One ALSBO budget examiner talked of communication with agency people over the telephone, "Over the years I've met with several of them. Some of them I still don't [meet with], I've never met with. But I know their voices and personalities, that's it." Several confirmed that meetings with agency personnel depend upon the circumstance and are often a function of the overall fiscal climate or related to aspects or problems specific to a particular agency. According to one ALSBO budget examiner:

> My agencies are not in the top three or top ten. They don't get a lot of money, they don't deal with a lot of controversial issues and they never run deficits. So the kinds of things they ask for are usually the things they have asked for in the past and haven't gotten. *So I generally don't get involved before I get their request.* However, when agencies want to know, "How much should I ask for? What's the best approach to take?" I'll come and talk to them about those kind of things, tell them about our priority listing and how much money has been given for certain things in the past. (italics authors' emphasis)

An examiner from the education section of the SCSBO talks of attending commission meetings to learn about the education-funding formula and visiting educational institutions to meet the finance officers. When asked about initiating contact with agencies, another SCSBO budget examiner stated that such contact is mainly through phone calls. "Sometimes I meet with them. It depends on the whole scenario that has been set for the year. Some years, we tell them, 'Don't request more than 5 percent of your budget or only send us your top three budget requests.'" When there is little money to spread around, as the range of choices for spending is pressed, these budget examiners find less of a need to meet with agency personnel for anything other than budget control. Also, containment of communication with those higher up keeps examiners in the role of guardian of the public purse and conduit of information to and from the agency and the executive, exclusively.

In Illinois, examiners expressed a greater propensity than did those in Alabama or South Carolina to meet with division chiefs and program directors. However, meetings with department heads remain dependent on the situation and individual. When asked, "Did you meet with the transportation secretary?" one budget examiner responded, "I have not met with him other than where it's been meetings between the budget office and the DOT. It's not like he knows me." ILSBO budget examiners do claim that meetings with division directors help them to understand agency priorities and goals, thus helping them with the social rationale behind agency budgets as well as a bit about political rationale. Stated one examiner, "I talked with them, different program staff over there, about the services that they have, found out which ones they considered really highly and asked them what problems they saw coming out, trying to find out as much as I could in a short time." Another sought answers from agency staff to long-range planning questions, such as: Where do the agency directors want to see the agency over the next few years? Do they have a long-range plan? Where are they related to that plan? What are the reasons that they may be behind, on target, or ahead of these plans?

As illustrated above, when afforded the opportunity, budget examiners in control-oriented budget offices do ferret out information on the social and political rationales behind their assigned budgets. In fact, the ILSBO examiners illustrate selective behavior in terms of searching out different pieces of information from different agency personnel. According to one examiner from ILSBO, in order to get program detail, "I talked with the people closer to the program." Division and program directors in the agencies can help budget examiners to understand agency priorities, while fiscal staff help with information about agency spending, accounting, and financial projections.

While examiners communicate with agencies to determine the "why" behind what agencies are spending or want to spend, they understand that the link goes both ways. A SCSBO examiner explains, "We are like their contact between them and the other world. We all work for one government, and all of our interests should be for the betterment of the state." According to another, "We communicate with [agencies] and let them know even as the budget cycle is being worked out whether or not the revenue is soft or if it's going to be excess revenue, that kind of thing. And the more sophisticated agencies have a real good idea from the beginning. [We] tell them informally that it would be a good idea if you don't allocate about 3 percent of your general fund revenue and hold it in a reserve on an interim basis until we have a clear picture. So that happened quite a bit."

In the end, however, much of the contact that these budget examiners have with agency personnel is restricted to the budget and finance staff rather than agency heads, and conversation centers on the fiscal rather than social or political aspects of agency activities. For example, one ILSBO examiner noted that in the case of one of her agencies, "they're just so big, that I don't even meet directly with their budget director. I meet with [pause], how far down does he go? I deal ordinarily with somebody who's like, two levels below him." Another examiner lamented, "I did not see [the agency head] for probably my first six months. She tends not to go to meetings and not to show up at hearings and things like that. So I never really met her until I was pretty well entrenched in what I was doing." Thus, the successful examiner hopes to develop a close and trusting relationship with the agency budget and accounting officers. Developing such a relationship greatly informs the examiner. An examiner from Alabama explains, "You learn about their funding situation, you learn where they get their money and how many funds they have and what kinds of program they have and where most of their money goes."

Making Site Visits

From a budgeting standpoint, site visits help the examiner connect concrete with dollars. And as discussed in the previous chapter, they can provide an overview of the functions of a department as well as a human perspective on the budget associated with that department. Site visits also help the budget examiner develop a relationship with individuals in agencies in order to ask intelligent questions. Budget examiners claim to "have a better feel for what they are doing, what kinds of programs are involved," when afforded the chance to make site visits. Regrettably, we find the same sort of "lock" on control-oriented budget examiners regarding site visits as we do regarding communication flows with agency personnel. That is, budget examiners in control shops are more restricted (often literally) regarding making site visits than their counterparts seem to be in policy-oriented SBOs. For example, in Illinois, budget examiners talked about having no travel money with which to make site visits:

> If we could have more travel money, I would go visiting some places in Chicago, but basically I have to stick to here.

Q: There's no division travel money for site visits to go out in the state?
Examiner: Basically no. There's some travel money that goes for division chief meetings in Chicago. All of the analysts try to bum rides if they're going someplace where the agency is going. Then we kind of bum rides with the agency staff.

And, true to form, budget examiners in control-oriented budget shops often expressed the need to make site visits for budget execution purposes, more so than for budget development. That is, examiners seem to use site visits to find out what agencies are spending money on (fiscal) rather than what agencies want to do or seek to accomplish (programmatic). One ILSBO examiner explained, "Most site visits [I have made] concerned capital projects which I didn't make recommendations on." Budget examiners use site visits to confirm or validate how agencies are spending money in relation to their appropriation and program mandates as opposed to researching the results of spending or its connection to policy.

In Alabama budget examiners explained that they may visit the agency or vice versa. The ALSBO deputy director expressed his belief that site visits are good for examiners "to see just where the physical space is, what they're having to work out of. It's hard to conceive that some folks are working in a basement of a building with no windows and they've got typewriters that are twenty years old, stuff like that." However, it was noted by more than one ALSBO budget examiner that as state government has become increasingly centralized with agencies locating in Montgomery, "we visit those around town." Further, "site visits are more a function of problems with budget [execution], for cash flow analysis problems, than preparation of requests."

Generally, however, there did not seem to be as strong a push for examiners in control-oriented SBOs to get out of the office and visit agencies to witness agency infrastructure, projects, programs, and activities as that for examiners in policy-oriented budget offices. On the other hand, control-oriented examiners sense that site visits provide essential information about agencies that is unavailable by paper, telephone, or even through meetings. Examiners use such contact to better understand the social facets of agency budget problems. One examiner emphasized:

I do make site visits. It's important to me. I was on one yesterday and I got, as a result of that visit, I have better insight in terms of the programs they talk about. [In setting up visits this year] I pretty much said I want to talk more to the program people. I find that to be most helpful, especially when you are doing impact statements, because it's just not enough to have those numbers there. You have to know why you need those numbers, what they are for, and how are they tied into the program that is of concern.

As noted earlier, a distinction in the conduct of site visits for these examiners, compared to those in a policy-oriented SBO, involves the predominant focus on budget execution over development. Thus, where the examiner and agency staff meets is often determined by the problem at hand. An examiner from the ALSBO illustrates this:

> And now when they have a problem, if it's an operations plan problem, they need to come here because we have access to the system, we can look up, if they say, well, this bill isn't clearing, why? And we can look up on the system. Whereas if we go to the agency, they many not have access to that. If it's a problem that needs to be fixed, we can do it while they're sitting in our office on our computer. Whereas the agency wouldn't have the capacity. They wouldn't have the clearance to get into the system to do what we do. So now we still go out and visit when an agency has spending problems, and we need to just sit down with them and say, "OK, we understand you've got a problem, tell me what your problem is." Then it is better if we go to them, and that way if they need to produce more documents, they can always run back to their office and get it. If we have budget hearings, maybe asking them to explain or just give us an overview of why they're asking for what they're asking, maybe we're not questioning if they're asking for too much or too little or whatever, but we just want them to give us more information, maybe we'll have them come here.

We have seen that John's entrée into the world of the budget examiner begins similarly to Mary's. He is overwhelmed with documentation, swamped by spreadsheets, legislation, old budgets, memoranda, and other "hard copy" related to the agencies to which he is assigned. Coming in several months prior to the budget development phase, he gets his feet wet by working through such papers while questioning other examiners about budgeting in general, looking to his section manager for guidance, and at the same time initiating contact with his agencies. His work pays off regarding knowledge about the legal and social facets of budgeting in his agencies. Within a few months, he should have a feel for why his agencies and programs exist, their funding sources, mandated activities, and budget trends.

Nevertheless, we have witnessed that the distance between examiners and top policy decisionmakers in the agencies makes it hard for these examiners to hunt down the political reasons behind budget problems. According to the comments of examiners from the Alabama, South Carolina, and Illinois budget offices, they are most likely to establish and maintain contact with the "agency budget people" rather than the department secretary, agency head, or even program director. According to one ALSBO examiner, "We're in pretty much constant communication with the financial people from the agencies so they pretty much tell us what's going on." In the next section we will see that the distance between these examiners and the governor is equally frustrating to their ability to understand and provide policy direction. Below we evaluate the ability of examiners from control-oriented budget offices to learn about the politics behind the budgets they review.

Political Facets of Budget Problems

John can expect that his contact with agencies, to a certain extent, will occur in a political vacuum. That is, while examiners may meet or be introduced to top policy decisionmakers along the way (particularly in the beginning of an assignment to provide a broad brush of an agency, for example), examiners often do not know the flavor of decisions going on at high levels within agencies or much past the level of state budget director. According to an ALSBO budget examiner, "The agency submits letters to us requesting stuff. Usually, just about every time, the director [of the agency] has already spoken with the finance director or has had a meeting with the finance director—a special meeting, because that's the person who gives the OK. Sometimes I am included in those meetings, but mostly, a lot of times, not."

For a number of reasons, it is very difficult for John as a budget examiner in a control-oriented budget office to gain equal footing with Mary regarding the political rationale behind his assignments. Many examiners from the three budget offices considered here admit that they do not know all the aspects of the politics behind their agencies' functions, programs, and spending. Stated one ILSBO examiner, "I am over here to understand the numbers, understand the programs, and relay those to the director and let them make the political justifications." Another examiner points out that politics is "not really something that's a big consideration at our level." Several offered that while an examiner may, in time, "see things on a bigger scale," such vision does not and even should not influence his or her preparation of agency spending plans. In some respects, for the examiner in a control-oriented budget office, learning about the politics related to an agency is unnecessary. Note the following exchanges with Illinois budget examiners:

> Q: Was it important for you to know the politics of the budget requests?
> Examiner: No. That didn't even come up. That wasn't even supposed to be a consideration at our level. We were just supposed to look at the facts and look at the needs. The politics, those kinds of decisions were occasionally

made at the director's level, but a lot of times I think they just sent them on to the governor and let them make the [decision], unless there was something, like I say, that had come up before, wouldn't fly, and what's the point of banging your head against the wall. But for the most part I was never told, never suggested to change things for political reasons, ever.

Replied another,

Q: Are you aware of the politics of the issues?
Examiner: Not all the time.

Q: Do you try and learn what it is?
Examiner: Yes.

Q: Why would you do that?
Examiner: It's interesting, like reading the tabloids. But that, I mean, it has no impact on my analysis.

Q: So even if you were aware of the political issue . . . you'd just ignore the political information anyhow?
Examiner: Correct.

Agency Priorities

As explained earlier, during predevelopment and concurrently with budget execution, examiners in control-oriented budget offices are often restricted in their ability to learn about agency priorities. They do so by communicating primarily through meetings and site visits with agency staff, and by asking questions of the director of the agency or program such as "Where would you like this program to be?" In spite of the fact that the examiners in Alabama, Illinois, and South Carolina indicated being fairly confined by no-growth budgets, they still sought to break down agency budgets to those components most important to the agency. An Alabama examiner talks about putting agencies under a bright light, shining it in their eyes, and asking, "What do you really need?" in order to shake out "pie in the sky" requests. An examiner from the ILSBO explains the process for finding out about Board of Education priorities:

I could get some ideas from either talking with the superintendent, talking with his assistant, or going to the board meetings, in terms of where they wanted to see money, where their emphasis was. The [current superintendent], his big emphasis was trying to equalize the system, make sure that everyone was treated fairly in the overall system. That was the big thing he pushed for. The superintendent prior to him, I didn't really get a feeling from him as to what his big thing was other than we need to get more money for education. The [current superintendent] was pretty definite on his wanting to equalize the system and make sure everybody was treated fairly.

Still another concurs that where a site visit is held helps to focus the examiner's attention to problems and issues important to the agency:

We did site visits [in corrections]. I think that was a very good way to establish where the priorities are going.

Q: How so?
Examiner: Because of the choice of where we went. We went to [a maximum-security prison] and they wanted to get the point across to me that maximum-security institutions are the most volatile, dangerous institutions in the state. They are our priority. It's really their actions. Actions talk about priorities.

Such responses further support our contention that examiners, especially those in control-oriented budget offices, are at the mercy of program directors and other agency staff in terms of the communication flow and spending recommendation strategy. If these budget actors are not forthcoming regarding their agencies' priorities, it is impossible for the examiner to incorporate such desires into a viable spending request, or to communicate such information to those higher in the administration.

On the other hand, these examiners are hardly in the position of coming up with various options for doling out surplus funds. Nor do they see their job to be finding money for agencies. While they recognize the need to "go to bat" for those agencies that carefully and clearly express a need, examiners ordinarily scrutinize individual requests without becoming too parochial regarding their agencies. For, according to an Alabama examiner, "I'm paid by the Finance Department, not by the Health Department or Public Safety." Another illustrates the examiner's discerning eye. "We have agencies that have good reputations and those who have bad reputations. A lot of them will cry wolf and you just listen to them and go on."

SBO Priorities: Communicating with the Section Manager

If John learns anything about the political facets of his agencies' budgets, it will probably be from his section manager. Most examiners from the control-oriented budget offices studied here had no contact with the governor, little (if any) with the director of finance, and often very limited interaction with the budget director. "Mostly what we are expected to do is dictated to us through the budget officer. We don't, I personally do not have much contact with the finance director himself," stated an examiner. Another from the ALSBO admits, "My first allegiance is to the division director. I don't really see that I am working for the governor. I guess because I answer more directly to my division chief." Thus, examiners learn to prepare research for their section manager and to "read" their managers carefully regarding information forthcoming about the examiners' agencies, as well as any directives coming from farther up in the executive branch. According to one examiner in the ILSBO, "as far as policy significance, whenever I've been unclear about what the [budget] bureau response might be, I've taken it to [my section manager]."

The examiners' role as information conduit becomes very clear at this stage in the budget cycle. From an examiner in Alabama:

> We usually will, [my section manager] and I, put together work sheets of all the agencies involved, and come up with a list of what we feel the priorities are, of questions and policy decisions that we need, go to [the deputy director] and [the budget director] with them, sit down and get their feel of what they should be, and then [the budget director] will take it from there.

Another explains he is constantly checking back with his section manager as he moves through budget development:

> If an agency has more than one program, usually, with of course my supervisor's permission, I'll call the agency and say, "Hey, you're gonna be cut, do you have any preference of where you'd like to cut?" Because most times they want to cut back the administrative sections and save the services.

It is at this critical stage of preparing information for presentation to others higher up in the administration that the SBO examiner can have an impact on the agency's budget. That is, having an understanding of the social, legal, and political facets of the budget problem at this point in the budget cycle is vital if the examiner is to be successful regarding a policy or funding initiative. Not surprisingly, we find this unrealistic in the control-oriented budget office because communication flow remains murky. For example, an examiner from Alabama claims that if she knew what the priorities were of either the finance director or the governor, it would certainly influence her approach to the budget request and help her better realign agency priorities with those of higher administration. When discussing changes made to budget recommendations, she added, "It may be that they have more information than I do. If I were privy to the information they have, I might not still be opposed [to their change in the budget recommendation]."

Further, once the budget information moves up the chain of command—to the finance director, the chief of staff, and the governor—priorities can and do change. More than a few examiners questioned the logic of conducting in-depth analysis of agency needs and desires when these officials "bump or realign our priorities" anyway. For example, one examiner talked of the experience of working through her first budget:

> It really opened my eyes too. Sometimes you feel that you do a lot of work and when the politics start coming into it, all common sense is thrown out the window. So that's one thing that really opened my eyes was that first time, and the effort that you put into it, and the solid budget that you think you've come up with, just to have somebody arbitrarily say, "OK, we need some money back and we're going to take it from here, now you live with it and make it work."

So as not to waste time, it is vital that John learn as much as he can from his section manager and keep the lines of communication clear between his agencies and the manager. He will learn about agency priorities from the agency itself (meetings and site visits) as well as from the manager. One of his only means of gathering information about the priorities of those higher up in the executive branch is to constantly question his manager as to whatever filters down. John should not expect that the priorities of the governor would be as clearly communicated to him as they are to Mary. To do his job, John will have to fully "mine" the legal, fiscal, and technical documentation he has collected, develop a good relationship with his agency (particularly in his capacity during budget execution), and communicate frequently with his section manager. One other avenue for John to pursue in order to learn about the politics of his budgets includes attendance at executive or legislative hearings. We see below that hearings offer some support to John, although they afford more prospective information on agencies. That is, the information that John picks up from hearings will help him to better understand his agencies for budget execution purposes, and regarding future rather than current budget development.

Gubernatorial Priorities

It is interesting that the three budget offices identified as control-oriented in this study each exhibited transition regarding the relationship with the governor. As explained earlier in the chapter, the ILSBO is defined as temporal control in orientation, given its attention to the details of the budget over a stronger focus on policy development and assessment before 1994. In this state, an examiner talked of "remaining apolitical by working for the Office of the Governor rather than the individual who is governor." Another agreed, identifying the changed role as "we're supposed to supply fiscal analysis to help the governor, whoever the governor is." In South Carolina, examiners were unsure about their role, due to creation of a new executive budget system. Several noted that they did not understand how their governor would use the budget information that they provided; one examiner speculated that the governor would create his own budget staff within his office. In Alabama, a budget office examiner explained how office orientation and function changes with new administrations:

> We were asked, I think, when the Hunt administration came (he had a lot of people that just did not know anything about state government), how to track legislation. We got very involved in tracking legislation, key legislation as well as appropriation bills and administration bills, and seems like we were trying to look for everybody, kind of taking on the governor's liaison duties in addition to what we were supposed to be doing as a budget office. This new administration seems to feel like they just want us to administer right now and we have not gotten nearly as involved.

Because of the policy distance from the governor, short revenues, and the confusion regarding role transitions (certainly in Alabama and South Carolina), it is hardly surprising that these examiners were most comfortable with control functions over policy initiation. Communication flow to and from the governor's office was often poor in comparison to that found in policy-oriented SBOs. That is, in policy-oriented budget offices, the governor's agenda is communicated through a number of formal and informal means—the State of the State Address, issue papers, memoranda by the secretary of finance, the budget director and section managers, the media, and perhaps directly in meetings with the governor or in casual conversation when walking down the halls of the budget office. In control SBOs we find that the governor's agenda does not filter down nearly as cleanly, and often is not even formally articulated to these examiners during predevelopment. According to one, "I don't really know, this governor has only been in fourteen or fifteen months, I don't know what his policy is." Another lamented that "the governor's agenda usually comes down from above and it's usually after I've done half my work and discovered that a lot of it is now useless."

The level of uncertainty about gubernatorial priorities among these examiners helps to explain their constricted rationality when reviewing agency budget requests. Explains one examiner:

When there is money, knowing the priorities from administration, we can sit here and do our best job, saying this is the little money we have and this is how we think it should be spread. But once you get up to the governor and this is how we think it should be spread and say this is how I want it, everything we do is completely shelved and we have to start over from scratch. If we knew what his needs were from the beginning, which, like I said, [is] based on who the administration is [our job would be easier].

In the following exchange, another examiner from the ILSBO illustrates that examiners do not consider the politics of budgeting as it pertains to their agencies to be a necessary component of their decision-making about spending recommendations. When the discussion turned to making cuts to agency budgets, we asked:

Q: Do you take that into account when you're analyzing the department requests and formulating recommendations? Do you keep the politics in mind?
Examiner: No. If they're going to take it out, they're going to take it out. So why should I worry about it now? They'll have their chance, and this is our budget, and they'll have a chance to take it out as soon as they get it.

Q: How about the governor's politics about the department?
Examiner: Once again, I make my recommendation here and when it goes across the street, if they've got any governor's politics in it, they'll take it out then. I always just sort of put it up on his desk and if they don't take it out, let them take it over there. I don't want to do that here. If you come up with a budget, you can back that budget because you think this is the best we can have. If you come up with a budget where you start taking things out because [the budget director] doesn't like this, it's very hard to explain that budget to somebody. So just go in and do it the best way between you and the agency and the division chief or whatever, and put it down and if the front office wants to take the money out, let them take it out. Let them explain.

When asked about examiners' understanding of the politics behind spending decisions, another from the ILSBO responded:

You mean like the politics of public opinion, the legislature, what the governor's agenda is, that kind of thing?
Q: Yes.
Examiner: Well, frankly I haven't known about a lot of it so far until recently.

Q: Because your options don't fit into the parameters?

Examiner: Just because they'll out of hand dismiss something, and again, I guess I'm thinking of when the agency is doing their request. They'll just, it's like, if you would have just out of hand dismissed this, like, weeks ago, I could have done something else.

Again, a policy orientation is unrealistic in an environment in which priorities are hard to decipher. Further, the conduct of analysis of agency budgets by examiners with the intent to "work" the request further up the hierarchy often wastes precious time.

Budget Hearings

Examiners from the three SBOs investigated here did mention hearings as another means to learn about the politics behind agency budgets. Executive hearings may be held during budget development (usually in the fall). The governor or the budget office will call on agencies to defend their spending plans. Agencies will use hearings to explain past expenditures and to cultivate support for funding old programs at increased levels, expanded or new programs, capital improvements, or personnel changes.

Holding executive hearings is not altogether certain, however. There can be two sets of budget hearings in Alabama; it just depends on the governor and the director of finance to hold finance department hearings separate from those held later by the legislature. According to one ALSBO examiner, "we are allowed to have budget hearings, executive budget hearings. It depends on the political climate as to whether we have separate budget hearings at the executive level or sometimes we combine them with the legislative side and have them all at once." Sometimes the governor will call in cabinet secretaries and their budget staff to discuss spending and program requests with him; he may or may not include anyone from the budget office in these meetings.

On the other hand, the legislature sponsors annual hearings with legislators from the Finance and Taxation and the Ways and Means committees and staff from the legislative fiscal office. Examiners usually attend these appropriations hearings "simply for note taking and information purposes." Given that executive budget hearings may not be held, those conducted by the legislature may be one of the only places in which examiners gain some insight into the political facets of their agencies' budget problems. This happens in South Carolina and Illinois as well. Note the following exchange with an ILSBO examiner:

Q: Do you know what the priority would be of [the assigned agency]?

Examiner: Well, right now they're kind of in, they have a couple of things they're trying to move at this point. One is that they've just started alternating examinations and things with the federal government. One year they do the banks, the next year the Feds do it, and how that's going to impact their agency as far as overlapping. They won't need as many people for any length of time, or if they could depend on the federal government to be there in the year, they have to give exams, and how that's going to impact their budget and their staff levels. There's also concern with the legislation in Congress dealing with national charters converting to state charters and vice versa and how that's going to impact. So they're kind of uncertain about those things right now.

Q: They really don't have a priority?
Examiner: Well, their priority is to examine the banks, trust companies, and that type every year. They have to do that.

Q: That's more like a mission.
Examiner: That's their mission, right. It is important to do those things every year, but this other aspect of it is, how it's going to affect what they do.

Q: How do you know all this?
Examiner: Through talking with the agency, appropriation hearings.

While the political facets are not as clear to these examiners, compared to their counterparts in policy-oriented budget offices, they need to know their agencies and budgets thoroughly before going into hearings, regardless of where they are held and by whom. One ALSBO examiner warned, "You should not be surprised during hearings." Certainly at the stage of executive hearings, examiners must understand agency budget problems. For instance, if an agency is about to finish building a new prison, a request for additional personnel is sure to follow and will need to be explained. Luckily, given their day-to-day focus on the control of agency spending, these budget requests generally hold few surprises for the examiners. According to one, "During the year you're in contact with [agencies], you get some ideas of the problems they're having, and kind of expect what they're gonna send in."

Development-Phase Analysis

Receiving the Agency Budget Request

According to one examiner, predevelopment activities entail "a lot of reconciling, adding to make sure that everything reconciled. Then, once you get through the historical data, the rest is detective work." Once agencies submit their spending plans to the SBO, John will use the budget request document itself as a major source of information, for it provides at least three years' worth of verifiable data. Combine this with the documentation that he has collected already about his agencies' budgets and problems, and John is very close to reaching the expert status regarding his agencies and budgets that is imperative for him to last on the job.

John will now analyze his budget requests for accuracy. Such requests normally include actual and proposed expenditure data for the last two fiscal years, the current fiscal year and the budget or requested fiscal year. Examiners verify the accuracy of the current year expenditures against what is recorded in the budget tracking system. Then, they go through the budget request column-by-column and line-by-line, checking the continuation or base budget first, looking for significant changes in spending amounts or among categories from the previous year. The focus of the examination is on program inputs, not program outputs or outcomes.

Next John will look at the improvements component of the request, where agencies present their request for new or expanded programs, additional equipment, or funding for new projects. If the agency is planning to purchase new computers, is that allowed under current budget policy? And has the agency processed the request through the information-technology-approval channels? If the agency is requesting funding for a new position, do the calculations include twelve-month or nine-month funding (since the latter is more realistic, allowing time for filling the position and saving 25 percent of the salary in the first year)? If the agency is proposing another trade office, for example, are the cost calculations consistent with the costs of operating existing trade offices, and if not, why not? What evidence does the agency present in these cases to justify the estimated costs presented in the request? Have they requested more than the rate at which commodity costs have increased? The questioning of requests will be rigorous and intensive, with detailed scrutiny expected by section managers and the budget director as well as agencies. The emphasis is on justification of the calculations, not on justification of the proposed activity itself.

John gets some insight into agency and program efficiency (aside from what he has picked up from meetings and site visits) by looking at the agency's budget requests included in their budget request package. In addition to fiscal trend data, the request may include workload and performance data indicative of agency efficiency and perhaps illustrative of agency goal attainment over the last year. Graphs, charts, and tables may be included here that provide a quick view of quantitative measures regarding agency performance based on data that the agency collects and maintains throughout the year. The request package often includes a capital expenditure form showing whether or not the agency anticipates building a building or purchasing automobiles or buying equipment for the office. The budget request also indicates staffing plans, describing additional employee needs if there is a new program they are considering implementing or that has been mandated to be implemented.

It is important to recognize the questions that the control-oriented examiners are *not* prone to ask as they review these requests. As illustrated earlier, there is no requirement to understand the underlying policy rationale for a request. Rather, the focus is on the documentation and quality of evidence presented in support of the request. The goal at this stage of budget development and for these examiners is to be able to support the numbers that have been produced. The policy merits of a particular request are evaluated higher up in the SBO or in the governor's office. And should John be able to free up any money through his calculations, these budget actors will decide where to reallocate the money.

The Revenue Constraint

Undoubtedly, the fiscal scenario in each of these state governments at the time contributed to a focus on guardianship and cutback management over policy initiative on the part of examiners. The prevalent theme of government—that needs far outweigh how much money is available—was a familiar tune played in Alabama, South Carolina, and Illinois in 1994. According to one examiner, "Tight economic times require agencies to go back to their original missions." Most examiners from these offices explained that the revenue situation precluded the creation of options for spending when reviewing agency budget requests and helping to prepare the budget. Such an environment renders issues of social value or consideration of economic rationality impractical. "Most of the things we do, fiscally based, there's just no money for it. I don't think I've been involved in anything where you pick one program or the other based on its social value or its ethical merit. I don't think I've had any part of that," claimed an ILSBO examiner.

Another examiner illustrates how constrained budget rationality becomes when money is tight. For this examiner, the technical and legal rationalities overshadow all others (social, political, and economic) as "the last three years, the [state budget] bureau has been cutting because we don't have much money, so that's the perspective I have. When more money floats to the top, and say revenue growth is up and there's more money to spend, we delve into programs and look into where to get the biggest bang for the buck, so to say, within certain programs." Yet, a multiple rationalities approach can be thwarted even in flush periods. Often new money is swallowed up or annualized by formula funding or entitlements, or applied to fulfill debt service requirements. According to one examiner, "We take all the agencies' requests and put them together, see how much they are out of whack with the revenues that are coming in, and then we have to make decisions from there and that's when the tough part comes in." In the end, we will see that it is no wonder that the politics of such budget problems is left by these examiners for others to grapple with.

Crafting a Recommendation

We witness that John is very much cornered into a traditional, incremental decision strategy when reviewing budgets in a control-oriented SBO. Because needs outweigh fiscal resources, because he is unclear about gubernatorial and other important budget actors' priorities, and because his focus is on reconciling spending with legal constraints, there is hardly an avenue for John to research agency-spending alternatives or options for the governor. In South Carolina, an examiner explains that while the office is "intimately involved from day one" with budget preparation, they do not consider themselves to be providing recommendations to the governor. On the other hand, they are not surprised by the recommendations that come out of the governor's office because it is the budget office that provides the research about agency requests that feeds into his decisions:

> There were no surprises. Not even their recommendation was a surprise because they involved us from day one. The governor had a three-person staff. And so we provided all the research that they needed done in order to make their recommendations. Now they didn't ask us to make a recommendation. I mean, they may ask us to make a recommendation. They may ask us, "What would you do about this?" or something like that, but there was no formal recommendation that we had to make. It was sort of informal working. The governor's office came over and met with each team, each functional team before they finalized their recommendation so we were intimately involved in the process.

The SCSBO examiners provide information and budget recommendations to the governor's staff, and it is this staff that makes final recommendations to the governor. "They determine what his budget would look like." Prior to the establishment of an executive budget process, the five members of the Budget and Control Board needed to reach agreement about the budget before sending it on to the General Assembly. Now, stated this examiner, "it is totally [the governor's] budget" and:

He can consult his wishes with the comptroller general or the treasurer, and the other two members of the board are going to get that budget anyway because one's the chairman of Ways and Means and the other chairman of Senate Finance. It's pretty much the governor, his staff that's going to come up and write his budget message for him and what priorities he's going to spend.

This differs from historical budget-making in South Carolina when the budget office would come up with recommendations based on available revenues. The director of the BCB would then talk with key members of the board individually as recommendations were being developed. Then the board would meet and the recommendations would be presented by the SCSBO. At that meeting and perhaps one or two more, the priorities of the board would be "hashed out," with the final recommendation indicative of the board's agreement on priorities.

Examiners in control-oriented SBOs are primarily information conduits and, as noted above, are not chiefly concerned with preparing recommendations of a policy orientation. According to an ALSBO examiner:

We are somewhat active in the recommendation of the governor, but not very much. The Budget Management Act spells out what we are supposed to do, and with the staff we have by getting the budget document together. Once that's done, once the budget is passed, then our job is administrative. We just have to watch the agencies to make sure that they don't overstep their legislative authority; that they don't get themselves in trouble if we can help it, doing things we would recommend they not do. It is not fiscally creative. I feel that [it is] more our job to administer the budget once it is passed. Not so much getting involved in the recommendation of it.

Therefore, we are not puzzled that John is not conducting analysis on a par with that required of Mary in a policy-oriented budget office—that is, with an eye toward developing or supporting policy initiatives or with the intent of bringing the governor around to a particular point of view. Rather, John will be looking at the reasonableness and validity of his agencies' requests as they move forward in the budget cycle; he will approach recommendations predominantly from the fiscal and technical perspectives. An SCSBO examiner discussed the checklist that each examiner runs through when putting together his or her budget recommendations:

We have to go through suggested priorities looking at constitutional requirements, annualizations for the next year, any type of statutes, new initiatives, new major policy issues, certain uncontrollable type items such as our rent, employee contributions which we have to make sure are fully funded, and then any type of new expansion or new initiative budget request. We have to look at the lapses for the past several years, any type carry-forwards, keep up with our transfer activities in case there are certain things that need to be applied to that, any type of mandated type provisos, statutes, or whatever. We have to also see if the agencies can work within their own funding availability. And then also we have to consider, "Well what if they do not get the funding? What will happen?" And then look at any type of reductions that has been discussed with the agencies that they really do need these programs anymore, the funding anymore.

When discussing budget recommendations, one examiner responded:

We have a lot of leniency in being able to [make recommendations]. If we think it is a valid request, then we go forward with it or not. Oftentimes if [the agency] comes in and says they need $20 million for overtime, I'm like, "Come on, now, you had $2 million last year; we have to talk about this." So generally I will go to the fiscal staff or the fiscal officers and try to talk them through this, saying, "You know that's not a reality, so why did you even press the issue?"

We see the fiscal and technical focus of another examiner in the next exchange. The examiner notes that the recommendation was made not from a policy perspective but from a fiscal one—to curb further contracting of the budget. It is insightful that knowledge of gubernatorial priority vis-à-vis this agency's specific initiative does flavor the examiner's decision to push forward with the request.

Q: So you were an advocate for them to get their request as the reward for their activities?
Examiner: I don't know if it was a reward, or more or less to stop the bleeding. They weren't asking for an awful lot, it was a very reasonable request. And I felt that another year or two of continued reductions would sidetrack the initiative, which, when they first announced it, the governor wrote a letter or a little news release, I believe, and supported it, mentioned it a few times. Well, if he wanted to support it, you should back that up.

Examiners seem less likely to "go to the wall" for agencies regarding spending requests, predominantly because they are unclear about the preferences of those higher up. Yet, while some steadfastly deny any role other than that of objective researcher and information provider, others do claim to throw out options "regardless of the politics" and let those higher up decide. And, even if the recommendation is not going "to fly," examiners seem comfortable making them as long as they can back up their numbers. Certainly given their focus, they can. An example is provided in the following exchange. Again, the fiscal and legal perspectives overshadow others in this examiner's rationale behind the additional spending for the agency requested:

> I think maybe two or three years since I've been here, we had money to, what I'll say "give away," what I mean, to give money over and above what they got before. And we've actually been able to go in and look at the agency and say, "OK, I think this agency really needs the money because they need to hire more people because they've got this new statute requiring them to do more things and they have to have more people."

So it typically comes down to the examiners' ability to defend the budgets they have reviewed and checked for their agencies. According to one examiner, they are advocates for the budgets and not necessarily the agencies or programs therein:

> Once we get that budget into the legislature, we think we've done a good job of whittling, of taking money out where it needs to be taken out, where they don't need those resources, and increments. Basically you annualize those programs and people that you think are necessary for them to continue what they're doing. You've taken out money for components of programs or people that we don't think are serving a useful function anymore. Then we added increments and initiatives to try to better the agency and maybe save money in the long run for a lot of things. So once we have that budget in, I feel like that's my best effort and their best effort to say this is one of the lowest levels we could live at and still effectively perform our function. So at that time, yeah, we both, I feel like I am advocating for that budget.

And of course, the revenue situation will overshadow any presentation of options or initiatives on the part of the examiner and the agency. One examiner explained:

> Usually it's one of two different scenarios: either "these are the revenues we project to have and it looks like we're gonna cut everybody 5 percent, so you prepare where we should cut your department," or it could be "OK, this is total revenue we project and it looks like we have $18 million to spread." Look at your agencies and see what you feel is important and which agencies you think should get some dollars and how much. For instance, there's an agency requesting some special forensic equipment or something, or they're building a prison, or if public safety is implementing

a new automatic fingerprint system, they have to have some million-dollar computer. So, I would go back to my budgets and look and see what special things were requested above level funding and make my recommendations from that. The past few years have been simply cutting. There has been no extra money. Survival.

Essentially, there is no resetting the recommendation after the governor's review. Rather, examiners explain that changes are often made to budgets after they are funneled farther up the SBO, to the governor's staff and to the governor. When changes are communicated back down to the examiner, it is his responsibility simply to pick up the pieces and move on. He will have to recalculate the numbers to work within whatever parameters have now been placed on the request; either money has been added to—or more likely cut from—the request. Agencies do go directly to the finance director or the governor's office if they have specific needs that they feel should be redressed. It would be a rare event, however, for an examiner to act as advocate for the agency at this stage in the budget cycle.

Such advocacy on the part of the examiner would have occurred much earlier in budget development, perhaps even during budget execution when the examiner is exposed to budget problems first hand. In Alabama, for instance, examiners claim that continual assessment of the operations plans enables them to find out about agencies' critical needs, information that examiners use when reviewing requests later in budget development. In South Carolina, examiners stress that much of their work during budget execution involves problem-solving, such as managing agency deficits. One examiner provided the following example of attention to problems during budget execution:

> We've had cases where the [state] treasurer was holding up disbursing money out of a particular fund. And I went to the fund area of the statutes to see if there was any reason why the treasurer should be doing that. In consulting with our legal people, we decided there was no reason why the treasurer should have been putting their nose in it, that there was no authority in the statutes that said that they control that money. They should disburse it.

Examiners may also solve problems for their agencies during the legislative session. An ALSBO examiner explained:

> We in essence go through every bill that's introduced to make sure, mainly to see if it's financially related. But there may be, and a lot of times what we've done, we call it a house cleaning. There may be just some technical

problems with the bill, and in the way that we could administer it in the past. And those are the kind of things we usually initiate. And of course we get approval to try to get those amended from [the budget director] and [the finance director] and the governor, if necessary. A lot of times an agency or legislator may want to create a fund to do some service, and there may already be a fund out there that can do the same thing, so we may work with them to alleviate the problem of double funding, or just like I say, administrative. Sometimes they will want to transfer funds from this fund to that fund to the other fund when there's an easier way to do it administratively. That's just house cleaning amendments.

In South Carolina, the budget division actually types the appropriation bill, uploading it into the computer system. "Any changes Ways and Means as a committee does, we implement, we keep track and implement that. But the Ways and Means staff will work with our staff on budget issues and budget questions and get a lot of information from us," stated one SCSBO examiner.

Summary: Constraints on a Multiple-Rationalities Approach to Budget Decisions

Unlike examiners in a policy-oriented SBO, we cannot expect that those within a control-oriented budget office can or will "ensure the governor's policy staff are aware of all the interested parties in a decision and the alternatives available to the governor." This is because, as pointed out previously and as we have seen here, examiners' communications with other budget actors in control-oriented SBOs are curtailed (sometimes severely so) to section managers and maybe the budget director and agency fiscal staff. Direct communication with agency secretaries, the governor's policy staff, and the governor is often nonexistent and very much at the discretion of these actors. The chief activity of the control-oriented budget office is *to compile* agency budget requests into the governor's recommendation to be submitted to the legislature.

Given such an orientation, it is unlikely that these examiners can be "out front" on an issue. An SCSBO examiner is emphatic regarding the role of the control-oriented examiner by stating, "My main responsibility is the technical side of getting the budget put together and printed and balanced and keep it balanced as it goes to the legislative process." In fact, we have witnessed that these examiners may not even know what the issues are. At the very least, they may be uncertain regarding what is most important to the governor. As one ALSBO budget examiner explained, "Before we can get the book published, the last thing we do is wait on recommendations to come back and then that's when we go through, we do every page and put in the governor's request. And, a lot of times the governor's request will change from the time we sent the book to the printer and the time we actually do the bill."

This is not to say, however, that these budget examiners are any less aware of state government operations and activities than their counterparts in a policy-oriented SBO. Essentially, they are experts on the flow of state dollars. What we witness is a very narrowly defined role that constricts examiners to the technicalities of budgeting—such technicalities involve checking agency spending plans and heavy involvement in the execution of the budget through expenditure oversight and legal review. As noted earlier regarding the many reasons that budget examiners look to state statutes and administrative rules for information on their agencies, we find those in control-oriented SBOs to be focused on the more mundane aspects of budgeting in terms of accountability and the legal requirements of spending. According to an ALSBO budget examiner, "We deal with agencies on a year-round basis, help agencies struggle through in making payroll and meeting all their budgetary requirements." Another remarked that their job could be divided into three components—assisting agencies in preparing their spending plans, entering these plans onto the system before the beginning of the fiscal year, and "just miscellaneous activities during the fiscal year." Without the governor, a finance secretary or the budget director taking the reins, so to speak, to include the budget examiner in developing policy initiatives, traditional control functions will preclude examiners' "involvement in substantive discussions and decisions regarding state policies affecting their agencies" that is reflective of a policy orientation. Murky communication flow, the mechanics of putting the budget together, and balancing (often in light of a poor revenue forecast) all constrict examiners in their ability to even begin to develop a policy orientation.

Note

1. Typical of southern states, South Carolina and Alabama have traditionally exhibited strong legislatures vis-à-vis the executive in budget matters. This has been somewhat muted, of course, by individually aggressive governors, and in Alabama given the program budget format, fund structure, and biennial budget cycle. Also as noted in chapter 1, South Carolina specifically legislated an executive budget system in 1993. In general, the emergence of partisan politics in the South has contributed to weakening legislative bodies in these states, and at least allows for the possibility of greater policy leadership on the part of the governor. It is interesting that the states in this study characterized as predominantly control-oriented exhibit partisanship across the branches; each had a Republican governor by the end of 1994, with a Democratic or split legislature.

8

Changing Roles:
From Guarding the Purse
to Guarding the Policy

Historical Evolution of the Budget Examiner Role

In previous chapters, we have noted that policy problems become budget problems when they require funding, and that this nexus of budget and policy decisions critically shapes the way in which budget decisions are made. We have argued that SBOs are the institutional gatekeepers in the budgetary process, and subsequently described budgetary decision-making in a policy environment that requires a multiple-rationalities approach to budget recommendations. We followed the decision-making of two different budget examiners to see how they invoked the various rationalities in their decision-making. We have seen how the critical distinction is governed by the degree to which the examiners operate in a policy-oriented SBO.

In this chapter, we pursue the distinction between the control-oriented and policy-oriented SBOs with respect to how this difference affects the roles budget examiners play with respect to their assigned agencies. To what extent do the examiners continue to play their traditional role as guardians of the purse? Are there other roles that the examiners play with respect to their agency assignments? If so, what is the relationship between the roles, the decision context, and the rationalities employed at various steps in the budget process? We now explain traditional roles of budget examiners.

Role orientation for central budget examiners has changed with the evolution of executive budgeting in the United States since the turn of the century. Howard (1973, 287) notes that the classic caricature of a budgeter is "a tight-fisted, penny-pinching bureaucrat who grubs over accounting figures and counts stamps at the end of each work day." This classic gatekeeper role is attributable to the formative period of budgeting, when its roots were firmly

planted in accounting and central clearance, and the budget office "was supposed to say no to everything" (Schick 1987). It was common practice to
give the central budget office control over execution of the budget: (1) to
prevent budget deficits, and (2) to ensure legislative intent (Schick 1987,
289). Such purposes were manifested in several types of control measures,
including reporting and oversight activities to promote efficiency and legality.

Budget examiners in state budget offices are the individual gatekeepers in
the budgetary process. They are the "eyes and ears" of the governor regarding operating departments and agencies, and the "ears and eyes" of departments and agencies regarding the policies of the governor. As we discussed
in chapter 2, SBOs are the institutional gatekeepers in the budgetary process.
Often attached directly to the governor's office, they are the central intermediaries between the governor and state agencies in the executive budget process. While the SBO is the reservoir into which flows the multitude of agency
requests, it is the individual examiner who largely controls the information
and requests that will flow onwards for consideration by the budget director,
the governor, and eventually the legislature.

Wildavsky's (1964, et. seq.) incremental budgeting model argues that decisions by principal budgetary actors are influenced by budgeters' anticipation of the choices made by *other* budgetary actors. Regular actors in the
budgetary process are expected to fill certain roles that become institutionalized. For example, agency budgeters are expected to be acquisitive and in-
flate their budget requests to the central budget office; the budget office is
expected to cut the budget requests before recommending a budget to the
governor; and the legislative appropriations committees are expected to guard
the treasury by cutting the governor's recommendation still more. These institutional decisional roles thus serve as a basis for predicting budgetary
choices. Although largely a macro-level model of budgetary decision-making, incrementalism predicts certain decisional roles in state budgeting: agencies are focused on budget improvement, the SBO budget examiners are
focused on percentage increases of agency requests over the base, and legislators are focused on the percentage change in the governor's recommendations for agency base budgets.

The predominant view of the budget examiner as "cutter" and "guardian
of the treasury" appears in numerous studies, including Ira Sharkansky's
(1968a; see also 1965) study of budgeting in American states, and Thomas
Anton's study of budgeting in Illinois (1966). For example, Anton (1969,
122) explained that "whether or not agency administrators are in fact expansive in the preparation of budget estimates, it is reasonably clear that the
persons who review estimates believe them to be expansive. . . . Recognizing the strength of built-in pressures to expand budgets, then, and believing

that these pressures will be reflected in budget requests, reviewing officials *naturally* see themselves as 'cutters.' "

"In one way, there is no point in denying, the budget function is preponderantly negative," New York budget director Appleby (1957) admitted. "It is on the whole rather strongly against program and expenditure expansion. This approach is desirable, because the programmatic agencies and most of the potent pressure groups are so expansive that there will be little danger that the undeniable values they represent will be overlooked or smothered by examiners" (Appleby 1957, 156).

On the other hand, while the budgeting orientation is rooted in control activities, we have noted that in many states, for example, it has evolved through management and planning eras into a policy orientation. With this change in focus and budgeting environment came new roles for budget examiners in the central budget offices (Schick 1966). Along with saying no in a high percentage of cases, there was a new requirement to consider alternative and better ways of accomplishing the objective(s) of the chief executive. Management analysts were added to budget offices to analyze program effectiveness and efficiency in the management era (ca. 1950–1965). Planning analysts were added during the planning era for estimating longer-term impacts of current spending decisions (ca. 1965–1980). The tension between using the budget as a constraint on government growth, yet alternatively as a means to search for new spending opportunities, increased the influence of economics and politics in budget development. "Thus, the results of the annual (or biennial) budget cycle depended more on the political and economic environment in which budgeting was practiced than on the procedures used" (Schick 1987, 4).

Appleby (1957, 156) explains that such consideration means that "a budget organization that is always and wholly negative is something less than ideal. There are ways to save money by spending more. . . . Nor should budget personnel be so blind to values other than their own that they do not see imaginatively and sympathetically the public service values behind the figures they deal in" (Appleby 1957, 156). Robert Cornett (1965, 174), a budget director for Kentucky, agreed: "If a budget agency is merely the institutional 'no' agency, then all that is necessary is that revenue estimates be conservative so that you make sure you collect enough. . . . Our job is tougher than this if we are really to lay out policy issues in the proper perspective."

The few extant studies that investigate relationships between state budget examiners and agency budgeters reveal a more complex profile, suggesting that successful relationships are based on mutual respect and trust (see Shadoan 1963a, 1963b, 1965; Howard 1973; Duncombe and Kinney 1987; Thurmaier 1995b; Thurmaier and Gosling 1997). Arlene Shadoan (1963a,

229) found that "in many states a primary aim of budget offices is to show agency personnel how budgeting is useful in fulfilling program aims. This is accomplished through extensive analyst-agency contact. . . . The analyst may aid the agency in establishing an internal budget process . . . whereby agency priorities are ironed out among the various divisions in an agency and a unified agency budget is presented for budget office and gubernatorial consideration." Howard (1973) recognized that the relationships between budget examiners and agency staff varied widely. At the federal level, Davis and Ripley (1969, 76) found that "personal relations also affect the relations between agencies and the Bureau of the Budget [OMB]. Respondents in both the Bureau and in the agencies stressed the importance of personality. . . . A good 80 percent of what gets done is based on personality." And in 1999, senior VASBO examiner Robert Lockridge (1999) lectured new budget examiners at a national conference that good working relationships are a *prerequisite* to good budget analysis.

Certainly, we have heard from the examiners in this study that a trusting relationship with the agency precludes good budget analysis. For example, in response to the question, "What makes an agency a pain?" one seasoned analyst from Alabama offered, "A lot of times personality conflicts. Or an agency that's always in a financial strain. Or an agency that's always involved in high-profile issues." Regardless of budget office orientation, the examiners questioned here realize the importance of establishing good "one-on-one" relationships with their agencies in order for them to complete their work, whether for budget development, budget execution, or both. An examiner from the SCSBO explains that a conversation about golf was one avenue to cooperation:

> You keep in contact with them the whole time. That's why I think it's good to meet the people up-front. That's what helped me, because I established a relationship, put a name with the face, and over the course of the last year, I haven't had any trouble with my contacts. I get information as I need it pretty quick, even from [that agency]. Everybody that's ever had them had to struggle with them but I've got my cup pretty quick from them, talk about golf with them.

In VASBO, an examiner carefully explains the importance of cultivating good agency relationships:

> I feel it's important to work in an open environment, and that is no surprise to agencies. We are very dependent upon agencies for accurate information. An agency could make our job absolutely miserable if they choose

not to cooperate. It has always been my commitment to agencies that I'll be as open as I can with you, with what I'm going to recommend, as long as you don't take that knowledge and go and try to lobby outside of our relationship, lobby with the secretary or lobby with the governor or particularly lobby with adversary groups with regard to the approach. I don't want to be in a situation where I recommend something and it turns out that I didn't have full knowledge of the issue for you, and the agency had to come in and say that they didn't know about this. And here I am sitting with egg on my face publicly because I got a bad recommendation out there. And I've got to either back down or else try somehow to save face and dig in. We can always differ over the issue, but we shouldn't differ over the facts. And I need to have all the facts in order to—there's an old saying that everyone's entitled to their own opinion but no one is entitled to their own facts. As I mentioned earlier, I'm totally dependent upon the agencies in making sure that I have all the facts, it's important, and that's why I try not to operate in a very closed-door atmosphere.

Establishing a trusting relationship with agencies is a primary step for an examiner, a precursor to a number of roles potentially played in the budget cycle. Other examiners in Virginia highlight the multiple roles of the examiner vis-à-vis agencies: "we are there for guidance to agencies." Alternatively, when assessing spending plans, "we assess how valid they are, how unrealistic and politically motivated." In South Carolina an examiner stated that "while examiners are sometimes perceived as the hawk," for the examiner, "the agency is perceived as the hawk." Roles are very much a function of perceptions and expectations evident throughout the repetitive, cyclical, timely yet dynamic process of budgeting.

As central budget offices began to assume a larger role in the policy process (especially since the late 1970s), budget examiners have increasingly adopted the role of policy analyst. Gosling's (1987, 1985) studies of Midwest budget offices found WISBO analysts serving a routinized policy role. Policy development was an important aspect of Wisconsin budgeting, especially for noncabinet agencies, such as education and natural resources. Wisconsin's governor turned to the WISBO examiners to develop policy initiatives in those areas because these independent agencies generated their own policy priorities for legislative consideration. The budget and policy processes required early identification of policy issues by analysts so that issues could be prioritized and studied as preparation for the next budget development period (Gosling 1987, 1985).

At the federal level, Davis and Ripley (1969) also found that agency budgeters categorized the attitudes of OMB budget examiners toward their programs as advocacy, neutrality, or hostility, with neutrality being the norm and hostility and advocacy being the exception. "Neutrality appears to be the normal stance of the examiners, as seen by the agencies. This is certainly the attitude for which the Bureau of the Budget strives. But agencies have also perceived examiners as being either hostile non-supporters or advocates for their programs within the Bureau. . . . But most did not feel that examiners became advocates (Davis and Ripley 1969, 71–72).

Similarly, Shelly Tomkin (1998) identifies at least four different roles for OMB examiners with respect to agencies, including:

- Cutters: absent a political imperative, hold back spending and growth in government.
- Neutral policy analysts: simplifying budgetary decisions to manageable dimensions for the CEO, "narrowing the bounds of ignorance" for executive decisions.
- Information conduits: passing information back and forth between agencies and CEOs, organizing the information for comprehensibility at top and bottom (a translator service).
- Policy advocates: a relatively new role seen by some as "politicizing" the examiner's role and compromising the "neutral competence" inherent in the conduit and policy analyst roles.

More recently, Tomkin (1998, 239) points out that President Clinton used OMB's institutional memory (and long-running list of "wasteful" programs) to cut 300 programs partially or totally, highlighting OMB's informed "naysayer" capacity for the president. Over time, Tomkin finds an increasing practice of examiners "percolating" policy options, especially at the beginning of a new administration, and then reading and interpreting the feedback from the administration as policy cues that guide their budgetary decisions. In this way, objective analysis gets policy and political feedback, which then is transformed to workable policy systems. Examiners may be involved actively in the development of budget and policy alternatives for programs that are a presidential priority (Tomkin 1998, 74–78).

On the other hand, the evolution of examiner roles has not been uniform, and certain administrations have used OMB much differently than others. For example, David Stockman used OMB examiners to "crunch numbers" that he needed for policy initiatives and legislative lobbying, greatly diminishing their "policy percolation" role. As their role in budget and policy formulation decreased, these examiners compensated for such a loss of power and influence by increasing their control role with respect to agency budget implementation. They still had some discretion in this part of the budget cycle (Tomkin 1998, 90–92).

A key finding of Tomkin's study is that the multiple roles of the examiner have been institutionalized in many cases, although the emphasis on one role or another seems to vary across time and place. Deciphering complex roles is itself a complicated task. The classical "no" bias is alive and well, but not uniform or uninformed (Tomkin 1998, 24). Identifying which factors influence role dominance (if any) is not a straightforward task. Transmitting neutral information *and* politically sophisticated advice from OMB to the president are not *necessarily* mutually exclusive, but the task requires "delicate and difficult balancing acts" and staff able to "negotiate their way through troubling role conflicts" (Tomkin 1998, 60).

Studies of state budget examiners also suggest multiple roles and the same potential conflicts. Janet Pittard explains that at the end of the 1990s, "especially with the advent of performance-based budgeting, the responsibilities of the budget analyst have shifted from that of an accountant to a more sophisticated, expansive set of skills, including: technological expertise, political savvy, knowledge of policy, historical perspective, legal awareness, and communication" (Pittard 1999). Lockridge (1999) also suggests that the examiner role requires a complex set of personal traits. An examiner needs to be:

- A self-starter who exhibits initiative;
- Assertive and direct;
- A "doubting Thomas" or devil's advocate;
- Detail-oriented;
- Adaptable to respond to changing priorities and deadlines;
- Highly tolerant of ambiguity;
- Creative;
- Inquisitive; and
- Objective, but mindful of politics.

More generally, the evolution of the role of the modern government finance officer has been recognized as a melding of two distinct orientations—one typical of policymakers focused on program initiation and management, the other typical of finance officers focused on the control and accountability of public funds. For example, Irwin David (1998) explains that technological advancements have "freed" both policymakers and finance officers to embrace a more comprehensive view of both the management and funding of public programs. Certainly, advanced technologies and the possibilities for information sharing through the Internet have the potential to free finance officers from mundane aspects of record keeping and allow more time for strategizing. Likewise, policymakers must look to more creative methods of financially supporting program activities just as finance officers must better link funding with the performance or results of agency and department activities. Lawrence O'Toole (1997) writes that the more complex environment of government activity today stretches the role of budgeters to the point where even technical competence coupled with agency advocacy is not sufficient for truly informed decision-making about public budgets. Both David (1998) and Miller (1991) conclude that the traditional role of finance officers (with responsibility for tracking and controlling funds) coupled with a new attention to policy initiative places them in very powerful positions. That is, their role orientation has evolved from a concentration on transaction processing to other functions such as analysis, design, forecasting, evaluation, and guidance.

Thus, just as we find multiple institutional roles in our sample of SBOs, it is not surprising that we find multiple roles for the budget examiners making decisions inside those SBOs. We recognize that examiners function at a different (lower) level than finance directors. On the other hand, their close connection to both the agencies for which they review budgets and (potentially) to the chief executive provide these budgeters with real possibility for taking on the multiple perspectives mentioned above. Nevertheless, as we witnessed in the last chapter, examiners in control-oriented SBOs are quite restricted in their knowledge of the political rationale behind their agencies' budgets.

Examiners in control-oriented SBOs are more likely to revert to an adversarial, control role that is expected from the incrementalism model. Examiners in the policy-oriented SBOs, in contrast, are generally afforded better, more direct communication with the governor, primarily in learning about the politics of agency budgets. These examiners are more likely to exhibit multiple roles and in fact largely eschew the "cutter" role. The focus of these examiners is on the policy consonance of agency requests with the governor's agenda, not percentage changes in agency requests. We will explore these roles in greater detail below, having provided a review of the evolution of the role of the budget examiner in American government.

The Roles Typology from Examiner Interviews

Considering the historical evolution of budget examiner roles in the United States discussed above, we explored several questions in our interviews with examiners in the eleven SBOs, specifically:

- Under what conditions does the SBO examiner act as watchdog or "naysayer" to agencies?

- Under what conditions does the SBO examiner act as a neutral intermediary between the budget director (and governor) and operating agencies?
- Under what conditions does the SBO examiner act as an advocate for
the assigned agency's programs?
- Does the role of the SBO examiner change with the different phases of
the budget cycle? For example, does s/he play a different role in budget
development than in budget execution?
- How important are personal relationships in defining these roles?
- How important are the SBO examiner's professional and educational
backgrounds in defining these roles?

We explored the role definitions of SBO budget examiners in our sample
states in two ways. In many cases, we directly asked examiners whether they
saw their role with respect to their assigned agencies as adversaries, advocates, or something else. We also asked a number of questions about the
activities of examiners vis-à-vis agencies during all phases of the budgeting
cycle, interjecting prompts regarding proportion of time spent on various
activities; what was most important to them regarding budgetary decisions;
and at what stage did they need or provide certain information. Researchers
attempted to adhere closely to the sequence of the interview protocol. Yet,
given the loosely structured format and in order to respect the examiners'
either substantive response to a specific question or questions, or their devia-
tion from the protocol at any point, some questions were never asked directly. If the question about roles was not asked of an examiner directly, we
thus coded the variable, "role," based on inference of examiners' responses
to other, related questions. That is, we coded role based on the examiners'
descriptions of their interactions with assigned agencies and other remarks
they made in the interview that indicated the roles they play in the budget
process with respect to their assigned agencies. Direct responses about examiner roles created initial role types. Indirect responses were then matched
to these role types. Both authors agreed to the role types identified for each
examiner.

Content analysis for role definition was therefore conducted in the following manner for those examiners not asked directly about the role or roles
that they play by virtue of their position in the SBO. The variable role was
coded as "adversary" if an examiner indicated skepticism about agency requests, verbalized a comprehensive or state view over agency or section perspective, or if they indicated a traditional guardianship role ("just say no") as
opposed to a budget "problem solver." Examiners were coded as illustrating
a "conduit" role if they spoke of the requirement to maintain communication
of information back and forth between agencies, the SBO, or the governor.

The "facilitator" role was indicated if the examiner expressed notions of helping to communicate information back and forth between agencies, the SBO, and the governor, as well as placing agency needs and desires in the best light throughout such communications or, rather, making sure that agencies present their best foot forward with spending requests. The "policy analyst" role is indicated by examiners who expressed the necessity to conduct objective analysis of public policies and agencies' requests with respect to their fit with the governor's agenda. Finally, examiners were coded as taking on an "advocate" role when they expressed commitment to agency goals and objectives, and talked of molding requests to accommodate agency needs and desires so that requests feed directly into the governor's agenda.

Regardless of the method for identifying the budget examiners' roles, it is evident that most examiners see themselves as performing multiple roles with respect to their assigned agencies. We now describe each of the major role characterizations revealed through our discussions with SBO staff that includes examiners, section managers, and budget directors.

Adversary

Recent studies of budget examiners suggest that the inherent cutter bias is alive and well. Thurmaier (1992, 1995a) found that absent a political imperative to protect or augment a program, budget examiners will reduce expenditures to adjust for a poor fiscal climate or to "improve" technical efficiency. Tomkin (1998, 74) found a similar bias in OMB: Absent a political imperative, examiners are inclined to hold back spending and growth in government. This behavior fits the expected examiner role in the traditional incremental model. "To explain the apparent negativism of budget review officials solely in terms of their mistrust of agency budget estimates," Anton (1969, 122) argues, "would be to overlook the *personal and political stake* they have in doing what they do. Review officers, too, must play to several audiences, including agency administrators, the governor, and the legislature. *Their failure to make the cuts others expect them to make would challenge the grounds for the existence of specialized review agencies and thus threaten the jobs they hold*" (emphasis added).

Some adversarial roles are played according to the classic incrementalism model, because the examiner expects classical behavior from the agencies. According to a VASBO examiner, "agencies have tunnel vision. I have a broader perspective." Another from the GASBO stated that "agencies know we have to cut them. They ask for everything in the world and then I have to spend a lot of time figuring out where they pad." In SCSBO, examiners are equally suspicious: "You have to be conscious that agencies are trying to pull a snow job on you." Such role expectations were revealed as well by this ALSBO examiner:

> Let's just say agencies ask for a pie in the sky because of the old adage "if you don't ask for it, you'll not get it." But once you get down under the wire and actually make them sit down and put them under the bright light shining in their eyes and say, "What do you really need?" That number gets changed and it's the same now as it was back then. . . . You can't blame an agency for asking. If they ask for the same amount of money, they're going to wind up getting stuck in that category that "this agency doesn't ever need any more. Skip over them."

Some activities are more adversarial than others, and regardless of the role this ALSBO examiner wishes to play, the adversarial role may be required by the office's control orientation:

> I have actually had to go through and look at individual vouchers and say this is extraneous travel. . . . Well, this is getting too detailed in my mind, but when we're asked, we can. But that's actually getting into individual vouchers that the agencies are writing, which are very detailed; and I don't think that we're supposed to do a general overall budget and we're not supposed to say, "Don't go to Denver to save money." But if we have to, we will. But I don't feel like we're supposed to be monitoring. That's what we're doing, [what] our budget officer has asked me to do now.

Other ALSBO examiners describe a role that is very technical, focused on detailed monitoring of agency expenditures and waiting for others to make decisions. Tasks include

> surveys, end of the month reports, a series of reports that we do to reconcile with those appropriations that have been out through the comptroller's office. You know: cash is reconciled, appropriation authority is reconciled and we also do a drawdown schedule, which I do to give to the Comptroller's Office. The bigger agencies that draw money in such huge lumps every month along with our [operations] plan at the beginning of the year, they submit a request of how they want this money drawn down by month. And we put the whole total picture together with all the agencies that receive general fund money, along with the revenues, along with the carry forward balance from the month before, to make sure that we have enough money that's gonna come in that month to give everybody their needs. And if that's not the case, we will get on the phone, and start calling them and asking them what portion they can postpone until the next month. And so

we do a lot of monitoring when it comes to the actual cash in the State Treasury and what the agencies are to receive.

An examiner from an SBO in a state in transition from a control to a policy orientation related stories about colleagues who seemed to like the adversary role.

> When I came here, the person who used to have my job came and we all went out to lunch with some of the other people, and I guess we kind of talked about it before too, but one of the [examiners] who's been here for awhile, he was talking about some of the things you need to do. "You've got to make sure they're not trying to do this and they're not trying to pull this over on you." And when he left, [my manager] said, "You have to understand that people look at that differently." And that's probably why I trust [my agency] to some extent, is that [my manager] said that these people for the most part, they might make mistakes, but they generally seem to be pretty up-front. And that's been my impression in dealing with them too. . . . I think I can be more effective if they don't feel like I'm out to get them necessarily.

She also retold a discussion that occurred during a training session on a new accounting system when "one of my colleagues said something like he was going to go 'stomp all over them [his agencies] and see what they're trying to get away with.' A, I think that's a poor attitude if you're going to be building relationships with people; and B, I don't really think there's a lot to find."

For the most part, however, examiners were reluctant to acknowledge any sort of adversarial role with respect to their agencies. When they did, they tended to emphasize that it was for a brief period as a necessary part of the budget process. For example, a KSBO examiner explains the adversarial role:

> Depends on the time of year. Around November 10 we'll definitely be antagonists because that's when Division of Budget recommendations come out. Then they'll submit their appeals. They know that I'm the one that's presenting the appeals to the governor and I'll get phone calls and they'll plead their case. Then once the governor's recommendations come out, it really depends if they got what they wanted. If they did not get what they wanted, if their appeal wasn't met, they do not like to openly criticize the governor, but they'll often openly criticize the Division of Budget. It must have been the Division of Budget that twisted the governor's arm and said, "Don't fund this." At least that's the way they present it in legislative committee.

Q: When they appeal, it sounds like you're still the antagonist. So when do you stop being the antagonist?

Examiner: With some agencies, you never do. They just do not like the Division of Budget and the whole process. With others, usually after the governor's [recommendations] come out, provided that they're accepting of the recommendations. If they fared well, then they'll even ask for background information from me so they can use it in their legislative presentation. . . . During the legislative session, we're also defending the governor's recommendations. In subcommittee hearings sometimes I'm asked questions point-blank, "What was the governor's reasoning behind this recommendation?" Later in the spring when it comes down to salary plan and any other special pieces, appropriation items, or other legislation that's passed, then it turns into a helpful mode. Like salary plan, it's been decided by the legislature, it hasn't been decided by us. They want our help so that they get their money. Then it becomes more friendly. Then during the summer, it's like the best because they want to discuss their issues with the budget analyst; they want to plead their case as much as possible to see if they can have their budget request received favorably.

Another KSBO examiner "sometimes" sees himself "as a watchdog . . . the antagonist . . . when you don't agree with what the agency feels will occur. Generally I'm not. We're supposed to be considered the expert for the governor on that agency, unbiased. We're to provide the governor with all the information we have, not just the information that sounds good or sounds bad. Agencies always don't present both sides of the coin, sometimes just one. Make sure you're there to present both sides."

Another reason examiners cite for an adversarial role with respect to agencies is due to a generally poor relationship with the agency. Sometimes there is a historical relationship between the SBO and the agency; it is less often a personality clash between the examiner and the agency officials. A senior WISBO manager stated a dominant view among examiners across the states:

My view is adversarial relationships are earned, and I don't think we should start that with them. Basically, the only time I will find myself in an adversarial position with an agency is when they are bullheaded enough to overrun budget policy, budget directives, and are steering very hard down their own course. And we have had cases where agencies have done that. Then it becomes adversarial. The other thing is if it's adversarial, it's almost poisoned. The whole working relationship's poisoned. And I have offered, whatever happens, to give up the agency and hand them over to somebody else. In particular, that was an agency where we started with a rocky relationship, but worked extremely well. They came up with a new executive director, it goes downhill fast. As it turns out, fortunately this guy's fired. It is now so smooth, you would never notice it, would never think that there was any kind of animosity ever between the two agencies.

An MNSBO examiner sometimes sees himself as an antagonist and sometimes as an advocate, depending on the situation. In general, he stated, "There's this continuum where agencies can have too much power and not provide information. For instance, there was a computer system that was developed a few years ago. They ended up running significant deficits without providing information to some of the people here who should have known. In that case I'd be an antagonist. Sort of the power's swung too far." On the other hand, this examiner recalled other situations where "sometimes people will get into a chopping frenzy and will just snap at programs or administrative budgets without understanding the repercussions on the people that are ultimately getting served. In those cases I have to swing back to sort of a different, more protagonist, defender of the agency" role.

Conduit

Shadoan (1963a) found the primary role of management-oriented SBOs in the early 1960s to be a conduit between the executive and the administrative agencies. Similarly, Tomkin (1998) characterized many OMB examiners as information conduits providing a translator service, passing information back and forth between agencies and the chief executive, and organizing the information for comprehensibility at the top and bottom. Neither advocate nor antagonist, examiners in the conduit role think, "We should serve sort of as a go-between, between them and our management here, but that doesn't mean that we're their advocates. We're supposed to be writing independent analysis, what's called for, of their proposals. . . . I think we should know what the agency's position is and maybe make the best case for it, but also be able to criticize that case." The focus of conduit examiners is often "just to write constructive criticism." The trick is to make sure that antagonist is not the primary role. "In fact," notes one examiner, "with some of the agencies I have now, there's sort of bad relations between their senior management and ours. My boss wants me to be in there, sort of helping to placate some of that sometimes. Even though on the other hand there is a lot to be critical of the agency, I also have to try to keep a balance there because sometimes they get short shrift by management here because of the personality conflicts or whatever between the folks at the top level." This neutral stance is often helpful, he argues, when "the agencies are their own worst advocates because they don't make that best case through their own programs. . . . Some of that's going to happen anytime you're analyzing something. But I don't think that's a primary role, to be an antagonist."

Maintaining a neutral, conduit role is apparently not easy, as suggested by this KSBO examiner:

> As much as you like to think you're neutral, I don't think you really are. We're a communicator of information, I think, primarily. It's our job to go out to all these agencies, gather all this information, and then have it right here in this little cubicle for when the budget director or somebody from the governor's office wants information, they can call my cubicle and get it. Well, that's tough because sometimes you have the accurate information, like I said when the agency trusts you and they feel that it's going to be used to their benefit or whatever. Other times, depending on the issues, you're not going to have the right information because somebody didn't level with you down the road and you can't really blame them because they're sensitive issues or political issues or whatever. If I were them, I probably wouldn't want to tell me either. . . . So it really just depends on the attitude of the agency people. I have agency people who'll tell you anything that you ask them. They know that if somebody's going to get them politically that it's not going to be me that's going to break their backs. It's going to be somebody else, somebody with more power than me. But then on the other hand, you have agency people who'll play the game, they'll call their own legislators and they'll just do everything they can to make the budget analyst look bad. I had one like that last year and it just drove me nuts.

The key to the balancing act of the examiner as conduit was captured by an examiner from the VASBO: "We can differ in opinion, but not over the facts." He added, "People have a lot of respect for the individual (either agency staff or examiner) when the information flow is open."

Facilitator

Examiners who see themselves as facilitators are generally more active helpers of their assigned agencies than the conduits. Still, they are not agency advocates, because they still highly value their "neutral" position in the process. This is the dominant view of the KSBO examiners, who do not view their role vis-à-vis agencies as antagonists, nor are they advocates. A senior KSBO manager captured the essence of the facilitator role for many examiners across the states: "I try to emphasize a positive attitude with the agencies, positive relationship with the agencies, a relationship that says not necessarily that I'm here to help, but I'm here to understand." The balance is tricky:

I don't think we're here to help them get their requests through. We're here to make sure they put it down right. We help them in technical ways, but we're not here to help them sell their budget. We're going to evaluate their budget and present it in an objective way. I try to get my folks to make sure they develop a positive attitude with the agency that allows them to be respected and allows them to obtain information because the agency knows it's to their advantage to keep the analyst well informed, but yet doesn't get in bed with him. "I respect you but I don't love you," that kind of deal. . . . So you have to be skeptical, but you have to be positive and objective. So I emphasize that more than anything.

For some, defining the role is "kind of difficult. I ask myself the same question. I look at it as more of a . . . I guess as a facilitator. They put together their budget; they know what their agency does. The best thing I can do is learn the most about their agency and what's behind the decisions in their budget. I just pick it up from there, and follow any other kind of parameters. We're also somewhat of a watchdog, not too much. We fill a lot of roles. [Asking agencies], "Have you thought of this?" That kind of stuff. You get to facilitate ideas. It's kind of a fine line because I can't go in there and play management analyst."

To some degree the examiners who play the facilitator role are acutely aware that the adversarial aspect of their role is grounded in the SBO as the institutional gatekeeper, for which they see themselves as an agent charged with ameliorating the negative aspects of their institution. An IASBO examiner explains:

Obviously the Department of Management, there's a certain amount of that conflict kind of thing. I don't really think they [the agencies] would list as an individual an antagonist because I really do try to, in my particular style as well, I try to work *with* the departments as opposed to working *against* and as opposed to working *for* the departments. I think our role kind of bounces back and forth. When I first had [an agency], I had concentrated particularly on that department, which also is an elected official's department. The prior analyst who worked with that department, I think it's safe to say, had many personality conflicts with most and many of the budget and fiscal people there. And there was, in my estimation, very much a lack of communication with the department. I went out of my way to increase communication with that department, and a lot of it just includes just picking one's rear end up and going over there and talking with them, instead of sending information or budget prints or monthly. . . .

I tried to make a special effort, even oftentimes taking prints over, monthly reports or something, taking it over to them, having the discussion, the meeting with them, making a special effort to actually communicate with them. I think it's helped tremendously. I jokingly say [the agency budget officer] doesn't tell me to "go to hell" near as often as he used to. But that's just his particular nature as well there, too. [He] is one of the fiscal people at [the agency]; doesn't get along with most people. [On the other hand] I've worked with them a lot. We've changed a lot of the way that we did some of the things in their budgets, tried to get them cleaned up, make things a little more clearer.

Policy Analyst

There is no consensus definition of policy analysis, and this can confuse the discussion of examiner roles. Abdulkarim Al-Nahas (1998) reviews multiple definitions of policy analysis and identifies the common trait of providing informed advice to policymakers to help them make decisions about public policies. Such a reduction may seem tautological, but Al-Nahas argues that the dilemma stems partly from the divisions within the field of policy sciences. The roots of policy analysis are in the positivist, micro-economic orientation of the 1950s, but this has been modified by the emphasis on the political and value-laden nature of policy analysis in the late 1980s and into the 1990s. The result is a general division of two major policy analysis roles. *Policy researchers* are institutionally oriented or disciplinary in focus, tending toward long-term studies and heavily quantitative in methodology. *Policy analysts* are more client-oriented and usually work in the same organization as the client, often on short-term assignments. Although the major textbooks in policy analysis urge students to strike a balanced approach, their emphasis remains rooted in the micro-economic roots and methods (Al-Nahas 1998; see also Weimer and Vining 1992; Patton and Sawicki 1993; Durning and Osuna 1994).

Howard (1973, 4) and others were early advocates of incorporating policy analysis into budgeting because "budgeting occurs in an arena of conflict between goals, values, and power." Regardless of the fiscal climate, Howard argues that policy analysis can make complex issues more understandable to the responsible decisionmakers. Policy analysis is viewed as a way of filtering decision items to focus on priorities and important issues, exposing and highlighting the underlying values and decision criteria, explaining why one alternative is preferred over another (Gosling 1997).

The consensus read in public policy formulation, notes Howard (1973, 32), "does not normally mean that agreement must be reached among a majority of all citizens. Rather, *consensus typically means obtaining a majority among the vocal participants who are taking part in the process of deciding a particular issue*" (see also Behan 1970). Thus, the policy analyst is one who is willing and able to view the politics of an issue without necessarily engaging in politics generally. Howard (1973, 161) observes that "analysis is not a technique so much as it is a way of looking at problems, a frame of mind, a disposition, or an attitude." Rationalistic budgeting requires "rational partisans, advocates who are informed of the potential consequences of their positions and their possible alternatives." Analysis must be applied "opportunistically," with administrators and political leaders, including the governor, deciding which opportunities will be exploited.

Lockridge (1999) maintains that budget examiners in the role of policy analysts are all named Thomas, as in "doubting Thomas." But they also have a high tolerance for ambiguity. This is important, Majone (1989) explains, because decision-making under uncertainty is the typical environment for policy decisions. Majone (1989, 18) writes,

> Even in formal decision analysis the explicit recognition of uncertainty forces a significant departure from a strict orientation toward outcomes. Under conditions of uncertainty different alternatives correspond to different probability distributions of the consequences, so that it is no longer possible to determine unambiguously what the optimal decision is. Hence, the usual criterion of rationality—according to which an action is rational if it can be explained as the choosing of the best means to achieve given objectives—is replaced by the weaker notion of consistency. The rational decision maker is no longer an optimizer, strictly speaking. All that is required now, and all that the principle of maximizing expected utility guarantees, is that the choice be consistent with the decision maker's valuations of the probability and utility of the various consequences. Notice that consistency is a procedural, not a substantive, criterion.

The key responsibility of examiners in this role is that they must be able to separate the *important* from *unimportant* issues. Oftentimes, they are willing to settle for the best available alternative instead of the theoretically "perfect" alternative. Given politics, it is objective analysis coupled with satisficing behavior. Tomkin (1998, 6) found this role exhibited in OMB: Examiners preferred the role of neutral policy analysts, simplifying budgetary decisions to manageable dimensions for the chief executive, "narrowing the bounds of ignorance" for executive decisions. A senior WISBO manager offers a concurring description of the policy analyst role:

> I would call it more like an analyst with the simple objective of "what is the best for the government, the administration, the people," whatever standard you want to call that. And realize that in some respects we are all in the same boat and that our role is basically just to reconcile all the various

agency requests with whatever money we have, and then set priorities within that. There are times that you are and should be an advocate for the agency. And there are times you are and should be their harshest critic.

On the other hand, Arnold Meltsner (1976, 10) believes that "the policy analyst is a political actor." Policy analysis is a form of *advice* regarding policy problems that are either chronic or crisis in character. The image of the policy analyst as objective and neutral is important, he argues, lest their basis of expertise be undermined. However, "if they are not political in a grand way, they are certainly so in a small way. Whether they know it or not, they make a number of political decisions" (Meltsner 1976, 11).

Meltsner identifies three types of policy analysts in the federal bureaucracy. The *technician* is "an academic researcher—an intellectual—in bureaucratic residence. . . . Politics is somebody else's business. His main business is research which is linked to policy making, and if left alone he will faithfully adhere to an internal standard of quality" (Meltsner 1976, 18). The technician thinks of politics as nonrational, and often omits, or is blind to, the political consideration in analysis. Meltsner found this role to be dominant among the federal policy analysts. Alternatively, the *politician* is focused on pleasing the immediate client. Lacking the analytical skills of the technician, the politician relies on skills of communication and coordination; his/her main tools are trust, confidence, and persuasion. The politician thrives on the short-run perspective and acceptance by the client. They tend to be high-level bureaucrats (Meltsner 1976, 49).

The *entrepreneur* is both a technician and politician. "As a purveyor of knowledge, he does not let his immediate client constrain him. . . . He sees the public interest as his client, . . . has strong normative views of the scope of government activity, . . . is concerned about distribution as well as efficiency, . . . [and] is much more aware than other analysts that his preferences guide the selection and solution of analytical problems" (Meltsner 1976, 36 and 37). Although this combination of technical and political skills is relatively uncommon, these policy analysts play an important function because of their greater sensitivity to political issues. They want the power to "make a difference," to be "inside" the decision-making core. The policy analyst is there to shake the system, to take risks, in the firm belief that knowledge is power, and that analysis makes a difference (Meltsner 1976, 37–39).

Policy entrepreneurs blend expectations to be the fire fighters on political issues with a belief that analysis will have a future payoff. Unlike technicians who view politics as a policy constraint, entrepreneurs are more likely to convert political constraints into opportunities. Their long-term goal is establishing a good relationship with their client. A short-run measure of success is "their impact on the budget," but that is set in the context of a continuing concern for policy implementation and feasibility (Meltsner 1976, 39–42).

Al-Nahas (1998) reviews several other policy analyst typology schemes, including those of Jenkins-Smith (1982, 1990) and Durning and Osuna (1994). He tests these typologies at the state level with a study of policy analyst roles in Virginia's bureaucracy. His research reveals several important aspects of policy analyst roles: first, that there are multiple types of policy analysts, perhaps dependent on the type of organizational role played in the policy process; second, that there is little empirical analysis of policy analyst roles in government, with the Al-Nahas (1998) and Durning and Osuna (1994) studies providing a glimpse of policy analyst roles at the state level. While the specifics of the definitions among typologies vary with each author, similarities are evident. For example, Al-Nahas (1998) finds concurrence with three general types of policy analysts found in the other studies he investigates: objectivity oriented, issue oriented, and client oriented. Where Meltsner (1976) defines technicians, politicians, and entrepreneurs, Jenkins-Smith (1982 and 1990) discusses objective technicians, client advocates, and issue advocates. Durning and Osuna (1994) recognize these three types as well, in addition to ambivalent issue activists and client helpers. Al-Nahas (1998), however, dismisses these last two typologies as lacking substantial empirical support.

The main interest to our study of state budget offices is the salience of these definitions to budget examiners who characterize themselves as playing a policy analyst role. Not surprisingly, the answer is somewhat complex. The dominant traits expressed by the examiners are "value objectivity" and "client service." Our analysis suggests that SBO examiners most closely resemble the client-oriented (CO) role, especially the "client counselors" (CC) described by Durning and Osuna (1994). These policy analysts highly value objective neutrality, while at the same time they acknowledge that their legitimacy derives from their clients, the governors. Their success as analysts thus depends on their ability to serve as agents for their clients by producing policy arguments (based on objective analysis) that will be used by their clients in policy debates. Moreover, both COs and CCs consider their personal policy preferences as subordinate to those of their clients. However, they acknowledge that the former have some influence on their work. For instance, client counselors are more willing than COs to be involved in the internal policy-making games.

This characterization fits the general role revealed by SBO examiners as they describe their policy analyst role. A WISBO examiner tells us that "the governor and the secretary of administration look on us to do all of the in-depth analysis on specific proposals, or if they have a proposal they want to forward, we're the ones that put it together, saying how it's going to work, develop, putting together the numbers, that sort of thing. So, yeah, that's definitely a focus." The objectivity prized by other policy analysts is evident in these SBO examiners as well:

> It goes back to asking the right questions at the right time. . . . Perfect example of this, of what I think is a good policy analyst: There were four of us sitting in a meeting last year trying to put together a legislative proposal. This one guy who's very, very conservative started to advocate for not cutting as deeply as the other three of us were proposing, not cutting the program as deeply because it was going to affect a number of [agency] clients. And I just stopped and said, "I'm surprised to hear you say that because you're so conservative," and he usually is saying, "Cut, cut, don't spend more." And he said, "Well, that point of view wasn't being represented in the discussion." And I said, "Yes, that's exactly what a good policy analyst does." You try to stay away from the "groupthink" whenever possible and you just ask the hard questions of each other with respect, not as an antagonist. So that your objective is to come up with the best policy you can that expends public dollars most wisely to get the effect you want.

The complex nature of the task of being responsive to the client, the governor, and maintaining objectivity is revealed in this extended discussion with an MNSBO examiner:

> Senior management has been very focused on us during the legislative session, advocating very much that we play a policy kind of role, and that we get in there and ask the right questions and try to keep a macro-level view of what was happening and those kinds of things. I don't know that that's exactly the way it's possible for us to run, to operate in our jobs, because it seems to me to be a real break between what's happening at the very top of our agency versus what we know. . . . It's this weird kind of thing that keeps on coming in and out of discussions. In our training sessions, for example, one of the things that was stressed early on was that our role was not to be political as budget officers. We are to be objective and our credibility rests on the fact that we are objective and not political players, and for the most part, to the greatest extent possible, we would be insulated from the political piece of that. Certainly from what I saw during the legislative session, if we were really going to be effective in the other piece of it—which was to be *entrepreneurial* as we were told to be, to sort of keep an eye out for what was happening policywise, and try to play a

role and let people know what was happening—it wasn't possible to be nonpolitical and do that.

Q: To be political in what sense?
Examiner: Have to be aware of the implications of certain [pause]. For example, there was a big to-do in the [legislative] committees about a proposal that would have had $50 million in the next biennium, at the last minute. This was something that clearly was not going to fit in. The bill would have been vetoed by the governor if this had stayed on there. When I heard . . . rumors that this was going to be added on in conference committee, this last piece that was going to have all this spending attached. . . .

Q: You got the rumors from?
Examiner: The legislative staff. In that case I guess it was the [political party] senate researcher who said they had big tails, watch out, they're going to stick that thing on there.

Q: This is the minority party in the legislature, but the governor's party?
Examiner: The governor's party, right.

Q: Where did you hear about a governor's veto?
Examiner: Through the whole process there had been a lot of very soundly worded letters from the governor to the legislature talking about the fact that there would be a lot of vetoes if the spending stayed at the levels that it looked like it was going to. And the governor in fact started to veto a lot of things and the bill [on which I worked] was the only one that survived without any line item vetoes or being vetoed in total. [One agency budget] was vetoed in total. So it was in such an environment where people were very concerned that this bill wasn't going to make it. Throughout the whole process, every time that any piece of it came up, people would say, "Will this make it? Will the governor veto this?" It's hard to sort of respond to those questions in a nonpolitical, objective way. You can discuss with them what we were looking for in terms of no spending in '96–'97 and all of those things. As I tried to talk about it, I realized what I would consider sort of overtly political [pause]. There isn't a lot of that, but I think to not acknowledge that everything you do when you're operating in such a political environment, that it's hard to make a distinction of political and nonpolitical.

Q: So you were thinking about the political aspects, implications of what, amendments?
Examiner: Of taking pieces of it, for example, that spent more than we

would have wanted them to spend. But it was the majority leader's initiative, things like that which certainly weren't my decision to make in terms of what we did with them. But I think in order to be useful to people in saying, "Look this is $15 million we might want to look at, but be aware that it's [a legislator]'s baby." I think you're required to be somewhat political as you're evaluating those and passing on that information, if it's of use.

Several examiners disclaimed a policy analysis role because their definition of policy analysis was more quantitative and in-depth than they found budget analysis. A KSBO examiner, for instance, thinks "policy analysis takes more of an in-depth look and you have to be familiar with the subject area, or get yourself familiar with it pretty fast. But probably more important than the subject area is if you have the analysis tools, whether it's survey research or good performance measures or something to determine whether these policies and programs are actually effective. I don't think we do that much." From her vantage point, "We ask the agencies to give us performance measures for their programs and we look at what they give us and we maybe consolidate them, refine them, pass them on. But they don't go anywhere beyond here. So while we might look at them a little bit, probably more than half the measures aren't any good anyway. So if the measures aren't any good, all I can say is that we don't—I haven't seen us really get into developing performance measures better, helping the agencies with that."

SBO examiners with a policy analysis role are willing to win some and lose some based on the principles at stake:

> Every once in a while I will say to an agency that comes up with a request, I'll say, "Can you see me selling that to the governor?" They want sixteen positions or something. "Do you think the governor's going to buy that?" And that's a factor. In a perfect world, it probably isn't because you do policy analysis and base it strictly on policy. But the fact that I'm focused, maybe focused is a bad word, but I'm cognizant of what the anticipated reaction of the governor or the secretary is going to be.

> Q: Have you made recommendations that you know are dead on arrival at the secretary's desk or at the governor's desk?
> Examiner: Yeah. I've made recommendations to the governor knowing that he will reject it. The way I look at it, we're to do policy analysis. Policy analysis is one part of the equation the governor looks at. He has a separate staff that does political analysis. Our job really is to make the policy recommendation. On occasion that will be overruled for political considerations. That doesn't bother me. I think that's the way the system's de-

signed. Case in point, in the most recent legislative session there was a bill, a pure pork bill to give the city of [XYZ] $4 million for sewer systems that no other city got. There's no rationale for it other than the fact that the senator from [the city] lived in [the city], was a [political party of the governor], and figured he could get away with it. We recommended it be vetoed early in the process.

Q: It was something stuck in from the legislative budget side?
Examiner: Yeah. We recommended early in the process it be vetoed. The budget director agreed. The governor's office came back and said, "We're not going to veto it." And I understood, we kind of expected that. So then what we started to do was chip around the edges, we'd make it a little more restrictive, we'd come up with something to give it a little less money without doing quite as much violence to the concept of public policy. So we started to try to work the issue. And basically, in that case, never did. They got their money. We lost that one.

In fact, some recognize that the adversarial or facilitative role functions hand-in-hand with policy analysis, if the process itself is to be effective. A WISBO manager explains:

In general *I think we have by design a somewhat adversarial relationship with the agency.* And I mean adversarial in sort of a good sense of the word. Not that we're bad-mouthing each other, but I think that the agency makes its case, and I think this is true even for cabinet agencies, this isn't just unique to [his budget office] team, the agency is set up to make their best case for their budget initiatives and I think one of our jobs is to be as critical as possible of what the agency is asking for and seek alternatives and look for ways to reduce the cost. And I think somehow you hope out of that debate good policy will emerge. And I think the fiscal bureau (our counterpart for the legislature), they do the same thing. And I think that all is healthy. . . .
    I think that we represent the governor. There's such a thing in there as legal counsel, there's such a thing as budget counsel. That's sort of what we are and we operate as budget counsel to the governor. *So I see that our role is to make the best case for the governor, even if on a particular issue or whatever we don't agree personally.* I still think it's like an attorney representing a client. The opinion the attorney has of a client is sort of irrelevant. You do the best job you can. And there may even be points where you're thinking, I don't think this is good policy we're pursuing. But I'm going to still make the best argument I can. And if you were the fiscal bureau staff, I would say that the best policy is going to emerge by

me making the best case I can for this policy, and then hoping you can make a better case. That if I can bring up, these are the reasons we need to do this, the reasons we need to get rid of this program, or the reason we need to put more funding into this program, and really think hard about it and make a good case, then that forces you to make a better case for why we should do something else.

Hopefully the process works best if we're all doing our job as well as possible. Then I think you get the best public policy. I think if I were, or you were, trying to play both sides of the fence, trying [pause]. If I was feeding you information as to why I thought the policy wasn't a good policy or whatever, I think that in the long run, on an individual issue, maybe something beneficial will come out of it, but in the long run, government's stronger for us playing our roles to the hilt. (italics authors' emphasis)

His view compares favorably with the role expectations of the classical incrementalism model of budget process.

Advocate

Many examiners reported that, in the past, examiners had a distinctly adversarial relationship with departments, but recent budget directors have tried to reformulate the examiner role definition to be advocates for their agencies' needs. This is not to say that they will no longer say "no," but they are expected to be as cooperative as possible with their agency counterparts to develop a list of "mandatory" funding needed by the departments to carry out assigned missions. Most examiners are trying to avoid the "antagonist" role of the past. This was particularly evident in MOSBO and IASBO.

This MOSBO examiner's description of activities in the previous budget cycle is representative:

> For a good part of the year my role was as an advocate for the department, when we were preparing budget recommendations. Not an advocate in the sense that I was trying to get everything I possibly could for them, but an advocate in the sense that . . . it was up to me to present the items that were their highest priorities, [and] that I felt were the most important, in the best light to give them the best chance to achieve funding. Then shortly after the governor's recommendations came out, my role shifted somewhat to more of an advocate or representative of the governor's office.

Meltsner (1976) observes that the policy analyst who recommends a particular alternative cannot avoid becoming an advocate since he is trying to convince others to adopt a course of action. The analyst must determine "whether he is a responsible or irresponsible advocate" (283 and 284). There is no simple answer to this question for "the roots of the problem lie in the basic incompatibility between the roles of analyst and advocate. The more the analyst pushes the client's preferences, and the more he tries to be persuasive and gain acceptance, the more he will encounter ethical choices. The more active he is politically, the more he will be in conflict with his analytical standards of behavior. . . . The more the analyst has to support a policy, whether he believes in its objectives or not, the more he will have to struggle with himself to determine where to draw the line" (Meltsner 1976, 285).

The Iowa secretary of management plays a strong role in budget development, and she was instrumental in reshaping the IASBO from a control to a policy orientation. The key to the balance of advocacy and objectivity, as she sees it, "is developing relationships of mutual trust so that our budget analysts can know as much as possible about the agencies that they're working with, that they get involved early, early, early on in the process so they are involved in departmental level meetings, making decisions about budget requests. They're involved in the policy development, they're involved in the planning. Then, in turn, the department staff staying involved after the budget gets here and we're working with it as we're developing the governor's budget recommendations." This stands in sharp contrast to the past, when "the agencies would do their thing, drop it at the door here. Our staff would have very little background information. We'd be expected to evaluate these things and make recommendations to the governor, which often we did without really consulting the departments very much. It was a black box." This characterization echoes the sentiments of several other budget directors in policy-oriented SBOs investigated here.

Duncombe and Kinney (1987) suggest that the advocacy role may depend on a good working relationship with examiners and their agency counterparts. A GASBO examiner compared advocacy for two of her agencies:

> It does influence advocacy because for me, I cannot go in and recommend to the governor something that I am not totally sure should be recommended. A lot of times with [agency one], they provided me any and all information that I needed in order to say OK they really need this. When I go in there and the governor says, "Why should this be recommended?" I would be able to tell him based on all the supporting information that I have. Whereas with [agency two], a lot of times they say it would take a month or two months before I can get you this information. You never really knew why you should recommend something, and I didn't feel comfortable. I told the fiscal officer that I didn't feel comfortable going in there and arguing [agency two's] case when I don't have the supporting information that I need in

order to do that. It really influenced me. I was more of an advocate for [agency one] in terms of being able to lay on the table why they needed this as opposed to [agency two]. I just didn't have the information a lot of times.

These comments also distinguish the advocacy role from that of policy analyst. The examiner as policy analyst must make the best case to the governor, regardless of how the examiner feels about said issue and the agency to which it regards. The examiner as advocate must believe in the numbers and rationale behind the issue or, rather, feel secure in moving the agency's case forward to the governor. That is, there seems to be more ownership of agency priorities in the case of examiner as advocate versus examiner as policy analyst.

Nonetheless, fiscal constraints have a dampening effect on the number of items that can receive support from the examiner. The examiner is constantly faced with a judgment about how important an agency request ranks relative to other priorities, both of the agency and of the governor. As this examiner explains:

> I don't know. It's kind of hard because I want to say contradictory things. I think that I advocate. I think it depends on the decision items sometimes, and it depends on where the decision item is on their priority list. If it's at the bottom of their priority list, I'm not going to advocate it very strongly. Given limited [general funds], you can only get so much. So I'm likely to advocate pretty hard for their top-listed items, and like I said, less so for the bottom ones. . . . There's constraints that go into that, though. If I know that (I don't want to make this too cut in stone), if I think that it's very unlikely that the secretary [of administration] or the governor will approve of a particular item, I'm not real likely to recommend for it. There are exceptions to that.
>
> If I feel very strongly on something, I will advocate it despite my anticipation that they won't like it, or vice versa. But that's reasonably rare. The one that comes to mind is [the commerce department] wants a Mexico trade office. They've got one in Germany, they've got one in Seoul, they've got one in Hong Kong, Japan, I think, as well, maybe not all three places. Anyway, they wanted one in Mexico and they gave me this big spiel about how our imports to Mexico out of [our state] are going through the roof and they've soared this much astronomically in the past five, ten, one year. So my question is, "Well, if they're going great guns, what the heck do we need a trade office for?" So I recommended against it and [my manager] went, "Whoa, really? The governor really wants that." And I said, "I don't know" but he said, "Leave it in, that's all right. They'll change your decision, but nobody's going to get mad or anything. So it's not a problem and

maybe you ought to bring this to their attention." I was reversed later and that's life around here.

The Issue of Neutral Competency

The evolution of examiner roles from controllers to planners and policy analysts has not been without controversy, especially as examiners are increasingly seen as advocates. Although there have been relatively few studies of budget examiners in central budget offices, the exceptions have concerned one of the more controversial issues surrounding budget examiners, that of "neutral competence." Of primary concern to several scholars is whether the historically "neutral" examiners in the federal BOB/OMB were becoming "politicized" because they were increasingly associated with the president's policies in an increasingly public way (see Heclo 1975; Johnson 1984 and 1989; Tomkin 1998). Heclo (1975, 81) defines neutral competence as: "A continuous, uncommitted facility at the disposal of, and for the support of, political leadership. It is not a prescription for sainthood." "Neutrality does not mean the possession of a direct-dial line to some overarching, non-partisan sense of the public interest. Rather," he insists, "it consists of giving one's cooperation and best independent judgment of the issues to partisan bosses—and being sufficiently uncommitted to be able to do so for a succession of partisan leaders."

Heclo (1975) believes that neutral competence provides budget and policy analysis to the chief executive with three important features: smooth communications, institutional longevity, and impartiality. Neutral competence "smoothes communication and thus improves the capacity of elected leadership to get what it wants out of the government machine." It also "accumulates informal sources of information within the bureaucracy, sources which can be the key to governing the sprawling executive machinery and which are otherwise unavailable to transient political appointees." Neutral competency also has a "vested interest in continuity . . . a special concern that initiatives be capable of being sustained for the period ahead. . . . They [budget examiners who are neutrally competent] worry about administrative feasibility because they do not want to have to deal later with problems of administrative breakdown." Finally, neutral competence contributes "a quality of impartiality to be set against other, more sectional appeals in government. Its viewpoint is no more pure or unbiased than anyone else's, but the axes it has to grind are broader than most. Its analysis is less concerned with the short-term political ramifications of who believes what how strongly, and more concerned with the substance of the policy issues themselves" (Heclo 1975, 82).

According to Heclo (1975, 97), the essence of neutral competence is that the chief executive "needs to know things that even (and especially) his best friends will not or cannot tell him. He needs his own lines into the agencies and his own independent source of advice." Therefore, the most appropriate use of a budget agency such as OMB "is as an independent source of analytic advice and governmental coordination in line with expressed [executive] desires." It is in this last vein that the controversy surrounding examiner roles erupted. The distinction between policy analysts and political analysts has been blurred at times, especially under dynamic budget directors such as David Stockman, who served as OMB director under President Reagan.

Johnson (1984, 506) describes how the Reagan administration used the budget "as the primary element of its domestic policy" and this gave OMB "unprecedented power as an instrument for advancing budget policy." On the other hand, as Tomkin's (1998) work later reveals, while OMB's star was reaching its apex, the power of most individual examiners was reaching its nadir, with many of them "crunching numbers" to fill Stockman's spreadsheets (Johnson 1984, 506).

Heclo (1975) and others admonish presidential administrations to be wary of making policy analysis in the budget office too politicized, as it endangers the long-term credibility of OMB examiners and their ability to provide smooth communications, a long-run viewpoint, and impartial analysis. Essentially, the successful crafting of policy analysis in the budgeting framework requires the acknowledgment that one can politicize the specific budget and policy issue without politicizing the budget office itself.

Veillette's (1981, 66) experiences as budget director in two states suggest that neutral competence is a professional tradition sacred to SBOs:

> The traditions of the two state budget offices in which I have served, those of Connecticut and New York, enshrine the tenet of "neutral competence"— the hypothesis of the early thinkers in public administration that a career staff can serve policy makers of differing political persuasions with equal diligence and responsiveness. In my experience the hypothesis has been amply confirmed. Social ideologues outside of the office become neutral professionals on the job.

This description agrees with the findings of Al-Nahas (1998), Durning and Osuna (1994), and Meltsner (1976) in their studies of policy analysts in state and federal bureaucracies. A dominant theme throughout these works is the nearly universal desire by policy analysts to reject pressures to "shade" their analyses to fit client preferences or their own personal policy agendas. Furthermore, given the roots of policy analysis in microeconomic theory, it is not surprising that many policy analysts hold strong preferences for spe-

Table 8.1

Role Identifications for Examiners in Eleven State Budget Offices

Name	Count	Percent of Responses	Percent of Examiners
Adversary	51	13.7	29.1
Conduit	89	24.0	50.9
Facilitator	62	16.7	35.4
Policy analyst	46	12.4	26.3
Advocate	99	26.7	56.6
Other	24	6.5	13.7
Total responses	371	100.0	212.0
Total examiner staff	175	(Counts staff with a valid, coded response.)	

cific values such as economic and technical efficiency in their analyses. From this foundation, they are able to "take advantage of analytical uncertainty" to emphasize one policy option over another (Al-Nahas 1998, 25).

Examiner Role Complexity

As a general rule, our interviews suggest that most SBO examiners find themselves taking on multiple roles. All of them highly value the objectivity norm dominant in the policy analyst role studies cited above. For many but not all examiners, this objectivity norm is often in tension with the norm of serving the client, principally the governor but often agencies as well. As we explore this dynamic in the rest of this chapter, we will see that this tension and these roles are defined partly by the phase of the budget cycle, partly by the orientation of the SBO, and partly by the professional and educational backgrounds of the examiners.

Table 8.1 presents the frequency distribution of roles identified for examiners across the eleven states. Several features are worth highlighting. First, there are twice as many responses to role identification as there are examiners (212 percent). We shall explore the patterns and roots of the multiple role responses embedded in this table. Second, the adversary role is a distinctly minority role for most examiners. As suggested above, SBO directors and examiners have tried to change markedly their perceived role as agency adversaries or antagonists. Only 51 of the 371 SBO staff responses (14 percent) were identified as an adversarial role, indicative of only 29 percent of the examiners. Third, the least frequent role indicated is policy analyst, with approximately 26 percent of the examiners identified with this role. In fact, the two highest frequency roles are advocate and conduit. The high response for advocate is surprising, and will receive scrutiny below.

Table 8.2

Average Number of Roles, by Role Type, by State

State	Advocate	Policy Analyst	Facilitator	Conduit	Adversary	Other	State Mean
Grand mean by type	2.7	3.0	2.6	2.7	3.1	1.4	2.1
Control SBOs	2.7	3.1	2.4	2.2	2.8	2.9	1.9
Alabama	2.0		2.0	1.6	2.0		1.5
Illinois	2.3		1.7	1.6	2.5	1.6	1.5
South Carolina	3.4	3.1	4.0	2.9	3.3		2.9
Policy SBOs	2.7	3.0	2.6	3.1	3.2	3.1	2.1
Georgia	3.3	3.4	3.5	3.4	3.8		3.1
Iowa	2.0	4.0	2.0	2.0	2.7	2.0	1.8
Kansas	2.7	2.0	1.4	1.8	2.5	1.0	1.2
Minnesota	2.0	1.4	2.0	2.0	2.3	1.4	1.5
Missouri	1.8	2.0	1.3	2.5	2.3		1.7
North Carolina	2.7		2.3	2.5	3.0		2.3
Virginia	3.8	4.1	4.0	3.7	4.0		3.7
Wisconsin	1.9	1.7	1.6	3.0	2.5	2.2	1.6
Case Count	$n = 99$	$n = 46$	$n = 62$	$n = 89$	$n = 51$	$n = 24$	$n = 51$

Table 8.2 presents the average number of roles identified for each examiner, by role type and state. Common characterizations for roles are arrayed from left to right according to an underlying continuum that ranges from positive to negative relationships between budget examiners and their assigned agencies. The "other" category falls outside the continuum and represents responses that did not easily fit into the other role categories. Looking at case count, it is surprising that 99 of the 175 SBO staff (57 percent) are identified with advocate as at least *one* of their budgetary roles. In a close second is the conduit role, with 51 percent of staff identified as having this as at least one of their roles. Only 29 percent of the examiners identified adversary as at least one of their roles, a sharp contradiction to classic incrementalism expectation.

In Table 8.2 we note that the highest average number of roles (grand mean = 3.1 roles) is attributable to the adversary role. This is not surprising in view of the many testimonies that examiners eschew this role and take it only when forced by agency relationships or necessarily due to fiscal conditions. Interestingly, the policy analyst role is also identified with a higher number of multiple roles. Notice that examiners in the policy-oriented SBOs tend to have higher numbers of multiple roles on average than do their counterparts in the control-oriented SBOs. This is particularly true with respect to the conduit (and adversary) roles. The conduit examiners in the policy SBOs tend to count this aspect as one of about three roles they play, compared to conduit examiners in control-oriented SBOs, who count this as one of only two roles they play with respect to their assigned agencies. Meanwhile, Virginia, Georgia, and South Carolina examiners identify with a higher number of multiple roles than examiners in other states. We will return to this point later.

Figure 8.1 illustrates the complexity of the examiner roles by looking at the distribution of multiple roles by type. For example, conduit and facilitator roles are held predominantly by examiners who identify only one or two roles, and these are the modal categories of examiners who play only a single role. In contrast, the policy analyst role is dominated by examiners exhibiting four or five roles (44 percent). The data supporting this figure indicate that of the 64 examiners identified with a single role, 32 (50 percent) were either conduits or facilitators. Only one examiner (in South Carolina) is identified as playing an adversary role only. Of the 114 examiners identified with a double role, conduits (18 percent) and advocates (32 percent) include a combined 50 percent of the examiners.

A VASBO examiner put the matter succinctly: "It's very easy to get confused in this environment because you're playing so many roles, wearing so many hats, you have to have authority to wear the different hats and not feel like you're confused or there is a problem." In a similar vein, a senior WISBO manager agreed that "at different times on different issues and depending on your viewpoint, the examiner-agency role could have been everything from adversary to advocate." In his view, the examiner works *with* the agency, but not *for* the agency.

> The distinction is important in that at times I would advocate for their position on an issue; but on the other hand, I have a certain independence. I'm here as staff to the governor and I hope that they wouldn't view it as antagonistic. But there were times when the agency just couldn't understand why we weren't embracing what they wanted, or they would make a good case, but we still couldn't fund it for one reason or another. And sometimes the reasons are not that obvious. Sometimes the reasons may not be seemingly all that strong. . . . But different situations, different issues, you're going to play a number of different roles and all the ones that you said I'm sure I played at times. But I certainly wouldn't say that my role was antagonistic. It's more accommodating. I think we want people, and I'm not sure I would say this is a change, but we want people here to be helpful to their agencies. We don't want to be viewed as roadblocks; we don't want to make more work for agencies, although we may need to if

Figure 8.1   **Distribution of Roles by Roles Type**

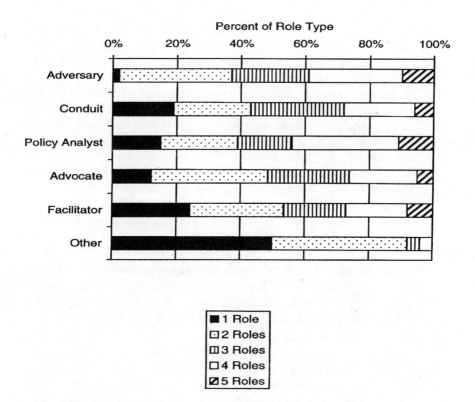

there's something that we just need that they have to provide us with. But we're here to serve agencies, but our primary clientele is, I think, the governor and the taxpayers of the state. Their views on things are not necessarily going to be the same as the agencies' who are looking pretty much at their clientele groups.

Similarly, the KSBO budget director wants examiners to avoid the roles of both adversary and advocate.

> I would like to think that they are all being analysts without being advocates or adversaries. I think we should be working with the agency to help the agency accomplish their goals while at the same time being many times a reality check for the agency as far as what resources are available to them, whether they be positions or dollars, and keep that sort of balance in there. I don't think it's appropriate for an analyst to be taking on an agency. I don't want them to do that. On the other hand, I don't want them to be advocating for the agency. The agency can advocate for itself and should, that's why the agency head's there, the cabinet secretary, whoever it might be, and in many cases advocacy groups help out with that. That's fine. The analyst shouldn't be doing that and should be working with the agency and presenting always a fair, accurate portrayal of what the agency's doing and the resources they have or need or desire to have to do that. So I say no advocacy relationships and no adversarial relationships and that balance in between there. . . . We do policy analysis, we do management analysis. As plans become appropriate, we may or may not analyze and involve ourselves. . . . The agencies do more of the planning and the policy development. We're doing the analysis.

To better understand examiner role complexity, we created a role index to combine the number of roles identified with an examiner and the type of roles s/he plays. First, a role score was constructed as the sum of the weights assigned to each role type, with adversary = 1, conduit = 2, facilitator = 3, policy analyst = 4, advocate = 5, and other = 0.50. The score continuum recognizes the greatest distance between the adversary and advocate roles, moving from least to greatest score indicative of the evolution of examiner role from traditional agency antagonist to advocate. The role score for each examiner was then divided by the number of roles identified for each examiner. This deflates the role score and also creates a crude index of role complexity. A low role index value is most likely indicative of an examiner with one or two roles identified as an adversary or conduit, while the highest index value is most likely generated by an examiner identified with four or five roles, including the roles of advocate and policy analyst.

The role score ranges from the least complex (Score = 0.5 for someone with a single role identified as other) to the most complex (score = 15 for someone with five roles including all but other). The role index ranges from 0.5 to 5.0. Cursory checks comparing the score and index values with individual data coding verified the variable characteristics. Both variables are normally distributed, with the median and mean for the role score = 6, and the median and mean for the role index = 3. As a result, we can compare the role complexity of examiners in the eleven states with the general orientation of their SBO and their educational and professional backgrounds. These tools allow us to propose a model that describes examiner roles based on these factors.

A Model of Budgetary Roles

The model presented in Figure 8.2 suggests that the roles identified for SBO examiners is a function of the degree of policy delegation they are given within the SBO, and their personal bias and style. The model further suggests that the examiners' roles affect their budget rationality and inevitably the effectiveness of their recommendations to the budget director and governor. We will refine the model shortly to further condition the interaction of roles and budget rationality upon different stages of the budget process.

When we discussed the decision context in chapter 5, we argued that the various decision contexts initially suggested by Schick's (1966) analysis could be reduced to a typology of control-oriented SBOs or policy-oriented SBOs. This is represented by the arrow "degree of policy delegation." As we discuss in detail below, one is unlikely to find an examiner in a control-oriented SBO characterizing his or her role either as an advocate for an agency during budget development or as a policy analyst. They are much more likely to describe themselves as a conduit or facilitator or even an adversary with respect to their assigned agencies. Not surprisingly, an adversarial role on the part of examiners in control-oriented budget offices seems to go hand-in-hand with poor fiscal condition as well. Such a role is not necessarily a volunteered one; recall the examiner from Alabama discussing the occasional requirement to go into agencies and make cuts, describing the activity as "not something we ought to be doing, but if asked, we can do it." In contrast, budget examiners in policy-oriented SBOs are more likely to characterize themselves as policy analysts, advocates, and conduits. This speaks to their greater involvement *researching* budget problems and solutions. Rarely do they describe themselves as adversaries.

The *range* of roles one observes in a given SBO is also a function of the general control or policy orientation of the SBO. The wide range of analytical demands on budget examiners in policy-oriented SBOs forces the policy-oriented budget examiners to wear a larger number of hats, switching roles as the various stages of the budget process require them to view agency budget problems in a different light. Consequently, most of the budget examiners in the policy-oriented SBOs saw themselves as playing all four roles at some point in the budget process. In contrast, budget examiners in control-

Figure 8.2   A Model of Budgetary Roles and Decision-making

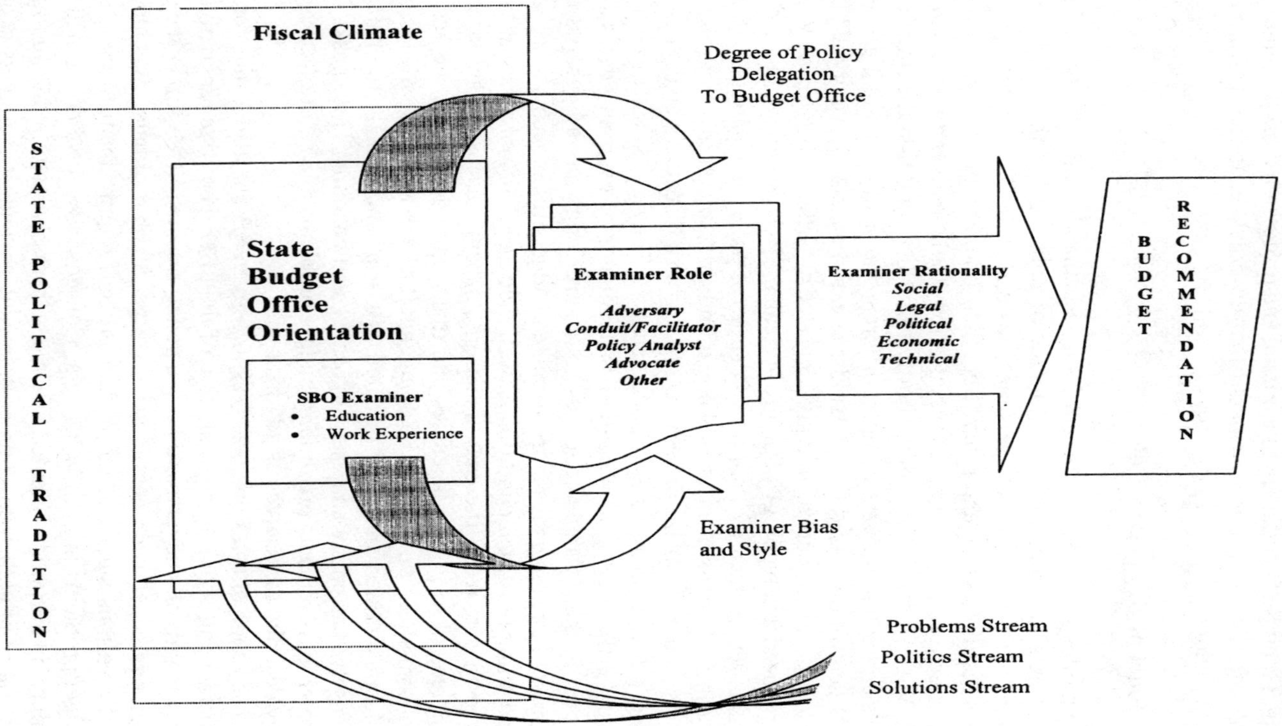

oriented SBOs are largely restricted to a conduit/facilitator role or an adversarial or advocate role. The range of roles is restricted by their rather narrow mission of monitoring execution or "crunching numbers" to be fed into policy analyses at higher levels in the SBO or in the governor's office.

Different Budget Phases Require Different Examiner Roles

As should be evident from our discussions of policy-oriented and control-oriented SBOs (chapters 6 and 7), there are distinct phases of the budget process, but the orientation of the SBO affects the degree to which the phases are markedly different, and consequently the degree to which there is a pronounced shift in examiner roles with changes in the budget process. Put simply, there is less variation in roles identified for control-oriented SBOs than for policy-oriented SBOs. There is a pronounced shift in behavior and budgetary tasks in policy-oriented SBOs as budget "seasons" change. The KSBO manager could never see himself as "a great adversary of the agency, but I think it is part of the role that you play, to challenge, to question. But it's done in a dispassionate sort of way, a professional sort of way. It's never intended to engender any sort of hostile feelings, certainly not of any long duration or [to] damage your relationships with the agencies. They won't give you any information anymore."

Recall another KSBO examiner who acknowledged a strong adversarial role. She also noted a shift to a different, more informational role once the governor's budget had been proposed. She changes roles to something more positive during the summer's predevelopment phase of the budget process:

Q: How about in the summertime?
Examiner: During the legislative session, we're also defending the governor's recommendations. In subcommittee hearings sometimes I'm asked questions point-blank, what was the governor's reasoning behind this recommendation? Later in the spring when it comes down to salary plan and any other special pieces, appropriation items, or other legislation that's passed, then it turns into a helpful mode. Like salary plan: it's been decided by the legislature, it hasn't been decided by us. They want our help so that they get their money. Then it becomes more friendly. Then during the summer, it's like the best because they want to discuss their issues with the budget analyst, they want to plead their case as much as possible to see if they can have their budget request received favorably.

Q: When they're pleading their case and being friendly, what's your role?
Examiner: To listen politely and not make promises . . . and also critical questioner.

The balance in favor of advocate roles over adversarial roles results from the relatively short period of the process where examiners may have conflicts with their agencies' goals and priorities. An IASBO examiner admitted some degree of antagonism in his role with respect to agencies because "we have to ask those hard questions. On the other hand, once we've talked with the department and have heard what they have to say about a particular program that they want or a particular spending pattern, and if we're convinced that that's the way it should be, then we're, like I said earlier, an advocate for the department up until the governor says yes or no. We'll do that also as we write." He was pressed to clarify his answer. "I believe for the most part we're advocates for the department more than we're antagonistic." If he believes that an agency's request is reasonable, then he becomes an advocate until the governor says yes or no. If the governor says yes, then he is an advocate for the governor's budget, essentially with respect to the legislature.

Even for senior examiners, the role definition may be obscured by the multiple demands of the job. A senior IASBO manager did not know whether an examiner is "an advocate or an antagonist. Budgeting is just trying to fit the programs that the governor or whoever want to include within the amount of dollars available. So it's a means of massaging to make it work. I don't know if that's an advocate or an antagonist." And "at times" he finds himself in the position of advocating for the departments' programs to the budget director or the governor. "Although in some respects we're trying to be neutral in the sense that we're providing information and letting [the governor and his staff] make their decision, but at the same time trying to steer them so that they understand all the ramifications."

Veillette (1981) suggests the role shift is to be expected, and should be done professionally. The shift in attitudes between budget formulation and execution "is best facilitated when each group is able to recognize the legitimacy of the other's concerns, has empathy for the broad goals of the 'adversary,' and trusts and respects the other professionally and personally. As a practical matter, the budget examiner should strive to create a relationship based on rationality (or at least reasonableness) and on an awareness of respective roles." The reasonableness test, he continues, "does not preclude tough action when required or desirable to meet high policy objectives, such as insuring maintenance of a balanced budget" (Veillette 1981, 65). By the same token, Pittard (1999, 3) reminds the examiner that "when you present your governor's budget, you become an advocate for that budget, whether you liked the items the governor put in his or her budget or not. Your role changes from the objective reviewer to the advocate."

The classical model of role shifting, as suggested by these remarks, is that the examiner first reviews the agency request forms to see whether they are properly executed and all budgetary directives are followed. The second step is to "weigh the estimates of expenditures against budget policy. Do the requests, for instance, implement the governor's policy pronouncements, comply with federal regulations, or follow other stated program objectives?" (Mathews 1965, 38) When the governor's budget is before the legislature, the examiner is an advocate of the governor's program, not the agency's. But is this pattern necessarily the case in every SBO? If an element of control remains in every budget office, then some degree of adversarial relationship is likely during the budget review. That is, denying a request is not viewed by either agencies or budget examiners as advocacy for the agencies. Moreover, implementation suggests cooperation, but can also be adversarial; monitoring and oversight suggest conflict. The primary factor governing this role shift may depend on how *much* control exists in an SBO orientation.

Different Decision Contexts Require Different Roles

The discussions of policy-oriented SBOs and control-oriented SBOs in previous chapters suggest that examiners in these SBOs face different expectations of their work. Examiners in control-oriented SBOs are largely restricted to control and monitoring functions and thus are less likely to fulfill a policy analyst role with respect to their assigned agencies. Further, advocacy by these examiners would likely take place during budget execution, not during budget development. Many examiners from control-oriented budget offices explained a confined set of activities, predominantly technical, during the period of agency budget review. In fact, quite a few were emphatic that they did not prepare recommendations, rather they checked budget requests, distinguishing between continuation and expansion budgets, and then running through a checklist of criteria related to agency budget request preparation for the budget director.

Examiners in policy-oriented SBOs, on the other hand, have a wider range of duties, including responsibility for assessing the compatibility of agency requests with respect to gubernatorial policy. Policy-oriented examiners also may behave differently than control-oriented examiners during implementation (predevelopment) phases, assessing agency program implementation in terms of how they are achieving gubernatorial policy goals rather than how much money is being spent or transferred between line items (typical activities of examiners in control-oriented SBOs). We explore the relationship between decision contexts and examiner roles more fully below.

Several tests of differences in total roles scores between states and SBOs of a control or policy orientation suggest that a relationship exists. For example, the Analysis of Variance (ANOVA) test for roles scores between states

Table 8.3

Roles and Roles Scores by State

	Advo-cate	Policy Analyst	Facili-tator	Con-duit	Adver-sary	Other	Row Total	Mean Role Score
AL	4		1	5	2		12	4.4
	(33.3)		(8.3)	(41.7)	(16.7)		(3.2)	
GA	15	9	13	14	4		55	10.1
	(27.3)	(16.4)	(23.6)	(25.5)	(7.3)		(14.8)	
IA	9	1	5	1	3	1	20	6.3
	(45.0)	(5.0)	(25.0)	(5.0)	(15.0)	(5.0)	(5.4)	
IL	6	0	6	14	6	9	41	3.1
	(14.6)	(0.0)	(14.6)	(34.1)	(14.6)	(22)	(11.1)	
KS	3	2	7	4	2	2	20	3.9
	(15.0)	(10.0)	(35.0)	(20.0)	(10.0)	(10)	(5.4)	
MN	6	5	1	5	4	7	28	3.9
	(21.4)	(17.9)	(3.6)	(17.9)	(14.3)	(25)	(7.5)	
MO	12	1	3	4	6		26	5.8
	(46.2)	(3.8)	(11.5)	(15.4)	(23.1)		(7.0)	
NC	7		9	8	1		25	7.2
	(28.0)		(36.0)	(32.0)	(4.0)		(6.7)	
SC	8	10	3	14	6		41	8.8
	(19.5)	(24.4)	(7.3)	(34.1)	(14.6)		(11.1)	
VA	18	12	9	19	15		73	10.9
	(24.7)	(16.4)	(12.3)	(26.0)	(20.5)		(19.7)	
WI	11	6	5	1	2	5	30	5.3
	(36.7)	(20.0)	(16.7)	(3.3)	(6.7)	(16.7)	(8.1)	
Column total	99	46	62	89	51	24	371	6.3
	(26.7)	(12.4)	(16.7)	(24.0)	(13.7)	(6.5)	(100.0)	

Note: Percentages in ( ).

is significant at $p \leq\ = 0.05$. Table 8.3 presents the mean total roles scores for each state. Note that ILSBO has the lowest total score (3.1), while GASBO and VASBO have the highest scores (10.1 and 10.9, respectively). Recalling that an "other" roles scores 0.5 points compared to 5.0 points for an advocate role, one can see how ILSBO's score results from the dominance of the conduit and "other" roles. Most of the ILSBO examiners were loath to label their role with respect to agencies as adversary, but, as will be seen shortly, the "other" type of role in ILSBO and ALSBO also has strong control characteristics. ALSBO, another control-oriented SBO, also has a very low (4.4) mean roles score. Nearly two-thirds of the ALSBO examiners are identified with either the conduit or advocate roles.

In contrast, VASBO and GASBO have no examiners identified with an "other" role, and a high share of advocate and policy analyst roles associated with their examiners. In addition, there are a fair share of facilitator and conduit roles in these states. South Carolina examiners contribute to a mean roles score of 8.8, just behind VASBO and GASBO. Although we have described this state as control oriented, it is evident that there is a wider range of roles in SCSBO, including a fair share (45 percent) of advocate and policy analyst roles alongside about a third of the examiners identified with a conduit role. NCSBO's mean score of 7.2 reflects the 28 percent of examiners identified with an advocate role with fewer examiners associated with the adversary role (only 4 percent).

It is interesting that these three southern states (Virginia, Georgia, and South Carolina) exhibit a high number of roles, especially given the distinction between the GASBO and the VASBO as policy oriented, and the SCSBO as control oriented. Yet the numerous roles of examiners in these offices can be explained. Certainly, as we have seen in previous chapters, the environment and decision context of the SCSBO is unusual compared to the other states included in this study. Even with a newly prescribed executive budget system in 1994, examiners in this office seemed more attuned, perhaps more cognizant of legislative than gubernatorial priorities (especially those of members of the money committees). They just as easily conducted fiscal note analysis at the behest of legislators via legislative staffers as for the governor's office. This can account for their heavy emphasis of a policy analysis role. In relation to the governor, however, these examiners do not claim a policy orientation; only one of fourteen examiners indicates a policy orientation.

Georgia provides a contradictory environment as well that might speak to the numerous roles that examiners found themselves involved in. Governor Zell Miller was notorious for his close, yet combative relationship with budget examiners in the GASBO, especially during budget development in order to learn about spending alternatives and possibilities. Essentially, this governor was diligent in keeping the communication between him and examiners free flowing, thus greatly advancing his budget and policy priorities. Yet, by virtue of budget law and traditional practice (and in spite of current reforms), this state still passes a line-item appropriation bill that severely constrains examiners during development regarding analysis of the base or continuation budget. The fiscal scene in 1994, as well as a gubernatorial focus on cutback management (redirection), also explains the heavy maintenance of a control orientation in this SBO. Thus, these examiners were in many ways split among a number of roles to maintain a control orientation, as well as to foster the policy one.

The many roles of Virginia's budget examiners may be explained by the "one-stop-shop notion" fostered in this office by section managers. And, at the time of this study, in addition to a number of traditional functions of budget offices, there was a mandate in the VASBO regarding oversight of

Table 8.4

Mean Total Roles Scores by State

	Mean Roles Score	Roles Index Score	State N
IL	3.1	1.99	28
KS	3.9	2.58	14
MN	3.9	2.47	18
AL	4.4	2.77	8
WI	5.3	3.55	19
MO	5.8	3.59	15
IA	6.3	3.59	11
NC	7.2	3.09	11
SC	8.8	2.97	14
GA	10.1	3.33	18
VA	10.9	2.96	20
Total	6.3	0.30	176

regulations that kept many of the examiners running. Again, the almost con-tradictory nature of this state's environment regarding gubernatorial strength, at once empowering (budget process and format) yet hindering (placement of budget office, tenure, and veto restrictions), may explain why these exam-iners found themselves operating in a number of roles throughout the budget cycle.

What of the other states characterized as policy oriented? The mean roles scores of IASBO and WISBO belie the high proportion of examiners with the advocate and policy analyst roles. In IASBO, they combine for 50 per-cent of all role responses, while in WISBO they account for a combined 57 percent of responses. The conduit and adversary roles account for only 20 percent of IASBO and 10 percent of WISBO role responses. The advocate and policy analyst roles account for 50 percent of the MOSBO role re-sponses, and almost 40 percent of the MNSBO responses. KSBO examiners do not fit this pattern, as their roles are diverse and the facilitator role is the modal response. Still, 25 percent have the advocate and policy analyst roles and only 10 percent have the adversary role.

ANOVA tests reveal that there are significant differences in both total roles scores and the roles index values across the states. Results in Table 8.4 group the SBOs according to Tamhane's ANOVA post-hoc test on the mean roles scores of the states. GASBO and VASBO scores are distinctly apart from the other SBOs. ILSBO, KSBO, MNSBO, and ALSBO are distinct from the other states. Yet, when the SBOs are compared based on the mean roles index score for each state, the Tamhane post-hoc test reveals that ILSBO remains distinct from the other states (except Kansas, Minnesota, and Ala-

Table 8.5

ANOVA and Tamhane Tests, Total Roles Scores and Orientation

Total Roles Score	Sum of Squares	df	Mean Square	F	Sig
Between groups	77.03079	2	38.5154	2.507255	0.08475
Within groups	2411.768	157	15.36158		
Total	2488.798	159			

Tamhane Post-Hoc Tests on ANOVA	Dep Var: Total Roles Score			
(I) Policy or Control Orientation	(J) Policy or Control Orientation	Mean Difference (I − J)	SE	Sig
Control orientation	Policy orientation	0.21	0.73	0.99
	Control and policy	−1.44	0.80	0.24
Policy orientation	Control orientation	−0.21	0.73	0.99
	Control and policy	−1.65*	0.78	0.09
Control and policy	Control orientation	1.44	0.80	0.24
	Policy orientation	1.65*	0.78	0.09

*The mean difference is significant at the 0.10 level.

bama SBOs). These tests establish that the variety and number of examiner roles vary by states.

We also tested whether the roles scores and roles index varies according to how the examiner viewed his or her SBO (whether control, policy, or control and policy orientation). The ANOVA and post-hoc tests reveal a significant relationship between the SBO's general orientation and both the roles score and the roles index ($p = 0.08$). Table 8.5 presents the Tamhane post-hoc tests for the total roles scores and SBO orientations. The roles scores for those in a policy-oriented SBO are significantly different than for examiners in control-oriented SBOs or SBOs with control and policy orientations. The mean roles index averages for each orientation are presented in Table 8.6. The ANOVA and post-hoc tests confirm that the policy orientation has a significantly lower mean roles index than the control and policy orientation ($p = 0.006$).

Finally, Table 8.7 presents Spearman's correlations for roles and orientations. Several interesting relationships are noteworthy. We first note that the control orientation is moderately related to the adversary and conduit roles, but only weakly related to the policy analyst and advocate roles. This finding contrasts with the policy orientation, which is moderately correlated with the policy analyst and advocate roles, only weakly correlated to the facilitator role, and unrelated to the adversary and conduit roles. As might be expected, the policy and control orientation is weakly correlated with both the

Table 8.6

Mean Roles Index by SBO Orientation

Orientation	Control	Policy	Control and Policy	Grand Mean
Mean roles index	2.5	3.1	3.2	2.9
Total count	55	62	42	159

conduit and the advocacy roles. The policy and control orientation is strongly correlated with the policy orientation (rho = 0.694) and there is a negative sign associated with the control orientation. The management and planning orientations are most strongly correlated with the facilitator role, and are also weakly associated with the policy analyst and advocate roles. We recall that these two orientations are identified almost exclusively by the budget directors and team managers, so these relationships largely reflect how their views of roles are conditioned by their perspectives on SBO orientations.

Examiner Roles in a Policy-Oriented SBO

Enthusiastic about the changing nature of the central budget staff in the glow of the planning, programming, and budgeting (PPB) reforms of the late 1960s, Howard (1973, 278) waxed that "as the budget becomes a more or less comprehensive compilation of policy statements, the traditional budget examiner becomes a policy analyst. Budgeting increasingly focuses on policy development; budgets set the agenda for discussion of policy objectives." Howard's job description for a policy-oriented SBO included a need to compare competing values (using an objective methodology to establish priorities) to produce a budget that "has both fiscal and political balance" (1973, 50). He admonished SBO examiners that it was not possible to disregard what agencies do and to concentrate only on how much money they request. The future did not augur well for the budget officer who saw his role in such terms. Yet he recognized that it would not be that simple for the central budget staff to break out of the "detailed control cocoon and become a policy and development butterfly" (279).

This encouraging but cautionary prodding by Howard followed Shadoan's earlier admonition that the development of the budget from primarily a control device into a positive tool for achieving aims has increased attention to the needs of budget office staff capable of transmitting and interpreting gubernatorial policies to the agencies. The emphasis is on "analytical ability" that "encourages the individual to consider alternative solutions to problems"

Table 8.7

Spearman's Correlations of Examiner Backgrounds and Roles

Spearman's rho Correlations	Roles Score	Role N	Roles Index	Type of Under-grad Degree	Previous Experience	Most Recent Experience
Role N	0.905**					
Roles index	0.509**	0.124				
Type of undergrad degree	0.008	0.032	-0.075			
Previous professional experience	-0.039	-0.052	-0.193**	-0.035		
Most recent professional experience	-0.127*	-0.124	-0.046	-0.122	0.113	
Number of years at SBO	0.217**	-0.162*	0.203**	0.187**	0.008	0.006

*Correlation is significant at the .05 level (1-tailed).
**Correlation is significant at the .01 level (1-tailed).

(Shadoan 1963a, 230–231). This policy orientation results in budget examiners' shaping and emphasizing budget issues, and in so doing, they "take on the often unrecognized moral responsibility of defining for other people the reality of what is occurring in various state programs," a somewhat metaphysical role (Howard 1973, 279). The sense one gains from these proponents of linking the policy and budget processes is that SBO examiners should actively think of their roles in terms of a policy analyst. Our discussions with examiners in policy-oriented SBOs nearly thirty years later suggests that this role is a significant component of the policy-oriented examiner's identity.

Let us briefly retrace the process with our policy-oriented examiner, Mary, this time with a focus on how her roles change at different stages of the budget process. Figure 8.3 graphically presents the budget process flow and maps the roles identified by examiners at different stages of the process. This stylized flowchart shows that the examiner roles are more complicated than the simple adversary role assigned in the classical incrementalism model. Moreover, the role shifts more often than simply from adversary during agency request review to governor's advocate in the legislative phase.

The most striking feature of this figure is the dominance of the policy analyst role throughout the budget process. The schematic exaggerates the presence of this role as identified by the examiners in our field study. One justification for this emphasis is that we have incorporated many of the "other" roles characterizations into the policy analyst role in this schematic. The presence of the policy analyst role throughout the process in a policy-oriented SBO also incorporates the notion that the policy focus of the SBO is never far from a concern of the examiner. The policy-oriented examiner "is in a unique position in state government," charged with "looking at the big picture" (Pittard 1999, 4). The policy analyst role also emphasizes Howard's (1973, 48) point that "the most critical calculations in budgeting entail judgment, not mathematics."

In the policy-oriented SBO, the policy analyst role begins for the budget examiner when she starts reading the old budgets and agency budget requests, and the statutes and codes that define the agency programs and priorities. Reading these documents and visiting agency operations in site visits reveals to her the policy priorities of the agency, and hopefully the policy agenda of the agency as well. Discussions with former budget examiners and team managers complements the discussions with agencies by establishing how the agency policies and priorities have been reconciled (or not) with those of the governor. The policy priorities embedded in the budget instructions are relevant and important components of her future analysis of the agency requests that will arrive on her desk in the near future. When she evaluates those requests, the feasibility tests include whether the requests

Figure 8.3   **Examiner Roles in a Policy-Oriented SBO**

Adversary	Conduit/ Facilitator	Policy Analyst	Advocate	Analysis Stage
				Read Old Budgets and Agency Requests
				Read Statutes, Code
				Visit Agency Head
				Visit Agency Staff
				Visit Agency Operations (Site Visits)
				Read Old Audit and Evaluation Reports
				Talk with Former Budget Examiners or Team Leaders About Agency Issues
				Develop Budget Instructions
				Get Governor's Priorities
				Get Revenue Forecast
				Get Spending Targets for Agencies
				Get Budget Requests for Agencies
				Evaluate with Respect to Governor's Agenda
				Discard "No Fly" Requests, *Unless* . . .
				Develop Alternatives to Requests
				Align Policy Priorities with Spending Target
				Within SBO Sections
				Across SBO Sections
				Recommend Agency Budgets
				To the Wall . . .
				Reset Recommendations After Governor's Review
				Monitor Legislative Amendments
				Veto Analysis and Recommendations
				Budget Execution

align with the gubernatorial policies and priorities. Recommendations on the agency budget requests depend on the policy alignment or misalignment. This also holds true of any veto analyses that she may conduct at the end of the legislative phase. The budget execution phase brings her back to more agency visits and policy discussions.

An essential requirement for policy-oriented examiners, according to Shadoan and Howard, is to translate political values into specific decisions. The principal method for accomplishing this is to heed the values expressed by the governor. To see and interpret gubernatorial priorities is a guiding rule for policy-oriented budgeting. This is manifest in the energy that examiners invest in developing and creating alternatives that meet political and budgetary feasibility criteria. Retaining a policy analysis perspective throughout the budget process provides the examiner in a policy-oriented SBO with essential tools. First, the analysis can take a long-run view. If examiners incorporate this factor into their recommendations, it may consist of a phased implementation of a program or policy, accommodating the political reality while projecting long-term strategic thinking and planning with the agency bureaucracy in mind. This method contrasts with the interests of the elected political officials, who tend to have a short-run view, with a focus on the inputs into the budget process, especially as it concerns their effects on powerful input-oriented interest groups (Howard 1973, 139–140).

The policy perspective complements a second tool, that budget examiners wield influence by virtue of their subject-matter expertise. "It is the examiner who is the expert with regard to his particular program area and who also understands the intricacies of programs well enough to generate or not generate issues which might otherwise remain unnoticed by supervision" (Tomkin 1983, 44). In order to develop and create alternatives to agency requests, the expertise of the examiner needs to be broader than the technical numbers associated with various line items. The year-round attention to the policy aspects of agency budgets produces "sophisticated agency budgeting so that the agency can handle more and more aspects of budget administration with the minimum of budget office control and is able to utilize the budget as a management tool in accomplishing program goals" (Shadoan 1963a, 229). This approach increases the odds that "analysis should improve, not annihilate, the political process" (Howard 1973, 139).

Incorporated into the policy analysis role, as it has been developed here, is a modest role for Meltsner's technician model of policy analyst. Anton (1969, 129) puts the technical aspects of budgetary accounting into perspective for budget examiners: "However fuzzy the thinking behind any given figure may have been, its representation as a specific dollar-and-cents figure implies precise measurement of quantifiable factors, leading to this—and no other—sum. For those who are closest to the centers of decision—and who are therefore in a position to know how unscientific the budget can be—it is not the document which offers symbolic satisfaction, but the process of putting it together." If the fuzzy numbers are more symbol than precise technical measure, it is useful for the examiner to have a good working relationship with the agency budgeters who can deliver that precision. Pittard (1999, 5) advises new budget examiners to develop a rapport with the people who actually crunch the numbers at the department level, the "worker bees," as well as their managers.

What of the advocate role for policy-oriented examiners? Tomkin found ample evidence at OMB "that there was an overall institutional norm which allowed, if not encouraged, the expression of dissent on the part of the examiner. Eighty-eight percent of the 60 examiners and branch chiefs interviewed on this point expressed the willingness to disagree with politically set policy and to allow such expression by their subordinates" (Tomkin 1983, 44C). As we discussed in chapters 5 and 6, the advocacy position of an examiner is a delicate one. Examiners seek to retain neutral competency with respect to the governor, and they also seek to avoid the label of a blindly loyal advocate for their assigned agencies. While the advocate label is generally shunned by budget directors and budget examiners, it is sometimes absolutely "necessary" for some budget examiners to advocate for their agencies. This is particularly evident as examiners develop alternatives to agency requests. As they craft their recommendation to the budget director and governor, they reach the decision point where they deny the request or prepare to "go to the wall" for the agency on this one. It is easier to justify in some agencies than in others, as was the case for this examiner:

> I'm definitely an advocate. The judiciary pretty much takes care of themselves. They have the contacts that they can call and twist arms. Everybody gives the judges some of what the judges want. Nobody wants to spend any money on the public defender or on criminals. That's just not a popular budget. So, if there are things that the department needs to do their job, I don't think they're going to get them unless I can present their case for them. I'm also critical. They frequently ask for things that I don't think are essential, and if they can't convince me, I mean, that's their first job is to convince me that they really need something. And if they can convince me, then I will advocate for them throughout the budget process. And as you work in the Capitol for awhile, legislators and staffers get familiar with who you are and where you're coming from. I am on occasion asked questions in hearings when I'm just there as an observer. The department is presenting the governor's recommendations, the chair will turn and say, what was the rationale on this, why did you recommend this?

The key, as Pittard wryly suggests, is to "know when to hold 'em, know when to fold 'em," and that judgment tends to come with experience (1999, 8).

The conduit/facilitator role is not absent from the policy-oriented SBO either. The emphasis is on the facilitator role, and the budget directors in the policy-oriented SBOs encourage examiners to have active engagement with their assigned agencies. "It is highly desirable that there be a close working relationship between the budget staff and the operating departments. Ideally, the members of the budget staff have strong professional relationships with the operating department personnel and possesses an intimate knowledge of agency operations. As a general rule, the budget personnel are welcomed in department program planning sessions, and very few departmental requests catch the alert analyst by surprise" (Mathews 1965, 37–38). The facilitator role is particularly important in the early stages of budget development, when budget instructions are being drafted by the SBO and sent to agencies, and examiners are helping agency budgeters interpret the guidelines for the impending agency requests.

Control is a low priority in a policy-oriented SBO, but it is not an absent value. The low emphasis on control, however, helps examiners minimize the adversary role. An IASBO manager echoes the sentiments of several policy-oriented examiners. He believes "a lot of times I'm perceived as an antagonist by some, because there are times I will play the role of the devil's advocate. I will bring up things not particularly because I believe in it, but because I want to be sure it's been thought of." Constraining the adversary role to those moments in the budget cycle when there are winners and losers reduces the zero-sum calculus to professional differences within an acceptable method of deciding funding to support some public values over others. It is a light touch of control that contrasts significantly with the control and adversarial roles in the control-oriented SBOs.

Examiner Roles in a Control-Oriented SBO

Howard (1973) notes that the SBO examiners are expected to be more sensitive to the budget balance requirement than are agencies, to have a comprehensive and coordinated viewpoint that places SBO examiners in the role of cutting agency budget requests. In the control-oriented SBOs, the simplifying rule is to focus on short-run fiscal management and expenditure control, fulfilling the classical "cutter" role of the incrementalism model. Agencies may justify requests with programmatic arguments, but the examiners judge the requests with respect to budgetary targets. The control tactics can become quite onerous for agencies, as this IASBO manager recalls of the Iowa budget office before its reorientation to a policy emphasis:

> We had a point in time when [the agencies] couldn't hardly move away from their desk to the next office without us knowing it. We were approv-

ing everything: approving travel, purchases, hiring. During that time we didn't have any money and we were trying to find ways to save money. At that point in time, I still felt, though, the relationship I had built with those departments remained intact. I tried to do everything that I could to make them feel [pause]. I didn't feel antagonistic. I didn't feel that that was my role. I never have. But I can see where the departments perceived us as being more antagonistic during that time. Since then, I don't know, perhaps if we go through another budget cycle like that, for a few years we have no money and budgeting is a much larger problem, perhaps we're going to be back into that mold. I don't know. But we have moved away from that significantly.

The adversary role may seem more pronounced in the control-oriented SBO because the examiners lack the balance between their assignment to ensure tight control of spending limits and an off-setting requirement to advocate for "true" agency needs within the general constraints of the state budget. The balancing act can be practiced by the policy-oriented examiner who has a broader mission than simply number crunching. But during budget development, decisions of the control-oriented examiner are based on mathematics more often than judgment.

In the control-oriented SBOs, control is a constant and primary responsibility of the examiners. The adversary role is viewed by many examiners in these offices as an unfortunate reality that comes about initially when developing budget instructions. The examiner roles then change only slightly as the budget cycle proceeds through the fiscal year. As seen in Figure 8.4, the greatest role for the control-oriented examiners is as the conduit between the governor and the agencies. They are the intermediary, but with a heavier flow of top-down information than bottom-up intelligence on program effectiveness or agency "needs" as opposed to "requests."

To a large extent, the control-oriented examiner is more of a conduit than a facilitator, with the emphasis placed on a technician role, the proverbial number cruncher. This aspect of the conduit role in OMB has received the most attention with respect to the Stockman era, when Tomkin explains that the president lost the "honest information" source of the examiners, and their recommendations were more frequently overturned. Stockman used OMB examiners to crunch numbers he needed for policies and legislative lobbying. Budget examiners were increasingly used to justify or fill in the details on decisions that had already been made by political appointees, rather than to provide advice and information to support decision-making in progress. While less time was being spent on the preparation of careerist analysis, more time was spent on other types of work assignments such as "numbers exercises" (Tomkin 1998, 47). Field trips and in-depth agency studies were

Figure 8.4 **Examiner Roles in a Control-Oriented SBO**

Adversary	Conduit/ Facilitator	Policy Analyst	Advocate	Analysis Stage
	▓			Read Old Budgets and Agency Requests
	▓			Read Statutes, Code
	▓			Visit Agency Head
	▓			Visit Agency Staff
	▓			Visit Agency Operations (Site Visits)
	▓			Read Old Audit and Evaluation Reports
	▓			Talk with Former Budget Examiners or Team Leaders About Agency Issues
▓	▓			Develop Budget Instructions
▓	▓			Get Governor's Priorities
▓	▓			Get Revenue Forecast
▓				Get Spending Targets for Agencies
▓				Get Budget Requests for Agencies
▓	▓			Evaluate with Respect to Governor's Agenda
▓	▓			Discard "No Fly" Requests, *Unless* . . .
▓	▓			Develop Alternatives to Requests
▓	▓			Align Policy Priorities with Spending Target
▓	▓			Within SBO Sections
▓	▓			Across SBO Sections
▓				Recommend Agency Budgets
▓				To the Wall . . .
▓				Reset Recommendations After Governor's Review
▓	▓		▓	Monitor Legislative Amendments
▓			▓	Veto Analysis and Recommendations
▓	▓		▓	Budget Execution

greatly reduced. While the examiners' role of the mid-1970s was primarily one of "proposing" policy alternatives, under Stockman it shifted toward becoming largely "reactive." Consequently, the OMB staff increased their control role because they still had discretion there, even as their formulation role decreased (Tomkin 1998, 90; see also Johnson 1984, 512). As we have noted earlier, this phenomenon at OMB paralleled the behavioral patterns at ILSBO.

There is little opportunity for examiners in the control-oriented SBO to be an advocate for assigned agencies during budget development because, as a rule, they do not meet with top agency people to see the "big picture," do not recommend directly on agency budgets, and do not brief the governor (if they even brief the budget director), so they do not have the opportunity to argue with the governor or the budget director on behalf of an agency request. However, these examiners are generally attuned to agency problems and concerns during the legislative session (for example, how new or changed legislation may change agency funding flows or the like) and budget execution. These examiners recognize that agency staff know their job best, and examiners believe that they can provide support for implementing programs and activities through budget administration. According to one ALSBO examiner, "budget management is up to the agency, to take the budget and run with it. And if they've got a problem there, if they want our assistance, we will help."

What can we tell John, our examiner in a control-oriented office, about the roles typical of his cohorts during his first full year of work? Certainly, he can have the most significant impact regarding budget decisions by fostering and maintaining free-flowing communication between his agencies and his section manager and hopefully with the budget director (such flow is unlikely to the governor directly). Thus, as noted in chapter 7, John needs to continually prod his section manager for information about communications higher up. And it would not hurt for John to be diligent in reading anything he can regarding gubernatorial priorities and considered initiatives that are provided internally through memoranda as well as those provided externally via media spots and newspaper articles and the like. Essentially, John must be self-directed in keeping abreast as best he can of the priorities of the agency and the governor. Communication flow is stilted, and so he will need to do more than reconcile numbers if he truly wants clarification on the political rationale behind his agencies' budgets and their requests.

John must remember, however, that there are a couple of spots in the budget cycle in which he does not have an avenue for communication. For example, because examiners in control-oriented budget offices usually do not have access to the full range of rationalities during budget review, they do not advocate for agency budgets when backed against gubernatorial priorities. Thus, we notice no role activity for the period that might deal with "no fly" requests. Further, at the point of developing alternatives to requests and again when resetting recommendations after the governor's review, examiners related to agencies from a guardianship standpoint—usually asking them to give up some (more) money. Maintaining a strong conduit role is certainly important during these stages.

In the end, as illustrated in Figure 8.4 and discussed in chapter 7, John can learn to take advantage of his roles during legislative deliberation of the budget and during budget execution to gain perspective about agency priorities to help with budget development in subsequent fiscal years. He is able to act as an advocate to agencies during these stages by recognizing potential budget problems during review of legislative as well as gubernatorial and agency initiatives during the session. And, in his day-to-day monitoring of agency spending, he can witness problems and potential problems, help (when asked) to solve these problems, and shore up this knowledge for future reference as the cycle begins anew when budget request guidelines are sent to agencies again.

Compare and Contrast: Control- Versus Policy-Oriented SBOs

Tomkin concludes that OMB examiners' decision-making is influenced by their gatekeeper role and the choices they make regarding which data and issues are to be pursued—and which will be ignored or excluded. Their decisions determine the structure of analyses and the options reviewed by senior officials in the process. When feedback from political officials is slow or absent, examiners are able to increase their policy roles. Neutrally exercised, an increased policy role gives the examiner the responsibility for "policy policing," which is a different type of controlling role from the traditional "no" bias. In the latter case, a presumption of "no increase" applies to all budget requests. In a policy-policing role, however, agency requests are judged with respect to whether they are in accord with the president's policy priorities (Tomkin 1998, 74–79).

Figure 8.5 allows us to compare the variations in examiner roles in the policy-oriented and control-oriented SBOs through different phases of the budget cycle. There are several steps in the process where the examiners hold similar roles. There is an adversary role for all examiners at key points of the process. It is worthwhile to note that the chart does not capture the intensity or character of the adversary roles. As previously noted, the character of the adversary role in the control-oriented SBO is focused on technical routines to "find" the mistakes or "tricks" embedded in the agency requests, while the character of the role in the policy-oriented SBO is in the context of skeptical policy analysis that forces better and more complete arguments from agencies to support their requests.

Figure 8.5   Comparison of Examiner Roles in Control- and Policy-Oriented SBOs

Adversary	Conduit/ Facilitator	Policy Analyst	Advocate	Analysis Stage / Control — Policy	Adversary	Conduit/ Facilitator	Policy Analyst	Advocate
				Read Old Budgets and Agency Requests				
				Read Statutes, Code				
				Visit Agency Head				
				Visit Agency Staff				
				Visit Agency Operations (Site Visits)				
				Read Old Audit and Evaluation Reports				
				Talk with Former Budget Examiners or Team Leaders About Agency Issues				
				Develop Budget Instructions				
				Get Governor's Priorities				
				Get Revenue Forecast				
				Get Spending Targets for Agencies				
				Get Budget Requests for Agencies				
				Evaluate with Respect to Governor's Agenda				
				Discard "No Fly" Requests, *Unless* . . .				
				Develop Alternatives to Requests				
				Align Policy Priorities with Spending Target				
				Within SBO Sections				
				Across SBO Sections				
				Recommend Agency Budgets				
				To the Wall . . .				
				Reset Recommendations After Governor's Review				
				Monitor Legislative Amendments				
				Veto Analysis and Recommendations				
				Budget Execution				

Second, the impetus for the activities in these steps of the process is different in the two types of SBOs. The actions of the control-oriented examiner are more likely instigated by team management at the behest of the budget director or the governor's policy staff. They are "finding a number," adjusting budget requests to "fit" the upper level decision(s), or applying some across-the-board decision rule to the agency budget request. The policy-oriented examiner, in contrast, is working with much greater independence in both evaluating the agency requests and aligning the requests with spending targets and gubernatorial policy objectives. The context for these decisions is ongoing policy analysis.

The examiners also play similar conduit/facilitator roles in discussions with agency personnel and conveying and interpreting budget instructions for assigned agencies. The top-down and bottom-up communications are an essential component of the impending budget decisions. The differences in these conduit/facilitator roles are subtle and not so subtle. First, the policy-oriented examiners are likely to meet with agency heads and engage in high-level policy discussions as part of their agency visits. The control-oriented examiners are more likely to meet with the agency fiscal officer and budget staff. The effect is communications within the context of policy analysis in the policy-oriented SBO, and a more technical level of discussion in the control-oriented SBO. Later in the process, the policy-oriented examiner can view the budget problem from multiple perspectives, while the control-oriented examiner is focused on technical aspects of the agency budget request.

The most striking contrast in roles between the control-oriented SBO examiners and the policy-oriented SBO examiners is the limited variety of roles in the former. The control-oriented SBO examiners are restricted to the adversary and conduit/facilitator roles primarily, with a bit of the advocate role possible following budget development and strongest during budget execution. There is a distinct shift in roles as described in the classical incrementalism literature, as the examiners finish gathering and conveying information between the budget director and the agencies and begin to apply to their agency requests the decision rules developed by the budget director and the governor's policy staff.

In the policy-oriented SBO, the examiners shift back and forth among several roles throughout the budget process and may even play multiple roles simultaneously. This is particularly true as they develop alternatives to agency requests. As seen in Figure 8.5, they will match the adversary role of their control-oriented SBO counterparts with respect to some agency requests later in the process. However, they may also be an advocate for other budget requests, all the while conducting the analysis of the requests in the context of policy analysis. To the extent that fiscal and other policy constraints allow, they may also try to work with the agency as a facilitator, to help them adjust their request so that it is more consonant with gubernatorial priorities.

The policy analysis thread that lingers throughout the policy-oriented budget process is manifested during the legislative phase as examiners typically monitor legislation affecting their assigned agencies, and often craft fiscal analyses of the bills to estimate the impact of the bill on the state budget (if it were to pass). Of course, the fiscal notes can be crafted to estimate costs so high as to impede passage, or so low as to increase the political feasibility of passage. The main value of fiscal note activity to examiners, however, is that it keeps them intimately familiar with the political forces pressuring their agencies' programs for changes. The examiners need to constantly assess those pressures for change in light of gubernatorial policies and priorities.

In a control-oriented SBO such as ALSBO, the legislative phase is not an opportunity for the examiner to conduct policy analysis. Fiscal notes are crafted by the legislative budget office, not the executive budget office. The ALSBO examiners rely on that analysis for their own studies, as explained by this examiner:

> There's some kind of reconciliation done between our office and [the] legislative fiscal office, usually on big issues, costwise, to make sure everything is in sync and everybody agrees. They do fiscal notes a lot of times on bills. We don't do any fiscal notes here. And we use that information a lot when we're given special analysis to do. We're doing that always. All during the year we're preparing special analysis for something that [the budget director] or somebody made a phone call, say to the director's office, they need, the director wants, the most updated information on this or that *so he can give out correct information.*

If and when the agency budgets are subject to veto analysis and recommendations, the policy-oriented examiner is as likely to be advocating for departmental needs as to be antagonizing the department with veto recommendations. The permutations on roles and role shifts are simply more numerous and likely in the policy-oriented SBOs than in the control-oriented SBOs.

The key distinction between policy- and control-oriented SBOs in examiner roles and role changes is that policy-oriented examiners often have a seat at the policy decision-making table, and they are aware that they will be expected to contribute to the policy decision at some point in the process, even if they do not directly brief the governor. Tomkin found the impact of the "seat at the table" to be very influential on OMB examiners. The direct exposure of OMB staff to President Carter had a big impact on usefulness and influence of OMB. Examiners personally defended recommendations to the president and they were highly motivated to excel in their analyses (Tomkin 1998, 53–54). The impact is no less motivational on state examiners. Witness the pride in this examiner:

> I know with the DOT the governor was quite happy with my recommendations because he told me. I walked around with a big head for quite a while. Because with DOT they have a tendency to ask for a lot of things.

He just simply told me that he was "really happy with the recommenda-tions. I thought they were really good." He told me that in a meeting, and then he was standing out there, and I was in my office, and he said that I had really done a good job on my recommendations. He told me.

As we shall see momentarily, the demand for—or the flexibility of—mul-tiple roles during the budget process influences the rationalities that examin-ers can apply to the analysis of agency budget requests. Before we turn to this relationship, we pause to consider the extent to which professional and educational backgrounds in the examiners influence their roles.

Educational and Professional Backgrounds of Budget Examiners

Our model of budgetary roles (Figure 8.2) suggests that examiner roles are influenced by their professional and educational backgrounds. The empiri-cal basis in budgetary literature for this linkage is a collection of mixed re-sults. Lee, Schick, and others have chronicled the changing backgrounds of examiners in SBOs (Lee 1991; Schick 1966; Thurmaier and Gosling 1997; Willoughby 1991a and 1991b). The general trend has been changes in two dimensions: the level of education and the types of education. Lee (1997) reports that the share of SBO staff with master's degrees has increased from 17 percent in 1970 to 48 percent in 1995. This compares with evidence from scattered studies at the state and national levels. For example, Kenneth Oldfield (1986) found that 56 percent of the 1980 MOSBO staff and 80 percent of the 1985 ILSBO staff had at least a master's degree.

Lee (1997) also reports substantial changes in the educational degrees of SBO staff. The share of SBO staff with accounting degrees has fallen from 29 percent in 1970 to only 12 percent in 1995, and the share of business administration degrees has fallen from 37 percent to only 26 percent in the same period. Meanwhile, the share of public administration degrees has in-creased from 15 percent in 1970 to 25 percent in 1995, and the share of economics and other social science degrees has increased in that period from a combined 5 percent to a combined 18 percent of staff. Similarly, other professional disciplines have grown from only 2 percent of staff in 1970 to 8 percent of staff in 1995. These changes suggest both an increased capacity of—and preference for—examiners who can conduct broader policy analy-sis instead of technical accounting and financial analysis. Indeed, Lee (1997) found a concomitant increase in the use of program information and analysis in SBOs between 1970 and 1990, although he noted some "backsliding" between 1990 and 1995.

In addition, there has been some research on changing professional backgrounds of examiners at the national and state levels. People bring extra-organizational cultures into the organization, for example, Hispanics or accountants. Such employees inject social and professional norms into organizations and can act as catalysts for subculture development, although they may be a transient or intermittent subculture (Martin 1992, 111). Accounting and business management backgrounds may foster a control orientation, the watchdog approach. Social science and MPA backgrounds may foster a management and policy analysis orientation, the intermediary and advocacy approaches. Experience in a state agency prior to work in the SBO may infuse the budget office with bureaucratic norms that reduce flexibility and initiative. These budgeters may feel attached to particular agency programs and policies. Pittard (1999) cautions that state budget examiners who come from an agency must learn to view their SBO assignment in terms of its impact statewide, to unlearn the ownership of programs and budget connected with the agency or departmental level.

Our field study of SBO examiners finds little support for the proposition that examiner roles are conditioned in part by their educational backgrounds.[1] Only the conduit role is specifically correlated with the type of undergraduate degree held by budget examiners. It is weak (rho = 0.192) but significant at $p = 0.01$. This suggests that budget examiners with accounting and business degrees are more likely to see themselves as conduits than those with social science or humanities degrees. As seen in Table 8.8, there is no statistical relationship between the roles scores (or the roles index) and the type of undergraduate degree held by the examiner.

There is a weak relationship between the total roles score and the examiner's most recent professional experience, and between the roles index and the examiner's previous professional experience. The negative signs associated with both relationships suggests that higher roles scores and roles index values are associated with backgrounds in private businesses and state agencies compared to backgrounds in the legislature or examiners going into the budget office directly from college. One interpretation consistent with the interview discussions is that those coming directly from college degree programs into the SBO are more focused on serving as policy analysts than more senior examiners who were rooted in business and accounting backgrounds but have had to evolve their roles as SBO orientations have changed. To support this interpretation, we note that roles scores and the roles index are both positively correlated with longer tenure at the SBO. In addition, the positive correlation between SBO tenure and undergraduate degrees suggests that senior examiners are more likely to have business and accounting degrees than more recently hired examiners (who are more likely to have social science and public administration degrees).

Table 8.8

Distribution of Bachelor's Degrees by Type, by Level of Roles

Number of Roles	Humanities	Business	Social Sciences	Accounting	Physical Science	Other	None	Total
Percentage of Bachelor's Degrees by Type, by Level of Roles								
5			4	5	7			3
4		12	13	10	14	100		12
3	18	15	11	33	7		50	16
2	27	33	36	19	29		25	32
1	55	39	36	33	43		25	38
Total (n = 167)	100	100	100	100	100	100	100	100
Average Number of Roles by Bachelor's Degree Type and Level of Roles								
5			3.0	3.0	3.0			3.0
4		2.8	3.0	3.4	3.1	3.0		3.0
3	3.7	2.9	3.0	3.1	3.3		3.7	3.1
2	2.7	2.9	3.0	3.1	3.3		3.5	3.0
1	2.2	2.7	2.8	2.6	2.7		5.0	2.7
Average	2.6	2.8	2.9	2.9	3.0	3.0	4.0	2.9

Table 8.8 is ordered from left to right according to the average number of roles in each type of undergraduate degree. Notice that there appears to be little or no difference in the number or distribution of roles between those with social science and those with business and accounting degrees. This corresponds with the insignificant correlation between B.A. types and roles in Table 8.8.

The lack of significant or strong relationships between the types of examiner roles and the educational and professional backgrounds of the examiners in our field study may be an artifact of the way we have defined the role types, plus the complications of analyzing multiple response data. On the other hand, it may also be true that the SBO culture (whether it is a control-oriented SBO or a policy-oriented SBO) may be so strong that examiners shed the subculture backgrounds they bring to the budget office. Although we do not explore the phenomenon in this study, some of the discussions with examiners suggest that each budget team or section may develop a distinctive subculture within the budget office (Martin 1992, 107). Various attempts to find statistical relationships between the type of agencies assigned to an examiner and his or her decision-making, role identification, or view of SBO orientation were not fruitful. However, our discussions with the SBO staff suggest that there may be a "welfare team subculture" that shapes the analytical approach to welfare programs and that is distinct from the "regulatory team subculture" that shapes the analytical approach to revenue and licensing agencies, for example. The former may be more policy oriented and the latter more control oriented. This in turn will affect their role perceptions and the range of rationalities that they apply to budget problems. We conclude that the differences we observe in examiner roles are likely to be most influenced by factors other than educational and professional backgrounds.

Different Roles Require Different Types of Decision-Making

The pervasiveness of the policy analysis approach is also due to the fact that various polities can face a common problem, analyze the same solution set, and reach different decisions because of the variations in politics surrounding the problems and solutions. Thus, the rational examiner looks at each budget and policy problem with a multifaceted approach because the solution set is realistically set, in part, by the politics surrounding the problem (Kelley 1987). Decision-making in a policy-oriented SBO demands a broader range of analysis tools than does decision-making in a control-oriented SBO. We have noted that the distinction between politics and policy is an important one, even if it is imprecise.

Diesing argues that political rationality focuses on structuring decision-making so as to balance the requirement for broad input (for legitimacy) with the requirement that the locus of decision-making is narrow enough to permit a decision to be made. A decision structure improves decisions as it embodies both of these characteristics to a greater degree. "First, the greater the variety of the presented facts, values, and norms, and the greater the variety of proposed alternatives a structure is able to produce, the more effective its decisions are likely to be. The reason is that decisions are made necessary by problems, and complex problems require complexity of treatment for adequate solution." The omission of key factors "from consideration means that the decision will have unanticipated consequences and perhaps quite different total results from those intended, and will be rational only by accident" (Diesing 1962, 177–178).

The requirement for analytical breadth, however, is balanced by the need to synthesize the factors into a decision. "The more intricate and subtle the ways of unifying presented factors are, the more effective the decision" about a complex problem is likely to be, Diesing notes. "A complex problem is likely to give rise in discussion to a variety of contradictory factual reports, differing values and norms, and conflicting suggestions for action. An adequate decision will have to note and embody most of the contradictory material and also relate it to the previous commitments of the group; but this is possible only through an intricate process of combination, evaluation, modification, and elimination." The difficult balancing act for the examiner is that "As the two characteristics are progressively embodied in a decision structure, they come increasingly into conflict with each other. The greater the variety of suggested facts and opinions, the harder it is to reach agreement; and the swifter and more certain the resolution process is, the harder it is to get varied and unusual factors presented to group awareness" (Diesing 1962, 178).

To the control-oriented examiner, the problem may appear only technical in nature: Did the agency meet the budget target? To the policy-oriented examiner, on the other hand, how the agency reaches the budget target is perhaps more important than whether they reached the target. In the sorting of the facts and values, the examiner in a policy-oriented SBO may find himself or herself an advocate for the agency and its priorities. An MNSBO examiner was very comfortable with this role, receiving support for this position from his team manager:

> I would say definitely that our role, from what I've picked up, is definitely more toward the advocate side.
>
> Q: How'd you pick that up?
> Examiner: Mainly from our team leader. It's his position, it was made pretty clear, that he doesn't view our job as being obstructionists, that we're here to make sure the [agency] doesn't do anything outrageous, but we're here to help them accomplish their mission. Whatever we can do to help that happen is our responsibility. We may be in a luxury of having a budget surplus in the last year, so there hasn't been the natural antagonism of a budget office having to cut a budget, and that may be a luxury that you can have when you're not having to cut someone's budget. But I think he's generally committed to that. There seems to be a shift that you've probably picked up from talking to people in this department away from kind of a controller status or real accounting oriented to more of a policy or procedures or management type of analysis. I think his attitude is kind of along with that.

The examiner suggests a relationship between his role in the budget process and the rationalities he applies to analyzing budgets. Howard observes that "budgeters are eclectics, deriving ideas and help from whatever sources they can," that budgets represent a strategy that lies somewhere between what is expected of programs and what programs hope to accomplish (Howard 1973, 20). A bias that favors "getting things done" is a natural support for an advocate role with respect to agency budget requests. As Howard recognizes, the examiner in a policy analysis context needs an open horizon of alternatives that can be matched with agency requirements for effective policy implementation. The multiple-rationalities approach to decision-making is a natural fit for an advocate role for examiners. The same is true for the policy analyst role.

It is important to note that the policy analysis required in the SBO is grounded in a special obligation to inject fiscal value in political decision-making. Appleby (1957, 156) describes this well:

> The budgeting function, like any other particular one, is a specialized way of looking at problems in decision-making. Any specialized way is parochial, in that it is a million—or innumerable—ways of not looking at the problems. But the budgeting function is *not* only valid technically; it represents one set of important values. Fiscal sense and fiscal coordination are certainly values. The budgeting organization is designed to give representation in institutional interaction and decision-making to this set of values.

An examiner with an advocate or policy analyst role cannot focus exclusively on the effectiveness rationalities (social, political, and legal) to the exclusion of the efficiency rationalities (economic and technical). The scope of analysis is necessarily large when one is charged with managing the "big picture." As Mathews comments, "The final phase of the budget estimation process results in a product which is a compromise based upon the interplay of both the political and professional forces. The product must be one designed to weather both legislative scrutiny and public opinion" (1965, 39).

Examiners with a conduit role, on the other hand, have lesser requirements for decision-making scope. In part, this is true because they have fewer decisions to make. To the extent that they provide initial inputs into higher-level decisions, they can focus on the technical and legal rationalities that are endemic to the control orientation.

The adversary role will apply different rationalities, depending upon whether the examiner is in a control-oriented SBO or policy-oriented SBO. In the control orientation, the adversary role arises as the examiner applies technical and legal rationalities to agency requests to determine if they conform to existing law and budget instructions issued by the budget director. As they find discrepancies, they adjust the requests accordingly. Since this often is done apart from discussions with the policy staff at the agency, the analysis is restricted and generally excludes an assessment of the programmatic outcomes of such adjustments to the agency budget.

In the policy-oriented SBO, the examiner's adversary role arises in the context of *policy control* rather than strictly financial control. The policy-oriented examiner must approach the budget problem mindful that "a decision to make a particular expenditure, whether a new car for the family or a building for the state, involves value questions. There are few problems for which there are single right answers clearly and simply revealed by technical analysis. The broader the jurisdiction—the larger the 'family'—the more complicated the values involved" (Appleby 1957, 119). The adversary role arises as the examiner replaces agency policy priorities and objectives with those of the governor. As we have discussed, this antagonism will be most evident in the few areas where the governor is actively pursuing policy objectives, for those programs that have risen to the top of the budget decision agenda. Programs that lack this visibility are less likely to conflict with gubernatorial policies, and the examiners are more free to advocate for agency priorities and programs to the extent that fiscal resources allow. An OMB manager in the early 1990s confirms that "80 percent of the institutional realities and public policy dilemmas do not touch on party politics or ideology," which makes the distinction between policy analysis and political analysis more routinely negotiable for the examiner (Tomkin 1998, 108).

Decision Context Matters

We have noted that the classic image of the central budget office analyst is "the bad guy," the "No-man," the agency's adversary who stands in the way of the agency's getting the money it needs to provide services. The last thing an agency wants to do is make the SBO examiner angry. A smooth and productive working relationship with the budget examiner is seen as an effective way to get the fiscal needs of the agency met (Duncombe and Kinney 1986; Gosling 1985 and 1987). On the other hand, agencies historically have been unlikely to characterize their SBO examiner as an advocate for their needs. That would undermine their traditional role as a key gatekeeper in the budgetary process.

However, our interviews with examiners suggest that they commonly view their role as multifaceted, shifting somewhat according to the stage of the budget cycle but increasingly characterized as facilitators—if not advocates—for agency needs. Examiners in policy-oriented SBOs are the primary conduit for macro-budgeting and micro-budgeting decisions between the governor and agencies. They confer and translate governors' policy directives to agencies and then report agencies' plans for complying with policies to governors. The influence of the SBO examiners in the process is evidenced by their ability to recommend spending requests that differ little from those the governor submits to the legislature. One of the keys to this feat is examiners' ability to play a role that meets the needs of both governors and agencies.

Our earlier discussion of the differences between policy-oriented and control-oriented SBOs indicates that the essential elements to this balancing act include a direct link between the examiners and the governor's policy staff. The strongest link, enjoyed by examiners in Georgia, Kansas, and Wisconsin, is when individual examiners brief the governor on their agency budgets and have the opportunity to "learn" how he or she thinks about things. The Missouri and Iowa budget staffs have the opportunity to sit in briefings, but they are somewhat marginalized because the focus of the discussion is between the governors and the budget directors, with the examiners present to provide technical details and backup. The budget directors in these states nurture a budget office culture that permits a free flow of communication between the governor's office and the budget staff, while still reminding the examiners that their focus is not on the politics of the issue but on the policy aspects of the issue. Examiners in the policy-oriented states seem to have no difficulties with the division, and the "neutral competency" norm is so strong that it is something that new examiners learn very quickly.

Heclo's analysis of the politicization of OMB under President Nixon was that communications from top-down had suffered from a transmission/translation layer between the president and budget examiners (telephone effect), increasing the remoteness of political leaders. Bottom-up communications also suffer because budget examiners are unsure of what happens to their analyses and recommendations upon transmittal to the policy staffers (pols) surrounding the chief executive. This field study finds little evidence of such politicization in the eleven states, with the possible exception of Illinois. The ILSBO examiners describe characteristics that correspond to the dysfunctionality that worried Heclo in his analysis of OMB. The examiners are unaware of political "deals" struck by the pols, and they are unsure of what happens to their analyses when they are dispatched from the budget team manager to the "front office." Impartial brokerage between agencies and pols is more difficult when pols upset agency folks. Most importantly, the examiners do not hold a long-run view of the state's fiscal health and budget policy. They are number crunchers in the classic sense of the word and greatly resemble the OMB examiners under the Stockman era, as described by Tomkin. The task for budget examiners in these situations, according to Heclo, is to cultivate "the reputation of an honest intermediary who balances loyalty to his political superiors with a fair presentation of the agency's case and his own analysis" (Heclo 1975, 94).

Relationships Matter

One of the factors that seems to be implicit in all of the previous discussions is that examiners must have strong professional relationships with the operating department personnel, the governor's policy staff, and other members of the SBO staff. An examiner's relationship to the budget director may also influence their role in the process. There is a familiarity in some offices where the budget director is referred to on a first-name basis. In others, the budget director is referenced in organizational terms, as in "the front office." To the extent that the budget director is a mentor, encouraging growth and increased responsibility from each examiner to explore budgetary alternatives that are consonant with the governor's policies and priorities and still meet agency needs, the examiner may be expected to identify with the policy analyst and advocate roles, and to apply a broad range of rationalities to budgetary analysis. To the extent that the budget director is remote, or viewed as an arbiter of agency budget problems, the examiner may be expected to identify with the conduit role, passing along information as the junction box between the departments and state "management." In all cases, it appears that the budget directors are viewed as the "fount of political knowledge" and the principal source of guidance on political issues, regardless of the control or policy orientation.

Meltsner (1976) argues that "who the client is" matters for the role taken by policy analysts. This field research explores the relationship between governors and examiners. It is clear that in some states, such as Wisconsin, the examiners serve the governor, full-time, all the time, even when they advocate for agency needs. In this state and similar ones, the examiners brief the governor on budget recommendations and establish a familiarity that encourages them to challenge the governor's policy positions when the examiner feels they conflict with the "best public policy" embedded in an agency budget alternative. In other states, the linkage to the governor is more indirect, even remote. In some states, the examiners officially become servants of the legislature once the governor has submitted a budget to them. The consequences of this relationship are not lost on the examiners, as reflected in these recollections of past governors:

> I guess I would say that over the last few years, I think the budget staff has been less participatory in a lot of the processes. And I'm looking at this over a fifteen-year period, OK? Back when I first started, it was not uncommon with [the governor], if they were going to talk about the courts budget, it might be at eleven at night and whoever had that budget was to be there. We don't do that stuff anymore. It's more a situation of certain people meeting and then you get an answer back. "Oh, by the way, put another $1 million in here." We were much more involved in the process previously. Now, it made you work weirder hours and probably longer hours, but I thought the advantage to that was you understood more rationale of what was going on.

Whatever the case, "the budget office determines in very significant ways (but not, of course, to the complete exclusion of other information sources) what information is given or released to various participants" (Howard 1973, 266).

Summary: Decision Context, Communication, and Budget Roles of SBOs

This chapter has explored the changing roles of SBO examiners in the eleven SBOs. The classical role of "guarding the purse" that is essential to the incrementalism model is found only in the control-oriented state budget offices, and even then it is only one of several roles played by control-oriented examiners. In the policy-oriented state budget offices, when examiners play an adversarial role their priority is "guarding the policy." We have also seen that the decision context of the examiner has important effects on both the number and the variety of roles played by examiners.

Policy-oriented examiners are more likely to have a larger number and a wider variety of roles than examiners in control-oriented SBOs. The narrower range of roles in the control-oriented SBOs is directly related to the narrower range of rationalities exercised by examiners in these SBOs. Focused on technical and legal rationalities, the examiners most often find their roles in the budget process restricted to conduit and adversary roles. The execution phase may give them an opportunity to be an advocate for agency needs, to make sure the agency gets their entitled allocation.

The contrast with roles and rationalities in policy-oriented SBOs is profound. At every step of the budget process, the roles presented in Figure 8.2 are different in subtle and not-so-subtle ways. The adversary role played by policy-oriented examiners is a policy control role, enforcing the governor's policies. The conduit role is more likely to include bottom-up flows of information from agencies to the governor and governor's policy staff than in control-oriented SBOs. Moreover, the policy-oriented examiner is more likely to act as a facilitator than a conduit, with the important implication that they are trying to help the agency accomplish its mission within the budget and policy constraints of the day. Finally, the policy-oriented examiners are more likely to view themselves in a policy analyst role, part and parcel of their constant mission to assess budget problems as policy problems—and to assess requests with respect to deviance or consonance with the governor's policies and priorities.

Underlying the examiner roles in both control-oriented and policy-oriented SBOs is the affirmation of earlier federal and state studies—good working relationships between agency budgeters and SBO examiners are critically important to agencies getting the resources they need to run their programs.

Note

1. The education and experience variables were coded on ordinal scales to suggest educational and professional dimensions. The education dimension ranges from broad social science to narrow business finance and accounting degrees. The professional experience dimension ranges from those coming with no experience or state agency experience to those with private-sector (business) experience. The professional experience scale probably has less statistical validity than the education scale. The underlying nominal nature of the education and experience variables allows us only the suggestion of a relationship.

9

Conclusion

Why Examine Examiners?

The role that states play in our federal system today, both financially and regarding policy development and implementation, warrants analysis of budgeting practices at this level of government. State governments are responsible for a larger and larger share of total government spending in the United States. In the year this study was conducted, state expenditure, as a proportion of total government spending, was 36 percent, up 10 percentage points from 1980! Direct expenditures by states predominantly cover activities and programs related to public welfare and education, yet also include heavy emphasis on health care, transportation, the environment, public safety, and corrections. State revenues have increased as well, although much less dramatically, making up 29.7 percent of total government revenues in 1980 and increasing to 33.5 percent by 1994. By 1994, state revenues comprised 63 percent of state and local revenues combined (U.S. Bureau of the Census 1997, 299–300). These revenues are derived primarily from taxes, insurance trust (including unemployment compensation, employee retirement, and workers' compensation), and charges. Any way you look at it, states are at the center of governmental activity that directly impacts citizens and their lives in the United States. Research about how these governments both raise and spend the public's money is therefore essential; we learn from the past in order to project into the future regarding each side of the budget equation. Our research has concentrated on the spending side to enlighten budget actors and the public alike about how spending decisions are made at the state level.

We have concentrated on the decision-making activities of the state budget office examiner for good reason. We view the state budget examiner as central to state budget decisions; the examiner is a vital link between micro-

and macro-level decisions, and between budget and policy decisions. In policy-oriented SBOs, the budget examiner works within the "hidden cluster" of policy actors to influence state spending—and state policy—by framing budget problems, developing recommendations, and taking advantage of "windows of opportunity" to acclimate the governor to a particular point of view. In policy-oriented SBOs, budget examiners serve in a number of different and important capacities throughout the traditional budget cycle. During budget execution, examiners monitor, yet support, agencies and their spending, often helping agencies to define their problems and consider solutions that can be deliberated later during budget development for the following fiscal year. During budget development the examiner provides an essential connection between agencies and the governor, at best cognizant of both gubernatorial and agency priorities throughout the process of developing budget recommendations for the governor. Once the governor's budget is presented to the legislature, budget examiners provide support, clarification, and other information to the governor regarding legislative and agency initiatives as well as budget issues.

We have investigated the decision processes of the examiner during budget development and budget execution, as it is at these stages in the budget cycle that the nexus between budget and policy decisions is most evident. It is at these stages that agency spending desires as well as program and capital initiatives can be taken forward by SBO examiners to the governor. The governor is chiefly responsible for the budget agenda. This budget agenda, dramatically flavored by the governor's policy focus, then influences legislative deliberation later on in the budget cycle. Therefore, the responsibility of examiners to review agency spending requests, and their ability to mold requests into an effective recommendation, very much shapes subsequent legislative debate and, ultimately, final appropriation bills. We have defined effective recommendations to include the degree to which the recommendation is acceptable to the budget director, perhaps the finance secretary, and ultimately the governor.

Examiners' work during budget execution very much influences future spending and therefore state policy. It is during this stage of the budget process that examiners get a "hands on" look at how and for what agencies spend money. Much of what examiners do while involved in budget execution is facilitate agency functioning through expenditure monitoring. (We see this is particularly true of examiners in control-oriented SBOs.) In so doing, the examiner gains valuable knowledge about program operations, management priorities, and, importantly, agency problems. When considering agency budget requests during the development phase, examiners can take the information they garnered during budget execution to fill in details of agency spending and operation. And direct assessment of agency problems during execution can help examiners to fully understand the foundations of need that agencies spell out in their budget requests during the development phase. The savvy examiner soon realizes that every day counts in terms of preparation for budget development and beyond.

Methodology, Sample States, and Decision Environment

Our method of study has been direct and descriptive. We conducted face-to-face interviews with examiners to allow them to discuss in their own words how they go about their job, where they look for information, which bits of information are important to them and when during the budget cycle, and what factors help or hinder their chief task of preparing spending recommendations for the governor. We interviewed most of the budget examiners from each office we visited, giving us a rich dataset that allows for cross-referencing and checking regarding characteristics witnessed in individual examiners that can be expanded to correctly characterize specific state budget office orientations.

We recognize that the decision-making we investigated occurs within a certain budgetary environment and decision context. This research assessed the decisions of examiners from a variety of state government environments, with the understanding that the circumstances within which these budget actors operate influences their ability to be successful in terms of budget recommendations. Generally, state governments provide political, economic, social, and demographic as well as organizational environments that have the potential to either enhance or hinder the examiners' abilities to influence gubernatorial decisions about the budget and thereby influence policy. In fact, the states included in this study provide a kaleidoscope of political, fiscal, and organizational environments within which their SBOs and the examiners employed therein operate. In turn, we witness a varying degree of budget powers afforded to the chief executives of the sample states.

Table 9.1 illustrates a number of the variables discussed in the introductory chapter that contribute to the decision-making environment of the budget examiner and that can strengthen (or weaken) a governor in terms of policy success during his or her tenure. Considering all the factors together, we found that several states rank as providing or experiencing circumstances strengthening the governor in 1994. These states include Illinois, Georgia, North Carolina, Missouri, and Virginia. Nonetheless, such categorizations are not definitive. For example, Virginia greatly weakens the power of the governor by limiting tenure and (relative to most of the other governors represented here) veto ability. Likewise, North Carolina's governor is greatly

Table 9.1

Factors Affecting the Strength of the Governor

Strengthens the Governor → Weakens the Governor	Executive and Legislative Branch Party Makeup	Tenure / Succession	Budget Office Location	Appointment of Budget Director Is by	Budget Format[b]	Revenue Forecast	Veto Authority[a]
	Branches Are Same Alabama Georgia North Carolina Missouri	**4 Years / Unlimited** Illinois Iowa Minnesota Wisconsin	**Governor's Office** Georgia Illinois North Carolina	**Government Alone** Georgia Illinois[a] Iowa[a] Kansas North Carolina[a] Virginia	**Program** Alabama Illinois Iowa Kansas Minnesota Missouri North Carolina South Carolina Virginia Wisconsin	**Executive** Georgia Illinois Minnesota Missouri[c] Virginia	**Line Item, Item Veto of Appropriations, Selected Words, and Meaning of Words** Illinois
	Split Legislature Illinois Iowa Wisconsin	**4 Years / Limited** Alabama Georgia Kansas Missouri North Carolina South Carolina	**In Another Dept. or Office** Alabama Iowa Kansas Minnesota Missouri South Carolina Virginia Wisconsin	**Dept. Head with Government Approval** Alabama Minnesota Missouri Wisconsin	**Zero-Based** Georgia Iowa Virginia	**Consensus** Alabama Iowa Kansas South Carolina[d] Wisconsin[e]	**Line Item, Item Veto of Appropriations, and Selected Words** Georgia Missouri Wisconsin
	Branches Are Different Kansas Minnesota South Carolina Virginia	**4 Years / Not Allowed** Virginia		**Budget and Control Board** South Carolina	**Line Item** Alabama Georgia Kansas Minnesota Missouri North Carolina South Carolina Wisconsin	**Legislature** North Carolina[f]	**Line Item and Item Veto of Appropriations** Iowa Kansas Minnesota South Carolina
							Line Item Virginia
							Very Limited Or No Veto Power Alabama North Carolina

[a]Budget director is a cabinet member.

[b]According to NASBO, (October 1999), *Budget Processing in the States*, Table N: Budgeting Procedures, p. 45.

[c]While the executive may work with the legislature to develop the revenue forecast, it is not required by law and it is the governor who revises the estimate.

[d]The Budget and Control Board, a quasi executive-legislative body, is responsible for preparing the estimate.

[e]Executive forecast required by law; forecast can be revised by the Legislature's Joint Committee on Finances.

[f]According to the Council of State Governments, *The Book of the States 1994–1995*, Table 6.4: Revenue Estimating Practices, p. 322.

[g]According to NASBO, (October 1999), *Budget Processing in the States*, Table J: Gubernatorial Veto Authority, p. 29. This table indicates that Alabama's governor is limited in veto authority during legislative sessions to returning bills "without limit for recommended amendments for amount and language" (p. 30). In North Carolina, "bills are subject to veto by the governor except for bills addressing amendments to the state or U.S. Constitution, joint resolutions, bills containing general assembly appointments to public office, revising senate or representative districts, and certain local bills. If the governor returns a bill, it is to be accompanied with objections and a veto message stating the reasons for the objection" (p. 31).

weakened given that (at the time of this study) the legislative branch generated the revenue forecast and the governor has no veto power. States with circumstances most hindering to the governor *on all counts* are rare, although we acknowledge that South Carolina falls to the bottom on four factors and closer to the bottom than the top on several others.

While currently state coffers are receptacles of the largesse of the sustained economic boom of the past decade, in the period of this study, many were in poor fiscal health, operating in environments of scarcity that we found even the strongest of states (politically and organizationally) could not overcome. Although confined to just two regions of the United States, our sample states do represent a range of demographic and economic environments. We have included very populous states such as Illinois, as well as much smaller states such as Kansas. Growth rates in the sample states range from 11.2 to 2.3 percent. Regarding economic health, the sample states range in per capita income from ninth (Illinois) to forty-fourth (South Carolina). Finally, Alabama, Illinois, and South Carolina ranked highest among the states studied on per capita federal aid. On the other hand, when examining per capita general fund revenues and expenditures, South Carolina falls above the U.S. average in 1994 (Minnesota, Wisconsin, and Iowa are ranked highest of these states on these two variables), while Alabama, Georgia, Illinois, and Virginia all ranked below the U.S. average on these two fiscal variables.

Essentially, we find among these sample states a mixed bag of budgetary environments. Often states have characteristics that conflict regarding empowerment to the governor. It is difficult then to completely characterize each state as "strong governor" or "weak governor." Rather we have illustrated that the environment in each state is complex at best, and must be explained and understood clearly when assessing budget examiners' comments. In any given state, certain of the factors may provide great strength to the governor regarding policy success, while others may weaken the governor's position (vis-à-vis the legislature).

Characterization of SBO Contexts on a Control-Policy Continuum

From our interviews with 182 budgeters, three-quarters of whom were budget examiners (the remainder being section managers, budget directors, and one secretary of administration), we are able to characterize the SBOs in this study on an orientation continuum from strong control to strong policy.

It is interesting to consider these results in light of the decision context each state provides. For example, South Carolina's political environment in 1994 weakened the governor (governor and majority party in the legislature are of different parties); so did several of the budget power indicators, most importantly, the location of this state budget office within the Budget and Control Board. Such an environment was certainly constricting to the SBO and examiners in terms of their relationship to the governor. As noted in Figure 9.1, 93 percent of the examiners and other budgeters interviewed in SCSBO indicated a strong control orientation for this office. Yet 7 percent of the budgeters indicate a policy orientation. The anomaly of this state is the fact that location of the budget office fostered a close relationship between the examiners and the legislature, and particularly with staff associated with House and Senate money committees. The examiners in the SCSBO considered their greatest avenue for influencing state spending (and thereby policy) was through the provision of research and information on budget and other issues to such committees and their staff upon request.

Other states illustrate equally complex environments and orientations. For example, Illinois is a state that provides a very empowering budgetary environment to the chief executive, yet fiscal and other circumstances relegated examiners in the SBO in 1994 to a strong control orientation. On the other hand, Iowa can be characterized as fairly empowering to its governor, ranking at the top on a few factors in Figure 9.1, while toward the middle of the pack on most others. Different from Illinois, the orientation of Iowa's SBO reflects perhaps the strongest policy orientation vis-à-vis control. Several other states with fairly strong policy orientations also retain a control orientation (some significantly so). Kansas, Missouri, and Minnesota each indicate a policy orientation with some vestiges of control remaining. Yet Iowa, Wisconsin, Minnesota, and Kansas all rank in the middle to top in fiscal condition.

Finally, it is interesting that Virginia and Georgia (two states that afford their governors fairly strong budget powers) maintain significant and conjoined control and policy orientations. These two states provide good examples of conflicting environments regarding the fiscal, political, and other factors. Both provided fairly strong budget powers to their chief executives (in Virginia's case, with caveats) and Georgia was politically a one-party state in 1994; yet each state experienced fairly severe fiscal environments in 1994.

In 1994, North Carolina was a state with an extremely popular governor; both branches of the legislature were of the same party; a fairly advanced budget format and process were in place; and the state ranked fiscally at the top of the states studied here. This SBO illustrates the only one with a predominant (62 percent) orientation toward management (not recognized in Figure 9.1). However, the control perspective remains important, and a policy orientation is acknowledged.

342

Figure 9.1   **SBO Orientation: SBO Placement Along Control-Policy Continuum**

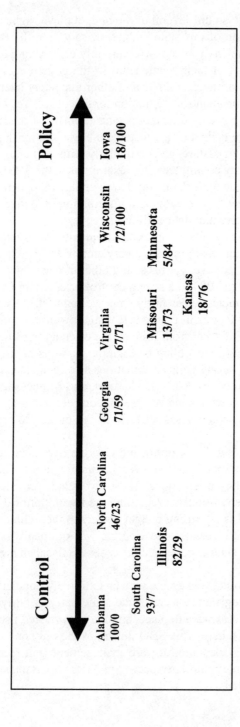

Note: Numbers below each state indicate the proportion of examiners indicating a control/policy orientation of their SBO.

Research Questions Answered

While these comparisons of states and their SBOs provide broad characterizations as either control or policy oriented (or some mix of the two), we specifically interviewed individual budget examiners to answer the following questions: *How do public budgeters (in this case, state government budget examiners) make decisions? Can we describe a model of budget rationality that reflects this decision-making activity? And under what conditions does this model apply?*

To answer the first question, we have outlined the budget problem and then discussed the numerous rationalities employed by budgeters approaching these problems. We have explained how the effectiveness and efficiency facets of budget problems involve different types of information and different types of reasoning.

We find that framing budget problems is particularly applicable to the budget rationality exhibited by state budget examiners as they explained it to us. First, the governor is responsible for the budget agenda. In his or her capacity as chief executive, the governor can ill afford to take on numerous policy priorities reflected in the budget recommendation to the legislature. Realistically then, the governor and the governor's policy staff turn to the budget staff for information not only regarding those areas with which the governor is comfortable, feels strongly about, and is specifically addressing, but also (and especially) those areas with which the governor is less familiar, has limited knowledge of, or has little interest in. Essentially, the governor needs problem-framing on policy issues from the budget examiner to compensate for the limited scope of policy priorities that concern the successful governor. Such framing acknowledges politics, yet remains objective and "neutrally competent." It is important, in fact, that examiners recognize that politics is just one facet of the budget problem (albeit an important one); further, engaging this rationality alone when reviewing agency spending plans and preparing recommendations will not necessarily lead to effective recommendations and acceptance by the budget director and governor.

Our model accounts for different state government environments, organizations within and of the SBO and specific to the budget examiner. We recognize that fiscal capacity and politics will overshadow the SBO environment; that the characteristics of the SBO further shape the examiners' environment; and that personality or individual bias comes into play as well. Taken together, the circumstances in any given state during any given period of the budget cycle predispose examiners to certain rationalities and foster their flexibility or inflexibility in framing spending decisions, developing options, generating recommendations, and communicating results of decisions up through the chain of command.

To understand flexibility in framing, we compared prototypical examiners in a policy-oriented SBO and a control-oriented SBO, and distinguished the two environments as well as the applicability of different rationalities to examiners in each office. At the onset, we find that examiners approach budget problems (in this case, agency spending requests) similarly in terms of their initial analysis of historical fiscal data, attention to statutory code, as well as federal and state mandates. This review of history helps examiners flesh out the framework upon which decisions will have to be made. As the budget cycle continues, however, there are significant differences in the approach to budget problems that each prototypical examiner exhibits, in part reflecting the *policy distance* between the examiners and the governor. First, the shorter policy distance in policy-oriented SBOs enables examiners to secure a much clearer understanding of the political rationale of budget problems. These examiners are clearly apprised of gubernatorial priorities, often from direct contact during budget briefings. They also learn the priorities and preferences of the budget director and their assigned agencies. In policy-oriented budget offices, we often witness budget directors and section managers encouraging and enabling examiners to get out of the office and learn the politics of the issues specific to their agencies. By learning about priorities, examiners in policy-oriented SBOs can fully recognize the political environment, enabling them to see multiple facets of the agencies' budget problems. They engage each of the rationalities (at some point) that comprise both the effectiveness and efficiency facets of problems, and can more accurately frame budget decisions for effective recommendations to the budget director—and eventually the governor. Ultimately, budget examiners from policy-oriented SBOs are able to approach budget problems more completely than examiners in control-oriented SBOs. The budget rationality exhibited by these examiners enables them to craft effective budget recommendations that are largely affirmed by the budget director and the governor.

Examiners in control-oriented SBOs operate in a comparatively constrained environment regarding the communication flow to and from the governor. The policy distance is long in these offices; examiners rarely have any contact with the governor, and even have trouble actively seeking out information about gubernatorial priorities. Recall that one examiner from Alabama's SBO claimed not to know what was important to the governor, even after fourteen months of his administration! Examiners in these offices use the technical and legal rationalities predominantly when framing budget problems. They secure some information regarding social rationality, given their oversight of agency spending during budget execution. While the possibility exists for them to learn about agency priorities, their inability to get at the governor's priorities precludes full understanding of the political rationality of budget problems, and it prohibits their ability to exercise economic (allocative) rationality. Their framing of budget problems is incomplete, and therefore these examiners cannot realize the budget success possible of examiners in policy-oriented SBOs.

In addition to weak communication flows among executive budgeters, the control-oriented SBOs in our sample each experienced poor fiscal climates in 1994; on any number of economic indicators they fall to the bottom of the states included in this study. As our model indicates, fiscal climate affects state government operation, and in this case, SBO flexibility vis-à-vis examiners' relationships with agencies. For example, we found that the relationship of examiners in control-oriented SBOs to agencies is best defined by budget execution and *not* budget development. It was not unusual for examiners from these offices to claim a focus on working with agencies throughout the year to administer the budget, a concentration on the technicalities of spending over and above budget development, or the preparation of agency spending options for the governor to consider. With a mind toward "simply surviving" and a sense of perhaps isolation from understanding the policy priorities of the governor, examiners in control-oriented SBOs illustrate an accounting focus in which they can only go through the motions of budget checking during development.

Our multiple rationalities model of decision-making applies to examiners in both policy-oriented and control-oriented SBOs. The ideal type of budget examiner from a policy-oriented SBO is fully rational in that he or she assesses both the effectiveness and efficiency facets of budget problems. The rationality of the prototypical examiner in a control-oriented budget office is multifaceted as well, though limited; the technical efficiency and legal rationalities of budget problems dominate decision-making in control-oriented SBOs.

Nonetheless, examiners in policy-oriented SBOs cannot be thought of as political aides to the governor. In fact, they claim to refuse to compromise their traditional role of neutral competence—even given their framing activity. These examiners are not substitutes for the governor's policy staff. Moreover, the budget directors made it clear that governors *do not want* examiners to be political analysts; rather they require rational actors who present objective and cost-effective information that has a chance of succeeding through legislative acceptance later on in the budget cycle. Governors rely on budget staff to provide validity and reliability for their policy preferences. Governors do not want politicized budget offices; they want policy budget offices.

On what basis do budget examiners make recommendations to the gover-

nor? We find the answer to be: it depends. We witness distinctiveness in state environments that constrict or enhance gubernatorial powers and are then reflected in SBO operations and examiner decision contexts. We are thus able to characterize SBO orientations along a control-policy continuum and then illustrate the different rationalities that examiners use within each decision context. Importantly, the communication flow to and from the governor and examiners, chiefly through or involving the budget director, directly impacts the most important aspect of decision-making in a policy-oriented office—understanding political rationality, recognizing important budget actor priorities. When this flow of communication is murky, constrained, or constricted in some manner, it is difficult, if not impossible, for the budget examiner to engage this rationality. Such an examiner then approaches budget decisions incompletely, unable to view all rationalities and then frame a budget decision for the greatest effectiveness.

What is the practical value of this model then? Wildavsky (1961) argues, "If a normative theory of budgeting is to be more than an academic exercise, it must actually guide the making of governmental decisions." Although not our original goal, there are normative implications of our model. If a governor wants to use the *budget office* as a policy tool (which is different than using the *budget* as a policy tool), then our results suggest that there needs to be a short policy distance between the governor and the budget examiners, facilitated by examiners briefing the governor, or at least sitting in the briefings to learn how the governor thinks about issues and his or her general budget and policy orientations. Governors should challenge examiner assumptions and make it clear, personally and through the budget director, that they do not need another political policy staff. Rather, the examiner role is professional policy advice based on a comprehensive analysis of each budget problem, including other facets besides the politics of each issue.

How might this insight and knowledge help a newly elected governor to achieve greater policy success? Certainly it behooves a governor to scan the fiscal and political environment to understand how budget examiners in particular can be expected to react. It may be that in periods of fiscal stress, chief executives and other political leaders wish to keep budget priorities close to the vest, at least early in the budget cycle, in order to allow for greater flexibility later on (for declaring cuts, tax increases, etc.). In fact, vis-à-vis the budget office and examiners, a governor can expect the best support throughout the budget process when communication between him or her and these budget actors is free flowing. During periods of fiscal stress, a governor can use the budget office and the examiners to protect budget and policy priorities. SBO examiners with an understanding of the effectiveness as well as efficiency rationalities behind agency spending and requests can then best frame recommendations for success. While governors in states with control-oriented budget offices may hesitate to inject a policy orientation into the SBO, or even raise the level of policy orientation because they think it politicizes the office and the examiners who work in them, we find that *this need not be the case*. Throughout our interviews in policy-oriented SBOs, budget directors, section managers, and examiners alike claimed that they were not interested in partisan politics or the partisan politics of a given agency. However, they emphasized that they need to know the political rationality behind the agency budgets they analyze in order to do their job thoroughly and in order to craft effective recommendations for the governor to consider.

Thus, an important aspect of the findings presented here is that economic rationality is not the exclusive analytical basis for examiners' decisions. Nor do politics completely overshadow the "work product" of the examiner in the form of a budget recommendation. Rather, an understanding of the multiple facets of budget problems, including effectiveness (political, legal, and social) and efficiency (technical and economic), allows for the most complete approach to budget problems and fosters the greatest success for examiners in terms of framing problems for deliberation by other actors farther along in the budget process. And, as noted above, governors in states with control-oriented budget offices do have recourse to change orientation, even if circumstances work against a strong position of the governor vis-à-vis the legislature. The governor in an executive budget system (which most states have) sets the stage for legislative deliberations about spending. He or she has the ability to influence communication flows to more directly engage budget actors (in this case examiners) for purposes of understanding and protecting budget and policy priorities. In other words, maintenance of—or reversion to—a control orientation in difficult political or fiscal times *need not happen*. The governor can make the call.

Current Contextual Considerations

Today, the decision context in which the SBO examiner works is, in some instances, different from that experienced in 1994. We witnessed how the recession of the early 1990s dogged governors into raising taxes and cutting state programs. Because of this, many faced eroded popularity early in their tenure as chief executive (Beyle 1993, 11). On the other hand, by the end of the decade, most state governments are operating in flush environments. For example, in Georgia citizens reap the personal benefits of tax cuts of the last administration, while the state takes on more responsibility at much greater expense—expense, it seems, the state can handle. The governor's agenda for fiscal year 1999 included enhanced educational programs, teacher salary increases, and education buildings and facilities. One supplementary source of income contributing to these items is a lottery that has garnered millions of dollars over the last four years for specific spending initiatives. The governor also sought to extend health care to the poor and uninsured; total new monies required being $78 million ($20 million in state funds, $58 million in federal funds). And, similar to other states, Georgia will be increasing its prison capacity in the next year by adding 4,554 beds to its prison system, increasing total beds to over 40,000. The U.S. Violent Crime Control and Law Enforcement Act of 1994 provides the construction money, but does not cover the personnel and operating costs of such facilities. Thus, the 1999 General Assembly appropriated additional millions to open and run these facilities.

By the year 2000, in fact, many state governments are well off financially, yet emphasizing performance- or results-based budgeting that fosters the competition characteristic of declining resources (Melkers and Willoughby 1998). That is, even in a fiscally expansive environment, Georgia, like a majority of state governments, tinkers with budget format and process. For example, in 1993, the state imposed a legal requirement for a performance-based budgeting system. Such a system ascribes greater accountability to agency personnel regarding spending. The format attempts to gather information on the results, and not just amounts, of state spending. Georgia is a good example of a state with plentiful revenues and a strong chief executive in an environment that continues to foster frugality on the part of the governor as well as competition among agencies for redirected funds. Melkers and Willoughby (1998) point out that forty-seven of fifty states have some performance-based requirements (either legislative or executive), most which have been enacted within the last decade.

Interestingly, the role of the central budget office (and so that of the examiner within the office) is not as clear in this environment. In circumstances of scarcity, the control function of the central budget office normally would be strengthened through requirements for clearer prioritization of accounts, increased monitoring of spending patterns, and greater attention to revenue and expenditure estimates (Chapman 1982; MacManus and Grothe 1989). Traditional, heuristic criteria become less valuable, while objective measures of performance become a more necessary component of the budget document and can help rationalize budget cuts to citizens (Willoughby 1993a and 1993b). In the current period of budget surplus and results-oriented expectations, both types of information are important.

Nonetheless, some recent performance related reforms have included new oversight bodies or committees with responsibilities once the sole purview of the state budget office. Power may well rest with the developers of performance measures, often those within agencies, or formulated in conjunction with specially assigned committees that can even involve members of the general public (Melkers and Willoughby 1998). While the effects of resource scarcity on central budget office activities and orientation seem evident, the influence of budget reform on the activities and power of central budget offices remains less clear. These factors must be addressed with future research initiatives that consider decision-making of any budget actor at the state level of government. The principal orientations of the SBOs in the sample may have changed since the interviews, especially SCSBO and perhaps ILSBO, but the arguments we have made should be robust even so. The contexts of different SBOs shape the roles and decision-making of examiners.

Future Research Activities

We have only scratched the surface of possible research activities that could verify results found here. Replication of this research effort in other regions of the United States is certainly important and encouraged. While our sample states provide a good mix of political, economic, and organizational environments, greater inclusion of states from the rest of the United States can support the generalizability of these results. Also, revisiting some of the states in this study would be an avenue for checking the reliability of our results. It would be particularly interesting to return to South Carolina to note any progress toward a policy-oriented SBO, given that state's experience with an executive budget system since 1994. Alternatively, Alabama's budget office has remained stagnant in size. Current policy focus in this state regards the possibility for a lottery to generate money for new education programs (NASBO 1999). Given a highly constricting fund structure, and traditionally murky (often nonexistent) communication to and from examiners and the governor, it seems unlikely that this state can budge from its control orientation. Returning to Illinois would be interesting, given that long-term fiscal pressures have eased and gubernatorial administrations have changed. In Georgia, Roy Barnes's election as governor in 1998, his immediate use of reorganization and appointment powers to change state government, his appointment of a new budget director (from the Legislative Budget Office), and subsequent rapid turnover in the Office of Planning and Budget contribute to a confusing environment for novice and seasoned examiners alike. It would be interesting to see the impact of these changes in Georgia state government on budget office orientation and budget examiner decision strategy. We suspect that such activity has only enhanced the policy arm of the governor in this state.

A different approach to the study of decision-making of examiners, but one equally suitable to checking on the reliability and validity of our results, would incorporate a laboratory approach by using simulation to measure how budgeters make decisions compared to how they "say" they make decisions. Further, it would be interesting to compare decision-making strategies and SBO decision orientations across a variety of SBOs and compare the results against appropriation levels. That is, we still have not answered the question: *Do SBOs of different orientations foster different allocation decisions?* The second part of this lab approach to the study of budgeting would involve trend analysis of budget actors and their decisions, and tracking decisions with appropriations, accounting for a number of controls to illustrate any direct relationships between decision-making and appropriations.

Other avenues on which to extend this line of research include focusing on other budget actors in the budget process, specifically budget directors and finance secretaries, perhaps agency heads, program managers, and budget staff, as well as legislative budget examiners. An excellent avenue for clarifying communication flows among executive budgeters might involve a survey of governors, both past and present. Such research may stand alone in terms of focus on one type of budget actor across the many states, or use a case approach to study a number of budget actors from one or a few select states. Finally, a programmatic approach to the study of decision-making might try to uncover distinctiveness of decision strategies across a variety of program areas typical of state government operation, such as education, transportation, welfare, and corrections.

Summary: Enlightening Decision-Making in SBOs

Wildavsky observed in 1961 that "most practical budgeting may take place in a twilight zone between politics and efficiency. . . . It does not seem to me that the problem of distributing shares has either been neglected entirely or has been confused with the problem of efficiency to the detriment of both concerns." His subsequent theory of budgetary incrementalism sought to describe how budget shares are allocated. We have attempted to bring to light the decision-making activity of a hidden, yet important cluster of budget actors who contribute to how budget shares are allocated. The relative lack of attention by academics to state-level budgeting, and to budget examiner activities and decisions specifically, are primary reasons that we have focused our research on this level of government and regarding this particular budget actor. We hope our model, developed and refined on the basis of this initial fieldwork, is a step forward in the search for an answer to Key's fundamental question of budgeting—how one decides to allocate one sum for program A and another sum for program B. We have provided an entrée into the world of just one budget actor. Of course, there remains much work to be done.

References

Abelson, R.P. 1976. "Social Psychology's Rational Man." In *Rationality and the Social Sciences*, ed. S.I. Benn and G.W. Mortimore, 58–89. London: Routledge and Kegan Paul.

Abney, Glenn, and Thomas P. Lauth. 1985. "The Line Item Veto in the States: An Instrument for Fiscal Restraint or an Instrument for Partisanship?" *Public Administration Review* 42 (May/June): 66–79.

———. 1986. *The Politics of State and City Administration*. New York: SUNY Press.

———. 1997. "The Item Veto and Fiscal Responsibility." *Journal of Politics* 59, no. 3 (August): 882–892.

ACIR. 1994. *Significant Features of Fiscal Federalism: Budget Processes and Tax Systems*, vol. 1 (June). Washington, DC: U.S. Advisory Commission on Intergovernmental Relations.

Al-Nahas, Abdulkarim S. 1998. "Role Orientations and Types of State-Employed Policy Analysts in Virginia." Ph.D. dissertation, Virginia Commonwealth University.

Anton, Thomas J. 1966. *The Politics of State Expenditure in Illinois*. Urbana: University of Illinois Press.

———. 1969. "Roles and Symbols in the Determination of State Expenditures." In *Politics, Programs, and Budgets: A Reader in Government Budgeting*, ed. James W. Davis Jr., 120–133. Englewood Cliffs, NJ: Prentice-Hall. [Reprinted from *Midwest Journal of Political Science* 11 (1967): 27–43.]

Appleby, Paul. 1957. "The Role of the Budget Division." *Public Administration Review* 17 (Summer): 156–158.

Aronson, Elliot 1972. *The Social Animal*. New York: Viking Press.

Axelrod, Donald. 1995. *Budgeting for Modern Government*, 2nd ed. New York: St. Martin's Press.

Bahl, Roy, and Larry Schroeder. 1979. "Forecasting Local Government Budgets." Occasional paper no. 38, Metropolitan Studies Program, the Maxwell School, 9. Syracuse, NY: Syracuse University.

Barber, James D. 1966. *Power in Committees*. Chicago: Rand McNally.

Behan, R.W. 1970. "PPBS Controversy." *Midwest Review of Public Administration* 4, no. 1 (February): 3–16.

Berman, Larry. 1979. *The Office of Management and Budget and the Presidency, 1921–1979*. Princeton, NJ: Princeton University Press.

Bernick, E. Lee. 1979. "Gubernatorial Tools: Formal vs. Informal." *Journal of Politics* 41, no. 2 (May): 656–664.

Bernick, E. Lee, and Charles W. Wiggins. 1991. "Executive-Legislative Relations: The Governor's Role as Chief Legislator." In *Gubernatorial Leadership and State Policy*, ed. Eric B. Herzik and Brent W. Brown, 73–92. Westport, CT: Greenwood Press.

Beyle, Thad. 1993. "Being Governor." In *The State of the States*, 2nd ed., ed. Carl E. Van Horn, 79–114. Washington, DC: Congressional Quarterly.

Book of the States 1993–1994. 1993. Lexington, KY: Council of State Governments.

Bosso, Christopher J. 1994. "The Contextual Bases of Problem Definition." In *The Politics of Problem Definition*, ed. David A. Rochefort and Roger W. Cobb, 182–203. Lawrence: University of Kansas Press.

Botner, Stanley B. 1985. "The Use of Budgeting/Management Tools by State Governments." *Public Administration Review* 40 (June): 335–342.

———. 1987. "Microcomputers in State Central Budget Offices." *Public Budgeting and Finance* 7 (Autumn): 99–108.

Bozeman, Barry, and Jane Massey. 1982. "Investing in Policy Evaluation: Some Guidelines for Skeptical Public Managers." *Public Administration Review* 42 (May/June): 264–270.

Bozeman, Barry, and Jeffrey D. Straussman.1982. "Shrinking Budgets and the Shrinkage of Budget Theory." *Public Administration Review* 42 (November/December): 509–515.

Breneman, D.W. 1995. "Sweeping, Painful Changes." *Chronicle of Higher Education* 42, no. 3: B1–B2.

Bretschneider, Stuart I.; Jeffrey D. Straussman; and Daniel Mullins. 1988. "Do Revenue Forecasts Influence Budget Setting? A Small Group Experiment." *Policy Sciences* 21: 305–325.

Bretschneider, Stuart I.; Wilpen L. Gorr; Gloria Grizzle; and Earle Klay. 1989. "Political and Organizational Influences on the Accuracy of Forecasting State Government Revenues." *International Journal of Forecasting* 5, no 3. Special Issue on Public Sector Forecasting.

Bromiley, P. 1981. "Task Environments and Budgetary Decisionmaking." *Academy of Management Review* 6 (April): 277–288.

Buchanan, James M., and Richard A. Musgrave. 1999. *Public Finance and Public Choice: Two Contrasting Visions of the State.* Cambridge: MIT Press.

Burkhead, Jesse. 1956. *Government Budgeting.* New York: John Wiley & Sons.

Burkhead, Jesse, and Paul Bringewatt. 1977. *Municipal Budgeting: A Primer for Elected Officials*, 2nd ed. Washington, DC: Joint Center for Political Studies.

Burton, John E. 1943. "Budget Administration in New York State." *State Government* 16 (October): 205.

Caiden, Naomi. 1984. "An Interview with A. Alan Post, Legislative Analyst for the State of California, 1950–1977." *Public Budgeting and Finance* 3: 74–90.

Chapman, Jeffrey. 1982. "Fiscal Stress and Budget Activity." *Public Budgeting and Finance* 2 (Summer): 83–87.

Clynch, Edward J., and Thomas P. Lauth, eds. 1991. *Governors, Legislatures, and Budgets: Diversity Across the American States.* New York: Greenwood Press.

Cohen, Michael D.; James G. March; and Johan P. Olsen. 1972. "A Garbage Can Model of Organizational Choice." *Administrative Science Quarterly* 17 (March): 1–25.

Cohen, Percy S. 1976. "Rational Conduct and Social Life." In *Rationality and the*

Social Sciences, ed. S.I. Benn and G.W. Mortimore, 132–154. London: Routledge and Kegan Paul.

Conant, James K. 1989. "Stability, Change and Leadership in State Administration, 1970–1986." *State and Local Government Review* 21 (Winter): 3–10.

Connelly, Michael. 1981. *Budgeting and Policy Analysts in Missouri*. Ph.D. dissertation, University of Missouri–Columbia.

Cornett, Robert. 1965. "The Summing Up." In *The Budget Analyst in State Management, Partial Record of the First Budget Institute*, Lexington, Kentucky, August 2–7, 1964. Chicago: National Association of State Budget Officers.

Crecine, John P. 1967. "A Computer Simulation Model of Municipal Budgeting." *Management Science* 13 (July): 786–815.

Crew, Robert E. Jr. 1992. "Understanding Gubernatorial Behavior: A Framework for Analysis." In *Governors and Hard Times*, ed. Thad Beyle, 15–28. Washington, DC: Congressional Quarterly Press.

Cyert, Richard M., and James G. March. 1963. *A Behavioral Theory of the Firm.* Englewood Cliffs, NJ: Prentice Hall.

David, Irwin T. 1998. "The True Financial Manager." *Government Executive* 30, no. 7 (July): 58–59.

Davis James W., and Randall B. Ripley. 1969. "The Bureau of the Budget and Executive Branch Agencies: Notes on Their Interaction." In *Politics, Programs, and Budgets: A Reader in Government Budgeting*, ed. James W. Davis Jr., 66–67, 77. Englewood Cliffs, NJ: Prentice-Hall.

Diesing, Paul. 1955. "Noneconomic Decision-Making." *Ethics* 66 (October): 18–35.

———. 1958. "Socioeconomic Decisions." *Ethics* 69 (October): 1–18.

———. 1962. *Reason in Society: Five Types of Decisions and Their Social Conditions.* Urbana: University of Illinois Press.

Druckman, James N. 1999. "Who Can Frame? Source Credibility and Framing Effects." Paper delivered at the 1999 annual meeting of the Midwest Political Science Association, Chicago, April 14–17.

Duncombe, Sydney, and Richard Kinney. 1986. "The Politics of State Appropriations Increases: The Perspective of Budget Officers in Five Western States." *Journal of State Government* 59 (September/October): 113–123.

———. 1987. "Agency Budget Success: How It Is Defined by Budget Officials in Five Western States." *Public Budgeting and Finance* 7: 24–37.

Durning, Dan, and W. Osuna. 1994. "Policy Analysts' Roles and Value Orientations: An Empirical Investigation Using Q Methodology." *Journal of Policy Analysis and Management* 13: 629–657.

Elster, Jon, ed. 1986. *Rational Choice.* New York: New York University Press.

Eyestone, Robert. 1978. *From Social Issues to Public Policy.* New York: John Wiley.

Fessler, James W., and Donald F. Kettl. 1996. *The Politics of the Administrative Process*, 2nd ed. Chatham, NJ: Chatham House Publishers, Inc.

Fischhoff, Baruch; Paul Slovic; and Sarah Lichtenstein. 1980. "Knowing What You Want: Measuring Labile Values." In *Cognitive Processes in Choice and Decisions Behavior*, ed. Thomas S. Wallsten, 117–141. Hillsdale, NJ: Erlbaum.

Forrester, John P., and Guy B. Adams. 1997. "Budgetary Reform Through Organizational Learning: Toward an Organizational Theory of Budgeting." *Administration and Society* 28, no., 4 (February): 466–488.

Forsythe, Dall. 1991. "The Role of Budget Offices in the Productivity Agenda." *Public Productivity and Management Review* 15: 169–174.

_____. 1997. *Memos to the Governor: An Introduction to State Budgeting*. Washington, DC: Georgetown University Press.

Frank, Jerome. 1930. *Law and the Modern Mind*. New York: Brentano's Press.

_____. 1949. *Courts on Trial: Myth and Reality in American Justice*. Princeton, NJ: Princeton University Press.

Frost, Susan H; James C. Hearn; and Ginger M. Marine. 1997. "State Policy and the Public Research University: A Case Study of Manifest and Latent Tensions." *Journal of Higher Education* 68, no. 4 (July): 363–397.

Gerwin, Donald. 1969. "Toward a Theory of Public Budgetary Decision-Making." *Administrative Science Quarterly* 14 (March): 33–46.

Gibson, Quentin. 1976. "Arguing from Rationality." In *Rationality and the Social Sciences*, ed. S.I. Benn and G.W. Mortimore, 111–131. London: Routledge and Kegan Paul.

Gosling, James J. 1985. "Patterns of Influence and Choice in the Wisconsin Budgetary Process." *Legislative Studies Quarterly* 10 (November): 457–482.

_____. 1987. "The State Budget Office and Policy Making." *Public Budgeting and Finance* 7 (Spring): 51–65.

_____. 1991. "Patterns of Stability and Change in Gubernatorial Policy Agendas." *State and Local Government Review* 23 (Winter): 3–12.

_____. 1997. *Budgeting in American Governments*. New York: Garland Publishing.

Gove, Samuel K. 1992. "Jim Edgar, The New Governor from the Old Party." In *Governors and Hard Times*, ed. Thad Beyle, 107–126. Washington, DC: Congressional Quarterly Press.

Gray, Virginia. 1983. "Politics and Policy in the American States." In *Politics in the American States: A Comparative Analysis*, ed. Virginia Gray, Herbert Jacob, and Kenneth N. Vines, 3–26. Boston: Little, Brown.

Gray, Virginia, and David Lowery. 1999. "Where Do Policy Ideas Come From? A Study of Minnesota Legislators and Staffers." *Journal of Public Administration Research* 10 (3): 573–597.

Harsanyi, John C. 1986. "Advances in Understanding Rational Behavior." In *Rational Choice*, ed. Jon Elster, 82–107. New York: New York University Press.

Hartwig, Richard E. 1978. "Rationality and the Problems of Administrative Theory." *Public Administration* 56 (Summer): 159–180.

Heclo, Hugh. 1975. "OMB and the Presidency—The Problem of Neutral Competence." *Public Interest* 38 (Winter): 80–98.

Hogarth, Robin M., and Melvin W. Reder, eds. 1987. *Rational Choice: The Contrast Between Economics and Psychology*. Chicago: University of Chicago Press.

Howard, S. Kenneth. 1973. *Changing State Budgeting*. Lexington, KY: Council of State Governments.

_____. 1979. "Governors, Taxpayer Revolts, and Budget Systems." *Journal of State Government* 52 (Summer): 131–134.

Jacoby, William G. 1999. "Issue Framing and Public Opinion on Government Spending." Paper presented at the 1999 annual meeting of the Midwest Political Science Association, Chicago, April 15–17.

Jenkins-Smith, H.C. 1982. "Professional Roles for Policy Analysts: A Critical Assessment." *Journal of Policy Analysis and Management* 2: 88–100.

_____. 1990. *Democratic Politics and Policy Analysis*. Pacific Grove, CA: Brooks/Cole.

Johnson, Bruce. 1984. "From Analyst to Negotiator: The OMB's New Role." *Journal of Policy Analysis and Management* 3 (Summer): 501–515.

_____. 1988. "OMB and the Budget Examiner: Changes in the Reagan Era." *Public Budgeting and Finance* 8 (Winter): 3–21.

_____. 1989. "The OMB Budget Examiner and the Congressional Budget Process." *Public Budgeting and Finance* 9 (Spring): 5–14.

Kahneman, D., and Amos Tversky. 1979. "Prospect Theory: An Analysis of Decision Under Risk." *Econometrica* 47: 263–291.

_____. 1984. "Choices, Values, and Frames." *American Psychologist* 39, no. 4 (April): 341–350.

Katz, Daniel, and Robert Kahn. 1978. *The Social Psychology of Organizations*, 2nd ed. New York: John Wiley and Sons.

Kelley, E.W. 1987. *Policy and Politics in the United States: The Limits of Localism*. Philadelphia: Temple University Press.

Key, V.O. 1940. "The Lack of a Budgetary Theory." *American Political Science Review* 34 (December): 1137–1140.

Kiel, L. Douglas, and Euel Elliott. 1992. "Budgets as Dynamic Systems: Change, Variation, Time, and Budgetary Heuristics." *Journal of Public Administration Research and Theory* 2, no. 2: 139–156.

Kiewiet, D. Roderick. 1991. "Bureaucrats and Budgetary Outcomes: Quantitative Analyses." In *The Budget-Maximizing Bureaucrat: Appraisals and Evidence*, ed. Andre Blais and Stephane Dion, 143–174. Pittsburgh: University of Pittsburgh Press.

Kingdon, John W. 1995. *Agendas, Alternatives, and Public Policies*, 2nd ed. New York: HarperCollins.

Kliman, Al. 1990. "A Successful Budget Process." *Public Budgeting and Finance* 10, no. 2 (Summer): 110–114.

Lauth, Thomas P. 1986. "The Executive Budget in Georgia." *State and Local Government Review* (Spring): 56–64.

_____. 1992. "State Budgeting: Current Conditions and Future Trends." *International Journal of Public Administration* 15: 1067–1096.

Lee, Robert D., Jr. 1981. "Centralization/Decentralization in State Government Budgeting." *Public Budgeting and Finance* 1 (Winter): 76–79.

_____. 1991. "Educational Characteristics of Budget Office Personnel and State Budgetary Processes." *Public Budgeting and Finance* 11: 69–79.

_____. 1992. "The Use of Executive Guidance in State Budget Preparation." *Public Budgeting and Finance* 12, no. 3: 19–31.

_____. 1997. "A Quarter Century of State Budgeting Practices." *Public Administration Review* 57, no. 2 (March/April): 133–140.

Lee, Robert D. and Ronald W. Johnson. 1998. *Public Budgeting Systems*, 6th ed. Gaithersburg, MD: Aspen Publishers.

Lehan, Edward A. 1981. *Simplified Government Budgeting*. Chicago: Municipal Finance Officers Association of the United States and Canada (now GFOA).

LeLoup, Lance T. 1978. "The Myth of Incrementalism: Analytical Choices in Budgetary Theory." *Polity* 10 (Summer): 488–509.

LeLoup, Lance T., and William B. Moreland. 1978. "Agency Strategies and Executive Review: The Hidden Politics of Budgeting." *Public Administration Review* 38 (May/June): 203, 232–239.

Lewis, Verne. 1952. "Toward a Theory of Budgeting." *Public Administration Review* 12 (Winter): 42–54.

Lindblom, Charles E. 1959. "The Science of 'Muddling Through.'" *Public Administration Review* 19 (Spring): 79–88.

_____. 1968. *The Policy-Making Process.* Englewood Cliffs, NJ: Prentice-Hall.

_____. 1975. "Incremental Decision-Making." In *Public Budgeting and Finance,* 2nd ed., ed. Robert Golembiewski and Jack Rabin, 161–175. Itasca, IL: F.E. Peacock Publishers.

Lockridge, Robert. 1999. "The Role of the Budget Analyst." Presentation at the 1999 Introduction to State Budgeting Seminar, "Perspective of a Budget Analyst," Chicago, August 1999, National Association of State Budget Officers.

Long, Norton. 1949. "Power and Administration." *Public Administration Review* 9: 257–264.

Loomis, Burdett A. 1994. *Time, Politics, and Policies: A Legislative Year.* Lawrence: University Press of Kansas.

Lowi, Theodore. 1964. "American Business, Public Policy, Case Studies, and Political Science." *World Politics* 16 (July): 677–715.

Lynch, Thomas D. 1995. *Public Budgeting in America.* Englewood Cliffs, NJ: Prentice Hall.

MacManus, Susan, and Barbara P. Grothe. 1989. "Fiscal Stress as a Stimulant to Better Revenue Forecasting and Productivity." *Public Productivity Review* 4 (Summer): 387–400.

Majone, Giandomenico. 1989. *Evidence, Argument and Persuasion in the Policy Process.* New Haven: Yale University Press.

Mannheim, Karl. 1940. *Man and Society in an Age of Reconstruction: Studies in Modern Social Structure.* New York: Harcourt, Brace & World.

March, James. 1986. "Bounded Rationality, Ambiguity, and the Engineering of Choice." In *Rational Choice,* ed. Jon Elster. New York: New York University Press.

Martin, Joanne. 1992. *Cultures in Organizations: Three Perspectives.* New York: Oxford University Press.

Mathews, Harlan. (Commissioner, Department of Finance and Administration, Tennessee.) 1965. "Expenditure Estimates: A Tennessee View." In *The Budget Analyst in State Management, Partial Record of the First Budget Institute,* Lexington, Kentucky, August 2–7, 1964, 36–39. Chicago: National Association of State Budget Officers.

McCaffery, Jerry, and Keith G. Baker. 1990. "Optimizing Choice in Resource Decisions: Staying Within the Boundary of the Comprehensive-Rational Method." *Public Administration Quarterly* 14 (Summer): 142–172.

Melkers, Julia, and Katherine Willoughby. 1998. "The State of the States: Performance-Based Budgeting Requirements in 47 Out of 50." *Public Administration Review* 58, no. 1 (January): 66–73.

Meltsner, Arnold J. 1976. *Policy Analysts in the Bureaucracy.* Berkeley: University of California Press.

Meltsner, Arnold J., and Aaron Wildavsky. 1970. "Leave City Budgeting Alone: A Survey, Case Study and Recommendations for Reform." In *Financing the Metropolis–Public Policy in Urban Economics,* ed. John Crecine, 311–355. Beverly Hills: Sage Publishing.

Miller, Gerald J. 1991. *Government Financial Management Theory.* New York: Marcel Dekker.

Mortimore, Geoffrey W. 1976. "Rational Action." In *Rationality and the Social Sciences*, ed. S.I. Benn and G.W. Mortimore, 93–110. London: Routledge and Kegan Paul.

Mosher, Frederick C. 1952. "Executive Budget, Empire State Style." *Public Administration Review* 12 (Spring): 73–84.

Musgrave, Richard A., and Peggy B. Musgrave. 1980. *Public Finance in Theory and Practice*, 3rd ed., 63–73. New York: McGraw-Hill.

National Governors Association Online. 1999. "The Governors, Political Affiliations and Terms of Office, 2000." http://www.nga.org/Governor/GovMasterList.html.

NASBO. 1987. "Table D. Gubernatorial Budget Authority and Responsibility." In *Budgetary Processes in the States: A Tabular Display*. Washington, DC: National Association of State Budget Officers.

_____. 1999. *Budget Processes in the States*. Washington, DC: National Association of State Budget Officers.

Nelson, Barbara. 1984. *Making an Issue of Child Abuse*. Chicago: University of Chicago Press.

Newman, Isadore, and Keith McNeil. 1998. *Conducting Survey Research in the Social Sciences*. Lanham, MD: University Press of America.

Nicolaidis, Nicholas G. 1960. *Policy-Decision and Organization Theory*. University of Southern California Bookstore, John W. Donner Memorial Fund, publication no. 11.

Niskanen, William A. 1971. *Bureaucracy and Representative Government*. Chicago: University of Chicago Press.

_____. 1986. "Economists and Politicians." *Journal of Policy Analysis and Management* 5, no. 2: 234–244.

Nutt, Paul C. 1999. "Public-Private Differences and the Assessment of Alternatives for Decision Making." *Journal of Public Administration Research and Theory* 9: 305–349.

Oldfield, Kenneth W. 1986. "A Comparative Analysis of Executive Budget Analysts in Illinois and Missouri." Paper presented at the 1986 national conference of the American Society for Public Administration, Anaheim, California, April 15.

Oppenheim, A.N. 1992. *Questionnaire Design, Interviewing and Attitude Measurement*. London: Pinter Publishers.

Osigweh, Chimerie. 1986. "Program Evaluation and Its 'Political' Context." *Policy Studies Review* 6 (August): 90–98.

O'Toole, Lawrence. 1997. "Treating Networks Seriously: Practical and Research-Based Agendas in Public Administration." *Public Administration Review* 57, no. 1: 45–51.

Palumbo, Dennis. 1995. *Public Policy in America: Government in Action*, 2nd ed. Fort Worth, TX: Harcourt Brace College Publishers.

Patton, Carl, and David Sawicki. 1993. *Basic Methods of Policy Analysis and Planning*. Englewood Cliffs, NJ: Prentice Hall.

Pfeffer, Jeffrey. 1981. *Power in Organizations*. Marshfield, MA: Pitman Publishing.

Pfiffner, John M. 1960. "Administrative Rationality." *Public Administration Review* 2, no. 3 (Summer): 125–132.

Pilegge, Joseph C., Jr. 1978. *Taxing and Spending: Alabama's Budget in Transition*. Tuscaloosa: University of Alabama Press.

Pittard, Janet. 1999. "Perspective of a Budget Analyst." 1999 Introduction to State Budgeting Seminar, NASBO. Annual meeting of the National Association of State Budget Officers, August, Chicago.

Poister, Theodore H., and Robert McGowan. 1984. "The Use of Management Tools in Municipal Government: A National Survey." *Public Administration Review* 43 (May/June): 215–223.

Poister, Theodore H., and Gregory Streib. 1989. "Management Tools in Municipal Government: Trends Over the Past Decade." *Public Administration Review* 49 (May/June): 240–248.

Polivka, Larry, and Osterholt, B. Jack. 1985. "The Governor as Manager: Agency Autonomy and Accountability." *Public Budgeting and Finance* 5 (Winter): 91–104.

Rall, Edward. (Business manager, Centre College, and former deputy commissioner of finance, Kentucky). 1965. "The Official Literature of Budgeting." In *The Budget Analyst in State Management, Partial Record of the First Budget Institute,* Lexington, Kentucky, August 2–7, 1964. Chicago: National Association of State Budget Officers.

Ramsey, James R., and Merlin M. Hackbart. 1979. "Budgeting: Inducements and Impediments to Innovations." *Journal of State Government* 52 (Spring): 65–69.

Ransone, Coleman B. Jr. 1982. *The American Governorship.* Westport, CT: Greenwood Press. *Review* 52 (November/December): 594–599.

Rochefort, David A., and Roger W. Cobb. 1994. *The Politics of Problem Definition.* Lawrence: University of Kansas Press.

Rosenthal, Alan. 1990. *Governors and Legislatures: Contending Powers.* Washington, DC: Congressional Quarterly Press.

Rubin, Irene S. 1990. "Budget Theory and Budget Practice: How Good the Fit?" *Public Administration Review* 50, no. 2: 179–189.

———. 1997. *The Politics of Public Budgeting,* 3rd ed. Chatham, NJ: Chatham House Publishers.

Rubin, Laura. 1996. "The Fiscal Position of the State and Local Government Sector: Developments in the 1990s." *Federal Reserve Bulletin* 82, no. 4: 302–311.

Sabato, Larry. 1983. *Goodbye to Good-Time Charlie: The American Governorship Transformed,* 2nd ed. Washington, DC: Congressional Quarterly Press.

Scheberle, Denise. 1994. "Radon and Asbestos: A Study of Agenda Setting and Causal Stories." *Policy Studies Journal* 22, no. 1: 74–86.

Schultze, C.L. 1968. *The Politics and Economics of Public Spending.* Washington, DC: Brookings Institute.

Sen, Amartya K. 1986. "Behavior and the Concept of Preference." In *Rational Choice,* ed. Jon Elster, 60–81. New York: New York University Press.

Schick, Allen. 1966. "The Road to PPB: The Stages of Budget Reform." *Public Administration Review* 26 (December): 243–258.

———. 1971. *Budget Innovation in the States.* Washington, DC: Brookings Institute.

———. 1973. "A Death in the Bureaucracy: The Demise of Federal PPB." *Public Administration Review* 33 (March/April): 146–156.

———. 1983. "Incremental Budgeting in a Decremental Age." *Policy Sciences* 16: 1–25.

———. 1987. "Budgeting as an Administrative Process." In *Perspectives on Budgeting,* 2nd ed., ed. Allen Schick, 1–12. Washington, DC: American Society for Public Administration.

———. 1997. "The Changing Role of the Central Budget Office." *Organization for Economic Cooperation and Development, Paris* (OECD/GD(97)109, downloadable at http://www.oecd.org/puma/online.htm, April 30, 1999.

Shadoan, Arlene Theuer. 1963a. "Developments in State Budgeting." *Public Administration Review* 23 (December): 227–231.

———. 1963b. *Preparation, Review, and Execution of the State Operating Budget.* Lexington, KY: Bureau of Business Research, College of Commerce, University of Kentucky.

———. 1965. *Organization, Role, and Staffing of State Budget Offices.* Lexington: Bureau of Business Research, College of Commerce, University of Kentucky.

Sharkansky, Ira. 1965. "Four Agencies and an Appropriations Subcommittee: A Comparative Study of Budget Strategies." *Midwest Journal of Political Science* 9, no. 3 (August): 254–281.

———. 1968a. *Spending in the American States.* Chicago: Rand McNally.

———. 1968b. "Agency Requests, Gubernatorial Support and Budget Success in State Legislatures." *American Political Science Review* 67 (December): 1220–1231.

Simon, Herbert. 1947. "The Proverbs of Administration." *Public Administration Review* 6 (Winter): 53–67.

———. 1957. *Administrative Behavior: A Study of Decision-making Process in Administrative Organizations*, 2nd ed. New York: Free Press.

Singer, Eric, and Valerie Hudson. 1992. *Political Psychology and Foreign Policy.* Boulder, CO: Westview Press.

Skok, James E. 1980. "Budgetary Politics and Decisionmaking: Development of an Alternative Hypothesis for State Government." *Administration and Society* 11 (February): 445–460.

Smith, Harold D. 1945. *The Management of Your Government.* New York: Whittlesy House, McGraw-Hill.

Standard and Poor's DRI Regional Economic Service. http://www.dri.mcgraw-hill.com/regional/.

State Yellow Book, A Leadership Directory. 1998. 9, no. 4 (Winter). New York: Leadership Directories.

Stedry, A. D. 1960. *Budget Control and Cost Behavior.* Englewood Cliffs, NJ: Prentice-Hall.

Stewart, Thomas R., and Linda Gelberd. 1976. "Analysis of Judgment Policy: A New Approach for Citizen Participation in Planning." *American Institute of Planners Journal* 42: 33–41.

Stone, Deborah A. 1989. "Causal Stories and the Formation of Policy Agendas." *Political Science Quarterly* 104, no. 2: 281–300.

Stone, Donald C. 1985. "Orchestrating Governors' Executive Management." *Journal of State Government* 59 (Spring): 33–39.

Straussman, Jeffrey. 1979. "A Typology of Budgetary Environments." *Administration and Society* 11 (August): 216–226.

———. 1985. "V.O. Key's 'The Lack of a Budgetary Theory': Where Are We Now?" *International Journal of Public Administration* 7, no. 4, 345–374.

Straussman, Jeffrey D., and Kurt Thurmaier. 1989. "Budgeting Rights: The Case of Jail Litigation." *Public Budgeting and Finance* 9, no. 2: 30–42.

Thompson, Joel A. 1987. "Agency Requests, Gubernatorial Support, and Budget Success in State Legislatures Revisited." *Journal of Politics* 49: 756–779.

Thurmaier, Kurt. 1992. "Budgetary Decisionmaking in Central Budget Bureaus: An Experiment." *Journal of Public Administration Research and Theory* 2, no. 4: 463–487.

_____. 1995a. "Decisive Decisionmaking in the Executive Budget Process: Analyzing the Political and Economic Propensities of Central Budget Bureau Analysts." *Public Administration Review* 55, no. 5: 448–460.

_____. 1995b. "Execution Phase Budgeting in Local Governments: It's Not Just for Control Anymore!" *State and Local Government Review* 27 (Spring): 102–117.

Thurmaier, Kurt, and James Gosling. 1997. "The Shifting Roles of Budget Offices in the Midwest: Gosling Revisited." *Public Budgeting and Finance* 17, no. 4 (Winter): 48–70.

Tomkin, Shelly Lynne. 1998. *Inside OMB: Politics and Process in the President's Budget Office.* Armonk, NY: M.E. Sharpe.

_____. 1983. "OMB Budget Examiner's Influence." *The Bureaucrat* 12 (Fall): 43–47.

Tversky, Amos, and Daniel Kahneman. 1987. "Rational Choice and the Framing of Decisions." In *Rational Choice: The Contrast Between Economics and Psychology*, ed. Robin M. Hogarth and Melvin W. Reder, 67–94. Chicago: University of Chicago Press.

_____. 1981. "The Framing of Decisions and the Psychology of Choice." *Science* 211: 453–458.

U.S. Bureau of the Census. 1997. *Government Finances*, no. 5. Washington, DC: U.S. Bureau of the Census. See also, http://www.census.gov/prod/3/97pubs/97statab/stlocgov.pdf.

_____. 1999. *State and Local Government Finances and Employment 1997.* Washington, DC: U.S. Bureau of the Census.

Veillette, Paul T. 1981. "Reflections on State Budgeting." *Public Budgeting and Finance* 1, no. 3: 62–68.

Wallsten, Thomas S., ed.. 1980. *Cognitive Processes in Choice and Decisions Behavior.* Hillsdale, NJ: Erlbaum.

Weimer, David, and Aiden Vining. 1992. *Policy Analysis: Concepts and Practice.* Englewood Cliffs, NJ: Prentice Hall.

Wildavsky, Aaron. 1961. "Political Implications of Budgetary Reform." *Public Administration Review* 21 (Autumn): 183–190.

_____. 1964. *The Politics of the Budgetary Process.* Boston: Little, Brown.

_____. 1969. "Rescuing Policy Analysis from PPBS." *Public Administration Review* 29 (March/April): 189–202.

_____. 1974. *The Politics of the Budgetary Process*, 2nd ed. Boston: Little, Brown.

_____. 1978. "A Budget for All Seasons? Why the Traditional Budget Lasts." *Public Administration Review* 38 (November/December): 501–509.

_____. 1986. *Budgeting: A Comparative Theory of Budgetary Processes*, 2nd ed., 219–246. New Brunswick, NJ: Transaction Books.

_____. 1988. *The New Politics of the Budgetary Process.* Boston: Scott, Foresman/Little Brown College Division.

Willoughby, Katherine G. 1991a. "The Decision Making Orientations of State Government Budget Analysts: Rational or Intuitive Thinkers?" D.P.A. dissertation, University of Georgia, Athens, Georgia.

_____. 1991b. "Gender-Based Wage Gap: The Case of the State Government Budget Analyst." *Review of Public Personnel Administration* 12 (September–December): 33–41.

_____. 1993a. "Patterns of Behavior: Factors Influencing the Spending Judgments of Public Budgeters." In *The Handbook of Comparative Public Budgeting and*

Financial Management, ed. Thomas D. Lynch and Lawrence L. Martin, 103–132. New York: Marcel Dekker.

———. 1993b. "Decision Making Orientations of State Government Budget Analysts: Rationalists or Incrementalists?" *Public Budgeting and Financial Management* 5 (Winter): 67–114.

Willoughby, Katherine G., and Mary A. Finn. 1996. "Decision Strategies of the Legislative Budget Analyst: Economist or Politician?" *Journal of Public Administration Research and Theory* 6, no. 4: 523–546.

Willoughby, Katherine G., and Julia Melkers. 2000. "Implementing PBB: Conflicting Views of Success." *Public Budgeting and Finance* 20, no. 1: 105–120.

Wilson, James Q. 1974. *Political Organizations.* New York: Basic Books.

Yunker, Jon. 1990. "Managing a Budget Office." *Public Budgeting and Finance* 10 (Summer): 96–101.

Index

Revenue forecasts, 57–58
  top-down information flows and,
    57
Rights-based budgeting, 94–95
Ripley, Randall, 130, 270–271
Rochefort, David, 111
Rosenthal, Alan, 10
Rubin, Irene, 34, 41–42, 44–46, 85,
  90, 171

S

Scarcity, 99–100
Scheberle, Denise, 112
Schick, Allen, 129–130, 132–133,
  136, 166, 301
Section manager, 251–253
Sen, Amartya, 83
Shadoan, Arlene, 269, 280, 310, 314
Sharkansky, Ira, 132, 268
Short policy distance (strong policy)
  model, 170
Simon, Herbert, 72, 76, 107
Site visits, 184–186, 189, 204,
  246–249
Skok, James, 4
Smith, Harold D., 31, 108, 171
Social conflict, political feasibility
  frontier and, 90
Social decisions, 81
Social integration, 89, 96
Social norms, 73–75, 83, 89
Social-political-legal (SPL) analysis,
  209, 203, 215
Social problems, 82–84, 96, 106
Social rationality, 82–87, 106
  decision structure and, 88
Social values, 85, 87, 111
Southern states, 145–153
  Alabama, 146–149
  content analysis, 145
  control function, 145–146
  control orientation, 148
  Georgia, 146–147, 152–153

Southern states *(continued)*
  North Carolina, 146–147,
    150–151
  schematic of SBO orientation
    patterns, 148
  South Carolina, 146–147,
    149–150
  strong policy model, 151–152
  transition (weak policy) model,
    150–151
  Virginia, 146–147, 153
State agencies
  priorities of, 188
  working relationship with
    examiners, 181–184
State budget office (SBO), 5, 22
  affirmation rates of examiners,
    163–166
  bottom-up flows, 59
  communication flow patterns,
    166–170
  control orientation, 131, 148,
    233–234, 251–253
    policy-oriented vs., 320–324;
      see also control-oriented
      budget office
  current contextual considerations,
    349
  decision-making structure, 61, 106
  functions of, 13
  as gatekeeper, 54–57
  GCM-RTB-incrementalism
    synthesis and implications,
    49–52
  as governor's policy tool, 129–131
  information flow, 57–59
  Midwestern states, 133–144
  macro/micro decisions, 59–62
  organizational setting of, 12–15
  orientations of, 131, 133–153,
    159–163
  political decision and, 87
  synthesis of change models, 46–47
  task of, 174–176

Kurt M. Thurmaier is associate professor in the Public Administration Department at the University of Kansas. He teaches public budgeting, public finance, comparative public administration, and quantitative analysis of public-sector programs and policies. Prior to joining the academic community, Thurmaier was a budget and management analyst for four years in the budget office for the State of Wisconsin, advising Wisconsin governors on economic development, housing, industrial development, and tourism budgets. His research interests include how state and local budget office analysts make recommendations to budget directors and chief executives. He has also served in a number of international consulting projects for local government budget reform in Eastern Europe. His publications have appeared in *Public Administration Review*, *Journal of Public Administration Research and Theory*, *Public Budgeting and Finance*, *State and Local Government Review*, and *Administration & Society*.

Katherine G. Willoughby is associate professor in the Department of Public Administration and Urban Studies in the Andrew Young School of Policy Studies at Georgia State University in Atlanta, Georgia, where she teaches courses in public budgeting and finance, public-sector financial management, and public policy analysis. Her research appears in leading journals of public administration and budgeting as well as books on public administration, budgeting and financial management, and information technology. Such work concentrates heavily on public budgeting theory, decision-making practices in the United States, government and privacy, and state government policy process. Willoughby also has been involved in a number of consulting and international training initiatives related to local government management, budget systems, and fund accounting practices.